PROFESSIONAL
Hospitality

CORE COMPETENCIES

PROFESSIONAL
Hospitality

CORE COMPETENCIES

HOSPITALITY PRESS

LYNN VAN DER WAGEN

Copyright © Merilynn Van Der Wagen 2003

Pearson Education Australia
Unit 4, Level 2
14 Aquatic Drive
Frenchs Forest NSW 2086

www.pearsoned.com.au

Acquisitions Editor: David Cunningham
Project Editor: Kathryn Lamberton
Copy Editor: Kathryn Lamberton
Proofreader: Kathryn Lamberton
Cover and internal design by Bowra + Bowra, Bowral
Cover illustration by Steven Bray, Sydney
Typeset by Midland Typesetters, Maryborough, Vic.

Printed in Malaysia, CLP

3 4 5 07 06 05

National Library of Australia
Cataloguing-in-Publication Data

Van der Wagen, Lynn.
    Professional hospitality : core competencies.

    2nd ed.
    Bibliography.
    Includes index.
    ISBN 1 86250 524 1.

    1. Hospitality industry - Customer services - Australia.
    2. Competency based education - Australia. I. Title.

338.460994

Contents

Preface

I recently returned to Australia from a trip to Canada and the USA. What a pleasure it was to board a Qantas flight and anticipate a visit to a local cafe back home. I also began thinking of some of the features that make Australia a wonderful tourist destination: cleanliness (compare the smog in LA), warmth (compare Winnipeg in winter), variety, safety (the information left in the room in one motel warned me not to trust the staff) and value for money. The coffee in Australia is superior to any I was served in the USA. A latte in one instance turned out to be a sickly chocolate syrup with fake cream on top. However, the warmth and hospitality I enjoyed, particularly in Canada, was similar to that which a tourist would receive in Australia, although perhaps a little more formal.

Hotels are unfortunately the same the world over. In order to differentiate the tourism product, knowledge of the country and the history and culture of local areas is essential for tourism and hospitality employees. While in Canada I was given an introduction to some of the cultural beliefs and practices of the First Nations people living in the area of Bellville, Ontario. Unique features such as these are of great interest to tourists.

In this book you are encouraged to develop an understanding of your country, its people, its attractions, and its flora and fauna. Visitors really appreciate your volunteering this type of information and engaging them in conversation. Believe it or not, most tourists are quite shy. A stimulating conversation with staff from their hotel or their tour guide contributes enormously to their impressions and memories of the country or local region they have visited.

This edition of *Professional Hospitality: Core Competencies* has, like the last, numerous anecdotes, case studies and examples. The weighting given particularly to Part 1 (which is an introduction to the industry) mirrors the weighting given to the Hospitality Core Modules in terms of curriculum hours and provides a solid foundation for students sitting for TAFE and high school examinations. Theory is often taught as a sequence of steps, such as those for solving customer complaints. In real situations things are generally more complex, requiring knowledge and judgement. So as a student who has industry knowledge and who has come to grips with the relevant legislation, you are in a far better position to solve the problems you will encounter daily in this industry.

This is a dynamic industry. Every interaction with a customer is unique, and for this reason the industry needs people who are ready to meet that challenge, to cope with change on a minute by minute basis, to anticipate difficult situations long before they become problems. Meeting the needs of customers is the hospitality industry's main aim. These customers are bored with sleeping in their own beds, bored with eating their meals at home and bored with watching television. They are looking for accommodation, food and entertainment in an interesting environment. Your role is to create it for them.

Staff shortages for chefs, food and beverage service staff, room attendants and kitchen attendants are being experienced across Australia. The impact of new technologies has led to a shortage of hospitality staff with information technology skills. With front office computer systems, hand-held ordering systems, point-of-sale networks, sophisticated engineering and housekeeping applications for hotels, and multimedia applications for conferences, career opportunities for people entering the industry are endless. This is an industry in which attainment of supervisory and management positions can occur at a young age and, increasingly, attainment of these positions requires completion of a certificate, diploma or degree in hospitality-related studies.

These studies are the building blocks for a life-long learning process that accompanies a fast-track career in this dynamic sector. I hope that this text is the start of many interesting experiences in an industry in which every day is different.

Lynn Van Der Wagen

Acknowledgements

I would like to thank the management, staff and students of Northern Beaches TAFE for their ongoing support.

I would also like to offer my thanks to industry contributors: AAA Tourism; ACADEMIE ACCOR; ACCOR Asia Pacific; ACCOR Hotels; Australian Liquor, Hospitality and Miscellaneous Workers' Union; Australian Tourism Export Council; Bureau of Tourism Research; Casino Department of Wrest Point Hotel Casino, Hobart; Department of Gaming and Racing; Forestville RSL Club; Hamilton Island Resorts; Hilton Hotel, Sydney; Kentucky Fried Chicken; Manly Pacific Parkroyal; Novotel, Darling Harbour; Parramatta Leagues Club Ltd; Park Hyatt Sydney; Puffing Billy Railway; Qantas; Six Continents Hotels (previously SPHC); Star City; The Hyatt Hotel, Canberra; Tourism Training Australia; Tourism Training NSW; and Voyages Hotels and Resorts.

All diagrams and figures from the Australian Bureau of Statistics are Commonwealth copyright and have been reproduced with permission.

All Commonwealth award material herein is reproduced by permission but does not purport to be the official or authorised version. It is subject to Commonwealth of Australia copyright. The *Copyright Act* 1968 permits certain reproduction and publication of Commonwealth legislation. In particular, S.128A of the Act enables a complete copy to be made by or on behalf of a particular person. For reproduction or publication beyond that permitted by the Act, permission should be sought in writing. Requests should be addressed to Commonwealth Copyright Administration, Department of Communications, Information Technology and the Arts, GPO Box 2154, Canberra ACT 2601, or emailed to commonwealth. copyright@dcita.gov.au

To industry colleagues who told me the stories from which the case studies in the book have been prepared, my sincere thanks. Although the stories may have a basis in truth, they are largely imaginary and any resemblance to real establishments would be an extraordinary coincidence as locations and events have been changed beyond recognition.

Finally I would like to express my thanks to Kathryn Lamberton, my editor, and the enthusiastic team at Pearson Education Australia that has brought you this book, and to David and Jean Cunningham of Hospitality Press for their continued support over the years.

Lynn Van Der Wagen

PART 1

The Hospitality Industry

This book is divided into five sections. Part 1 is designed to give you an overview of the tourism and hospitality industry. It will provide you with an understanding of the different sectors of the hospitality industry and their relationships. It also covers legislation relevant to the industry, including your responsibilities as a hospitality employee, the role of trade unions and employers, and quality assurance. Skills in researching information are included to help you find your way around the industry.

COMPETENCY UNITS

DEVELOP AND UPDATE HOSPITALITY INDUSTRY KNOWLEDGE (THHHCO01B)

Elements

- Seek information on the hospitality industry
- Source and apply information on legal and ethical issues for the industry
- Update hospitality industry knowledge

DEVELOP AND UPDATE LOCAL KNOWLEDGE (THHGCS01B)

Elements

- Develop local knowledge
- Update local knowledge

SOURCE AND PRESENT INFORMATION (THHGGA03B)

Elements

- Find information
- Prepare and present information

PART 1 ALSO INCLUDES BACKGROUND INFORMATION FOR:

PROVIDE RESPONSIBLE SERVICE OF ALCOHOL (THHBFB09B)

PROVIDE RESPONSIBLE GAMBLING SERVICE (THHADG03B)

CHAPTER ONE

Introduction to the industry

OBJECTIVES

The aim of this chapter is to introduce you to the various sectors of the hospitality industry and to the important relationships between the hospitality industry and other industries associated with it. On completion of this chapter you should be able to:

- seek information on the hospitality industry
- explain the relationship between tourism and hospitality
- explain the relationship between the hospitality industry and other industries
- describe the various sectors of the hospitality industry and the services they provide
- update hospitality industry knowledge.

When I travel around Australia I like to stay in bed and breakfast establishments because they have a homely atmosphere. This type of accommodation is generally so much nicer than a motel if you are travelling frequently. However, I have to say that they are all quite different. They vary in terms of standard of accommodation, privacy, peace and quiet, and quality of their breakfasts. In some cases, the level of cleanliness and hygiene leaves a lot to be desired. In this respect, they are just like my own home! The proprietors, too, are different—some a little reserved and retiring, others just the opposite. My only really bad experience was with an owner who would not leave me alone. She started talking the moment I arrived and followed me everywhere with a constant barrage of one-way conversation. I felt that I was fulfilling some deep psychological need for companionship and felt boxed in within minutes. Some people might call it just being friendly, but it was too much for me!

The nature of the hospitality industry

This tells us something about the nature of the hospitality industry, the different types of hospitality operations and the varied approaches of the people who manage them. Although establishments in different sectors, such as clubs, hotels and resorts, share similar characteristics, which will be described in this chapter, they are also sometimes as unique as their proprietors. As with the customers visiting hospitality operations, it is with some caution that we stereotype establishments within different sectors. There are, for example, vast differences between two- and five-star hotels.

What is hospitality?

Providing hospitality means offering a welcoming environment to visitors, and the hospitality industry is without doubt a people industry. The warm welcome Australians give to visitors, the friendly, relaxed approach that is part of our culture, and our exquisite natural scenery are all attractions for people coming from overseas. This same hospitality is extended in the local club, when a member arrives at the bar for a drink after a game of golf, and by the staff who serve cappuccino at the local coffee shop. In these examples you will notice that this hospitality is offered to people who are away from home, some only walking distance, others many miles from home. This illustrates the diverse nature of the industry: it meets the needs of customers of both local and distant origin.

Since a tourist is generally someone who is travelling away from home, not all the people mentioned above are tourists. The golfer certainly isn't, nor is the shopper stopping for a cup of coffee. The hospitality industry should therefore be distinguished from the tourism industry. Tourists are travelling away from home, and they use the services offered by the hospitality industry, but so too does the local population. In many establishments customers are a mix of locals and travellers. The balance of customers may vary, from primarily a local market to primarily a tourist market, depending on a range of factors such as the location or the season. The overlap between tourism and hospitality is illustrated in Fig. 1.1, which shows that tourists (including business tourists) access accommodation, food and beverage, and other facilities provided by the hospitality industry. At any one time at any one establishment the balance of local patrons and tourists may vary.

Readers looking at the growth rate in expenditure by international visitors in Fig. 1.2 could conclude that the hospitality industry is gearing solely towards meeting

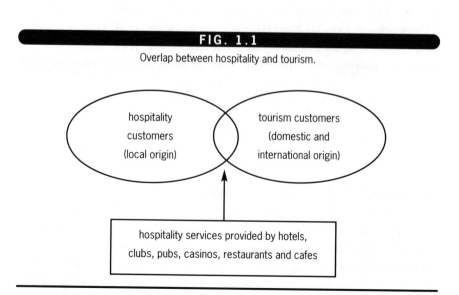

FIG. 1.1
Overlap between hospitality and tourism.

hospitality customers (local origin)

tourism customers (domestic and international origin)

hospitality services provided by hotels, clubs, pubs, casinos, restaurants and cafes

Economic impact of tourism 2000–2001

- Domestic visitors generated 78 per cent of tourism industry Gross Domestic Product (GDP) in 2000–2001 while international visitors contributed 22 per cent.
- Spending by international visitors accounted for 11.2 per cent of total exports.
- Tourism GDP amounted to $31.8 billion, a direct contribution of 4.7 per cent to total GDP.
- The tourism industry contribution to total employment was 6 per cent (551,000 persons) in 2000–2001.

Note: Further information can be obtained from the Australian Bureau of Statistics state office in your capital city.
Source: Australian Bureau of Statistics, Australian National Accounts: Tourism Satellite Account 2000–2001, Cat No 5249.0. Reproduced with permission.

the needs of those tourists. In actual fact, domestic tourists spend more than three times the amount spent by international tourists. Local tourists are therefore very important to the hospitality industry, even though this segment is not growing as rapidly as the international market segment, as also shown in Fig. 1.2. Add to this the fact that many hospitality customers are not tourists, but locals, and it becomes clear that the industry meets a variety of needs.

The nature of the tourism industry

The tourism industry is hard to define because there are so many businesses that contribute goods and services to the tourism product (see Fig. 1.3 on page 6). The sectors that are most often described as part of the tourism industry are:

- accommodation
- transport

FIG. 1.2

Expenditure by local and overseas tourists.

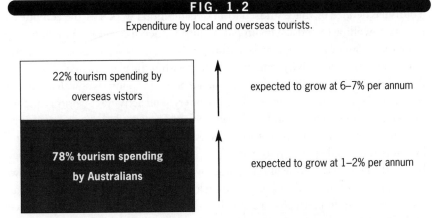

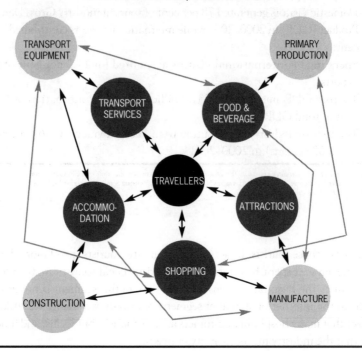

FIG. 1.3

Direct and indirect components of tourism.

TRANSPORT EQUIPMENT

PRIMARY PRODUCTION

TRANSPORT SERVICES

FOOD & BEVERAGE

TRAVELLERS

ACCOMMO-DATION

ATTRACTIONS

SHOPPING

CONSTRUCTION

MANUFACTURE

Source: Tourism Forecasting Council, June 1997. Reproduced with permission.

- tour operators
- tour wholesalers
- retail travel agents
- attractions and theme parks
- information services
- events, including business (meetings, incentives, conventions and exhibitions—MICE) and other events such as street festivals.

Tourism is defined by the World Tourism Organization (WTO) as 'the activities of persons travelling to and staying in places outside their usual environment for not more than one consecutive year for leisure, business and other purposes not related to the exercise of an activity remunerated from within the place visited'. This broad definition makes it possible to include tourism between countries as well as tourism within a country in our definition. Tourism refers to all activities of visitors, including both overnight visitors and same-day visitors. The economic impact of tourism is therefore felt across many sectors of the economy. The industries most affected by direct tourism demand are transport, accommodation, and food and beverage. Indirectly, however, tourism affects a much wider range of industries. This is known as the 'multiplier effect'. For example, when a tourist buys a meal, this has an impact on the restaurant from which it was purchased, the food wholesaler and the producer of the raw ingredients, the farmer.

Forms of tourism

There are two main classifications for tourism:

- Domestic tourism—travel within the usual country of residence (Australians travelling within Australia)
- International tourism—travel outside the country of residence (Americans, for example, travelling within Australia).

When referring to international tourism, the following distinction can be made:

- Inbound tourism—those leaving their country of residence to travel into the country of reference (tourists coming into Australia)
- Outbound tourism—the tourism of resident visitors outside the country of reference (Australians travelling overseas).

Although hospitality is included as a sector in the tourism industry (often as accommodation and food and beverage), the hospitality industry is also regarded as an industry in its own right since it meets the needs of customers other than tourists. The Australian Bureau of Statistics (ABS) has provided a useful definition for the hospitality industry:

> The hospitality industry comprises businesses whose primary activities are the provision of accommodation, selling of alcoholic beverages for consumption on the premises, provision of food and entertainment. (Cat No 8674.0)

The following types of businesses therefore fall under the hospitality umbrella (and can also be described as industries in their own right):

- accommodation
- clubs, pubs, bars and taverns
- cafes and restaurants
- casinos.

The above classification used by the Australian Bureau of Statistics forms the basis for this text. While it would be appropriate to talk about the tourism and hospitality industries, there is considerable overlap, so the term, 'the tourism and hospitality industry', or 'the industry', will be used throughout this book when referring to both.

This overlap between the tourism and hospitality industries is illustrated in Fig. 1.1 at the beginning of this chapter. As you can see, both domestic and international travellers use all the services shown. However, local hospitality consumers would use only the clubs and casinos and the food and beverage services. The amount spent on hospitality by local residents (as opposed to tourists) is highly significant, as we have mentioned. Research into household expenditure on food and non-alcoholic beverages has shown that of average weekly expenditure almost 27 per cent is spent on eating outside the home (see Fig. 1.4 on page 8) and there has been a steady upward trend in this spending in recent years. Expenditure on holidays within Australia and overseas accounts for 31 per cent of spending on recreation. (ABS Cat No 6535.0)

FIG. 1.4

Money spent on meals outside the home and takeaway food.

Source: Australian Bureau of Statistics, Cat No 6535.0. Reproduced with permission.

Sectors in the hospitality industry

It is useful to classify the hospitality industry into establishments that provide largely for sleeping (accommodation), eating (food services), drinking (beverage services) and gambling (casinos). While this is fairly simplistic, it sits comfortably with the standard definitions and statistical analysis of industry sectors provided by the Australian Bureau of Statistics. Of course there are many other types of establishment where the primary purpose is to provide entertainment, meeting facilities, sporting facilities and relaxation. However, these link closely with the culture and leisure classifications, and so will be listed separately.

Accommodation sector

Anyone travelling away from home needs somewhere to sleep and the range of options is enormous. Suites in the top hotels can cost in the region of $5,900 a night, and for this price the traveller at the luxury end of the market (usually pop stars and presidents) can enjoy the use of several rooms, including a bathroom the size of a small apartment, with marble from floor to ceiling and a spa almost as big as a swimming pool. Generally, this guest would expect to find a sitting room, bar, balcony and outstanding views, in addition to a number of other unusual features such as telephones in the bathroom and self-closing toilet lids. Original art and enormous floral arrangements often decorate the suite, and butler service is included to ensure that every need is anticipated. Confidentiality and discretion are also important aspects of the service.

In contrast, a backpacker might be looking for a room in the region of $20 per night. For this they could expect to share a room with several other people in dormitory-style accommodation, with additional charges for linen. The lodge might be closed for a certain period each day, which would entail packing away all belongings and storing them in a locker. The kitchen is generally the focal point in backpacker establishments where cooking facilities are provided and a convivial atmosphere is developed as travellers from varied destinations share information, stories and often food. Many other types of accommodation, such as camping facilities and institutional accommodation, will be described in Chapter 9. At the end of June 1998, there were 6,143 employing businesses in the accommodation industry. These businesses operated 6,496 separate accommodation establishments. Motel establishments (2,638) and caravan parks (1,709) accounted for 41 per cent and 26 per cent respectively of the total number of establishments. Other accommodation establishments included holiday flats, units or houses (486), licensed hotels (450), serviced apartments (377) and guesthouses (297). (ABS Cat No 1130.0)

Food services sector

This sector has undergone enormous growth in recent times. Most people eat food prepared outside the home at least twice a week. A packed lunch is almost a thing of the past as staff and student canteens offer sandwiches, pies, pizzas and hamburgers. Home delivery of prepared food became popular in the early 1990s. Eating breakfast in a restaurant, fast food outlet or coffee shop is also a very recent development. Many of the older generation would never have considered eating out at breakfast-time, and many would only have eaten a meal at a restaurant once or twice a year, on very special occasions such as birthdays and anniversaries. At the end of June 1999, there were 12,845 employing businesses in the cafes and restaurants industry. In addition, there were 1,716 locations operated by catering businesses,

which represented 12 per cent of locations in the industry. (ABS Cat No 8655.0)

The type of food available outside the home has also changed considerably. Slow-cooked food such as roasts, stews and baked puddings is available less often than fast-cooked food: Asian-style meals, pasta, Caesar salad, foccacia, polenta, couscous, curries and other delicacies are now appearing more regularly on menus. Many of these are very healthy and appropriate for our nutritional needs. However, oil-based cooking is still on the increase and our dependence on hot chips as a dietary staple is a major concern for nutritionists and other health professionals. The fast food business is growing rapidly. ABS results show that at the end of June 1999 there were 13,121 takeaway food businesses (Cat No 8655.0).

Food service also occurs in hospitals where nutrition and special needs must be catered for. 'Cook chill' is a method that has been developed to ensure that patient meals are as fresh and tasty as possible. Food is prepared in the armed services, in jails, on oil rigs and at many other unusual places, such as platforms on the Great Barrier Reef which cater for daily visitors. The need for qualified chefs to meet the growing demand for food prepared outside the home is a guarantee of a career for anyone interested in food preparation and presentation.

The food services sector includes establishments such as restaurants, bistros, cafes and fast food operations, as well as catering services for non-commercial facilities such as hospitals and commercial operations such as airlines.

Beverage services sector

In view of Australia's multicultural population, the range of beverage service outlets has increased enormously in recent times. The pub, or hotel, is still the traditional meeting place for people, but a wide variety of other outlets cater for specialised markets. There are wine bars and cocktail bars; Greek taverns, English pubs and American saloons; and even bars with the Internet on line for computer enthusiasts. All have different themes, decor, service styles and entertainment. Brasseries (not brassieres) serving good coffee and informal continental-style food are also extremely popular. Customer loyalty is a big factor in outlets that primarily serve liquor, as these venues are often the social meeting place for locals. The club industry, for example, meets the social needs of two primary markets, the local community and the elderly. Many clubs are non-profit organisations, which direct their poker machine profits to subsidising food, beverage and other services, as well as towards sponsoring local events. Their community involvement is high and their customer loyalty strong.

Responsible service of alcohol is an important issue in this industry and applicants to this sector need to know the guidelines on, for example, minimum age for service and refusal of service. Working in beverage service also requires an extensive knowledge of wines, spirits and cocktails. The Australian wine industry has an international reputation, and service personnel should be able to recommend wines based on customer taste and should also be able to describe grape varieties and regions. Mixing cocktails is another specialised skill, requiring an extensive knowledge of ingredients and recipes, as well as flair in preparation and presentation.

This sector includes establishments such as clubs, pubs, taverns and bars.

Casinos sector

At the end of June 2001, there were 13 casinos operating in Australia, employing a total of 20,413 people (ABS Cat No 8683.0).

Services in the hospitality industry

The hospitality industry also provides a range of services, which are connected closely to other sectors and operations in the industry, and these are outlined below.

Entertainment and nightclubs

Frequently, for example, the hospitality industry provides entertainment together with food and beverages. In some cases the entertainment is secondary, the fine food and wines being the main attraction, while in other cases the reverse applies, for example, the main attraction at a major concert would be the band, with catering as secondary.

Sporting events

Catering required for sporting events can be extremely challenging, given the size of the crowds at some of these and the demands placed on services, at half-time for example. Sometimes catering outlets are part of sports stadiums and catering services are provided regularly, giving operators the opportunity to fine tune their procedures. In other cases, such as the Formula One Grand Prix, the catering is a temporary arrangement for the one major event. This places enormous demands on the planning and organisational processes needed to prepare for such an event. Small temporary kitchens with minimum equipment and no access to supplies if anything is forgotten are some of the challenges in one-off catering.

Fairs and festivals

Oktoberfest is celebrated every year in the Barossa Valley and at The Rocks in Sydney. Traditional foods, beers and wines, as well as entertainment—all with a German theme—are provided. The annual Floriade in Canberra is an attraction to many visitors whose needs for food and beverage may be secondary to the viewing of the exquisitely colourful flowers, but nonetheless most important. The Adelaide Festival and the Melbourne Comedy Festival are also examples of festivals which attract both tourists and residents. In all situations where people are away from home, eating and drinking are important needs, and hungry and thirsty people become very frustrated very quickly. Quick responses, often in challenging situations, are required by staff because customer tolerance of delays is very much lower than it is in many other service situations, and skilled management is required to organise the preparation and service of perishable foods for such large crowds.

Business meetings

The meetings and exhibitions sector provides facilities and services for business tourists. On average, the in-country expenditure of a business tourist is higher than for most other tourists and for this reason the relevant associations work hard to promote Australia as a business tourism destination. The facilities are usually provided in large hotels and convention centres. Resorts are also popular. Conventions are often booked five years in advance and can include numbers in the thousands. Delegates need accommodation and transport if they are not housed at the convention site. Often there is a range of speakers from different countries, with last-minute requirements, some necessitating the provision of sophisticated technology. Room set-ups may need to be changed to suit varying styles of meetings, and often displays have to be erected by different operators with different needs.

Recreation

Resorts offer recreational activities in addition to accommodation and food and beverage services. These include daily activities suitable for a wide range of ages and cultures. Guests in resorts rely on staff to quickly build relationships for social interaction and to break down nervousness. Cocktail competitions, trips, walks and other activities help people to make new friends while on holiday and to enjoy their stay. Organised sports offered at resorts include tennis, aerobics, sailing, snorkeling, parasailing and adventure tours.

Information

Increased interest in ecology has resulted in a new breed of hospitality staff, those who are knowledgeable about the local culture, flora and fauna. Guides for walks and dives are often expected to have a scientific or historical background and, at the same time, to be able to communicate their knowledge effectively to the customer.

All staff working in the industry must be well informed about their organisation and its services, and the local area and its attractions, so that they are able to make suggestions to guests. Offering information to customers is part of the service expected: staff members should not wait to be asked, they should volunteer this information. Often visitors are unsure of themselves and don't know which questions to ask; quite often they are unaware of the many activities available.

Too few service personnel in the hospitality industry can remember their history lessons at school, but it is imperative for them to be able to talk about Australia's history, culture and attractions to visitors. This knowledge provides the opportunity to engage in conversation with our foreign visitors and to ensure that they leave with a taste of what we have to offer, as well as with a positive impression of Australian service, as the story below shows.

On a recent visit to one of Australia's superb pristine wilderness areas, Tasmania's Gordon River, a tourist was surprised to find that there was so little bird life and so few flowers in the forest. This she had not consciously noticed until it was pointed out to her. According to an explanation provided by the tour guide, it was due to the ice-age origin of the forest and a system of pollination in the area that did not depend on bird or insect intervention but rather on other vegetative reproduction. She also learnt that the ancient Huon pine trees growing in the region had been there for over 2,000 years, making them some of the oldest living things in the world. And that the timber from these trees could be used even after it had been under water for years owing to the preservative nature of its natural oils, making it ideal for shipbuilding. This tour generated a new level of interest in the region and in everything botanical for this visiting tourist.

Relaxation

One of the services associated with the hospitality industry is the provision of facilities for relaxation. These include massage, aromatherapy, yoga, and a range of other health-oriented services. In addition, guests need the assurance that normal daily chores, such as packing the dishwasher and making the bed, will be done by someone else. Room attending involves cleaning bedrooms and bathrooms with care, while public area cleaning ensures that lobbies and other guest areas are immaculate. This is very challenging in 24-hour operations. The Housekeeping Department in most hotels, motels and resorts is generally one of the largest. Turning rooms around between check-out time (usually 10 a.m.) and check-in time (usually 2 p.m.) when large numbers of guests are coming and going is difficult to say the least. Resident guests do not want to be disturbed by room attendants as few people can relax while watching someone clean their rooms. To ensure a relaxed time for guests, these aspects of service need to be performed discreetly. A holiday is often a time when people pretend that life is perfect and all the hard work that goes into cleaning rooms and preparing meals happens invisibly. In fact, one of Australia's leading island resorts has corridors underground so that staff cannot be seen pushing trolleys around.

Functions and banquets

These are often the most important and expensive events in a person's life. Absolutely nothing can afford to go wrong at someone's wedding as this event can sometimes cost almost a life's savings. Professional organisation and a high level of credibility are most important. Each event is unique and all aspects of the service, from the setting to the decor, food and entertainment, must meet the particular needs of the customer. A function that runs like clockwork requires infinite care in planning and preparation, anticipating potential problems or delays and responding proactively. Like management in all other aspects of the industry, function and banquet management, sometimes of hundreds of guests, requires extensive experience, knowledge and skill.

Commercial catering

Commercial caterers provide catering services for meetings and conventions, which range in size from small to very large. They also provide both on-site and off-site catering. Catering for weddings, for example, can be provided at a function venue or at a remote or unique location. Some caterers offer other special services, such as kosher catering. Commercial catering can be done on a large scale, with contracts at major tourist venues, or on a small scale in the home for small dinner parties.

Security

Guests staying at or visiting any type of establishment expect that both they and their belongings will be safe. Nothing ruins a holiday more than a security-related incident. Fortunately, Australia is one of the safest destinations in the world. Despite this, security services have to ensure that guests or members are not disturbed by intoxicated patrons and that they can leave with their large winnings accumulated at the gaming tables at the casino intact. Security staff play a discreet, important role in ensuring that guests are not exposed to any kind of safety risk.

Gaming

With the opening of several new casinos, Australia is offering gaming to both local customers and overseas visitors. Games include roulette, blackjack, Keno and two-up, which has a long history in Australian gambling. Poker machines, available in many clubs and hotels, range from the old-fashioned 'fruit machine' variety (although, to the disgust of many old-timers, nowadays you press buttons instead of pulling on the arm) to very sophisticated games with more complex rules. With the advent of virtual reality, gaming machines of the future will offer extraordinary entertainment. The wide range of gaming activities currently available will be described in more detail in Chapter 11.

Relationships with sectors of the tourism industry

Many of the sectors and services of the hospitality industry also relate closely to the sectors and services of the tourism industry outlined below.

Tour operators and wholesalers

Tour operators prepare their own tourism programs of destinations and activities. Tour wholesalers put together packages, which include accommodation, transport, tours and activities. These are the special packages that we see widely advertised. Inbound operators bring tourists into the country while outbound operators take tourists to overseas destinations.

Travel agents

Travel agents are responsible for recommending destinations and making bookings for travel and accommodation. People rely on their agents to recommend holidays that will meet their particular needs. This is extremely challenging, given the number of domestic and international possibilities and the importance of a careful match with what the customer is looking for. Very often a year's or a lifetime's savings will be spent on a major trip so careful questioning, listening, advising and ticketing is necessary to ensure the outcome reaches expectations. Travel agents work closely with the hospitality industry to keep up to date with services offered and special deals on accommodation, dining, entertainment and activities. The Australian hospitality industry also works hard to ensure that our attractions and services are sold overseas to inbound visitors.

Tourist information centres

These centres vary from large to very small. In fact, in the small snow-country town of Tumbarumba, the tourist information centre is run by local volunteers who are very knowledgeable and very entertaining. Often the information centre is part of a small shop selling local crafts, jams and souvenirs. One such centre in New South Wales is a caravan converted into a small museum, which shows something of the mining history of the nearby ghost town. Stopping for a visit, to pick up maps and brochures, as well as a cold drink, can lead to long conversations with two enthusiastic old people with extraordinary tales to tell. Guest books filled with hundreds of positive remarks demonstrate how much their enthusiasm and conviviality have been appreciated by visitors over many years. Children leave with ice-creams in one hand and pieces of fossilised wood in the other, and adults leave enriched by information and anecdotes.

Other tourist information centres are large and very busy, with demands on staff to answer diverse questions. In Australia's major cities, there are, as you can imagine, numerous places of interest and many different ways to get there. Knowledgeable, friendly service is most important. Again the hospitality industry relies on staff in information centres to correctly advise customers of the services it offers, such as accommodation and food and beverage.

Airlines

Qantas and Virgin-Blue are two airlines well known for their outstanding levels of service. However, there are also many small operators in Australia offering services to small towns. Hazelton Airlines (now Regional Express) is an example of one with a long record of serving people in the bush. Many people on board aeroplanes are travelling for business, while others are travelling for other reasons, such as illness in the family. The special needs of all these travellers must be met by an industry that provides hospitality under sometimes very difficult circumstances.

Transport operators

Other transport services include coaches and hire cars, taxis, buses and trains. In many cases it is hard for staff to pick the traveller from the commuter, but generally questions can give clues to their needs. Coach drivers have one of the most challenging tasks of all: getting a load of noisy people safely from one destination to another. In addition to this, the driver is also required to harmonise relationships between members of the group, entertain them and provide them with extensive information along the way. In fact, there are many personalities among Australia's coach drivers who are fondly remembered by overseas visitors.

Co-ordination between hotels and coach operators is necessary to ensure that arrivals are processed quickly and that everyone reaches their rooms with a minimum of delay. Checking out also needs to be handled professionally to ensure that a coach load of tourists is not left sitting outside the main entrance waiting for one missing person to resolve a problem with their account. Tours need to run on time as many Asian and European visitors become extremely concerned by even small delays.

Attractions

Warner Bros Movie World in Queensland is an example of a major attraction. This theme park, of which there are many in Australia, captures the excitement and magic of Hollywood. Other attractions include World Heritage Sites, such as the South West Wilderness in Tasmania, and built features, such as the Sydney Opera House. In both Australia and New Zealand, visits to natural attractions are combined with 'soft' and 'hard' adventure packages. In fact, nature-based tourism is a rapidly growing sector of the industry.

Retail outlets

Few tourists can resist the attraction of local souvenirs. The quality of the products now available on the Australian market is very impressive; for example, unique artworks are very popular with overseas visitors who are looking for quality locally produced merchandise for special gifts or personal keepsakes. Paintings, wooden crafts, glassware and clothing are all popular items, giving an outlet for local talent.

An American couple who settled on Dent Island in the Whitsundays over 40 years ago sell unusual coral art to visitors who come, not only to look at what they have to sell, but also to see the beauty of the environment in which they live. Surrounded by palms, the small shop, which is part of their natural accommodation, has a magnificent view of the turquoise sea. Their lifestyle and their enthusiasm to meet new people who arrive daily by yacht are admired and remembered by all visitors who have glimpsed their small paradise.

Tourist shopping areas, such as the Salamanca Markets in Hobart, The Rocks in Sydney and South Bank in Brisbane are magnets for visitors.

Influences on establishments in the hospitality industry

There are many external influences on the operation of hospitality establishments, but we will cover only the most important ones here (see also Fig. 1.5).

Market needs and expectations

The changing needs of consumers have already been mentioned. New foods, drinks and styles of operation are important to those customers who are always looking for a different experience. The enormous range of items available on today's menus is testimony to this. In contrast, other customers look for an environment in which they feel comfortable and know exactly what to expect. Many successful operators in the industry have offered the same style of food, entertainment or accommodation for many years. Loyal customers would be most disturbed by significant changes. Some families visit the same camping ground or country hotel year after year, meeting the same group of friends each time. This need for continuity and return to 'home' values is met by establishments that offer older-style accommodation and food. These can range from modest 'home stay' type accommodation to luxurious rooms in historic buildings filled with antiques and original artworks.

Anticipating changing customer needs and deciding whether to change to meet them are dilemmas for every hospitality operator. Staying in touch with the customer base, researching customer needs and expectations, and constantly asking for feedback are all ways in which establishments can ensure continued success.

Economic climate

The value of the Australian dollar has a major impact on the tourism industry. It affects the 'value for money' achieved by visitors from overseas, and has an impact on outward bound tourists who are seeking 'value for money' in other destinations. Tourism exceeds all exports, including coal and wool, in generating revenue for the country. Just as important as meeting the needs of these important

---

FIG. 1.5

Influences on the operation of establishments in the hospitality industry.

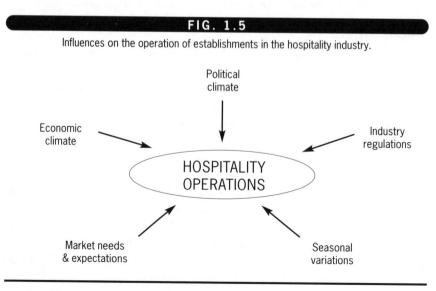

Political climate

Economic climate

Industry regulations

HOSPITALITY OPERATIONS

Market needs & expectations

Seasonal variations

revenue-generating inbound tourists is ensuring that local tourists are attracted to what is offered by the industry so that their dollar will not leave the country. Too many Australians have been overseas and have not seen anything of what Australia has to offer. Frequently price and economic factors influence these decisions.

Periods of recession are likely to have the largest impact on leisure spending, and the level of disposable income is also crucial to the viability of many parts of the hospitality industry. Gambling appears to be an interesting exception, with high revenue in both the good times and the bad.

Seasonal variations

Fortunately for most of Australia's tourist businesses, our climate is so pleasant that our off-season means a fluctuation in trade rather than a closing of operations. In many colder climates the winter season is so severe that the hospitality industry is only viable for half of the year. Our temperate climate ensures that we can offer holidays all year round. Peak times vary from establishment to establishment, depending on their markets. November is a popular month for Japanese tourists to visit Australia, and of course the summer holidays in December and January are always very busy. Some restaurants experience small seasonal variations in trade, but other sectors, such as the club sector, are busy all year round.

Industry regulations

Legislative requirements, such as licenses to serve alcohol and for pavement trading and gaming, have a big impact on the operation of hospitality enterprises. The need for a grease trap in a takeaway shop or small restaurant, and the requirements of the Food Act and the Occupational Health and Safety Act, all have an impact on the way in which an establishment can operate. In addition to legal obligations, hospitality organisations can face ethical problems if they introduce, for example, 'happy hours' and 'dollar drinks' as these can sometimes lead to seriously intoxicated patrons. The industry is working hard, through its associations, to provide guidelines on such issues. Smoking legislation is being implemented in a wide range of hospitality establishments to limit the risk of passive smoking to guests and staff. Gaming is another issue requiring legislation, and this is discussed in more detail in Chapter 11.

Political climate

The political climate and the general level of personal safety in a country are important factors in consumer decision-making. Despite having many attractions for tourists, some countries are perceived as being too dangerous to visit. The threat of terrorism is one aspect of the political climate that is taken into account by potential tourists.

Working conditions in the hospitality industry

Wages and conditions of employment in the tourism and hospitality industry are covered by a range of legislative guidelines, which will be covered in more detail in Chapter 13. It is important to note, however, that there are minimum wages and conditions that apply to all Australians working in the industry. Although these may vary, depending on whether staff are covered by awards or agreements, and which award or agreement applies in a particular workplace, these requirements do exist, and they can be explored by contacting the appropriate union, or state or federal Department of Industrial Relations, to find out more information.

One of the most important considerations when planning a career in the industry is the hours of work. Since the industry is mostly a 24-hour operation and primarily focused on leisure, it is necessary for staff to work shift work, weekends and public holidays. This can have both positive and negative effects on your family and social life.

Personal attributes required by the industry

Excellent communication skills and teamwork are essential in this industry. In all service industries, and the hospitality industry is no exception, positive customer contact is the key to running a successful operation. Employers are always on the lookout for staff who communicate well and show initiative in asking questions, providing information and anticipating needs by watching customers' body language. Communicating clearly with people of all ages, cultures and languages are attributes that are highly regarded.

Being able to work in a team is also important since most work in the industry is done in teams. Serving food or drink is the last step in a long line of procedures involving a number of staff. Checking out a guest is another example of team effort. Although only one staff member does the check-out, bookings have been made by someone else and the guest has been checked in by a third person. Errors made at the time of booking and not noticed or remedied at the time of check-in can leave a guest with a very bad impression of an establishment. When a receptionist explains to a guest at the time of arrival that only some methods of payment are acceptable, this ensures that the customer is not embarrassed when settling the account on departure.

Changeover of shifts requires staff to be punctual so that handover procedures and briefings can be done, resulting in a smooth transition from one group of staff to another. This is known as 'seamless service'.

Well known for high levels of staff turnover, the hospitality industry is now taking steps to build career paths for employees to retain them longer. This has significantly increased the professionalism of service provided in Australia. As a result, employers are looking for dedicated people who have long-term plans for career development. A commitment to improving the quality of service offered to customers is reflected in personal presentation. Tidy appearance, with the right level of formality to suit the style of the establishment, is recommended when going for interviews. Supervisors and managers find it frustrating to remind staff of the company's uniform code, and are looking for staff who take the image of the organisation seriously enough to present themselves flawlessly when arriving for interviews or work.

Honesty and discretion are other important attributes in an industry where breaches of security and confidentiality are possible. Revealing the name of a guest or their room number would be a serious breach of confidentiality.

Service ethos in the industry

A service ethos is a commitment to a certain style and approach to service. Some hospitality establishments have a very informal service ethos while others, at the luxury end of the market, have a very formal one. Words used in greeting reflect the service ethos of the establishment. Compare 'G'day, how are ya?' with 'Good morning, my name is Alison, may I help you?' Both are appropriate in different situations, so too are the level of familiarity and many other aspects of service. Generally, a company has a mission statement, which is a guide to their service ethos.

Management skills required by the industry

Running a hospitality establishment is far more complex than most people realise. For a start, the urgency to meet customer needs for food and beverages is far greater than it would be for camera repair or photograph processing. Tolerance levels for delays in service of food and beverages are very low indeed, as we have mentioned. Food and, to some extent, beverages are perishable, and careful stock control is essential. Imagine managing the stock for an island resort where all items take a minimum of three days to reach you!

Added to this is a very high level of customer transactions. Unlike at a supermarket, where you pay for all items simultaneously, customers in the hospitality industry tend to pay for one thing at a time. Also, the number of accounts being opened and closed daily in Front Office is often higher than the number that would be opened and closed in an entire year of an average small business with a 30-day credit period.

All these features of the industry require highly developed management skills, including planning, organising and controlling operations, while customer service requires outstanding communication skills.

Quality assurance in the industry

In order to maintain the quality of products and services available to guests and customers, most hospitality organisations have a quality service philosophy or a quality assurance program. Essentially this means that they monitor their systems and procedures and check the quality of their products. By seeking feedback from customers they can ensure that they remain responsive to customer needs and maintain their standards. For example, if a customer complains about the temperature of the food, staff can be advised and systems changed accordingly. Most quality systems go further and attempt to monitor feedback so closely that they are able to predict future trends and to respond to change more rapidly than their competitors.

The subject of quality management and the role you can play in providing quality service will be covered in more detail in Chapter 20.

Types of hospitality establishments

Some establishments are commercial, which means that they operate for profit. When a local restaurant closes down, it is no doubt because it did not make a profit. When, on the other hand, yet another outlet or fast food chain opens, it means that the company has a successful formula for staying in business and making a profit. Profits are only possible through management carefully controlling costs, planning orders and rostering staff, and of course through conscientiously monitoring customer satisfaction.

Non-commercial hospitality enterprises, including clubs, hospitals, canteens, and catering outfits in jails and institutions, are not in operation to make profits. Although not driven by a profit motive, these operations have to work just as hard at successfully managing costs, staff and customer satisfaction.

Key departments of hospitality establishments

Some of the key departments found in hospitality establishments, and their responsibilities, include:

Front Office	Reservations, check-in and check-out
Housekeeping	Maintaining cleanliness of rooms and public areas, linen and uniforms
Kitchen	Food preparation
Food and Beverage	Food and beverage service
Sales and Marketing	Promoting and selling products and services
Human Resources	Maintaining staff levels and staff satisfaction
Finance	Controlling costs and managing finances
Purchasing	Purchasing and maintaining stock
Gaming	Providing gaming facilities for customers
Leisure and Entertainment	Providing leisure activities and entertainment events
Maintenance Engineering	Ensuring the safety and sound operation of equipment, building maintenance
Security	Ensuring the safety of guests, staff and valuables.

These departments work very closely with one another. If a guest leaves something behind in the room after check-out, for example, Housekeeping staff will hand it over to Security, and Security relies on Front Office records to trace the owner of the lost property. As a further example, Kitchen staff responsible for food preparation are reliant on Purchasing for their supplies of perishable and non-perishable commodities. Negotiating the best price and freshest produce is the responsibility of the purchasing officer. Stores officers keep the stock until it is issued to the department that requests it. Kitchen staff preparing menus often use numerous stock items, and each gram and millilitre must be accounted for. Food is ordered in the restaurant, often on the recommendation of Food and Beverage staff. Service and customer feedback are also part of the role of restaurant staff. The team effort required to deliver flawless service is quite apparent from these examples.

The other important aspect of service (over and above those mentioned here) is the personal attention that customers are looking for from this industry. It is, after all, the 'hospitality' industry. And this is a role of every staff member. It is not unusual for a room attendant waiting at the lift to ask if you are having an enjoyable visit and to provide information on activities. This is a 'can do' industry and the words 'not my department' should never be heard in the hospitality sector.

Career paths in the hospitality industry

Looking for employment in the hospitality industry is easier than in most others. First, it is a growth industry and there are often opportunities for people who are prepared to work hard. Employers constantly complain about being unable to fill positions in housekeeping, stewarding and portering, and the shortage of trainee chefs is well known. A position in a restaurant, coffee shop or fast food outlet is a golden opportunity to learn about the procedures used in the industry and, most importantly, to develop experience in handling customers of all ages and from all walks of life. Research into the services provided by an establishment is straightforward, and brochures, advertising and a personal visit will all help to increase your knowledge of an organisation before attending an interview. Finally, the training offered in the industry is consistent nationally, with completion of competency units, either on or off the job, counting towards the achievement of a qualification. The Tourism Training office in your state will be able to give you a directory of recognised training providers, both public and private.

Activities

1 Give a broad overview of the various sectors of the hospitality industry by researching some of the hospitality establishments in your local area.
2 List the services provided by the establishments you have identified.
3 What are the primary markets of these establishments? (These are also called market segments.)
4 Choose one of these establishments and briefly discuss some of the external factors (such as the season or legislation) which may affect the operation. State whether it is a commercial or non-commercial organisation.
5 Using the same example, describe the attributes of the ideal employee working in this organisation.
6 Describe how two departments in this organisation would need to work together to meet customer needs.
7 Select an entry position (which would be suitable for an applicant with minimum experience) in this organisation, and describe the skills and knowledge that would be useful in applying for this position.

8 Prepare to answer the following question in an interview at your chosen establishment: 'How did you obtain information on work and training in the hospitality industry to prepare yourself for this interview?'

CASE STUDY

Geraldine and Samantha had always wanted to open their own hospitality business. Geraldine was a qualified chef and had run a small but expensive coffee shop in Sydney. Samantha, her lifelong friend, was a trained nurse. So, in 1997, they bought a remote property in the Northern Territory, accessible only to 4WD vehicles, and developed an ecotourism business for adults only.

The business is doing well, but not well enough. Permanent tents have proved to be very popular but only for a limited time of the year. They are now at a turning point, and are undecided about the services they should provide to attract a wider clientele. They are considering upgrading their facilities and accommodation.

Discussion questions

1 In which category would you place this hospitality operation?

2 Why, in your opinion, are remote locations attractive to tourists?

3 What kinds of external influences would affect this operation?

4 Various functions, such as reservations, would need to be performed in this business. List them and recommend the partner who would best be suited to them.

5 What would you do to increase business?

6 Describe the attributes of someone likely to get a job working for Geraldine and Samantha.

7 Discuss the benefits of working in a tourism or hospitality establishment such as this one.

8 If you were to work for Geraldine and Samantha, what hours would you work?

LINKS

Australian Tourism Datacard—
http://www.btr.gov.au/statistics/Datacard/datacard.html

Bureau of Tourism Research—http://www.btr.gov.au/index.html

Commonwealth Department of Industry Tourism and Resources—
http://www.industry.gov.au/content/root.cfm?objectid=1C66D24D-C9B8-4439-B3F3BA20F6C65C87

State and territory tourism organisations—
http://www.atc.net.au/research.asp?sub=6LIB#news)

World Tourism Organization—http://www.world-tourism.org/

CHAPTER TWO

Introduction to the customers

OBJECTIVES

The aim of this chapter is to give you an overview of the customers whose needs the hospitality industry aims to meet. On completion of this chapter you should be able to:

- differentiate between international and domestic tourists
- discuss the ways in which the hospitality industry meets the needs of tourists
- discuss the ways in which the hospitality industry meets the needs of local residents
- identify industry trends and influences
- use knowledge of the hospitality industry and its customers to enhance the quality of work performance.

Ladies who play Bingo at the Binawarra Club are usually waiting at the door before the club opens in the morning. They generally play three times a week, meeting old friends, having lunch afterwards and putting a little money in the poker machines before going home. Their enthusiasm is typified by Judy, an elderly lady of 75 who recently had a minor heart attack during her Bingo session. The staff administered first aid and an ambulance was called. Judy was advised to go to the local hospital for observation, but she was adamant that she was not prepared to leave until after Bingo, besides which she was feeling fine. The ambulance officers were not surprised and took out an indemnity form for her to sign and acknowledge that she was ignoring their advice.

This tells us something about the hospitality industry and the attraction it has for its customers. The customer is the key to the industry. A study of the industry is first and foremost a study of its customers. The services and products supplied by the industry are all geared toward meeting the needs of the customers. Astute operators and astute students planning a career in the industry are fully aware of this and put a lot of effort into learning about the people who use the industry for dining out, holidays and entertainment.

Judy, in the story above, belongs to one market segment—elderly widows with a comfortable income for entertainment and travel. She is one of many women who have a high enough disposable income to go on tours visiting attractions such as Uluru in Central Australia, Rotorua thermal springs in New Zealand and the Great Barrier Reef in Queensland. Cruises to Fiji and trips to London, Hong Kong and Vienna are other examples of annual highlights. Although not inspired by fast food, these women are likely to eat out at least six times a week at the club or at a local coffee shop.

A market segment is a group of customers who share similar characteristics. Each hospitality operation attracts certain market segments. Even if their scope is very broad, such as sales of hamburgers or fried chicken to all age groups, they tend to direct their marketing to particular segments. In the fast food industry, for example, much of the advertising is directed at the younger generation. Clearly not every customer will fit neatly into a market segment but, generally speaking, it is useful to describe the characteristics and spending habits of market segments in order to better understand and cater for their needs. However, there can be a danger in stereotyping customers. Grouping customers to identify how their needs can best be met must be balanced with a flexible approach to ensure that individual needs are not ignored. A study of the hospitality industry starts with a study of its customers (as groups and as individuals). It is followed by a study of the nature of the industry and the departments and processes within it.

Domestic tourism

While domestic tourism grew at only 1 per cent per year between 1988 and 1997, it still accounted for the highest level of demand for accommodation. In 1997 domestic visitor nights spent in hotels, motels and guesthouses amounted to 50.8 million. By 1999, domestic visitor nights totalled 294 million (see Table 2.1). In the same period, international visitor nights totalled 108 million, compared with 18.1 million in 1997 (Tourism Forecasting Council, February 2001).

Domestic tourism continues to be the 'bread and butter' of the tourism industry, currently accounting for around 73 per cent of visitor nights (see Fig. 2.1). However, as you can see from Fig. 2.2, this percentage is predicted to drop in the next few years to reflect the faster growth rate of international markets.

TABLE 2.1

Overnight travel by Australians in 1999.

Main purpose of trip	Trips ('000s)	Nights ('000s)	Expenditure ($m)
Holiday/leisure	32034	143975	17235
Visiting friends and/or relatives	23277	86881	6313
Business	14735	44194	8978
Other	2935	13604	1053
Total*	**72981**	**294266**	**33579**

* Includes purpose not stated. Components may not add to total as overnight trips may contain multiple visits undertaken for different purposes.
Source: Bureau of Tourism Research—http://www.btr.gov.au/statistics/Datacard/overnight.html

FIG. 2.1

Domestic and international visitor nights 2000.

International nights 27%

Domestic nights 73%

Source: Tourism Forecasting Council, February 2001.

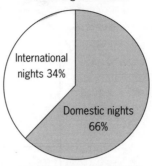

FIG. 2.2

Forecast of domestic and international visitor nights in 2010.

International nights 34%

Domestic nights 66%

Source: Tourism Forecasting Council, February 2001.

The history of domestic tourism in Australia is well summarised in this report:

> From relatively early days Australians developed a love affair with the beach. From early this century those who had the means and time to travel from the capital cities to relatively close beach access areas established beach 'shacks' for Christmas holidays and/or the occasional fishing trip.
>
> As in other industrialised countries, mass tourism did not emerge until after the Second World War and it was not until about the mid-1950s that it started to have an impact on style, location and quality of tourism accommodation. The first motel appeared at this time as did the Gold Coast 'high-rise' hotel (if only a few stories). Now the Gold Coast is one of the nation's major tourist attractions.
>
> Motels spread their way along major routes, such as the Pacific Highway between Sydney and Brisbane, the Hume Highway between Melbourne and Sydney, and gradually replaced the 'country pub' in rural locations. (Industry Commission, *Tourism Accommodation and Training*, 1996, pp. 4–5. Copyright Commonwealth of Australia reproduced by permission.)

Resort destinations emerged in the 1960s and early 1970s. Today's accommodation market is extremely diverse, taking in hotels, motels, guesthouses, home stay, caravan parks (best locations in the country), holiday units, resorts, backpacker accommodation, houseboats, trains and cruise ships.

One of the most recent trends in domestic tourism is towards exploration of pristine environments: four-wheel drive tourists, for example, are attracted to remote and underdeveloped sites. This trend away from the traditional beach holiday started only in the last decade and, as a result, more and more pressure will be placed on the environment. Australia's World Heritage Sites are shown in Fig. 2.3 on page 26. An investigation of these sites could provide some valuable background knowledge for anyone planning a career in the tourism industry.

FIG. 2.3

Australia's World Heritage Sites.

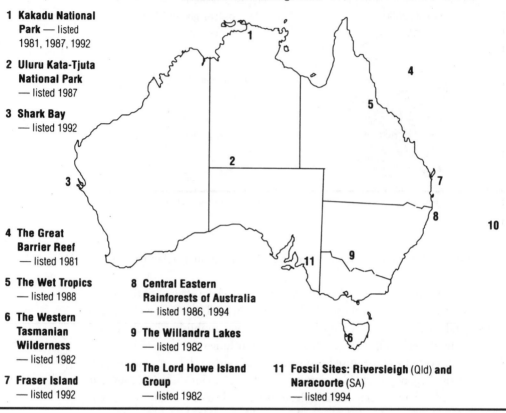

1 **Kakadu National Park** — listed 1981, 1987, 1992

2 **Uluru Kata-Tjuta National Park** — listed 1987

3 **Shark Bay** — listed 1992

4 **The Great Barrier Reef** — listed 1981

5 **The Wet Tropics** — listed 1988

6 **The Western Tasmanian Wilderness** — listed 1982

7 **Fraser Island** — listed 1992

8 **Central Eastern Rainforests of Australia** — listed 1986, 1994

9 **The Willandra Lakes** — listed 1982

10 **The Lord Howe Island Group** — listed 1982

11 **Fossil Sites: Riversleigh** (Qld) **and Naracoorte** (SA) — listed 1994

Source: Industry Commission, *Tourism Accommodation and Training*, 1996, p. 123.
Copyright Commonwealth of Australia reproduced by permission.

FIG. 2.4

Projected gains in the labour force participation rate for men and women 1993–2011.

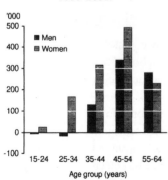

Source: Australian Bureau of Statistics, Cat No 6206.0. Reproduced with permission.

Influences on tourism and hospitality markets

Demand for holiday accommodation, for fast food, for home delivery, for fine dining and for entertainment has increased rapidly with higher disposable incomes and, in part, with the increasing number of women in the workforce who do not have the time to prepare meals. And this demand is likely to continue as the number of working women in the 45–54 age group is expected to double by 2011. In all age groups, except the 15–24 age group, labour force participation rates for women are expected to increase. The participation rate for women aged 25–34 is projected to grow from 66 per cent in the mid-1990s to 79 per cent in 2011, and the rate for women aged 35–44, from 70 per cent to 84 per cent over the same period. These participation rates, illustrated in Fig. 2.4, have important implications for prospective hospitality managers.

Some people are working harder to afford a lifestyle in which they dine out more than they dine in. Empty refrigerators, described in novels about New Yorkers in the sixties who ate out for breakfast, lunch and dinner (or occasionally ordered in to eat from a carton), are becoming increasingly common in local inner-city apartments. Australia has over 12,000 restaurants and cafes. Since the mid-1980s, the number of restaurants and cafes has grown by around 150 per cent, and the number of fast food outlets has more than tripled (ABS Cat No 8634.0). Although Americans spend more annually in restaurants and on takeaway and fast food than Australians and New Zealanders, this gap is narrowing.

Another major trend having an impact on the hospitality industry is the increased amount of leisure time available for recreation. Annual leave developments are illustrated in Fig. 2.5, with annual leave increasing from one week per year in the 1940s to four weeks per year in 2000. While this is true for Australians, many Asians still take only one week's leave per year. This has important implications for staff working in the hospitality sector as plans for spending leisure time are likely to differ markedly from one customer to another.

There have also been some interesting changes in the number of hours worked by Australians and it appears that full-time staff are now working longer than ever. Full-time employees (particularly married women whose workforce participation has increased) need to save time on chores such as shopping and cooking. The number of part-time and casual jobs continues to grow and these employees have more leisure time. All these factors contribute to growth in the hospitality sector; the industry wins on all counts.

Local market segments

There are numerous local market segments, groups of customers with similar characteristics who are consumers in the hospitality industry, so in this section we will describe a few trends which are having a major impact on the nature of the industry and its customers.

FIG. 2.5

Paid annual leave increases 1940–2000.

1 WEEK	2 WEEKS	3 WEEKS	4 WEEKS
1940	1945	1963	2000

Older consumers

Looking at Table 2.2 and Fig. 2.6, you can see that more people are living longer. The population aged 65 and over rises rapidly from 2.2 million in 1997 to a projected 4 million in 2021 and around 6 million in 2051. This represents a projected increase from 12 per cent in 1997 to around 18 per cent in 2021 and about 25 per cent in 2051. If planning a career or business in this industry, these projections would have an impact on your decision-making. Organisational strategic plans for the next 20 to 30 years would need to take these and other trends into account.

The National Population Council estimates that by 2020 the average male life span will have extended by two years and the average female life span by five years.

TABLE 2.2

Projected population ('000) in Australia by age group.

Age group (years)	1997	2011	2021	2031	2051
0–14	3920	3841	3858	3918	3898
15–64	12366	14222	14638	14749	15018
65 and over	2245	2952	4021	5052	6027
85 and over	216	368	440	612	1134
Total	**18747**	**21383**	**22957**	**24331**	**26077**

Source: Population Projections, 1997–2051, Series II, 3222.0 reproduced with permission. Australian Bureau of Statistics.

FIG. 2.6

Projected population structure of Australia 1997–2051 ('000).

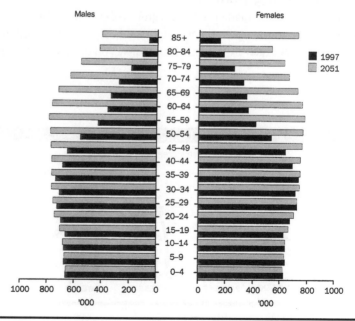

Source: Population Projections, 1997–2051, Series II, 3222.0 reproduced with permission. Australian Bureau of Statistics.

Women over 80 will outnumber men two to one. Market segments emerging from this scenario include:

Men aged 55–70	Substantial retirement income, with time to spend on leisurely travel. Belong to local clubs for sport and entertainment, including gaming. *Main interests:* sporting events, entertainment.
Women aged 55–70	Increasingly working until 60, these women are fit and keen to enjoy the freedom lost through child-rearing and later career development. Travel in groups to exotic locations, enjoy soft adventure. *Main interests:* natural and historical attractions.
Women aged 70–89	Retirement living with fine dining, leisure and entertainment facilities. Coach tours and cruises. *Main interests:* cultural events and indigenous flora.

Younger consumers

The average family with two children and, increasingly, with two incomes to indulge these children spends more than ever before on eating out, visiting adventure attractions and travelling. A plane trip to a resort, an impossible dream for many previous generations of children, will become a standard holiday for many in the next century. Attempts by parents to spend quality time with their children to compensate for long hours at work will increase their participation in the hospitality industry. Marketing efforts will target the children who influence the consumer decision-makers, the parents. Emerging consumer markets for the hospitality industry include:

Children aged 2–10	Like to eat out in colourful environments with recognisable characters and products. Food: easy to eat, highly sugared or salted. Activities and entertainment included. *Main interests:* colour and action. Parents are looking for a clean, safe and fun type of environment with a low food cost.
Teenagers aged 11–18	Maturing faster, this segment is looking for excitement. Challenging the boundaries of the body and the mind are a preoccupation. *Main interest:* escapism.

Hard-working consumers

High stress levels and long hours seem to be typical for the modern worker. Dining out and short holiday breaks are lifestyle choices made by these individuals whose fast-paced life does not give them much chance to escape. Emerging market segments include:

Young couples	With no children and two jobs, this segment has money to spend on health resorts, entertainment and overseas travel. *Main interests:* fitness, entertainment and the arts.

TABLE 2.3

International visitor arrivals 1991–2010 ('000).

Year	New Zealand	Japan	Other Asia	Europe	North America	Rest of World	Total ('000)	Change on previous year (%)
1991	480	529	389	531	325	117	2370	—
1992	448	630	506	577	312	131	2603	9.9
1993	499	671	704	637	332	154	2996	15.1
1994	480	721	927	721	344	168	3362	12.2
1995	538	783	1118	752	363	171	3726	10.8
1996	672	813	1311	799	378	192	4165	11.8
1997	686	814	1350	874	394	200	4318	3.7
1998	709	751	1081	951	446	229	4167	−3.5
1999	729	707	1211	1072	495	245	4460	7.0
2000	821	720	1351	1203	571	280	4946	10.9
2001	738	718	1402	1242	529	295	4924	−0.4
2002	**752**	**732**	**1494**	**1314**	**536**	**308**	**5136**	**4.3**
2003	**773**	**755**	**1676**	**1406**	**583**	**331**	**5525**	**7.6**
2004	**800**	**777**	**1895**	**1511**	**628**	**358**	**5968**	**8.0**
2005	**828**	**803**	**2127**	**1613**	**669**	**385**	**6424**	**7.7**
2006	**856**	**828**	**2406**	**1721**	**711**	**416**	**6939**	**8.0**
2007	**878**	**856**	**2725**	**1833**	**751**	**449**	**7492**	**8.0**
2008	**892**	**882**	**3077**	**1946**	**793**	**484**	**8074**	**7.8**
2009	**902**	**908**	**3469**	**2063**	**835**	**521**	**8698**	**7.7**
2010	**908**	**935**	**3913**	**2186**	**876**	**562**	**9381**	**7.8**

Notes: Numbers in bold are forecasts. Figures for 2000 and 2001 are based on preliminary Overseas Arrivals and Departures data.
Other Asia includes all Asian and Middle East countries, except Japan.
Source: Tourism Forecasting Council, October 2001.

TABLE 2.4

Length of stay and spending of international visitors 1999.

Region	Average length of stay (days)	Average expenditure per night in Australia ($)	Average expenditure per person in Australia ($)	TOTAL expenditure in Australia ($b)
Europe	38	69	2585	2.83
North America	27	88	2359	1.15
Japan	13	114	1424	0.94
Asia	30	94	2822	3.14
New Zealand	15	79	1168	0.82
ꞁ	26	83	2167	9.37

Source: Bureau of Tourism Research, International Visitors Survey (IVS), 1999.

Singles	Freedom from the constraints of relationships or children allows for extensive world travel to remote locations. *Main interests:* new cultures and new environments.

These are just a few trends and some of the emerging market segments. Other market segments have always been there and will continue to have their special needs. The disabled traveller, for example, may need wheelchair access to hotel rooms, stages and podiums; accessible control buttons in lifts; wheelchair accessible toilets and knee spaces under washbasins. People of different religious beliefs also need to be catered for. Muslims, Hindus and Jews, for example, have particular dietary needs. Kosher kitchens are available in some large hotels, while others have to be converted following strict guidelines. All such special needs have to be anticipated. Therefore, hotel reservations staff require an extensive knowledge of the needs of a wide range of guests and the strategies that can be put in place to meet individual needs not catered for by their establishment.

International tourism

Inbound tourism is the fastest growing sector of the Australian tourism industry. While domestic tourism continues to grow by a small amount each year, its growth is well outmatched by that of the international market. Between 1991 and 2000 arrivals increased by an average of nearly 8 per cent per year. In 2000, nearly 5 million tourists visited Australia and this number is expected to grow to around 9.4 million in 2010 (see Table 2.3).

As you can see from Table 2.4, visitors from Asian countries (excluding Japan) spend the most, which can be partly explained by the fact that they stay longer in Australia than other international visitors, apart from Europeans. By far the most popular reason for visiting Australia for all international tourists is for holidays, followed by visiting friends and relatives (see Table 2.5 on page 32).

Service and customer expectations

All visitors to Australia arrive with preconceived ideas about what to expect. Many are struck by the size of the country, finding that it takes longer than anticipated to travel from one attraction to another. They often expect to see the whole eastern part of the country within a week, including all capital cities, the Barrier Reef, Uluru and the Daintree!

From a service viewpoint, all customers expect efficient service. Where they tend to differ is in the level of formality and friendliness they seek. However, even though a visitor may expect formal service in their own country, they may be delighted with the open friendliness and informality of Australians. The level of acceptance will vary from individual to individual, of course, and some visitors may be offended by what they see as a lack of courtesy.

All tourism and hospitality customers, including international visitors, differ in terms of:
- expectations and needs
- interests and activities

TABLE 2.5	
Purpose of visit for international visitors for 1999.	

Reason	%
Holiday	56
Visit friends/relatives	19
Business	10
Convention/conference	2
Other	13

Source: Australian Bureau of Statistics.
http://www.btr.gov.au/statistics/Datacard/dcpurp.html
Reproduced with permission.

- cultural factors
- socio-economic factors
- available time
- health
- age
- personality/mood.

In every case effort must be made to anticipate customer needs and to remain responsive to feedback from the customer. This is not always easy as some Asian visitors, for example, do not like to complain. Saying 'No' is thought to be rude and impolite because it might hurt the other person's feelings. This is also the case with many Africans. If asked 'Do you understand?' they will tend to say 'Yes' because it would be a poor reflection on

Cultural diversity deserves more than lip service

LEN TAYLOR, AUSTRALIAN TOURISM EXPORT COUNCIL (FORMERLY INBOUND TOURISM ORGANISATION OF AUSTRALIA)

For more than a decade 'multi-culturalism' and 'cultural diversity' have been used as easy, catch-all descriptions for our unique blend of indigenous, European and Asian population.

But while we've adopted the jargon—we need to go further in embracing and promoting this cultural blend.

We need to show our new citizens that we recognise and want to draw on their language and cultural skills for the benefit of everyone.

For the tourism industry this means seeking assistance from our many ethnic groups so that we can keep up with visitors' changing language needs.

Up to one-third of Australia's overseas visitors are now Chinese, Indonesian/Malay, Korean, Japanese and Thai-speaking.

However, a recent survey on visitors' language needs indicates we are not responding quickly enough to these projected changes in our tourism markets.

The survey of 80 tourism organisations revealed that while German, French, Italian and Spanish-speaking visitors were less than 14 per cent of the total number of non-English speaking visitors, almost 30 per cent of staff were expected to be fluent in European languages!

The study also highlighted six major areas in tourism where staff fluent in languages were needed including tour guides, tour co-ordinators, front-of-house staff, flight attendants and marketing and sales staff.

As Australia's only body solely representing inbound tourism, the Australian Tourism Export Council (ATEC) believes our cultural diversity is as valuable an asset to tourism as our landscapes and indigenous heritage . . .

If we accept the fact that our tourism industry needs to upgrade its language and cultural skills, it is vital that tourism operators take a close look at their staff hiring policy.

In many cases, staff with foreign language skills are employed to do a job that does not call on these skills. What a waste!

ATEC suggests that tourism operators upgrade their companies' language skills by adopting the following recommendations:

- Be aware of how many of your existing customers are from non-English speaking countries as well as their current level of English skills.
- Develop a comprehensive language policy with commitment from the top.
- Make foreign language skills a recruitment criterion, and emphasise this in recruitment literature.
- Develop a training plan to improve staff language skills and cross-cultural understanding skills.
- Provide training programs that relate to cultural awareness.
- Provide visitor information in a number of foreign languages.

There is no doubting our cultural diversity gives us a significant competitive advantage over others in the international tourism industry. It is up to us to make the most of it, not only for our sake, but for all Australians.

Adapted from Len Taylor, Australian Tourism Export Council. *Tourism and Hospitality Update*, May/June 1997. Reproduced with permission.

the sender's communication skills if they were to say 'No'. It is most important for service staff to be aware of possible cultural differences.

Customers can also vary in temperament and mood, the two main factors playing a part in this being fatigue and hunger. The hungry or tired customer is, in fact, more challenging than most. Anyone who works behind a bar will appreciate the necessity of playing amateur psychologist to the customers they attend.

Examples of the various ways that employees can deliver high quality service include:

- communicating with customers in a way that promotes goodwill, trust and satisfaction
- identifying customer needs through body language and other cues
- being aware that body language is often culturally based
- ensuring that customer requests are met promptly
- providing service beyond the customer's original request
- selling the organisation's services and products in a positive manner
- providing useful information and advice to the customer
- displaying positive, polite and attentive body language.

Activities

1 Find out as much as you can about Australia's World Heritage Sites so that you can discuss them with international tourists.
2 With a group develop a questionnaire about Australians on holiday. Interview four Australians about their holidays, if possible in a particular market segment. (For example, you might like to interview parents on a tight budget.) Together, collate and analyse your findings and develop three profiles of domestic tourists.
3 With a group develop a questionnaire about dining out in Australia. Interview four Australians about their dining-out experiences (this can include takeaway or fast food). Once again, try to interview a particular market segment, such as singles in the 20–30 age group. With your group, analyse your findings and develop three profiles of local hospitality consumers.
4 Japan's population is expected to change numerically (reducing by 25 million) and demographically (ageing rapidly) in this century. At the moment the number of people over 65 outnumbers the number aged under 15. By 2050 the number of people 65 and over will account for around 32 per cent of the population. What are the implications for tourism in Australia?
5 List the needs of one group of international visitors and identify how the industry meets the needs of this market segment.

CASE STUDY

Anna and Mira, two Dutch visitors to Australia, were enthusiastically explaining their impressions of Australia. 'The space, we cannot get over the amount of space you have. Homes and gardens, farms and deserts. You can buy a brand new flat on the Gold Coast for less than $250,000—with views of the ocean. The average person in Holland cannot possibly afford a home with a garden or such a beautiful apartment. There is just no space left in Europe: every square centimetre has been developed. There is such diversity, in the cultures here and in the Australian environment. So much is unspoiled. The sights we have seen and the distances we have travelled! This has been such an experience for us.

'Australians have "no worries" written all over them. It is in their bodies, just to look at them. They are so tolerant and easy going, but at the same time very hard working.'

Discussion questions

1 What would attract a Dutch visitor to Australia?
2 In weighing up the pros and cons of visiting Australia, what would some of the 'cons' be for someone travelling from Europe?
3 How are lifestyles in Australia different from those in Holland?
4 What were the main impressions of these tourists?
5 Were these impressions accurate?
6 How were Australians perceived by these tourists?
7 Are these the impressions we would like tourists to have of our country and its people?

LINKS

Australian Bureau of Statistics, *A Century of Population Change: Year Book of Australia 2001*—http://www.abs.gov.au/ausstats/abs@.nsf/Lookup/NT0001768A

Australian Tourist Commission statistics— http://www.atc.net.au/research.asp?sub=6FOR

Department of Industry, Tourism and Resources— http://www.industry.gov.au/content/root.cfm?objectid=1C66D24D-C9B8-4439-B3F3BA20F6C65C87

Tourism Forecasting Council— http://www.industry.gov.au/content/controlfiles/display_details.cfm?ObjectID=80E72BA6-3584-4DAD-B55780EF35713968

CHAPTER THREE

Research – updating industry and local knowledge

OBJECTIVES

This chapter is designed to help you to improve your research skills. On completion of this chapter you should be able to:

- research hospitality industry and local knowledge
- identify and access sources of information
- use questioning techniques to obtain information
- sort and summarise information
- check currency and accuracy of information
- prepare and present information
- use knowledge to promote the tourism and hospitality industry
- use knowledge to assist customers with their choices.

An American couple visiting Australia asked me whether some Aboriginal people lived in reservations like the indigenous Americans. I was lost for an answer. I had heard of land rights but was not really sure what the words meant. I realised that I could remember very little from my history lessons and that I should have a better general knowledge. If I knew more about Australia and its people, I could be a better ambassador for my country. Most guests don't ask these sorts of questions but many would like to be given information so that they could get a feel for the country.

HOTEL RECEPTIONIST

Having explored some of the places and people in the tourism and hospitality industry, it is now appropriate to develop your knowledge as a basis for future communication in the workplace. This is most important. If you were to attend an interview and quote the number of predicted international arrivals for 2010 the interviewer could not fail to be impressed. If you were able to discuss the many different cultures from which these visitors were coming, all the better. Knowledge is also important in your interactions with customers. You can't be friendly and provide good service in a vacuum, and the best thing to talk about is the products and services available. In a broader sense, one of the products you are selling is Australia, so it is important to know something about it. You also need to know a little bit about the countries of origin of our visitors. Only then will you understand what sorts of things they are interested in and how not to inadvertently cause communication problems.

A further valuable outcome of this chapter will be the ability to find information when you need to. Learning to use a library and the Internet to find information is a key competency.

Industry knowledge

There are numerous sources of information on the hospitality industry. They include:
- the media
- reference books
- libraries
- unions
- industry associations
- industry journals
- the Internet
- information services
- personal observation and experience
- colleagues, supervisors and managers
- industry contacts, mentors and advisers.

Other related industries that you should stay up to date with include:
- entertainment
- food production
- wine production
- recreation
- meetings and events
- retail.

To remain up to date with trends in these fast-moving industries, it is important to watch the media closely and to keep a portfolio of press clippings. This will ensure that you are aware of topical issues and changes to legislation pertinent to all these industries.

Local knowledge

If you are working in the hospitality industry, you also need to develop your local knowledge since customers will be keen to know more about the region they are visiting. Most local libraries have a special section on local history and this is well worth consulting. Your local Tourist Information Office can provide lots of useful information, and participation in local tours is also helpful. And don't forget to read the local paper, listen to your colleagues and customers, and pay attention to the local media.

An organised portfolio of relevant information will help you to give customers advice on shopping, restaurants, attractions, museums, events and natural features in your local area. The information included in your porfolio should include:

- local maps and transport information
- specific shopping details and timing of local markets
- restaurants, cafes and other dining venues
- facilities and services such as hairdressers, dentists, travel agencies, post offices and banks
- theatres and entertainment venues
- sporting venues and fitness centres
- art galleries and museums
- places of local and historic significance
- local guided tours and trips
- local customs
- festivals and special events (local councils usually have a calendar of events).

When doing this research, it is important to look at things through the eyes of a tourist. Imagine also that you are a visitor from overseas, a visitor from another state, a very old tourist and a very young tourist. All have different interests, so you will need to be able to answer questions on a diverse range of topics.

Knowledge of the hospitality enterprise

The information discussed so far relates to the hospitality industry as a whole and to local areas. But employees working for hospitality enterprises need to know about the services provided by their organisation. For example, an employee working in a hotel should be able to answer questions about:

- food and beverage outlets and their menus
- housekeeping services such as babysitting and laundry
- fitness centre hours of operation and equipment
- business centre hours of operation and services
- room features such as Internet access
- current functions and events in the hotel and their location.

Identifying relevant information

One of the most difficult tasks when conducting research is deciding which information is relevant. For example, you might need to decide which topics to search for in a library. If you were looking for books on the subject of 'special events', you might find that there were fewer than you expected. If, however, you extended your research to cover meetings and conventions as well, you would find a lot of information relevant to your topic. On the other hand, there would be some topics for which there would be far too much information and you would need to narrow the subject in order to make the task manageable.

When we conduct research, we often find that we have a huge amount of information—from the library, the Internet and the experts. If we don't allow sufficient time to analyse the data, we are wasting our time. This is the reason why establishing a timetable for your research is important, a topic which will be covered later in this chapter.

Researching primary data

In addition to researching information using the sources suggested in this chapter, you might wish to gather your own data by conducting formal or informal interviews. With formal interviews, structured questionnaires are used, while informal approaches involve questioning and observation. There is much to be learnt from keeping your eyes and ears open when visiting hospitality establishments. You can observe the decor, lighting, music, advertising, range of products, service procedures, and much more.

When designing a questionnaire for a survey, frame your questions very carefully so that you secure information that is relevant to the topic. To do this successfully, you need to plan the structure of the final report. If, for example, you wanted to know how many holidays a sample of people took each year and how long they spent at each destination, you would not need to ask them their age, address, sex, marital status and number of children—not, of course, unless you intended to compare age groups or families and singles. For the latter, a reasonably large sample would be required.

While the subjects of statistics and sampling are beyond the scope of this chapter, you need to be aware that if you are making comparisons you need a large sample. For most quantitative research, the minimum number of people interviewed would be in the region of 200; for qualitative research a smaller sample can be used.

When seeking information, you also need to decide on the type of question to use. An open-ended question will provide interesting information, but it will make it difficult to compare information and calculate averages or other statistics. Most surveys include both closed and open questions. This is illustrated in Fig. 3.1 on page 40.

As you can see from the questionnaire, there are only four boxes to choose from, which does not allow the person responding to say 'don't know' or 'not sure'. You might like to include this option.

A question-based approach will help you to enlist the interviewee's support. If you start by explaining how long the questions will take, the topic covered and your reason for doing the research, you will more than likely find that people will be happy to respond. Careful design will ensure that you don't waste their time or yours.

Once you have the required number of completed questionnaires, you need to sort and summarise the information. Firstly, record the number of responses in each

Sample questionnaire, using open and closed questions.

	Strongly agree	Agree	Disagree	Strongly disagree
1 Tourism is good for the Australian economy.	☐	☐	☐	☐
2 I would support tourism expenditure by my local council.	☐	☐	☐	☐
3 I would go out of my way to help a tourist.	☐	☐	☐	☐
4 I would support the development of a hotel or resort in my local area.	☐	☐	☐	☐

How do you feel about the impact of tourism on the environment? _____

_____

box for each question. Then write a report, analysing the data and drawing conclusions based on the responses obtained. (Each question provides you with a section heading.) Graphs are very useful in supporting your conclusions.

The library

All libraries in Australia, and in fact in many other countries, use the Dewey cataloguing system, devised by Melvil Dewey and first published in 1876. This system allocates 10 classes to library materials. These classes are:

000 Generalities
100 Philosophy
200 Religion
300 Social Sciences
400 Language
500 Pure Sciences
600 Technology (applied sciences)
700 The Arts
800 Literature
900 Geography and History

These 10 classes are further subdivided into 10 divisions. Each of these 100 divisions is further divided into 10 sections. For example, 994 means Class 9 (Geography and History), Division 9 (Modern History) and Section 4 (Australia). This simply means that in any library you visit you will find Australian History at 994.

Each book has a number on the spine called the call number. Each book has a unique call number. If you are looking for a specific book, the first place to stop would be the catalogue, which allows you to search by title, subject, author and content. Computerised catalogues have now made searching much easier.

Books

There are several parts to a book and these are listed below.

Title page

This usually includes the title of the book, the name of the author or editor, the name of the publisher and the location of the publisher. These are all worth recording if essays and assignments are to be referenced correctly (more on this later).

Table of contents

If you are looking for an appropriate book, the table of contents will give you a broad idea of the book's contents.

Bibliography

This is a list of the books and articles referred to by an author when writing a book. It is useful for further reading on the subject.

Index

This is an alphabetical reference to all the important people, facts, events and issues that are discussed in a book. If you were looking for some information on the origins of multiculturalism, you would probably find this subject listed in the index of a book on Australian history.

As an example, here is an extract from a publication called *Images of Australia*, which was indexed under 'multiculturalism':

> Al Grassby, the flamboyant, British-born Minister for Immigration in the Whitlam Government was, as Liffman suggests, an important catalyst in the promotion and acceptance of the notion of a multicultural society. In 1973 he issued a statement entitled A *Multicultural Society for the Future*, which set out the concepts of ethnic heterogeniety and cultural pluralism . . . He advocated the concept of 'the family of the nation' as a means to stress the contribution of migrants to Australia and of the need to recognise, rather than dismiss, their distinctiveness. (Collins, 1992, p. 115)

Acknowledgements

Every time a passage from a book is used it should be quoted in inverted commas " " or indented, as above. Each quote should be acknowledged in the text or in the references with the author, date and page. The full details of the source should be listed in the bibliography. Notice that in the quote in the last paragraph the author, date and page are included in brackets after the quote. Turning now to the bibliography for this book, the Collins reference is listed in detail.

Most bibliographic entries are listed as follows:

> Van Der Wagen, L. *Professional Hospitality: Core Competencies*, 2nd edn. Hospitality Press, Sydney, 2002.

In the bibliography you need to record the author, title (in italics), publisher, place of publication and date. There are several different ways of presenting the information in a bibliography, but the most important point to remember is to remain consistent in the style used.

As long as the source is acknowledged, as described above, it can be quoted. All other writing should be in your own words. When someone else's work is presented as your own this is known as plagiarism. There are generally severe penalities for submitting non-original work without acknowledgement.

Students have presented my own writing back to me on more than one occasion. One student copied four pages from one of my books. It is hard to imagine that I would not recognise my own work!

The Internet

The Internet is a global network of computer networks interlinked with each other. They are physically connected by a wide variety of network hardware (fibre optics, modems, telephone lines, etc.). Part of the Internet is known as the World Wide Web. Your computer, when online, can access thousands of Australian and international 'sites' (other computers' locations on the Internet). Some of these are the sites of libraries and other official bodies; others are the sites of individual people. At the moment anyone can publish anything on the Internet.

Searching for information on the Internet

The Internet is growing at a rapid rate, and as technology evolves so does the amount of information available to users. Some of the information is very useful, while some, such as individuals' 'home pages', is mostly for fun. For this reason you need to search carefully and critically for the desired information. Bear in mind that, unlike with books, there is no editor checking the content and deciding whether the material is worthwhile or accurate.

A search for Japanese culture revealed this information contributed by Taiji Okada (http://www.su.ic.uk/clubs/osc/japan/articles/japanculture.html):

> In Japan it is illegal to gamble. To get around this problem, the Japanese have devised an interesting method around this. Pachinko is similar to the pinball machine, except it involves a lot more balls!! (literally thousands). Westerners have never taken to this game due to it being very noisy and illogical. If a gambler wins then he exchanges his balls for some prizes. He then crosses over the street and trades his prizes for hard currency. Pachinko is very popular in Japan, and it is rare to see them empty in the evening.

Another leisure activity is 'Karaoke'. This is the famous noctural pastime where Japanese have a chance to get intoxicated and come out of their shells. Karaoke is based on the traditional Japanese 'Enka' (traditional singing).

For the more active people western sports are becoming more popular. They are gradually becoming more popular in schools and as a pastime. However the two national sports still remains to be 'Sumo' and 'Yakkyu' (baseball).

A virtually universal pastime in Japan is 'Manga' and 'Anime', comics and animation. They range from the extremely young to the extremely adult topics. Japanese are brought up on Manga from an early age and it is not oncoming [sic] to see old Japanese businessmen reading Manga on the trains.

To conclude it can be said that although traditional and modern Japan are starkly different, the traditional values are still carried on. This is emphasised when one travels from the countryside to the modern inner city. We hope that this article has given you an insight into some of the many aspects of Japanese culture and gives a better perspective of this country.

When this Internet article was shown to someone who had lived in Japan it was found to be inaccurate in many respects. This illustrates the concern that many people have about information found on the Internet. In contrast to the Internet, where anyone can publish anything, books are usually written by credible authors, checked for accuracy and edited carefully, as we have mentioned. For this reason, information accessed on the Internet needs to be treated with caution.

When referencing information found on the Internet you need to record the author, the title of the story/information (in italics), the address and date of access to the page. Here is an example of how to do it:

Comcare Australia. *Changes to the Occupational Health and Safety Regulations.* http://www.comcare.gov.au/publications/factsheets/fs-fs23.html (8 March 2002).

Current and emerging technologies

In addition to developing industry knowledge and knowledge of trends and issues for related industries, such as the wine industry, it is also important to stay up to date with current and emerging technologies. Use of the Internet for research has been discussed briefly, but there are a number of other types of technological skills which employers in the hospitality industry find useful:

- web page design and maintenance
- computer network troubleshooting
- personal computer and printer troubleshooting
- use of point-of-sale systems (automated cash registers).

Some extremely sophisticated systems are in fact used in the hospitality industry. Two examples include high-tech laundering and catering solutions. In the larger hotels the wash loads are enormous and the whole system is computerised. The

Chef using touch-screen technology for cooking.

computer system manages processes based on information provided by the user, such as the type of fabric. The software manages the washing process such as selection of temperature, type of detergent, length of cycle, etc. Similar systems are used for large-scale catering operations where a chef stirring a pot is no longer a familiar sight. Instead, such variables as the amount of water required for cooking particular dishes are controlled by a touch screen. The whole system is closed once the ingredients have been loaded and the cooking process is managed again by sophisticated software. Industry magazines are good sources of information on these emerging technologies.

Research timetable

In conducting research, it is useful to develop a mind map before starting. As you can see in Fig. 3.2, the subject is written in the centre and related concepts are clustered together on the mind map using colour coding.

Having done this you will have a framework for the assignment you are writing. You may then decide to concentrate on one particular area.

Next, the steps involved in doing the work need to be planned and plenty of time allowed for 'problems' that might delay completion. Leaving a margin for error is also an excellent idea. When you finish your work before everyone else you will be able to look smug and relaxed.

Developing a timetable is a most effective way to get started. This is because working out what has to be done demonstrates how difficult it is to achieve the deadline comfortably.

Another planning technique is the Gantt chart, which allows you to schedule overlapping tasks. A Gantt chart is illustrated in Fig. 3.3 on page 46.

Below are some general tips for managing research and study:
- Identify your routines.
- Make study a routine (same time each day).
- Find your own style of learning.
- Organise your learning area and learning materials.
- Remove distractions.
- Focus completely on one task, however short the period.
- Reward yourself for achieving goals.
- Make a note of the time you waste and review this regularly.
- Revise your plans at the end of each day.
- Set achievable targets for the next day.
- Take regular breaks and do some stretches.
- Get plenty of exercise and eat healthy food.

In the activity that follows you will be required to source information on one of the topics and to prepare and present the information in such a way that it is

FIG. 3.2

Mind map.

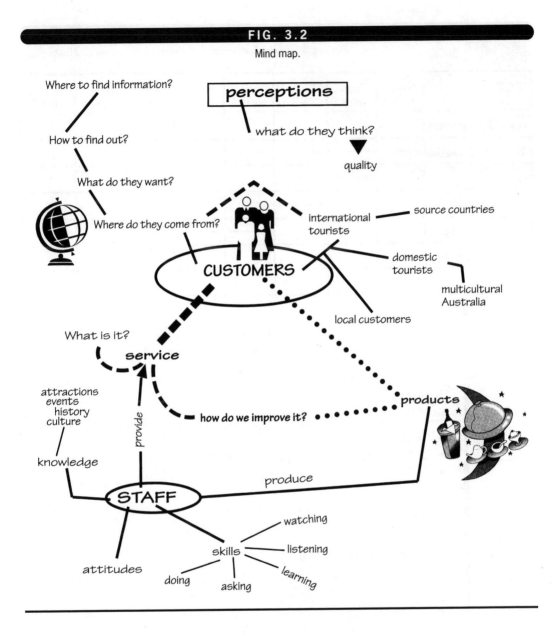

clear, concise and relevant to the audience (assume that you are presenting the information to the owner of the hospitality enterprise where you work—you may indeed have this opportunity soon). To do this you will need to:

- identify a range of current and accurate information
- decide on the relevance of this information
- draft a report/presentation including appropriate information
- ensure that you meet a prescribed deadline for presenting the information
- present the information to the appropriate audience and obtain feedback on its value

FIG. 3.3

Planning timetable—Gantt chart.

TO DO	Term week 1	Term week 2	Term week 3	Term week 4	Term week 5	Term week 6	Term week 7	Term week 8
Cultural Awareness								
Research information	←——————————————→							
Conduct surveys		←——→						
Collate information			←——→					
Prepare presentation				←——————→				
Practise presentation						←——————→		
Present								

- develop your own evaluation (for example, 'I did the following things well', 'If I did it again, I would do the following things differently').

Activity

Source and present relevant information in a meaningful way in relation to any one of the following topics:
- customer satisfaction in a specific hospitality enterprise
- workplace accidents and injuries in the hospitality industry and their prevention
- the value of emerging technologies to a particular sector of the hospitality industry
- historical and other local knowledge of interest to tourists to your region.

Discussion questions

1 Materials found on the Internet are both uncensored and unedited. Discuss the pros and cons of allowing anyone to publish anything in this forum.
2 Discuss the approach you would take if a guest asked you to recommend a restaurant in a major city in Australia.
3 If a client asked you to recommend an art gallery, how would you find the information necessary to help them?

LINKS

Australian Tourist Commission—http://www.atc.net.au/

chefmoz dining guide—http://chefmoz.org/Australia/

Restaurant and Catering Australia—http://www.restaurantcater.asn.au/

CHAPTER FOUR

Hospitality structures and relationships

OBJECTIVES

The aim of this chapter is to give you an overview of a range of hospitality establishments. A few of these will be illustrated by means of organisation charts, and you will be introduced to some of the departments, with special emphasis on some of the support departments. On completion of this chapter you should be able to:

- differentiate between the organisational structures of different hospitality establishments
- explain the services provided by different hospitality departments
- describe the roles of a variety of support departments
- illustrate career progression in one hospitality establishment.

Major hospitality divisions

In the first chapter we talked about the industry and in the second chapter we introduced the hospitality customer. Now we will discuss the internal structures of hospitality organisations to give you a better feel for the industry.

One of the departments of great interest is Human Resources and it and other departments will be discussed in this chapter, while departments such as Front Office and Food and Beverage will be covered in more detail later in the book. Without these descriptions of the various divisions and illustrations of hospitality organisations, readers often find it quite difficult to apply the concepts of teamwork, interpersonal skills and customer relations, which will be discussed in Part 2.

While there is enormous variation in the organisation structures of hospitality establishments (this will be illustrated later in this chapter through charts of actual organisations), there are some similarities. These are described briefly here and illustrated in Fig. 4.1 on page 48, which shows the Executive Committee of a large hotel. A hotel is useful for illustrative purposes because it combines food and beverage with accommodation.

Food and Beverage Division

The Food and Beverage Division may include a number of restaurants, bars, kitchens, banquets and room service. Each of these is a department, such as the Room Service Department, but outlets with names like the 'Captain Cook Lounge' do not have the word 'department' associated with them, even though they are

FIG. 4.1

Executive Committee of a large hotel.

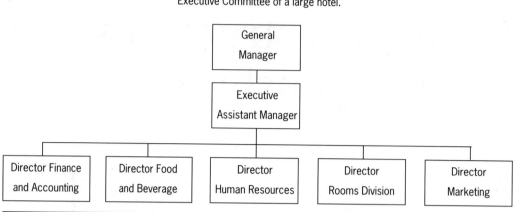

departments. Each department has a manager. All the managers report to the Director of Food and Beverage. In some establishments the Executive Chef reports to the Food and Beverage Director, but it is also quite common for the Executive Chef to be placed on the same level as the other directors.

Rooms Division

This division provides accommodation and associated services and includes the Front Office and Housekeeping Departments. Front Office is responsible for guest reservations through to guest accounts on departure. This department also provides a range of services such as car parking, messaging, information and luggage handling. The Housekeeping Department maintains the public areas of the hotel and the guest rooms. Like Front Office, Housekeeping provides a range of services such as valet, laundry, dry-cleaning and child-minding.

Marketing Division

This division is responsible for long-term forecasting, taking all types of external influences into account, and developing products and services that are best suited to customer needs. These products and services are then sold to individual and corporate (business) customers. Marketing strategies, such as direct overseas advertising and development of package deals in conjunction with airlines, are also handled by this division. In some cases there is a Sales Department within the Marketing Division, and each sales person would have certain corporate accounts to look after. There might also be a Public Relations Department, which would be responsible for communication with the press and the public.

Finance and Accounting Division

This division would argue that it is the most important division in the establishment because it monitors the finances and reports to department and division heads. Such reports detail revenue and gross and net profit for the year to date, and compare these figures with those for the same period in the previous year. Department managers turn to this division when they need help with their budgets. There could be a number of departments within the Finance and Accounting Division and for staff the most important one is the Payroll Department. Others include Accounts Payable (money owed by the establishment) and Accounts Receivable (money owed to the establishment).

Human Resources Division

Recruitment, selection and induction together make up the function called staffing. This means providing the organisation with the appropriate staff in the short and the long term. Recruitment involves attracting applicants to the organisation, selection involves choosing the best applicant and induction is the process by which new employees are eased into their jobs and told all about the establishment, its philosophy/mission, its history, its rules and its services to staff. There may be a separate Training Department within the Human Resources Division.

Support departments

There are several support departments which do not fit as comfortably as some of the others into divisions because they provide services to most, if not all, departments. Purchasing is a good example because this department does the purchasing for all departments.

Purchasing

The purchasing of food (many of the products are perishable) and beverages is a major part of the role of this department and a good relationship between the Purchasing Manager and the Executive Chef is essential. Housekeeping places demands on Purchasing for its cleaning and guest room supplies, and of course for furnishings. All other departments require stationery, most of it highly specialised, and equipment.

Engineering and Maintenance

Although it works most closely with Housekeeping, this department is responsible for all building maintenance, including air-conditioning and fire systems, energy management and repairs. Painters, electricians, refrigeration mechanics and carpenters all work in this department. Sustainable energy and waste management are important environmental issues, particularly where hospitality establishments are located on 'green' sites such as islands, reefs and forests where disposal systems are not available. Controlling use of electricity is a major issue for hotels, restaurants and clubs. The ANA Hotel in Sydney, which is fronted with glass, has computer systems to monitor the glare and lower the blinds when necessary. In many older hotels all rooms are air-conditioned, whether occupied or not. These days, sophisticated systems automatically turn up the air-conditioning or turn it on when a guest opens the door. Lights that can detect movement have been a great boon for security, at the same time saving electricity.

Security

Security is another support department for the whole establishment and its role is to monitor customer safety and security. Prevention is the main focus, achieved through regular patrols and early intervention. Sometimes things can get out of hand and in such situations the police are Security's next call. Hopefully they arrive in time to restore order before the mob celebrating in the bar destroys the grand piano in the lobby, as happened in one hotel. Fire, evacuation, theft, lost property and all emergencies are the primary responsibilities of this department. However, it does have its lighter moments, such as the one described in 'Column 8' in the *Sydney Morning Herald* on 21 January 1996:

> They look after their guests at the Novotel, Darling Harbour. Last September, we recorded the composure with which its reception desk greeted a naked (but for a strategically held *Herald*) man who had locked himself out of the room. Now this: About 1.40 yesterday morning, a security guard found a fully-dressed guest lying, sleeping peacefully, in a corridor. A quick search revealed his room key—after celebrating too much, he'd lost his way to his room on another floor and at the other end of the building. Now how to get him back there? The security man got a porter's trolley, and, with some help, wheeled the still comatose guest to his room and laid him out on his bed.

Systems Department

The Systems Department is responsible for all computer system troubleshooting and software support. Computer systems are used for all Front Office functions, for cashiering in all outlets, for locking systems and for energy monitoring. All security systems, including smoke detectors, are also monitored by computer. Guest telephone calls are logged and in most cases the data is routed directly to guest accounts. All of this involves integration between different computer hardware and different computer software. Back-up of all data is essential and this support role ensures that the dreaded 'system down' does not occur.

Activities and Entertainment

Sporting events, gala balls, cocktail competitions, nature walks, bands and live performances all need to be organised. Each event needs considerable negotiating and planning, and in the case of live performances there are the technological challenges of lighting and sound. Although most performers are reasonably well organised, there are usually last minute hiccups that need to be smoothed out. This department works closely with Marketing to promote special events.

Specialist sporting activities such as aerobics, water sports and mini golf are often run independently by contracted operators. The quality and service provided must be monitored to ensure that guests are satisfied.

Catering

In many clubs the catering is subcontracted, so that although the restaurant offers counter service, a buffet or table service, this is not the direct responsibility of club management. If the standard were not satisfactory to club members, this issue would be raised with the contractor.

The managers of the support departments have various reporting relationships depending on the needs and structure of particular establishments. For example, in some hotels, the Purchasing Manager reports to the Finance and Accounting Director, while in others he or she reports to the Executive Chef. By looking at some of the organisation charts provided at the end of this chapter, you may be able to track down these departments and the differences in reporting relationships. In smaller establishments the function is often performed by one person and not by a whole department.

Most of the organisation charts have been kindly provided by organisations to give readers some insight into the differences and similarities in hospitality establishments. These should also be extremely useful for career planning and for providing a context for the following chapters, which deal with general industry principles.

Suppliers

Although suppliers are not part of a hospitality establishment, they are partners in providing quality products and services. Suppliers must be able to support the organisation effectively. The hospitality operation looks at a number of factors—quality, price and availability. In some cases freshness is an issue; in some the product is unique (such as some bush foods); and in others the item purchased is designed and produced specifically for the hotel or club. Artworks for major hotels fit into this category. Many restaurants buy their cakes from external suppliers, and many clubs and cafeterias buy their 'wet food' from catering firms. Wet food includes meals like casseroles and curries, which are purchased ready made. Pastries, another familiar item, are sometimes only half baked when purchased, the baking being completed on site to produce a better quality product.

Consultants

In addition to suppliers, most hospitality enterprises employ an accountant to manage financial affairs including GST and taxation. An organisation chart for a small restaurant is illustrated in Fig. 4.2 (on page 52) in which the accountant is shown.

Activities

1 Develop a table to compare the organisations illustrated in the charts and the services they provide to customers.
2 Prepare an organisation chart for a small fast food outlet.
3 Plot a career path through two of the organisations illustrated.
4 Suggest some training options for developing the skills necessary for entry into a position in one of these organisations.

CASE STUDY

Kim's career profile was one of the most interesting of all the staff working in the club. She had started in the industry as a casual food and beverage attendant in the Banquet Department of a hotel while still studying at college. She had been promoted to the position of supervisor by the time she had finished her studies and was offered a full-time job by her manager. However, she could see that her experience was limited and her aim at the time was to start her own business.

Having obtained a Diploma in Hospitality Management, she decided that the fastest way to get some all-round experience would be to work at a country motel which had its own restaurant. Knowing the excellent reputation of a particular motel and restaurant, she accepted a position there as cashier. Within weeks she had been trained in many facets of the restaurant's operation and by the end of the year she had been promoted to assistant manager. A lateral transfer to an administration role in the motel occurred only six months later and it was not long before she was handling all accounting responsibilities for both operations.

When her mother became ill, she needed to move back to the city. A position advertised by the local RSL club appeared suitable as she would be working close to home. Within two years Kim had been promoted to secretary manager.

Discussion questions

1 Why do most organisations like to promote from within?

2 Why would someone with a management diploma not be placed at management level immediately after graduation?

3 How would Kim's experience be valuable if she were to start her own business now?

4 What further study would you recommend to Kim if she wanted to move back into the hotel sector?

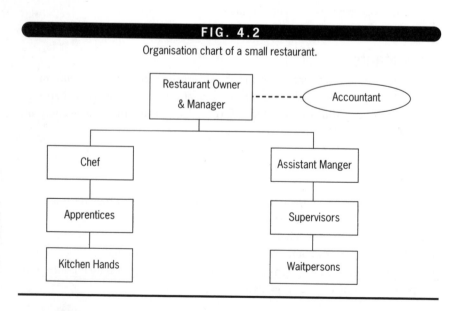

FIG. 4.2

Organisation chart of a small restaurant.

FIG. 4.3

Organisation chart of a large resort.

VOYAGES

HOTELS AND RESORTS

Ayers Rock Resort Organisational Structure

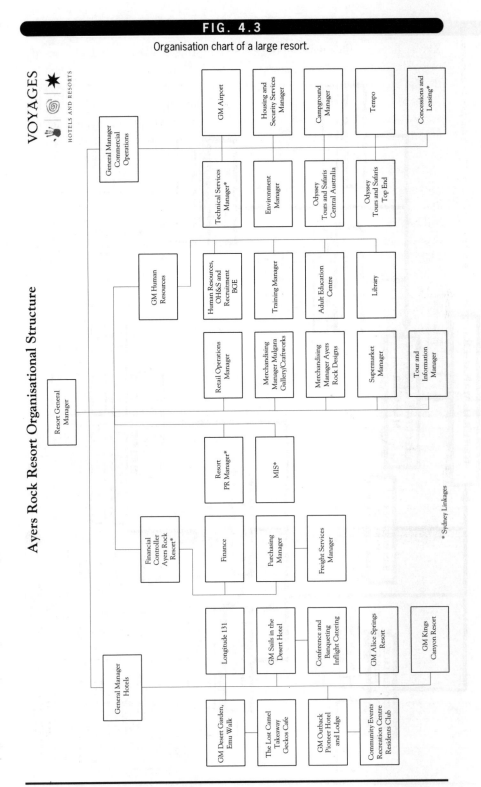

* Sydney Linkages

Courtesy Voyages Hotels and Resorts.

FIG. 4.4

Organisation chart of a large hotel.

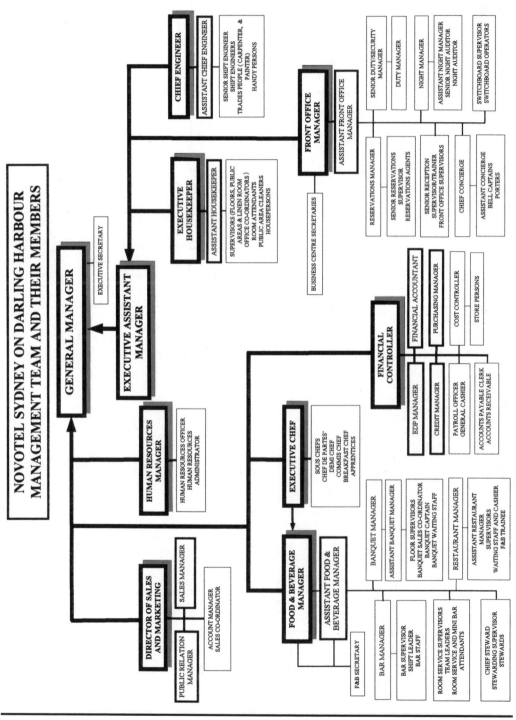

NOVOTEL SYDNEY ON DARLING HARBOUR
MANAGEMENT TEAM AND THEIR MEMBERS

Reproduced with permission of Novotel Sydney.

FIG. 4.5

Organisation chart of a large club.

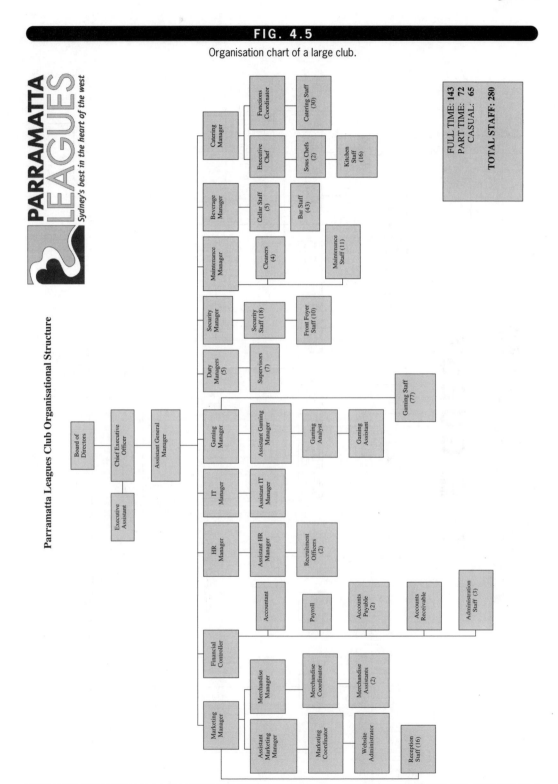

Parramatta Leagues Club Organisational Structure

FULL TIME: **143**
PART TIME: **72**
CASUAL: **65**

TOTAL STAFF: **280**

FIG. 4.6
Organisation chart of a large hotel.

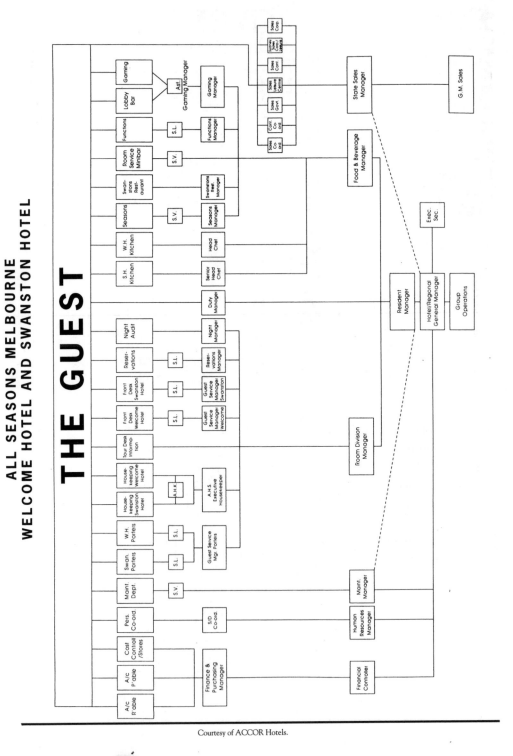

Courtesy of ACCOR Hotels.

CHAPTER FIVE

Food and beverage and RSA

OBJECTIVES

This chapter introduces the food and beverage dimension of the hospitality industry. The scope of this sector is very broad, taking in outlets both very large and very small. On completion of this chapter you should be able to:

- differentiate between different types of food and beverage outlets
- review the modes of operation and services offered by the food and beverage sector
- describe the roles and career paths in this sector
- review the attributes of a food and beverage operative
- explain the relationship between the food and beverage sector and other sectors of the hospitality industry
- outline responsible service of alcohol (RSA) guidelines.

The history of food and beverage service is an interesting one. In the 1800s suppliers of liquor were blamed for all sorts of social ills: crime, immorality, child abuse and prostitution. During the 19th century many acts were passed to restrict the sale of alcohol. The temperance movement emerged in the mid-1800s and it had a strong impact on public opinion, demanding prohibition of the manufacture, importation and sale of 'alcoholic liquors'. Much controversy surrounded the question of hotel opening hours, with some people advocating that closing should occur earlier than 11 p.m. In 1916 a riot involving soldiers who were to be subjected to longer training hours led to the wrecking of the bar of the Commercial Hotel in Sydney. The soldiers seized all the alcohol held by the hotel and continued their rampage through the streets of the city. This resulted in one death and several injuries.

This incident reinforced calls for restricted trading hours and a closing time of 6 p.m. was introduced. Early closing led to the uncivilised 'six o'clock swill' where patrons would rush to place their last orders before closing. Moves to extend trading were made on the grounds that longer hours and the serving of drinks with meals would lead to more civilised behaviour. The comments of Justice Maxwell in the *Sydney Morning Herald* of 23 February 1954 express public opinion at that time:

LIQUOR REFORMS

The Royal Commissioner, Mr Justice Maxwell, says in his report on the liquor trade, issued yesterday, that later closing hours for hotels should be considered.

'I am satisfied that the evidence requires the finding that there are evils associated with 6 o'clock closing which ought not to be tolerated in a civilised community', his Honor said.

'In addition, the present closing hour encourages sly-grog and after-hour trading at "blackmarket" rates.

'There is a clear need for provision for drinking at tables or seated—as against what is described as "perpendicular" drinking, for better facilities than very large bars, less secrecy and more openness attendant upon the present layout of many bars and, in addition, greater provision for either gardens or open-air bars.'

The judge said that there was evidence that many licensees were interested only in selling liquor, and disregarded the house side of the trading as an unprofitable nuisance. There was a need for making statutory provision to ensure that reasonable requirement of accommodation and meals were met.

Finally, in the same year, substantial changes were made in New South Wales, extending opening hours and service of alcohol with meals, though in Victoria six o'clock closing continued for many years. However, only 'bona fide' travellers could be served with alcohol on Sundays and public holidays. The formation of returned servicemen's clubs and sporting clubs brought about social changes which made liquor reforms essential, as reported in the *Sydney Morning Herald* on 25 November 1954:

LIQUOR ACT REFORMS

Hundreds of new club licences will be granted to social, sporting, ex-Service and workers' organisations under amendments to the Liquor Act. The amendments will extend hotel closing hours to 10 p.m. and permit restaurants and hotels to serve liquor with meals until midnight.

The nature of the food and beverage industry is constantly changing. The American idea of home delivery was unheard of in Australia until the 1980s. Eating out, especially for breakfast, was not common in Australia or New Zealand in the early part of the 20th century, despite being popular at that time in the United States. Having breakfast at a cafe these days has been a response to European influences on the Australian population, with cappuccino now the third most popular drink in Australia after milk and carbonated beverages. The Italians drink cappuccino only at breakfast and see the habit of drinking it at any time of the day as bizarre.

The multicultural influences on consumer habits in the food and beverage sector have been substantial, with new cuisines blending many of these influences. Emerging now is an Australian cuisine, which is increasingly using local produce and 'bush tucker'. Overseas visitors to Australia are more positive than ever about our menus, citing the food we offer as one of the best reasons to visit our country.

Some of the most popular locations for eating out in the major cities are as follows:

- Brisbane: Park Road, Milton; Brunswick Street, Fortitude Valley
- Sydney: Victoria Street, Darlinghurst; Norton Street, Leichhardt; Oxford Street, Paddington; King Street, Newtown
- Canberra: Franklin Street, Manuka
- Melbourne: Fitzroy and Acland Streets, St Kilda; Toorak Road, South Yarra; Brunswick Street, Fitzroy; Lygon Street, Carlton
- Adelaide: Rundle Street and Gouger Street
- Perth: James and Lake Streets, Northbridge
- Hobart: Salamanca Place
- Darwin: Cavanagh Street.

The city of Yarra (an inner Melbourne suburb), for example, has around 300 cafes and restaurants.

As we can see, a cafe culture has developed, with many young residents in inner city areas eating out several times a week.

Types of food and beverage outlets

Food and beverages are provided at a huge range of places, from cafes, bistros and restaurants to prisons, hospitals and boarding schools, as outlined below.

Restaurants

The range of restaurants in Australia is almost unlimited and the influence of many cultures is strongly felt. Chinese, Japanese, Spanish, Indian and Thai are but a few of the types of restaurants found everywhere, with sushi, tapas and satay sticks well known to many consumers. Culinary trends have also influenced the more traditional restaurants, with a leaning towards lighter and sometimes vegetarian food. Eating out at a fine dining restaurant will cost a couple at least $150, depending on the quality of the wines selected. On the other hand, Yum Cha (bite-sized Chinese delicacies served with tea) in a Chinese restaurant will cost in the region of $30 per couple.

Hotel and motel restaurants and bars

Smaller establishments might have only one restaurant or dining room and one bar while others have a range of outlets with different themes and pricing.

Bistros

Bistros traditionally offer reasonably priced meals in a simple but elegant environment. In many Australian clubs and pubs, bistros offer self-service and black-board menus.

Cafes

As mentioned previously, this is the fastest growing type of food and beverage outlet, with new cafes mushrooming in the larger cities. Cappuccino, latte, short black and many other varieties are popular with the increasingly experienced coffee consumer, and we will learn more about coffee and coffee-making in Chapter 6. With the introduction of babbaccino (all froth and no coffee) for little consumers, their education is starting young.

Coffee shops/tea lounges

The old-fashioned tea or coffee shop with home-made cakes and sandwiches is still popular, particularly in country areas.

Cafeterias

Supplying food for staff and students, cafeterias tend to offer low-cost, self-service meals, which are quickly prepared.

Fast food outlets

McDonalds, Pizza Hut, Kentucky Fried Chicken and Red Rooster are some examples of fast food outlets which can be relied upon for consistency and speed. They are very popular with younger consumers. Smaller fast food outlets are often family businesses, selling pies, sandwiches and hamburgers to office workers and people in a hurry who are looking for a cheap meal.

Function and convention centres

Conventions of 200 people or more place huge demands on caterers. The Convention Centre in Canberra is a good example, with the main dining area catering for up to 450 people.

Outside catering

Many small caterers cater for private parties including, for example, roasting a lamb or side of pork on a spit and providing all the accompanying salads. Others cater for large outdoor events such as races and sporting events. Weddings also provide profitable business for caterers.

Club dining facilities and bars

Clubs are popular dining venues, providing a range of food and beverage outlets. In most cases the food is very reasonably priced and this makes the local club a convenient place in which to eat or meet friends for a drink. Gambling and other entertainment are also provided. Revenue from gaming is often used to subsidise the food outlets.

Transport dining facilities

Eating on board the Country-Link XPT or the *Oriana* are two experiences most people would enjoy. On the *Oriana*, for example, the bakers prepare 300 loaves of bread and 3,500 rolls and pastries every day. Catering is done for airlines, trains, ships, boats and ferries. Dining on Sydney Harbour (for lunch or dinner) is an unforgettable experience for most visitors, appealing as it does to all the senses.

Hospitals

This captive consumer is becoming more discriminating and staff are working harder than ever to meet the needs of patients. 'Cook-chill' methods enable staff to prepare a wider range of food which is fresher and tastier than it used to be.

Nursing and retirement homes

The ageing of the population was mentioned in Chapter 2. Retirement homes are becoming increasingly popular from the age of 55 onwards. These now provide a range of food outlets including fine dining restaurants for people who have made a lifestyle decision to avoid the tedium of shopping and cooking meals.

Prisons

Catering for prison inmates is the role of prison staff. At times, when prison officers have gone on strike, prisoners have been treated to McDonald's three times a day.

Educational institutions

Boarding schools and canteens cater for a young growing clientele. Satisfying, nutritious and tasty food is the order of the day, with legendary meals like toad in the hole and bread and butter pudding becoming a thing of the past.

Armed services

The level of catering often depends on the rank of the officer in charge of the site. It can range from silver service to ration packs for soldiers in training.

All of the above food outlets offer beverage (drinks) service too. Where alcoholic beverages are concerned, the exceptions would be BYO (bring your own) restaurants and cafes and fast food outlets. Prisons, hospitals and educational institutions are other obvious exceptions. Where the outlet has a liquor licence, alcoholic beverages can be served. In some cases the category of licence allows for alcohol service only with meals, while in others, such as bars and nightclubs, beverage service only is permitted. In addition to the above-mentioned hospitality operations, beverage service (implying alcoholic beverage service) is also available in the following outlets.

Public bars

Australia is well known for its public bars, with the older variety still tiled from floor to shoulder height for easy cleaning. The 'no thongs or singlets' rule is very curious to overseas visitors as they seldom have any idea what thongs (they may well confuse them these days with thong underwear!) and singlets are.

TABLE. 5.1

Per capita consumption of alcoholic beverages 1997.

Country	Beer	Wine	Spirits	Total
	litres	litres	litres of pure alcohol	litres of pure alcohol
Luxembourg	110.8	52.0	1.6	11.2
France	37.5	60.0	2.4	10.9
Germany	131.1	23.0	2.0	9.5
Italy	25.4	53.5	0.7	7.9
New Zealand	84.1	17.0	1.0	7.3
Australia	**94.7**	**18.4**	**1.3**	**7.6**
UK	103.6	14.3	1.3	7.7
Poland	41.8	6.5	3.4	6.3
USA	83.2	7.4	1.8	6.6
Japan	54.7	1.0	2.2	6.6

Source: World Drink Trends, World Advertising Research Center, Oxfordshire, UK, 1998.

FIG. 5.1

Apparent per capita consumption of beer and wine in Australia 1978–98.

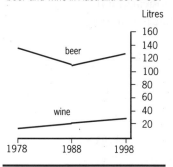

Source: Apparent Consumption of Foodstuffs in Australia, Cat No 4306.0, Australian Bureau of Statistics. Reproduced with permission.

Tavern bars

These are more sophisticated with better decor and higher prices.

Cocktail and nightclub bars

These bars are more expensive, offering a vast range of interesting drinks.

In addition to bars, many clubs and hotels have bottle shops or liquor stores associated with them. Australian drinking habits compared with those of other countries are illustrated in Table 5.1. Of those countries Australia was ranked sixth in terms of total alcohol consumption. On the whole, Australians are drinking a little less beer and a little more wine. This is illustrated in Fig. 5.1.

Variations in food and beverage establishments

Food and beverage outlets differ in terms of size, location, level of service, cost, target market and entertainment. The smallest outlet may serve takeaway or home delivery only, while others may also have a few tables or benches for customers. Larger outlets such as the Concourse Restaurant at the Sydney Opera House (which caters for up to 320 diners in the short time before shows) face enormous challenges as all meals have to be served in such a short space of time. A dinner for 300 guests would also require fast service to ensure that the entree is not being served at one end of the ballroom while desserts are being cleared at the other. Some outlets are located in unusual places, such as cafeterias on oil rigs and pubs in opal country, while many are in city and suburban areas. Of course some food and beverage outlets are on the move and in-flight catering, for example, demands quick service on short flights. The level of service and cost are other distinguishing factors and in many outlets in the lower price range self-service has been introduced to keep the price of food down. Finally, entertainment such as theatre, cabaret or live music may be offered in addition to food and beverage.

Although self-service is common in the lower price range, one would not expect it in a four-star hotel other than for buffet meals. On a recent visit to such a hotel in Fremantle, a customer was sent to the bar for a late lunch. As he had his family with him, he went through the bar to the outdoor area where tables were set up.

After a long wait he was obliged to go back into the bar, where there was not a single customer in sight, and ask for four menus. After he and his family had decided what to order and had waited optimistically but fruitlessly for someone to emerge to take the order, he had to go back into the bar to place the order. One would certainly expect a higher level of service from a four-star hotel.

Modes of operation in the food and beverage sector

Styles of food and beverage service differ. There is plate service where food is plated in the kitchen and self-service where customers help themselves from a buffet. Silver service entails service at the table; the waiter serves hot dishes with spoon and fork. It takes time to develop the skills and flair to do this properly, and trainees practise using potatoes and onions. Once this has been mastered, they move on to more difficult items such as asparagus. Try picking up asparagus with a spoon and fork held in one hand without looking clumsy! Gueridon service involves preparation of food at the table, generally using a mobile trolley, often with flaming brandy. Showmanship and style are important aspects of this flamboyant approach to service.

In some cases food and beverage outlets are now 24-hour-a-day operations. In most cases they are open seven days a week. In all cases their busiest times are the times when people celebrate: Christmas, New Year, Easter and other holidays.

Employment in this sector involves working shifts that coincide with invitations to be with family and friends. This is the downside of working in the industry. The upside is the opportunity to work while people are enjoying themselves. Compared with many industries, hospitality offers more variety, more people contact and more scope for travel. The industry needs people who have a sincere interest in providing the best service possible to please customers. This involves a commitment to hard work, to coping under pressure, to dealing with complex problems and to satisfying a wide variety of people, mainly at their best, but sometimes at their worst.

Attributes of a food and beverage employee

Some of the attributes sought by employers in the industry include initiative (engaging customers in conversation), warmth, humour, and an ability to express oneself clearly and to use positive body language to communicate confidence and reinforce verbal messages. Personal appearance must be immaculate, whatever the level of formality in uniforms. The ideal person would also be able to cope with pressure, solve problems and sell products. Patience, good judgement, and knowledge about food and beverage products and diet and nutrition are additional attributes on an employer's wish list.

Roles and career paths in the food and beverage sector

The Food and Beverage Department generally includes a number of sections/departments as illustrated in Fig. 5.2 on page 64.

This sector has the best employment prospects of all sectors in the hospitality industry. The sheer scope of catering activities and the services associated with

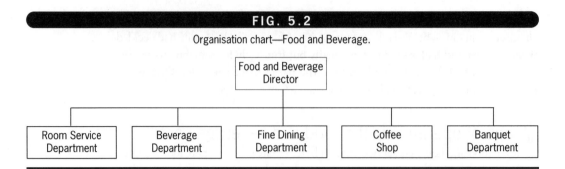

FIG. 5.2

Organisation chart—Food and Beverage.

```
                    ┌──────────────────┐
                    │ Food and Beverage│
                    │     Director     │
                    └──────────────────┘
    ┌──────────┬──────────┼──────────┬──────────┐
┌─────────┐┌─────────┐┌─────────┐┌─────────┐┌─────────┐
│  Room   ││         ││  Fine   ││         ││         │
│ Service ││Beverage ││ Dining  ││ Coffee  ││ Banquet │
│Department││Department││Department││  Shop  ││Department│
└─────────┘└─────────┘└─────────┘└─────────┘└─────────┘
```

them make this a potentially successful career path for anyone planning a career. The expertise and knowledge developed, including customer relations skills, are also transferable to other industries. The knowledge gained in food preparation and service, and in hygiene, health and safety, is invaluable. An understanding of food products and beverages, including wines and cocktails, can prove useful for both personal and professional reasons.

Some of the positions available for liquor service staff include:
- bar attendant
- drink/wine waiter
- cocktail bar attendant
- bottle shop attendant
- supervisor
- outlet manager.

Some of the positions available for food service staff include:
- waiter/food and beverage attendant
- host
- supervisor
- outlet manager.

The duties of food and beverage attendants are provided in Chapter 16 under the job description provided by The Hyatt Hotel in Canberra.

Food and beverage positions are graded under most awards and agreements. These grades relate to the level of service (fine dining and cocktail mixing being the highest) and to the training requirements for each position. Pay rates are not high in food service and bar service positions but the addition of tips makes the shift hours worthwhile. Penalty rates (for working at night and during weekends) are rapidly disappearing, given the nature of the industry.

Overtime is not uncommon and adds to the basic pay. Casual positions are easy to come by, especially for banquets and with large catering organisations. Opportunities to start one's own business are excellent.

Interrelationships with other departments

Departments in a hospitality establishment that work closely with Food and Beverage include Kitchen, Stores, Accounts, Housekeeping, Front Office and Human

Resources. In casinos, the Food and Beverage and Kitchen Departments work closely with the Gaming Department to meet the needs of gamblers. The food service role in this situation is secondary to the primary business, which is gaming. However, some time ago, Star City in Sydney changed its menus from the more traditional European style to include Asian and other influences to suit its clientele.

The relationships between Food and Beverage and other departments are summarised in Fig. 5.3. The closest working relationship is obviously with the kitchen. This relationship is sometimes stormy, mainly because of the pressures of fast service. There is little room for error. Illegible handwriting could, for example,

FIG. 5.3

Food and Beverage relationships with other departments and external agencies.

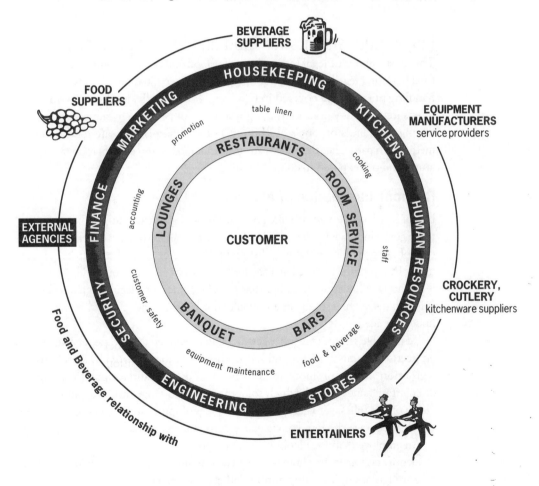

FOOD AND BEVERAGE INCLUDES THESE SECTIONS

OTHERS WHICH HAVE INTERRELATIONSHIPS WITH FOOD AND BEVERAGE

result in the wrong meal being served and an unhappy customer, particularly if the customer's companions had all received their meals. The chef would be most unhappy because the other meals would have to be brought back to the kitchen and kept warm while the correct dish was prepared.

Relationships with external agencies

Food and Beverage has relationships with many external businesses: there are food suppliers, beverage suppliers, equipment manufacturers and service providers, crockery, cutlery and kitchenware suppliers, and entertainers to be dealt with regularly in a large hospitality establishment. Even small operators have fairly constant contact with food and beverage suppliers in order to ensure that the produce they use is always fresh.

Legal requirements for food and beverage operations

The most important legal requirements for food and beverage outlets come under food handling legislation and liquor legislation (see Chapter 12). Hygienic food handling practices are covered in Chapter 24. Essentially, food service staff need to ensure that they practise the highest levels of personal hygiene (rinsing and wiping the hands on one's clothing is not adequate!) and safe food handling methods. In particular, this means ensuring that food is stored at appropriate temperatures and not exposed to contamination.

Responsible service of alcohol

Liquor legislation is very specific about where and when alcohol can be served and these guidelines need to be explained to service staff as they are dependent on the type of licence held by the establishment. Service of alcohol to patrons who are under 18 is prohibited (the legal age for liquor service in parts of the United States is 21) and staff need to be aware that they face fines for illegal service of alcohol (see Fig. 5.4). The establishment would also be fined and it would risk losing its liquor licence.

Responsible service of alcohol certification is required for anyone serving alcohol on licensed premises. In general terms, the regulations enacted by state/territory legislation aim to promote responsibility and to eliminate practices such as discounted 'happy hours', which sometimes lead to binge drinking, and the provision of test tubes, yard glasses, lay-backs, jugs of spirits and mixers, and shooters, which encourage the rapid or excessive consumption of liquor.

An employee serving alcohol is required to:
- identify customers to whom service may be refused in accordance with state/territory legislation, including minors and intoxicated persons
- where appropriate, request and obtain acceptable proof of age prior to service
- refuse service in a polite manner and state reasons for the refusal
- serve alcohol in accordance with the provisions of the relevant state/territory legislation, licensing requirements and responsible service of alcohol principles

FIG. 5.4
Responsible service of liquor.

PRINCIPLES of RESPONSIBLE SERVING OF LIQUOR

- no liquor to minors
- no liquor promotions that encourage binge drinking or drunkenness or are discriminatory or likely to appeal to minors
- no admission of drunks
- refusal of liquor service to drunks
- a duty of care for patrons and staff
- patron behaviour not to adversely impact on the neighbourhood

It is an offence to permit intoxication on licensed or club premises (section 125, Liquor Act 1982 and section 44, Registered Clubs Act 1976).

Gaming and Racing
A NSW Government Department

SIGNS OF INTOXICATION

- a notable change in behaviour (especially towards anti-social or inappropriate behaviour);
- slurring of, or mistakes in, speech;
- clumsiness, knocking things over (like a drink or an ashtray), or fumbling with change;
- a significant loss of co-ordination (usually swaggering or swaying); and
- a degree of confusion, a lack of understanding or ability to hear, and a difficulty in responding.

Physical signs include vomiting, violence and abusive language.

IF IN DOUBT

- no admission
- no liquor service
- consult with supervisor/manager
- remove from premises
- call for Police assistance

STRATEGIES TO PREVENT INTOXICATION

Management
- prominently display the intoxication sign
- promote low alcohol liquor and other non-alcoholic drinks and provide quality food
- develop and display house policies
- avoid unacceptable and illegal liquor promotions
- provide transport options
- provide security when appropriate
- provide quality entertainment
- promote and provide staff training

Management and Staff
- inform patrons and staff of their legal obligations regarding liquor to intoxicated people and expected behaviour
- intervene tactfully and peacefully
- seek assistance from the patron's friends

Staff
- politely refuse service and explain why
- interact with patrons
- ensure consistent standards of service

RESPONSIBLE SERVING OF LIQUOR OFFENCES

- permit intoxication or indecent, violent or quarrelsome behaviour on licensed or registered club premises
  Maximum Penalty $2,000

- sell or supply liquor to an intoxicated person on licensed or club premises
  Maximum Penalty $2,000

- sell or supply liquor to a minor
  Maximum Penalty $2,000

- allow liquor to be sold or supplied to a minor on licensed or club premises
  Maximum Penalty $2,000

Note: A complaint action can be taken against a liquor licence or certificate of registration where its continuation is considered not to be in the public interest.

Reproduced with the permission of the Department of Gaming and Racing.

- prepare and serve standard drinks in accordance with industry requirements
- when requested, give accurate information to customers on alcoholic beverages in accordance with enterprise/house policy and government regulation, including:
  types
  strengths
  standard drinks
  alcohol percentages in a range of frequently served drinks

- identify issues regarding service of alcohol to different types of customers and incorporate them into service
- encourage customers courteously and diplomatically to drink within appropriate limits
- recognise erratic drinking patterns as an early sign of possible intoxication and take appropriate action
- monitor the emotional and physical state of patrons for signs of intoxication and, where appropriate, offer food and non-alcoholic beverages
- politely decline requests for drinks to be dispensed in a manner which is irresponsible, or which encourages the rapid or excessive consumption of alcohol, and advise customers of the reasons for the refusal where appropriate
- refuse service to intoxicated customers in a suitable and consistent manner, minimising confrontation and arguments and pointing out signage where relevant
- assess intoxication levels of customers using a number of methods, including:
  observation of changes in behaviour
  observation of emotional and physical state of customers
  monitoring noise levels
  monitoring drink orders
- when assessing intoxication, take into account factors which affect individual responses to alcohol, including:
  gender
  weight
  general health
  rate of consumption
  food intake
  other substances taken
- politely make offers of assistance to intoxicated customers as appropriate, including:
  organising transport for customers wishing to leave
  assisting customers to leave
- where appropriate, give patrons a verbal warning or ask them to leave the premises in accordance with enterprise/house requirements, the specific situation and provisions of state/territory legislation/regulations
- use appropriate communication and conflict resolution skills in handling difficult situations
- refer difficult situations beyond the scope of individual responsibility to the appropriate person
- promptly identify situations which pose a threat to the safety or security of colleagues, customers or property, and seek assistance from appropriate colleagues according to enterprise policy.

The benefits of responsible service of alcohol reforms for the community and the enterprise include:
- improved patronage
- increased profits
- safer premises

- reduced government intervention (police, liquor authorities, local council)
- satisfied staff and patrons
- reduced community complaints
- improved image of premises
- reduced operational costs (for example, security, legal, repairs)
- improved attitudes and approaches to alcohol consumption
- better health status.

Activities

1 Find an example of an establishment in your local area for each type of food and beverage outlet listed at the beginning of this chapter.
2 Prepare an organisation chart for the different sections within the Food and Beverage Department of a large establishment.
3 List the type of information you would need to have at your fingertips to answer questions from customers in relation to food and beverage.
4 Draw a diagram to illustrate the relationships between the Food and Beverage Department and other departments.
5 Explain why good interdepartmental relationships are important in the industry, using the Food and Beverage Department as an example.
6 What are the attributes of a competent food and beverage employee?

CASE STUDY

The waiter greeted us warmly as we arrived, opening the door and cheerfully acknowledging the awful weather. She asked whether we wanted to be seated in the main area, which would be a little noisy, or in a quiet spot on the verandah. We chose to sit outside in a glassed-in area, which was very romantic. Elegant and old-fashioned decor, subtle lighting and classical music contributed to the ambience.

The waiter returned after a short time to assist us with our menu choices, explaining the dishes and their ingredients. She then left us for a little while to agonise over our selections. While taking the orders, she asked whether it was our first visit to the area. In conversation she was able to recommend some walks which were off the tourist track and somewhere to have lunch. Throughout the meal she was attentive but discreet. At one point she came back to the table, filled the glasses and asked what we thought of the wine. The pace of the service was just right. We were not in a hurry and wanted to savour the meal. Breaks between the entree and main and between the main and dessert were timed beautifully. If the timing had been any quicker, we would not have had room for the date and butterscotch dessert or the chestnut soufflé which were out of this world! To summarise, the food was superb, the service outstanding and the whole meal an unqualified success despite the exorbitant bill at the end.

Discussion questions

1 How did this establishment create its particular ambience (atmosphere)?

2 How did the waiter match the needs of her particular customers?

3 What approach might this waiter have taken if she were serving a family?

4 What factors would these consumers balance against the cost?

LINKS

Liquor Control Reform Act (Vic)—
http://www.austlii.edu.au/cgibin/disp.pl/au/legis/vic/consol_act/lcra1998266/?query=title+%28+%22liquor+control+reform%22+%29

Queensland Liquor Licensing Division—http://www.liquor.qld.gov.au/_sitemap/

CHAPTER SIX

Cafes and coffee-making

OBJECTIVES

This chapter will introduce you to the history of coffee, the various popular styles of coffee, and the art and science of coffee-making. On completion of this chapter you should be able to:

- briefly describe the history of coffee
- outline the stages involved in bringing coffee from cultivation to the customer
- outline the procedures for making espresso coffee
- describe the different types of coffee
- describe the different preparation styles of coffee.

*T*he story of how coffee growing and drinking spread around the world is one of the greatest and most romantic in history. It starts in the Horn of Africa, in Ethiopia, where the coffee tree probably originated in the province of Kaffa. There are various fanciful but unlikely stories surrounding the discovery of the properties of roasted coffee beans. One story has it that an Ethiopian goatherd was amazed at the lively behaviour of his goats after chewing red coffee berries. What we know with more certainty is that the succulent outer cherry flesh was eaten by slaves taken from present-day Sudan into Yemen and Arabia, through the great port of its day, Mocha, now synonymous with coffee. Coffee was certainly being cultivated in Yemen by the 15th century and probably much earlier than that. Venetian traders first brought coffee to Europe in 1615.

At first coffee was mainly sold by lemonade vendors and was believed to have medicinal qualities. The first European coffee house opened in Venice in 1683, with the most famous, Caffe Florian in Piazza San Marco, opening in 1720. It is still open for business today.

INTERNATIONAL COFFEE ORGANIZATION

The consumption of espresso coffee has grown worldwide, with the proliferation of coffee shops, cafes and coffee carts. By 1999, there were over 12,000 businesses classified as cafes and restaurants in Australia, with over one million seats available for consuming food on the premises. This figure does not include fast food or takeaway food/coffee outlets of which there were over 13,000 in the same year. (ABS Cat No 8687.0)

'Espresso' is one of the best known Italian words in the world. It was coined to express the special pressurised extraction of coffee from the whole coffee bean, which was ground just before preparation and brewed in a professional coffee-making machine.

So what is the difference between the coffee shop, the cafe and the restaurant where coffee is served? The definition of each of these is tricky; however the level of formality, quality and variety of food served does vary for each. A restaurant is a more formal food and beverage outlet, selling predominantly main meals or multi-course meals. Almost all restaurants have a liquor license. Cafes are more informal, providing less sophisticated meals and snacks throughout the day, while the focus of a coffee shop is coffee. Traditionally, a coffee shop served mainly sweet cakes and other coffee accompaniments, but these days they also serve light snacks. The fine line between a coffee shop and a coffee retail outlet is even more blurred. Many chains fit the retail mould since they have very limited seating and sell mainly takeaway coffee. Coffee carts are becoming increasingly popular, too, for espresso coffee on the go or at major events.

Whatever the outlet, the quality of the coffee is most important to the customer (although the Barista might disagree—see box below):

> 'The froth must be dense.'
> 'I like my coffee strong, with a slightly bitter after taste.'
> 'Black coffee is the only way.'
> 'The smooth creaminess of a latte is perfect for me.'

The art of coffee-making—or the art of communication?

There are so many, many coffee shops everywhere. For me it is ultimately not about the taste but more about the relationship between the Barista and the customer. It is amazing what you learn about people in two minutes each day. I see about 150 people each morning and I know more about everyone in the building than anyone else. I am a counsellor, news service and listening post for the grapevine and gossip. The relationships you have with the customers differentiate you from the competition. To do this you must have a stable staff, so that people see the same faces. This way you also know their coffee preferences and this helps with the service and the workflow. Even at other locations where it is a production line, with mainly new customers every day, personality still goes a long way. You need to serve with style.

Processing lots of orders during peak times is tricky—there are almost an infinite number of combinations just considering size, caffeinated/decaffeinated and type of milk, as well as all the different styles of coffee. Customers arrive in waves and you must serve people in order. However, from a speed point of view it is easier to group coffees when you are making the same type. You have to balance this so as not to annoy people waiting. If you have orders for six flat whites, when you call the order the person who reaches the counter may be out of sequence, upsetting a customer who has been waiting longer. In a high production environment you might consider a ticket system, calling 'cappuccino 9', for example. When there are masses of people and you lose one docket everything goes out of whack. The faster you go, the more stressful it becomes and quality is compromised. The extraction time and milk steaming processes cannot be hurried. However, if you are multi-tasking, doing several things at once, you can improve the workflow.

The grind of the coffee is important for optimal extraction when the water flows through the grinds (25–30 seconds). The results can range from too weak to too bitter. This also depends on the humidity, the temperature and the packing of the hopper. For this reason you might have to adjust the grind during the day.

Once the milk boils, the froth goes wispy and separates. Then it smells like baby vomit and the coffee is too hot to drink. Ideally the milk should be around 60 degrees with a creamy velvety texture. The froth should not be distinct from the milk. It should have a whirlpool effect with no large bubbles. The whirlpool effect works the bubbles out, as does a quick tap of the jug or a short period allowed for the bubbles to subside. The service temperature does depend on whether the customer is taking the coffee back to the office, in which case it needs to be a little hotter, or drinking it straightaway. The creamy texture (froth) relates to the fat content of the milk, with skim milk easiest to work with and soy milk the most difficult.

Pouring is also an art that needs to be mentored by an expert. You can make hearts and ferns. An easy one is half white and half black. You can write someone's name with a broken paddle-pop stick. For cappuccino, putting the chocolate on the shot of coffee and then adding the milk produces an interesting effect. Some places have their logos cut out on the shaker so that the chocolate is patterned with the logo.

However, as I have said, your relationship with the customer is what matters most. You can get good coffee at lots of places these days.

BARISTA

TABLE 6.1
Barista training.

Formare Barista	Trainee
Barista	Qualified coffee-maker
Avanzato Barista	Advanced coffee-maker
Maestro Barista	Master coffee-maker
Grand Barista	Winner Annual Gourmet Coffee Institute Barista Competition

Types of beans

Coffee belongs to the botanical family Rubiaceae, which has some 500 genera and over 6,000 species. *Coffea* is by far the most important member of the family economically (see Table 6.2).

Since Linnaeus correctly described *Coffea* in the mid-18th century, botanists have failed to agree on a precise classification system. There are probably at least 25 major species, all indigenous to tropical Africa and certain islands in the Indian Ocean, notably Madagascar. The two most important species of coffee economically are *Coffea arabica* (Typica coffee), which accounts for over 70 per cent of world production, and *Coffea canephora* (Robusta coffee).

There are several processes from coffee cultivation to service:

- harvesting the beans
- processing the beans
- drying the beans
- hulling
- polishing
- grading and sorting
- exporting
- roasting
- grinding
- brewing.

Preparation styles

Following are definitions of the most popular styles of brewed coffee:

- **Espresso** (simply 'caffe' in Italy): Small amount of dark, rich coffee; traditionally served in small, pre-warmed demitasse (half cup).
- **Doppio**: Double espresso (twice the amount of coffee and twice the amount of water; basically, two shots of espresso in one cup).
- **Ristretto** (literally, shrunk or short): More concentrated espresso made with the same amount of coffee but less water.

TABLE 6.2

Popular species and types of coffee.

Family	Species	Varieties	Examples
Rubiaceae	*Coffea*	arabica	Typica
		canephora	Robusta
		liberica	

- **Lungo** (long): An espresso made with more water than usual (sometimes called an Americano).
- **Macchiato**: Espresso 'stained' with a dollop of steamed milk on top.
- **Corretto**: Espresso 'corrected' with a touch of grappa, cognac, sambuca or other spirit.
- **Con panna**: Like macchiato, but whipped cream substituted for steamed milk.
- **Caffe freddo**: Iced espresso (chilled, sweetened and served in a tall glass, sometimes on ice).
- **Caffe latte** (latte): Espresso mixed with steamed milk and served in a glass; typically made with more milk than a cappuccino, with little or no froth on top. In Italy, the coffee in a caffe latte is made in a stove-top machine, rather than an espresso machine, and is not normally served in bars or restaurants. It is usually served at breakfast.
- **Latte macchiato** (stained milk): Steamed milk 'stained' with a shot of espresso coffee, served in a tall glass rather than a cup.
- **Cappuccino**: Espresso with foamed milk—one part espresso, one part steamed milk, one part froth.
- **Cappuccino scuro** (dry or dark cappuccino): Cappuccino prepared with less milk than usual.
- **Cappuccino chiaro** (wet or light cappuccino): Cappuccino prepared with more milk than usual.
- **Cappuccino freddo** (iced cappuccino): Cappuccino served over ice.
- **Skinny** (as in skinny cappuccino or latte): An espresso-based drink made with skim or non-fat milk.
- **Tall** (double or grande): A larger portion (not necessarily twice the size), as in tall latte.

Making a perfect cappuccino.

Preparation of coffee

Making and serving good coffee involves the following steps:

Preparation

- Organise the coffee workstation for efficient workflow, with all equipment and supplies readily available.
- Store coffee and other commodities in appropriate airtight containers and conditions to maintain quality and freshness.

Customer service

- Provide advice to customers about coffee types and characteristics where appropriate.
- Determine customer coffee preferences and requirements, and offer style choices and coffee accompaniments accordingly.

Grinding coffee

Select correct coffee and grind to correct particle size, according to blend and/or roast style required, as well as environmental and equipment variations.

Extracting coffee

- Ensure that appropriate cups or glassware are warm before preparation.
- Measure the required dosage and place into filter basket, tamping coffee evenly using correct pressure.
- Ensure that group head is clean prior to inserting group handle.
- Adjust the temperature and pressure of the machine between cycles, ensuring correct operational temperature.
- Assess quality of extraction visually.
- Check spent grounds ('puck' or 'cake') to identify any required adjustments to dosage.
- Flush the group head for next use.

Preparing milk

- Select correct milk and appropriate jug according to type of coffee and quantity required. Ensure that the jug is clean and cold.
- Expel excess water from steam wand, flush and wipe clean before and after use.
- Steam milk in accordance with milk type and specific order, ensuring that temperature and texture are correct.
- Pour milk using appropriate techniques, according to coffee style and customer preference.

Cafe latte decorated to perfection.

Decorating coffee

Add finishing touches such as chocolate and swirls for decorative appeal.

Caffeine content of coffee

According to the International Coffee Organization, caffeine is generally consumed in amounts less than 300 mg per day, roughly equivalent to:

- three to four cups of roasted and ground coffee
- five cups of instant coffee
- five cups of tea
- six servings of some colas or
- ten tablets of some painkillers.

Activities

1 Visit a main street in your town or city and count the number of outlets selling coffee.
2 Compare the quality of the advertising, promotional material and menus.
3 Compare the quality of the coffee according to your own taste. Look at strength, flavour, texture and presentation.
4 When you have selected the best coffee, interview the barista and ask for his/her secret for making good coffee.

CASE STUDY

Barry's Beans is a cafe selling a large number of takeaway coffees every day. Barry, the owner and manager, made a business-savvy decision to bulk-buy discontinued lines of takeaway coffee cups and lids. (Bulk purchasing means lower cost and therefore higher profit.) As the lids were not designed specifically for the cups, Barry checked to ensure that they fitted together before he made the purchase. However, day one of using the new takeaway cups saw Barry presented with an unfortunate situation. His customers appeared to walk away happy with their steaming hot coffee until their first sip sent scalding cappuccino right down their neck and clothes as the lids popped off the ill-matched cups. Although this dramatic spillage seemed to occur only a few times a day, it was necessary for Barry to consider the ultimate cost of his profit-inspired decision.

Discussion questions

1 Why was Barry's 'dry run' test of the cups and lids proven ineffective?
2 If you were a customer who had been scalded, what would your options be?
3 What are Barry's options regarding the complaining customers and the remaining stock?
4 How should Barry balance his concern for customer satisfaction with economic viability?
5 What are the legal and ethical issues involved in this situation?

LINKS

e-barista.com—http://www.e-barista.com/

The Espresso Index—http://www.espresso.com/

International Coffee Organization—http://www.ico.org/frameset/coffset.htm

CHAPTER SEVEN

The kitchen and catering

OBJECTIVES

This chapter introduces the professional kitchen, the kitchen in which trained staff prepare and present food of the highest standard of freshness and quality, the kitchen in which hygiene and safety are essential considerations. On completion of this chapter you should be able to:

- examine a range of kitchen operations and describe how they relate to other departments/functions within the same establishments
- describe a range of food production techniques
- examine the relationship between quality, presentation, cuisine style and cost control
- describe the varying staff positions that exist in a range of outlets
- review the duties of a kitchen attendant.

The world catering market grew by around 30 per cent in the second half of the 1990s to around A$1 billion, largely due to the lifestyle changes mentioned in Chapters 1 and 2, such as the trend towards dining out, the rise in consumption of takeaway and fast food, and the ever increasing numbers of women in the workforce. This growth trend is likely to continue.

Advertisements for chefs continue to dominate the newspapers. Top chefs, with the appropriate skills, qualifications and imagination, can command excellent salaries, some earning as much as $200,000 per year. According to Tony Bilson, 'Being a chef is no longer a wage-slave position, it's an art. The only difference is we're not subsidised. We don't come under the aegis of the Australia Council.' A recent article in the *Australian Magazine* referred to the 'deification of chefs' by the public: some of them have been raised to a god-like status in the eyes of the public.

Despite rosy predictions for career development in the catering industry, the pay rate for an apprentice chef is low and there is little compensation in the early years for the pressures of work in a hot kitchen and the irregular working hours. However, changes are occurring.

In the area of training there are still the traditional apprenticeships, but there are also traineeships with on- and off-the-job training, as well as certificates and diplomas at supervisory and management levels, some available through distance education. The old system of indentureship to one employer is evolving, with the advent of training companies. They employ apprentices and manage their employment, thus giving them exposure to more than one workplace during their training.

Catering opportunities exist in numerous types of establishment including restaurants, cafes, resorts, hotels, motels, gourmet and fast food outlets, convention centres, educational institutions, hospitals, prisons, clubs, cafeterias and pubs. In fact the scale of catering for air and rail transport is enormous, with quality and consistency being the biggest challenges as the food is prepared in advance and reheated. Catering in the army is another challenge. The Australian Army Catering Corps comprises 1,150 staff, with services ranging from silver service to field service under the most basic conditions. Working in the bush with makeshift kitchens and no lights or running water can be quite a task. Everything must be transported and set up—utensils, cooking equipment, fuel, fresh and dry produce, spices, to name but a few—and staff cannot afford to forget a thing. The Kitchen Field Mobile is a stove used to prepare up to a thousand meals three times a day, and is indispensable for such operations. Planning and efficiency take on a new meaning with army catering.

Some of the above operations, such as cafes and restaurants, are commercial (for profit), while others, such as catering for hospitals, are non-commercial (not for profit). Catering can also be provided in conjunction with other services such as conferences, entertainment and accommodation.

Relationships with other departments/functions

The kitchen and the restaurant have the closest working relationship. Teamwork is essential, with effective communication between departments about menus, customer requests, orders, food preparation times and sales contributing to the achievement of mutual goals. Kitchen staff need to inform restaurant staff of all dishes available, including their ingredients and methods of preparation. Restaurant staff should be given the opportunity to taste dishes prepared for customers so that they are able to sell them effectively. In some cases food service staff are encouraged by the management to 'move' certain items which, if not sold, will have to be discarded in a matter of days. This level of co-operation helps to ensure cost-effective use of fresh produce.

The Purchasing Department also works very closely with the kitchen (see Fig. 7.1 on page 80). Although it is responsible for purchases for all departments, it is the kitchen that places the greatest demands on this department. Availability and price of ingredients are important considerations in menu planning and waste minimisation is also essential to avoid blow-outs in food costs.

The Accounts Department is also involved in this cycle. Besides making payments for purchases of food and other kitchen requirements, the relationship between the kitchen and the Accounts Department relates to budgets, forecasts, expenditure and cost control procedures. To put this more simply, the cost of the food purchased and the cost of labour, plus other minor costs, must be met before a profit can be made. In the kitchen where waste is a big factor, with perishable food items and unmet demand for food purchased and prepared, this is particularly challenging.

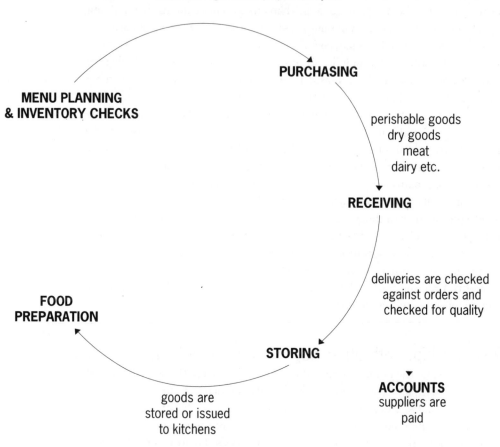

FIG. 7.1

The purchasing and food preparation cycle.

PURCHASING

**MENU PLANNING
& INVENTORY CHECKS**

perishable goods
dry goods
meat
dairy etc.

RECEIVING

**FOOD
PREPARATION**

deliveries are checked
against orders and
checked for quality

STORING

ACCOUNTS
suppliers are
paid

goods are
stored or issued
to kitchens

Quality, presentation, cuisine style and cost control

There are many considerations in planning menus. Nutrition is one aspect, and this was mentioned in Chapter 1. Quality and availability of food products are others. Customer tastes and food trends are yet others. The purchasing cycle for raw products is illustrated in Fig. 7.1. The kitchen requisitions foodstuffs after careful discussion about price, availability and quality, and the Purchasing Department places the orders with suppliers. Stocks are delivered and on delivery every item must be checked for quality, weight and quantity. Where relevant, goods are date stamped. The food items are then stored or issued directly to the kitchen. Careful monitoring is required to ensure effective stock control. Stock must be rotated, items which need to be used by a certain date must be incorporated in menus, portion sizes must be just right for customer needs, and waste in food preparation must be managed by using off-cuts in other dishes.

Working out the profitability of menus is complex but it is essential in order to establish which items are selling best and the profit ratio on each one. Analysis will show whether an item is a 'star' or a 'dog'. A star is a menu item which has low cost/high profit and sells well, while a dog is an item which sells badly (see Fig. 7.2). Chefs must constantly manage the quality of the food, the presentation, the cuisine style and the cost aspects of running a kitchen.

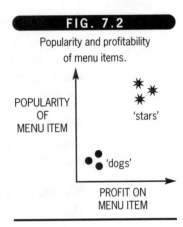

FIG. 7.2

Popularity and profitability of menu items.

Methods of food production

Knowledge of food production methods is essential for all service staff as customers often ask about the preparation of a dish. Naturally, qualified chefs are experienced in the use of all of the methods mentioned below.

Boiling

Boiling is used for cooking such items as potatoes, pasta and chicken stock. When this is done for very short periods, with vegetables for example, it is known as blanching.

Poaching

Poached food is cooked in hot water, which is kept below the boil. Examples of foods cooked in this way are eggs benedict, dried fruit and fish.

Steaming

The food is cooked by the temperature of the steam but is not immersed in the water. Items such as vegetables, seafood and puddings are placed in receptacles—such as the steam basket widely used in Asian cooking—in, or above, the boiling water.

Simmering

Dishes such as goulash and curry are cooked very slowly at a temperature below boiling, while stewing involves simmering meats at low temperatures in a thickened sauce.

Baking

Baking is done with dry heat in an oven. Where the oven has a fan to circulate the heat more evenly, it is known as fan baking. Cooking meat and poultry in this way is known as roasting.

Barbecuing

Generally done outdoors, barbecues are used to grill a wide range of foods, including meat and vegetables.

Frying

Frying involves cooking with fat or oil in a pan. For deep frying, the food is submerged in hot fat or oil, while stir frying involves cooking food very rapidly over a high heat with little fat or oil. Examples of food cooked in this way are Pad Thai and fried rice.

Grilling

Grilling involves cooking under direct heat. Fish and chops work well with this method.

Microwave cooking

This is a convenient method of heating and cooking, especially for pre-prepared foods.

Style and pricing of menus

Menus vary enormously in style, from the basic photocopied page to the finely detailed and beautifully presented menu of the fine dining restaurant. These days menus are often listed on blackboards, which used to be reserved for specials only. The graphic artist often provides outstanding illustration for this type of menu.

Table d'hôte is a menu which offers meals at a fixed price. Sometimes there is a choice, but the final cost for a three-course meal is the same. A la carte is a menu in which all items are listed and priced separately. The final bill is a reflection of the customer's choices.

Cuisine styles

Below is an outline of the main cuisine styles used in Australia.

Classic

The traditional or European style of cooking has its origins in France. One of the greatest chefs of all time was Auguste Escoffier who was the executive chef at the Savoy Hotel in London 100 years ago, working for general manager César Ritz. He wrote a book called *Le Guide Culinaire*, which became a classic, and he was recognised as the emperor of the world's kitchens. His culinary skills were well known in the finest hotels in Europe and his influence can still be felt today. One of his most famous sauces was Sauce Diable, which he served for the first time to the Prince of Wales and Kaiser Wilhelm. It evolved from the creative use of overripe mangoes. Escoffier saw cookery as an art form and developed it accordingly.

Modern

Responding mainly to health issues, many classic dishes have been adapted to better suit today's tastes and trends.

Nouvelle

This type of cuisine is based on the French cooking tradition but uses smaller portions and fewer fats and creams.

Minceur

Cuisine minceur is ideal for the kilojoule conscious and has developed in response to the needs of a more sedentary population.

Naturelle

Australia and New Zealand have some of the finest fresh produce in the world and cuisine naturelle, where food is cooked simply to retain its natural flavour and nutritional value, is popular in both countries. In fact visiting European chefs are often astonished by the variety of our fresh produce. Unlike the European menu, which is seasonal, menus here are able to incorporate most fresh products, as they are available the whole year round.

Ethnic

The range of ethnic restaurants in Australia is enormous. A study of the telephone book will reveal a restaurant of almost every ethnic origin, and Chinese, Thai, Indian, Moroccan, Japanese and Italian are just a few examples.

Regional

Regional cooking comes from a particular part of a country. In China and India, for example, the dishes from various regions are quite different.

Cook-chill

Perishable foods are put through a mild heat or pasteurisation process which extends the time they remain edible, provided they are kept in the temperature range, 0–4°C. Pasta, rice and soups are often prepared in this way for large catering operations such as airlines, banquet kitchens and hospitals. The products can be assembled after separate cooking of the individual components, or the meal components can be assembled, vacuum packed and then processed through pasteurisation to give them a longer shelf life.

Staff positions in the kitchen

The levels at which cooks and kitchen attendants are employed can be found in the relevant award, for example the Restaurant etc. Employees State Award (NSW).

Cook Grade 1 is generally an employee who cooks breakfast and snacks. Learning the basic skills of the profession, this trainee or apprentice is in the early stages of their career and may be employed by the bakery, butchery or pastry section. Cook Grade 2 has had some basic training and is able to apply skills and knowledge to cooking a wider range of foods. Cook Grade 3 has finished a traineeship or

apprenticeship in cooking, baking, butchery or pastry cooking. By this time the cook should have a wide range of skills. This position is also known as Commis Chef. Chef Grade 4 has completed all training and is able to plan menus and prepare many different dishes. Some chefs at this level have already specialised, while others have assumed responsibility for a small team. This position is also known as Chef de Partie. He or she would be in charge of ordering and stock control for a small section or kitchen.

The Sous Chef is the second in command in the kitchen and has an important administrative role. Management of most of the day-to-day running of the kitchen is the responsibility of this chef.

Executive Chef is the highest position in the kitchen. This person is responsible for ordering food, planning creative menus, managing finances, managing staff and planning for the future. Generally, he or she would attend meetings of senior staff regarding management of the whole operation and long-term plans.

There are also three grades of kitchen attendant and they are responsible for general cleaning duties in the kitchen, assisting with setting up ingredients for cooking and preparing basic foods such as salads and soups. In many kitchens this employee is known as a steward. The Stewarding Supervisor or Kitchen Attendant Supervisor is responsible for staff involved in cleaning, washing up and basic food preparation. This is quite often a large section, which works under pressure during busy service periods to ensure that all utensils, crockery and ingredients required by the chef are at hand.

The following article, kindly contributed by David Kallmeier, and published in the *Sydney Morning Herald* on 25 February 1992, sums up the dedication required for a catering career.

IT TAKES TIME TO COOK UP DEDICATION

The sight of raw chicken at 6.30 a.m. is not most people's idea of a good start to the day. It's not what I consider a particularly attractive view of the morning either, but as an apprentice chef, you become accustomed to such things.

In the world of catering, each day is as busy as the next. There will always be the need for mise-en-place (preparation of food), be it on a large or a small scale.

Remember the last time you invited friends for dinner, ummed and aahed over what to feed them for three courses, wandered the shopping centre for hours looking for the right ingredients, spent a fortune on obscure vegetables with names you could hardly pronounce, locked yourself in the kitchen all day and then panicked about whether to serve fresh fruit or that delightful sponge you made earlier?

For a chef, decision-making is an everyday occurrence, not a dilemma.

On this particular Monday I have officially completed my four-year apprenticeship and become a fully qualified chef. Not a chef in a hotel, not a chef in a restaurant, not a chef on a cruise ship or any of those other glamorous notions people seem to have about those who wear tall white hats—but a chef in one of the largest catering organisations in Australia.

I have spent close to the final 12 months of my apprenticeship at the Reader's Digest. The catering organisation I am employed by, Spotless Catering, is contracted to the publication company to cater for in-house functions such as board meetings, cocktail parties, executive dining rooms, grand luncheons, hot and cold buffets, not to mention providing at least 250 people with English and continental breakfast, morning teas and assorted lunch specialities.

The standards are high and the demands are tough for school-leavers who want to cook for a career. Interviews, examinations, practical demonstrations and endless scrutinising challenge your knowledge, ability and dedication.

I wasn't the type of child who baked biscuits on Saturdays and I wasn't particularly fond of my mother's apron strings. So why, I hear you ask, did I choose a life in the kitchen?

I don't know exactly, but the creativity provides a challenge. You are constantly learning, while the will to succeed and better yourself is intense. Maybe my love of food in general overrides any worries I had about becoming a chef.

Like any job, it has its ups and downs, but being judged NSW finalist for the Apprenticeship of the Year and participating in culinary competitions outside of working hours seems to bring out my best and make it all seem worthwhile.

Most people's reaction to my occupation is directly related to their passion for food. What they fail to understand is that a chef does not spend all day simply taste-testing and adding salt to culinary masterpieces. OK, so I enjoy the taste-testing. But there's also a wide variety of tasks that still have to be completed, such as ordering goods, balancing the books, changing and rewriting menus. Also, there is a seemingly endless stream of paperwork that has to be done.

Then there's the people side of things. Oh yes, a chef does deal with people besides other chefs and staff. Each client has a different idea of the type of menu he or she would like, each function requires a fresh approach and each diner has a different opinion and varying expectations of what he or she is about to receive. To meet all of these demands and survive with rave reviews from all sides takes patience, understanding and, at times, nerves of steel.

When you work with food, you play with one of the human race's most intimate and personalised idiosyncrasies—taste.

The inner turmoil a chef experiences while watching a diner take a bite of the first serving of any meal can only be likened to that indescribable feeling you get when you think the chair you're leaning back on is about to tip over backwards, but you save yourself at the last microsecond.

The greatest misconception the public has of chefs is that they will constantly hold dinner parties and barbecues, and even cater for other people's parties, simply because they like to cook. Sure, a bit of home entertaining is nice, but do accountants offer to tidy up their friends' finances or carpenters fix the squeaky hinge when they visit?

I enjoy catering, but I didn't train this long to make a weekend brunch for 20 people in the backyard.

For all of you that are of the opinion that domestic catering, like a dinner party, is time consuming and sometimes laborious, just think for a minute what a chef has to encounter in a day's work.

Sometimes it might be smooth sailing, but more often it is irate customers demanding their meal 'pronto', a small function suddenly doubling in size, a customer questioning a portion size or, on the odd occasion, a customer disputing the bill.

Admittedly the prime responsibility of a chef is to satisfy the customer, but have you ever stopped to think how demanding diners can be?

The next onslaught of hungry diners are on their way and the afternoon's gastronomic delights must be prepared.

One day, hopefully in the not-too-distant future, I'll be working with some of the best chefs in Europe . . .

Postscript: David achieved his ambition and travelled the world.

Recommended practices for kitchen staff

The primary considerations for kitchen staff should be hygiene, safety and cost control. Adherence to food hygiene regulations is very important, and following are recommended practices:

- Don't store food on the floor or leave it uncovered.
- Don't leave food out—it must be stored at the correct temperature.
- Don't refreeze food.
- Take care with chipped crockery and damaged food utensils and equipment as bacteria can grow in the recesses.
- Keep hair covered.
- Keep your hands clean and away from the hair and face.
- Avoid sneezing or coughing in the kitchen and never smoke while handling food!
- Do not eat on the job.
- Avoid cross contamination by handling foods and waste carefully.

Experienced chefs agree that the kitchen is a very dangerous place. Cuts and burns are common and care should be taken to avoid them. Careful handling of knives (a sharp knife is less dangerous than a blunt one as pressure does not have to be used) and saucepans is essential. Hot oil is particularly dangerous. An apprentice recently slipped while cleaning and his arm went into the deep fryer. This type of accident should be avoided at all cost. Safety shoes and professional cookery uniforms are recommended for good reason.

Good communication and teamwork are essential in this department, which works under enormous pressure at times. Managing work, by planning (mise-en-place) and scheduling tasks carefully, and working efficiently are also very important.

Quality and consistency in service are achieved by developing standard recipes. These are used as the basis for cost control and purchasing is done accordingly. It is therefore essential that each dish is prepared and presented according to the standard recipe. Such consistency is important for the customer and for the senior chef who has created the dish. Preparation should follow standard procedures and portion sizes should always be the same. In this way the chef can be assured of the quality of the food presented to the customer and the costs can be managed efficiently.

Australia—The place where food is happening

Australia is rapidly becoming recognised as the place where food is happening. Chefs from all over the world are looking to us for ideas and tourists are increasingly attracted to the food and wine we offer. King Island cheeses, Margaret River wines, Tasmanian lobsters and Queensland tropical fruits are just a few of the products that are inviting world attention. In using our fine products in unique ways, Australia's restaurants are achieving world-class standards, and Australia is fast becoming a food destination. The Victorian Government has led this new development, with its marketing of the Melbourne Food and Wine Festival, which runs for six weeks, as the world's best food fair.

Food, wines and beers are an important aspect of our culture, well appreciated by locals and visitors alike. Beer was first brewed in Australia by James Squire, who arrived at Port Jackson on the First Fleet in 1788. The first brewery was opened in 1811 and, since then, they have proliferated, with many boutique beers emerging in recent years. Our wine regions now produce many world-class, award-winning wines and export overseas.

Advising customers on the best wine or beer to go with a particular item on the menu is an important role for all food service personnel, who sometimes ask advice of the chefs who have created the dishes. Complimentary relationships between food and wine, or beer, are important in ensuring customer satisfaction.

Activities

1 Find some recipes which use the different cooking methods described in this chapter.
2 Visit your local supermarket and identify ingredients which could give a menu item an 'Australian' feel or appearance.
3 Explain how quality can be achieved by comparing meals which you have eaten at restaurants on the following principles:
   • use of fresh ingredients
   • use of standard recipes
   • use of standard procedures
   • use of standard portion sizes
   • standard presentation.
4 Explain why good interdepartmental relationships are important in the industry, using the kitchen as an example.

5 Discuss why the following industry principles are relevant to work in the kitchen:
- hygiene
- courtesy
- safety
- managing work flow
- problem-solving.

Discussion questions

1 Work out how many meals you eat away from home each week.
2 Conduct a survey of friends and relatives to find out how many meals they eat away from home each week.
3 What are the implications for someone planning a career in food preparation?
4 Can you predict any particular food trends?
5 How would you describe Australian cuisine?
6 Why are other countries interested in our ingredients and methods?

LINKS

Australian and New Zealand Food Authority (ANZFA) (Food Safety Fact Sheets)—http://www.anzfa.gov.au/mediareleasespublications/factsheets/foodsafetyfactsheets/index.cfm

Australasian Society of Clinical Immunology and Allergy (ASCIA) (Food Allergies)—http://www.allergy.org.au/aer/infobulletins/allergy_overview.htm

Food Lovers Guide to Australia—http://www.sbs.com.au/foodlovers/

CHAPTER EIGHT

Front office and club reception

OBJECTIVES

The aim of this chapter is to provide you with an overview of the work carried out by the Front Office of a hospitality establishment. On completion of this chapter you should be able to:

- describe the functions performed by staff in Front Office
- describe the interrelationships between Front Office and other departments found in hospitality establishments
- describe the relationships between Front Office and external agencies
- outline career path options in Front Office
- review the attributes of a Front Office employee.

A guest staying at a resort in the small country of Swaziland in southern Africa was taken ill in the early hours of the morning. He had eaten swordfish for dinner, which was possibly not a good choice since Swaziland is situated inland from the coast. However, the freshness of the fish was not considered until much later that night when it became clear that he was suffering from food poisoning. The guest and his wife describe it as the worst experience they have ever had in a hotel. Despite its size (350 rooms), not a single staff member could be raised. Their first step was to call the switchboard but there was no reply. Repeated attempts to get through to anyone on the telephone list were likewise unsuccessful. Reception did not answer and a frantic tour of the building at 4 a.m. did not reveal a single staff member at the front desk, or indeed anywhere else.

Functions of Front Office

The Front Office department is the main point of contact for all guests staying at a hotel, motel, resort or guesthouse. There are various functions performed by Front Office, and by the sections or departments within it, such as reservations, check-in, guest information and check-out (see Fig. 8.1 on page 90). The switchboard is also a Front Office responsibility. In smaller operations all functions are generally performed by one or two staff members who answer the phones, provide

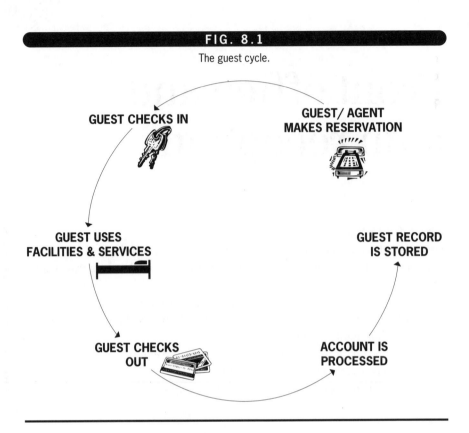

FIG. 8.1

The guest cycle.

GUEST CHECKS IN

GUEST/ AGENT
MAKES RESERVATION

GUEST USES
FACILITIES & SERVICES

GUEST RECORD
IS STORED

GUEST CHECKS
OUT

ACCOUNT IS
PROCESSED

information, take reservations and perform all the duties associated with Front Office. In the example above, none of the Front Office staff were available to provide much needed assistance.

Following is an outline of the work and responsibilities of the various sections or departments within Front Office (see also Fig. 8.2 on page 93).

Reservations

This department is responsible for taking advance bookings for accommodation. Achievement of high occupancy levels (number of rooms occupied) is the goal of any hotel or motel and this is only possible through careful attention to reservations. The Reservations Department works very closely with the Marketing Department to ensure that the highest levels are achieved at the best possible rates. If, for example, the Reservations Department were to receive a request for 100 rooms two years from now at a discount rate, they would need to know what occupancy they could expect at that particular time. It would be very foolish to sell 100 rooms at a highly discounted rate if they could be filled at normal rates.

On the other hand, empty rooms are disastrous for hospitality establishments and discounting is a sensible way to fill them during anticipated low occupancy periods. In most selling situations—in a clothing shop, for example—stock can be discounted in a sale and the money invested in the stock can be recouped, even if the stock has to be sold at cost price. In the hospitality industry, an empty bed is money lost—it can never be recouped at a later date. The aim of the industry therefore is 'heads on beds'.

Reception

The role of the Reception Department is to greet arriving guests and check them into their rooms. This involves looking up the reservation, checking the details, assigning a room number and having the guest sign the registration form. Another important function of this department is to arrange a method of payment with the customer, preferably before or on arrival. (Generally, hotels and motels like advance payment from customers to avoid 'skippers'.) In most cases the guest leaves a signed

credit card voucher at the Front Desk which guarantees payment to the hotel or motel. This can be discarded on departure if another method of payment is chosen. With this procedure the organisation avoids giving guests credit since it is time consuming to follow up bad debts. Registration of guests also provides an opportunity to sell the services of the establishment and to ensure that all special requests are met.

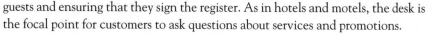

The Reception Department in a club has the important role of greeting members and guests and ensuring that they sign the register. As in hotels and motels, the desk is the focal point for customers to ask questions about services and promotions.

The duties of a club receptionist include:

- checking membership badges/cards upon entry to the club
- providing accurate advice and information on club services and facilities to customers and club members as required
- assisting guests to 'sign in' in accordance with government and enterprise requirements
- explaining club membership and club rules clearly, correctly and politely to the public and to members
- explaining membership application forms to applicants and assisting applicants to complete forms if required
- issuing correct membership badges/cards
- checking membership records to verify membership
- checking that members and guests comply with dress and age regulations, in accordance with enterprise policy
- referring disputes over entry to the club to security, a supervisor or other relevant person, according to enterprise policy.

Portering

This department takes care of guests' luggage and shows guests to their rooms on arrival. The staff of this department must be able to explain how to operate all equipment in the room, such as air-conditioning and television. This is particularly necessary where the guest can access their account and messages on the TV monitor. Showing guests to their rooms and settling them in also provides an opportunity to sell the establishment's other facilities, such as restaurants and bars. Luggage is often stored by porters for guests who have to leave their rooms for check-out by 10 a.m. but do not depart until later in the day. On departure the porters carry the guest's bags to the front of the hotel and call a taxi or arrange other transport if necessary.

Concierge

The role of the Concierge in large hotels is to provide information to guests on hotel facilities, local events and attractions. Making travel and theatre bookings is another service offered by the Concierge. Unusual requests, such as where to buy a black evening dress when the stores are closed, or how to find a dentist who will attend to a broken tooth in the middle of the night, are the kinds of things that the Concierge deals with daily.

Telephone/Communications

This incredibly busy department is responsible for all communications including incoming and outgoing calls, guest wake-up calls, paging systems and so on. Communications staff must be aware of all events and facilities and must be able to describe to callers where the establishment is situated, how to get there and the cost of parking. They have to respond to innumerable other questions and be able to direct callers to relevant departments and staff. The Communications Department is usually a small room with whiteboards covered in writing on each of the walls and switchboards, flashing lights and sophisticated telecommunications equipment. The Communications Department is usually the emergency centre for the establishment.

Records

All records, whether stored manually or on computer, have to be carefully maintained for legal and other reasons. Guest databases, for example, make it possible to select previous customers with specific profiles for new marketing campaigns.

Cashiering

The main function of this department is to process payment when the guest leaves. The bill (folio) is totalled, and the guest checks it to see if all the transactions are correct, then settles the account. This is often more complicated than it would first appear, since guests often run two accounts simultaneously, say one for business expenses and one for private expenses (the bar, for example). Likewise, some expenses may be met by the package deal, while others have to be met by the guest. Since there is generally a number of different guests, all with different package deals and different rates, this can become very complicated. The cashiers are also responsible for cashing travellers cheques, assisting with EFTPOS (electronic funds transfer point of sale) withdrawals and handling the day's takings for the various outlets.

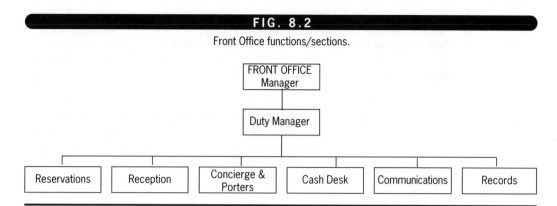

FIG. 8.2

Front Office functions/sections.

Legal or regulatory requirements for Front Office

Relevant legislation varies between states and territories and, of course, federal and common law also apply. The origin of these laws and regulations will be discussed in Chapter 12. The areas most relevant to the operation of Front Office are the importance of registering all guests, ensuring guest safety and the safety of their belongings, and providing the services advertised. Other relevant legislation deals with the confidentiality of guest information and records.

Duties of Front Office staff

Many staff in hotels, motels and resorts are multi-skilled and have titles such as 'Guest Service Agent' because they are able to perform most of the following roles. However, descriptions of the duties of staff in their specialised roles, as outlined below, is a useful way of getting to know what goes on in Front Office.

Reservations Clerk

Requests for advance bookings for accommodation can come from individual guests or from corporate customers (someone often books on their behalf). The Reservations staff have to be aware of the features of all rooms, as well as all the services and facilities the hotel, motel or resort has to offer. In some situations room rates are negotiable within limits and the staff in Reservations carry the responsibility for these negotiations. Clearly the aim is to sell the establishment at the best possible rate. Requests for group bookings are particularly challenging because packages and discounted rates often have to be negotiated. Efficiency, product knowledge, customer relations skills, selling skills and a good telephone manner are essential. A general knowledge of local events and attractions is also important as the range of questions asked by prospective customers is limitless.

Receptionist

Duties include allocating rooms prior to arrival, greeting guests on arrival, checking reservation details such as room rate and length of stay, organising the preferred method of payment, handing out a key (often a key card) and calling a porter to show the guest to their room. Enquiring about special requests and providing information are other important roles of Reception staff.

Porter

The porter carries luggage to guestrooms, demonstrates the operation of lights, air-conditioning, television and other equipment, explains some of the establishment's services and offers to make bookings for newly arrived guests. Handling messages, delivering newspapers, storing luggage and organising transport are some of their other duties.

Concierge

The head porter or concierge is in charge of all porters and advises guests on attractions, tours, events and shows. Key aspects of this work are providing information and offering services. Many of the requests are unique and unexpected, and the concierge is expected to assist wherever possible. Perks of the job include tips and invitations to attractions and events so that first-hand recommendations can be made to guests.

Telephonist

A telephonist, like all other Front Office staff, needs to know the establishment, its facilities and its services intimately. Food and Beverage outlets, entertainment, functions, promotions, hotel departments, staff and current guests (including VIPs) are all part of the information that must be at hand. Extensive knowledge and an ability to handle pressure are important aspects of work in Communications. As mentioned previously, this department is the emergency centre of the hotel, motel or resort and staff have to be able to respond quickly, calmly and appropriately to emergency situations.

Cashier

The cashier is responsible primarily for settling guest accounts and processing payment. Payment can be in the form of vouchers, credit cards, cash or travellers' cheques. Keeping the guest account up to date is necessary in establishments that do not have point of sale (POS) systems linked to Front Office. If this is the case, then charges are brought to the desk by staff from the outlets and these charges are posted to the guest account. Cashiers also cash travellers' cheques, convert currencies and handle EFT (electronic funds transfer) systems.

Night Auditor

Staff who work as night auditors generally work from 11 p.m. to 7 a.m. and during that time they close the books for the previous day's trading. The books must balance and any errors made by the day staff must be traced. These can include posting to the wrong guest account, using the wrong code, making data entry errors, and so on. With the huge number of daily transactions, mistakes do happen; however, with the advent of computerised point-of-sale systems, the night auditor's job has

Services offered by Front Office

The services offered by Front Office have already been discussed in the above sections. Just as a reminder, they include:
- reservations for advance bookings
- check-in on arrival
- room and key allocation
- portering and providing information
- security for valuables (safety deposit boxes)
- recommendations for hotel/motel/resort facilities and services
- recommendations for transport, attractions, entertainment, activities and events, as well as all types of other information
- onward reservations for travel and accommodation
- telecommunications, messages and newspapers
- business services such as word processing
- account payment and departure.

become much easier. Restaurant takings have to balance, including cash on hand and amounts charged to guest accounts. By morning, reports have to be ready for management to review the previous day's trading. This is an outstanding career opportunity for individuals who have a head for figures and the stamina to work graveyard shifts.

Supervisor

A Front Office supervisor is responsible for seeing that all tasks are performed efficiently and accurately. It is important for the supervisor to observe the work flow and to anticipate the arrival of groups so that staff can be allocated appropriately. The supervisor is generally very skilled on the Front Office computer system and can help staff with the more unusual functions. The supervisor can also assist with guests who have a particularly difficult enquiry or problem. Administrative tasks include developing staff rosters, supervising back-up of computer data, generation of reports, and so on.

Of course, the positions described above are those you would normally find in a four- or five-star hotel. A description of each is useful because the same roles would be performed in more modest establishments, but possibly all by the same person! Some of the different types of accommodation available are listed in the accompanying box. The challenges are just as great since all these tasks still have to be performed: reservations, check-in, room allocation, account management, advice and information, and check-out.

Different types of accommodation

youth hostels

backpacker accommodation

guest houses

bed and breakfasts

homestay

farmstay

caravan parks

holiday apartments

serviced apartments

boutique hotels

resorts

motels

hotels

CASE STUDY

The 'hotel' was in the New South Wales highlands and seemed as though it had not changed in 100 years. Indeed, it appeared that parts of it hadn't been cleaned in 100 years either! The general state of cleanliness was not assisted by the numerous indigenous animals and birds which overran the place. These were enthusiastically fed by the guests, who were overwhelmed when kangaroos turned up on the balcony for tea and scones and cockatoos drank out of the milk jug. The downside of this was the kangaroo droppings left around the tables at the guests' feet and the bird droppings on every railing. Despite everything, the owner was quick to explain that his return rate for guests was 75 per cent, which is something that a city hotel would envy. He and his family were completely multi-skilled. They all knew how to take and record reservations, send confirmation letters, check people in, take people to their rooms, explain local history, run activities, serve in the bar, post charges to guest accounts, check out departures and balance the books. In addition to all these Front Office duties, they saw their customer relations role as the most important of all as this was what made the place so popular.

Discussion questions

1 What were the attractions for guests at this establishment?
2 What are the risks involved in everyone being a jack-of-all-trades and master of none?

Attributes of a Front Office employee

Hotels, motels and clubs looking for staff to work on the Front Desk list the following attributes as important:

- ability to create a good first impression, verbally and non-verbally (posture and expression)
- ability to communicate fluently with a wide range of customers
- understanding of different customer needs and expectations
- understanding of different cultures and an ability to speak foreign languages
- attention to, and care for, detail
- punctuality
- impeccable presentation
- good voice qualities
- commitment to professional service
- ability to work as a team member
- extensive knowledge of the local area, events, entertainment, transportation, etc.
- ability to sell Australia, its culture and its attractions to visitors.

A successful guest stay is the result of teamwork, from reservation to check-in, from room cleaning to guest information, from dining in the restaurant to check-out. All these are linked in some way and employers look for staff with an ability to co-operate with other team members and departments, to anticipate problems and prevent them, to pay attention to detail and to communicate effectively.

Career path options

Career opportunities for staff who have worked in Front Office include positions such as Night Manager, Front Office Manager, Sales and Marketing Manager and Director of Rooms Division. Night-time positions provide good opportunities to learn about all aspects of the hotel since the number of staff is fairly low in the early hours and staff who are on duty have to cope with a wide range of different challenges. Think about it: most of the guests are in the hotel when most of the management staff are not. The Night Manager is often the most senior person around in the early hours if an emergency occurs. The graveyard shift is also the time when the books are balanced for the previous day's trading. This provides the opportunity to develop an overview of the hotel's or motel's operation.

Entry positions on the Front Desk in large hotels are rare as these jobs require an extensive knowledge of the hotel and its services. Extensive training is required on the Front Office computer system, and these days guest service staff are expected to be multi-skilled. This means that they need to be able to work in Reservations, Reception, Cashiering or Communications. Generally, new staff begin as porters, car-parking attendants or telephonists. Having developed a sound knowledge of hotel services and having demonstrated excellent customer service skills, they are then transferred to the front desk. Naturally, the ability to speak foreign languages is an enormous asset and, if they are fluent in the language(s) of many of the hotel's or resort's guests, the opportunities are limitless.

Interrelationships with other departments

To this point the different sections, or functions, of Front Office have been described. However, Front Office does not work in a vacuum; it works closely with some or all of the following departments.

Housekeeping

The Housekeeping Department, or Accommodation Services Department, as it is sometimes called, ensures that guestrooms are cleaned and that public areas are spotless. This is a challenging task since check-out time is generally 10 a.m. and check-in time is usually 2 p.m. This means that the rooms of departing guests have to be cleaned within four hours. Often, however, guests arrive by plane as early as 7 a.m. and want their rooms immediately. If the rooms are still occupied, Front Office has to advise Housekeeping as soon as they have been vacated so that Housekeeping can proceed with cleaning. If the previous guests leave early and Housekeeping is advised immediately, then the rooms can be prepared and the guests checked in before the official check-in time. All arriving guests are guaranteed a clean room by 2 p.m. so Housekeeping often has a busy morning. If Front Office is advised as soon as a room is ready, very often the guest can go straight to the room without waiting. Communication between the two departments is thus very important. With early advice from Front Office about arrivals and departures, Housekeeping can schedule cleaning more easily. Special requests for ironing boards, hairdryers, cots and additional blankets, for example, are generally made at the time of check-in and Housekeeping is advised so that the items can be taken to the room.

Food and Beverage

Front Office staff are often asked to recommend food and beverage outlets. For this reason it is important to ensure that information available is up to date, including special promotions, such as theme nights in the restaurant. Indeed, competent Front Office staff take a proactive approach in selling the outlets at the time of check-in and making restaurant reservations for the guests, rather than waiting to be asked.

In order to sell the hotel's services, staff need to have first-hand experience with what is available. In some establishments new employees are taken to one of the food and beverage outlets for lunch during orientation to enable them to better appreciate what the organisation has to offer. Others go a step further and allow staff who have passed the probationary period to stay at the hotel with a partner of their choice for a weekend. What an incentive! This contributes enormously to a sense of belonging in new employees and enables them to sell the establishment's services and facilities more effectively.

Kitchen

Guests on special diets generally discuss these requirements with either Reservations staff when making a booking or with Reception staff when checking in. Co-ordination with Kitchen staff should ensure that these special needs are met. One of the best examples that springs to mind is the wealthy lady who took up an entire floor of a large city hotel, accompanied by several poodles. Each of these animals had a particular diet and liking for different foods, all of which was spelled out in detail. Careful co-ordination with the kitchen was necessary to meet the special needs of these animals, needless to say to the great amusement of staff in both the Purchasing and Kitchen Departments.

Sales and Marketing

Sales and Marketing takes overall responsibility for attracting guests to the hotel and ensuring that occupancy (number of rooms occupied) and revenue (money earned) are maximised. Sales and Marketing is assisted in this by Front Office staff, mainly those in Reservations, who take on a sales role when speaking to prospective guests on the telephone. Marketing promotions and packages are generally aimed at presenting an attractive image of the establishment and ensuring that accommodation is sold, particularly at times when occupancy is expected to be low. In city hotels, for example, business people often use hotels during the week, resulting in high occupancy from Monday to Thursday. Sales and Marketing efforts in these enterprises are thus aimed at developing packages, such as luxury weekends away from home, which will bring in revenue during quieter times. Sales and Marketing managers also work closely with Reservations staff in Front Office on predicting occupancy rates, often many years ahead, to ensure that revenue is maximised. Although a booking for 300 rooms sounds attractive, a group of this size would expect a substantial discount and it may be possible instead to fill the hotel with customers paying the full price.

The Public Relations manager is employed by this division and is responsible for communication with the press and the public. While there are many events that need to be attended and guests that need to be met, the most important aspect of this role is the hotel's relationship with the media. This involves high-level communication skills for writing press releases and making statements to the various branches of the media.

Finance

While the Front Office staff manages daily revenue, the Finance Department is responsible for the overall financial status of the organisation. As described earlier, night auditors balance the books for the day's trading each night. The Night Audit staff therefore have dual reporting responsibilities, to the Finance/Accounts manager and the Front Office manager. Guests who pay on departure would pay at the front desk and cashiers would be responsible for 'collecting' the money. Guests whose companies have accounts would sign on departure (assuming that this had been previously authorised in writing by their company) and these amounts would be 'collected' by the Accounts Department by billing the company. Co-ordination and co-operation between Front Office and Finance and Accounting is essential.

Engineering

Problems in the room with, for example, the air-conditioning system or the plumbing are referred to the Engineering Department. Another area in which Front Office and Engineering work closely together is on the room locking system. Where keys are used, Engineering will produce new keys to replace those that have been lost or damaged. Sometimes the whole lock has to be replaced or reprogrammed if theft of a key is suspected. Nowadays, however, advances in technology have led to the use of key cards, which look like credit cards. These are given unique codes, which are used only for the guest allocated to the room. As soon as the guest checks out, the code is changed so that access is denied to everyone except staff and the new guest. In this way there is never unauthorised access to a room which cannot be checked by downloading information from the lock on whose card was used to gain entry.

Security

Once again, any problems experienced by guests, such as disturbances, theft or loss, are reported to Front Office staff who in turn contact Security. The Security Department is responsible for the safety of guests and their belongings. Most of the time their presence is so discreet that it is unnoticed by guests. A difficult case recently referred to Security by Front Office staff at a resort involved theft of items left lying near the swimming pool while the guests were swimming. After many months of investigation, the case was resolved when gardeners found a number of small valuables in a bird's nest. On a more serious note, Front Office and Security staff work closely together in cases of emergency such as fire and other threats to safety.

The reasons for developing harmonious relationships between departments are clear. Customer service is the role of every employee in the hospitality industry: when a staff member receives a request from a customer, he or she should deal with it personally by contacting the relevant department. Where departments support each other—for example, where Front Office staff recommend the chef's new menu—both guest satisfaction and increased sales will be the result.

Providing quality service is complex as each customer's needs are unique. One aspect of this service is clear communication, both with customers and with other departments. This is very demanding when guests' needs differ so enormously. In the space of ten minutes a Front Office staff member might have to deal with a family arriving to check in, an irate call requesting an iron which had been promised half an hour ago, a five-year-old who is wanting to come behind the desk and appears to have mislaid (or been mislaid by) her parents, and a visitor from overseas who speaks no English. Clear communication makes everyone's job easier and ensures the smooth operation of the establishment and the well-being of the guests.

The procedures laid down by the organisation are an important contributor to quality service. Each step must be followed carefully to ensure that mistakes are not made which might have implications down the track. Making a mistake with an arrival date can have serious repercussions if the hotel is full and the guest has arrived very tired in the early hours of the morning. A feeble excuse about the confusion in dates at 1 a.m. (did you book for the 21st or the 22nd?) would not go down well. Operational procedures exist for a reason and they need to be followed to the letter. Tasks have to be juggled, depending on the flow of guests arriving and departing, and the time allocated for 'chatting' to guests limited when working under pressure. Help has to be given to staff out of their depth, which often means calling on a more senior staff member to resolve the issue.

Relationships with external agencies

Front Office staff work closely with a number of other operators in the interests of meeting guest needs (see Fig. 8.3). These include travel agents who make reservations at the hotel on behalf of their customers and who take onward reservations requested by Front Office staff to assist resident guests who are making plans for further travel. Similar two-way relationships exist with the airlines, which provide both customers, including their flight crews who stay at the hotel, and assistance in making onward bookings.

Bookings for local entertainment, tourist attractions, tours and events are all done for guests. This involves working closely with other operators to make sure

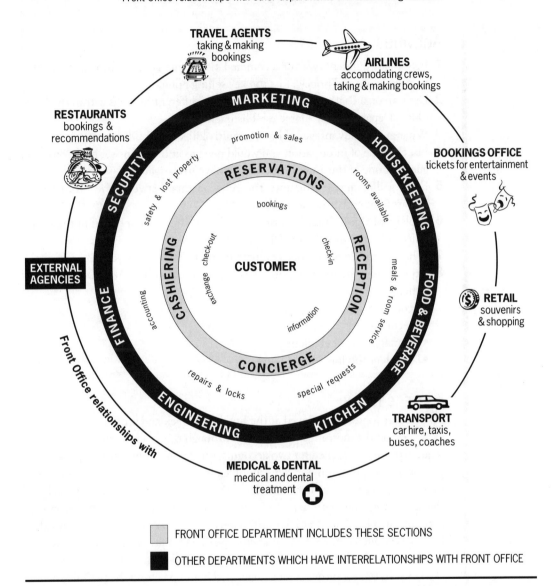

FIG.8.3

Front Office relationships with other departments and external agencies.

FRONT OFFICE DEPARTMENT INCLUDES THESE SECTIONS

OTHER DEPARTMENTS WHICH HAVE INTERRELATIONSHIPS WITH FRONT OFFICE

that the information provided to guests is up to date. At a resort, for example, guests might want to book anything from dinghy hire to a luxury day cruise. Many large hotels and resorts have retail outlets in the building, but shopping advice is sought by guests staying at all types of establishments. Front Office staff also work with transport operators, including taxi, bus, coach and car hire companies.

Work in Front Office in a hotel or motel is like a dance. Each step is defined and executed, and one person can let everyone else down. Each step is planned and practised many times, and all this careful choreography is directed at one aim—guest satisfaction.

Activities

1 Investigate different types of accommodation, ranging from 'cheap and cheerful' to 'prestigious and pricey'. List the key selling points.

2 Draw an organisational chart indicating the different sections within the Front Office Department of a large establishment.

3 What are the advantages of having multi-skilled Front Office staff?

4 List the type of information you would need to know to answer questions from guests at one of the establishments you have investigated.

5 Draw a diagram to illustrate the relationships between the Front Office Department and other departments.

6 Explain why good interdepartmental relationships are important in the hospitality industry, using Front Office as an example.

7 What are the attributes of a competent Front Office employee?

8 Explain how the following industry principles are relevant to work in Front Office:
- courtesy
- security
- managing work efficiently
- problem-solving.

CASE STUDY

Mr and Mrs Jonessy had stayed at the hotel for a week and arrived to check out at 10 a.m. on the morning of departure. Although they had not previously requested this, they asked for two accounts, one for accommodation and another for meals and entertainment. This involved transferring the transactions onto new folios. Once the cashier had created the two accounts, Mrs Jonessy paid for the accommodation with her VISA card. Mr Jonessy chose to pay the second account using his ATM card. Unfortunately his request for $748 was declined. Mrs Jonessy offered her ATM card, with the same result. Both customers were highly embarrassed, explaining that they had several thousand dollars in their accounts. In the meantime a long queue had built up behind them. Only then did the cashier realise that the daily limit on withdrawals of $400 might be the problem. The problem was resolved by Mr and Mrs Jonessy each withdrawing a smaller amount. Both were relieved and grateful for the tactful handling of this issue.

Discussion questions

1 At what stage of the guest cycle were these customers?

2 Why is this an important stage?

3 Why do you think the customers asked for two accounts?

4 What words would you have used to explain to the customers that their cards had been refused?

5 Is there anything that could have been done to alleviate the embarrassment caused to Mr and Mrs Jonessy by the other guests eavesdropping on what was being said?

LINKS

CMS Hospitality Software—http://www.cmshosp.com.au/

Hotel Software Systems—http://www.hssltd.com/pcs/

INNfinity Hospitality Systems—http://www.lodgical.com/

CHAPTER NINE

Accommodation services

OBJECTIVES

The aim of this chapter is to provide you with an overview of the work carried out by the Accommodation Services Department, or Housekeeping Department, of a hospitality establishment. On completion of this chapter you should be able to:

- describe the various types and standards of accommodation available commercially within Australia
- explain the functions performed by staff in Housekeeping
- describe the interrelationships between Housekeeping and other departments found in hospitality establishments
- outline career path options in Housekeeping
- review the attributes of a Housekeeping employee.

Standards and style are key words that could be used to describe the aims of the Housekeeping Department, or Accommodation Services Department, as it is known in larger establishments, acknowledging the scope of its role in a hotel operation. The standards maintained by Housekeeping are usually consistent with the type of accommodation and the price charged for rooms. In a five-star hotel the guest would expect the room to look as though it had just been redecorated. The guest would certainly not expect to see any sign of the previous occupant! The level of cleanliness in rooms of this standard is exceptional, far exceeding that of the average home. Tiles are cleaned, floors are mopped, mirrors are polished and linen is changed daily. Three-star motels, while still maintaining high standards of cleanliness, would not have the same luxury appointments in the rooms, making them easier to clean.

The other key word, style, is a significant feature of the Housekeeping Department, as its staff are responsible for the image of the establishment. In this description of Pangkor Laut in Malaysia, the style and ambiance of the resort is highlighted.

> My wife and I were led down the boardwalk to the sea villas and the luxurious Purnama Suite. Our first impressions were of a profusion of exotic flowers: colourful plants thriving in the garden, tropical blooms floating in large urns of water and vibrant orchids growing in attractive Asian earthenware pots on the boardwalk.

Soft music greeted us as we entered the cool interior of the magnificent suite. Comfortable oriental furniture, rich hardwood timbers and traditional woven bamboo created a relaxed atmosphere, while modern amenities such as a CD player, two televisions, electronic safe, refrigerator with fully stocked bar, tea- and coffee-making facilities and thermostatically controlled air-conditioning promised sublime comfort.

Our butler, Douglas, proudly took us through the suite, showing us the stylish bedroom, the elegant sitting room and enormous bathroom with separate toilet, shower and glassed-in bath alcove. The bath, which was easily large enough for two people, was filled with water, and flowers were floating on the surface.

GETAWAY INTERNATIONAL TRAVEL SUPPLEMENT, 1995

The housekeeping role of creating a stylish environment and maintaining high standards of cleanliness is an essential part of any hospitality operation, including restaurants, clubs, ocean liners, trains and serviced apartments. P & O Australia carries more than 30,000 Australians on South Pacific cruises every year, injecting around $55 million into the combined Australian and local economies (http://www.pocruises.com.au). During the peak cruise season, cabins and all other on-board facilities have to be maintained in shipshape condition.

Role of Housekeeping in accommodation establishments

The Housekeeping Department is often the largest department in the establishment and its functions include some or all of the following:

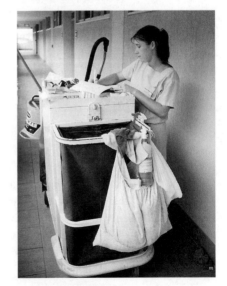

- ensuring that guest accommodation is clean and hygienic
- making sure that all fittings are in good working order
- checking that all supplies (such as toiletries and minibar stock) have been replenished
- ensuring that public areas (such as the lobby) are clean and polished
- making sure that furnishings and fittings, including light fittings, are clean and in good condition
- ensuring that windows are cleaned regularly.

One large city hotel employs a staff member for one job only: to replace light bulbs. The job is called Light Globologist! Like painting the Sydney Harbour Bridge, this is a continuous process, starting at one end and working through to the other.

Housekeeping is responsible for meeting requests for irons and ironing boards, laundry, babysitting, extra linen or towels, and numerous other items. Guest liaison is a key aspect of work in Housekeeping as staff are asked many and varied questions by guests.

Housekeeping is also responsible for decor, the selection of furnishings and wall coverings being very important. Thousands of dollars are spent on decor and these decisions are not taken lightly. A poor choice of floor covering could lead to accidents, or it could result in a very unsightly hallway if wear and tear showed up sooner than expected. Expensive wallpapers that could not be replaced when damaged would be considered a fundamental mistake. If light fittings could not be matched, and extra supplies had not been purchased at the time of installation, this could result in the replacement of all fittings, even if just one or two were broken.

As mentioned above, the Housekeeping Department is responsible for the image of the establishment, and as such it plays an important role in selling the organisation to the public. The housekeeping role is also performed in hospitality operations other than those that offer accommodation since clubs, restaurants, pubs and casinos all have to ensure that their premises are kept clean and highly presentable.

Types and standards of accommodation

Types of accommodation range from the budget end of the spectrum to the luxury end where artworks, floral arrangements and furnishings are opulent. Regardless of the decor, all hospitality establishments have a responsibility for presenting a good image to the customer and ensuring that all facilities are spotless. The following are examples of different types of accommodation.

Hotels

Offering many different levels of accommodation, hotels vary from very basic to very elegant. Licensed hotels provide meals, a public bar and lounge drinking facilities. Specialised hotels include casino hotels, airport hotels and extended stay hotels.

Australia's largest hotel, the Crown Towers in Melbourne, has 484 hotel rooms. The Crown Entertainment Complex, also Australia's largest, operates 350 gaming tables and 2,500 gaming machines. Star City in Sydney has a hotel complex with 352 rooms, 139 serviced apartments, seven restaurants and two theatres. On a world scale, these hotels are small: the MGM Grand in Las Vegas has over 5,000 rooms and, with Luxor, a huge casino and entertainment complex, provides 15,000 jobs. The atrium at Luxor is so large that nine 747s could fit in the lobby. There are some unusual hotels too. In Japan, commuters who do not wish to travel home at night can stay in sleeping capsules, each with individual air-conditioning and its own television. With not enough room to stand up, it is sleeping room only. Famous jails offer unusual accommodation; at the Unitas Hotel in Prague one can sleep in the prison cell occupied for five years by Vaclav Havel, a poet who became leader of the Czech Republic in the early 1990s. The open-air tree-top accommodation available in Australia's tropical forests sounds far less claustrophobic!

Motels

Motels, too, can range in quality and price, and are aimed mainly at the travelling market, generally offering car parking outside the room. Like hotels, they can be licensed or unlicensed.

Resorts

Resorts offer accommodation and food and beverage, as well as entertainment and a wide range of activities. These facilities enable guests to enjoy a holiday at one location. Resorts often provide water sports, but sometimes they include only land-based activities such as golf and tennis. Hamilton Island Resort, featured in many of the photographs in this book, is Australia's largest, with 750 rooms, eight swimming pools and numerous food and beverage outlets.

All suite hotels

These hotels offer longer term accommodation, generally with more than one guest room, a dining and lounge area, and a small kitchen. Serviced daily, this type of accommodation is ideal for business travellers who are likely to spend more than a few days and want to feel at home.

Private clubs

Some private clubs also offer accommodation for guests. One of the oldest of these is the Royal Sydney Yacht Squadron, which was established in 1862.

Serviced apartments

Holiday apartments are very popular, allowing guests to cook some meals and go out for others. They are serviced either daily or weekly and are very popular with families.

Hostels

Catering for the budget traveller, hostels offer cheap but clean accommodation with no frills, ranging from dormitory style to single, all at a low price.

Guesthouses

Bed and breakfast guesthouses are becoming increasingly popular, mainly because of the personal service they offer, the opportunity they provide for guests to get to know the host and hostess, and the insight they offer into Australian culture and hospitality. This trend is likely to continue as more people open their homes to paying guests.

Farmstay

Visitors who are attracted to Australia's vast outback are increasingly interested in visiting working properties and participating in activities such as sheep shearing, cattle mustering and other 'chores' which to them are a great novelty, coming as they often do from big cities.

Cruise liners

Everyone in Australia knows the *Fair Princess*, a popular ship for short but exciting and eventful cruises, which account for a large percentage of the Australian cruise market. The *QEII* also visits Australia regularly, the guests on board having spent more money than most of us dream about on the cruise of a lifetime. The flagship of Cunard's fleet, the *QEII* is a 13-storey city at sea, with five restaurants, eight bars, a golf driving range and a reference collection of 6,000 books. It accommodates 1,800 passengers.

Camping and caravans

Some of Australia's best real estate has been retained as camp sites. The camp site at Trial Bay Jail at South West Rocks in northern New South Wales has rolling lawns leading down to the water's edge and there are similar sites in many other small coastal towns in Australia. Camp sites are also found in Central Australia, in most national parks and on many islands. Fabulous climates and idyllic environments make camping and caravaning Australia's most popular and economical holiday.

Ratings systems

Accommodation ratings systems provide a guide for visitors on the level of service and facilities they can expect. Star ratings range from one to five star and ratings are done both for hotels and for motels. Following an initial inspection, the establishment is visited regularly to ensure that standards are maintained. Classifications are granted by the automobile associations in the respective states and the Northern Territory (see Table 9.1).

From the ratings guidelines it becomes clear that there are big differences between the types of rooms one would expect in a one-star hotel compared with those in a five-star hotel. Air-conditioning with individual control is one variation. Only three-star hotels and above have private bath/shower and toilet facilities. Five-star hotels have a choice of dining facilities. And the differences go on and on.

TABLE 9.1

Classification for hotels and motels.

★   Establishments offering a basic standard of accommodation. Simply furnished, adequate lighting. Motel units have private facilities. Resident manager.

★★   Well-maintained establishments offering an average standard of accommodation and furnishings.

★★★   Well-appointed establishments offering a comfortable standard of accommodation, furnishings, lighting and heating/cooling. Rooms would contain telephone, clock radio, tea and coffee making facilities with light breakfast available.

★★★★   Exceptionally well-appointed establishments with high quality furnishings and comfort. High standards of presentation and guest services with restaurant on site, air-conditioned rooms, comfortable lounge seating, hairdryer.

★★★★★   International style establishments offering a superior standard of appointments, furnishings and decor with an extensive range of first class guest services. A number and variety of room styles and/or suites available. Choice of dining facilities, 24 hour room service and additional shopping or recreational facilities available.

Note: The requirements of the lower classifications are included in the higher. Motel classifications follow a similar format. **Source:** AAA Tourism.

Hotels and motels must comply with a very comprehensive check list to ensure that they meet all the requirements for classification. It can be quite complex for owners who are renovating older properties or historic buildings. Providing private showers and toilets, air-conditioning and insect screens, for example, can be difficult if the historic nature of the building is to be preserved. For this and other reasons not all establishments have star ratings.

Room rates (the charge for a single night's accommodation) depend on the level of service provided or the star rating. A number of factors influence the price for a room, including the season, with room rates much higher in peak season. Room rates can also vary widely within a single hotel, depending on the size of the room and the view. As you could imagine, a room with an ocean view would sell at a higher rate than one with a view of a back alley. It is most important that the person who makes the reservation advises the guest of the reason for the cheaper rate, otherwise the guest might have expectations that cannot be met. The more information provided to the guest before they arrive, the greater the potential for a satisfied guest. A guest who has high expectations, which are not met, is likely to go away dissatisfied, while a guest who gets more than anticipated, in service and/or facilities, is likely to be satisfied.

The Governor Suite at the Park Hyatt Sydney, illustrated in Fig. 9.1, gives you an idea of the standard of accommodation you could expect to find at the top of the suite range in a five-star hotel. The room charge for this suite is around $5,900 per night and it enjoys a very high occupancy rate.

FIG. 9.1

Governor Suite, Park Hyatt Sydney.

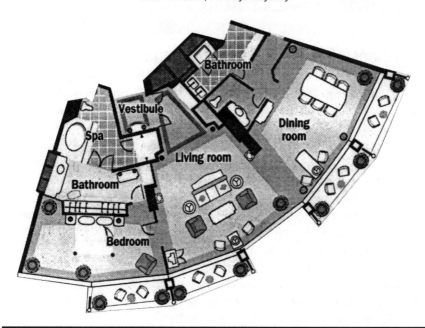

Courtesy of the Park Hyatt Sydney.

When a customer books budget accommodation, their expectations will be low. They will not expect expensive carpets or marble bathrooms. However, there are some minimum requirements, and these are that the rooms are clean, the shower and toilet facilities hygienic, and the staff friendly and helpful. The guest balances cost and benefit, the cost being the room rate and perhaps the extra effort of walking down the hallway to the shower/bathroom, and the benefit being the opportunity to save money and the possibility of meeting some interesting people in the kitchen or bathroom!

For very expensive accommodation a guest would have quite different expectations, including luxurious decor, discreet service and an enormous range of extras including shoe-polishing, babysitting and 24-hour room service.

Legal or regulatory requirements for Housekeeping

Under consumer law the establishment must provide facilities and services at the appropriate standard, as advertised. Looking at the ratings systems and at advertising brochures, it is clear that Housekeeping plays an important role in meeting guest expectations and the organisation's legal obligations to provide advertised services. The Housekeeping Department also works closely with Security to ensure the safety of guests, thus meeting a duty of care. The use of inflammable materials to reduce the risk of fire is one aspect of the department's contribution to customer safety; another is the installation of improved lighting and closed circuit television. Housekeeping is also responsible for keeping a watchful eye on guests who are ill. Security of guest belongings is essential and this has been much improved with the introduction of electronic room keys, as already mentioned in Chapter 8. Vigilance by Housekeeping, and indeed by all staff, is essential.

Functions of the Housekeeping Department

Working in Housekeeping in any hospitality establishment requires careful attention to detail and an in-depth knowledge of cleaning products and their applications. In five-star hotels some aspects of the work are very complex, such as operating the computer systems that manage the huge laundries. One aspect of the work common to all hospitality operations, and possibly the most important, is customer relations. In a five-star hotel this may involve organising laundry for guests, in a two-star country hotel it may mean giving information about horse-riding activities. In fact, in the latter, the room attendant may be the very same person who takes charge of horse-riding later in the day. Flexibility and stamina are necessary: the work is physically demanding and working under pressure is not uncommon during high levels of occupancy.

The primary functions of any Housekeeping Department are:
- cleaning establishment facilities and guest rooms
- providing laundry services (supplying, for example, towels to guests, or staff uniforms and table linen to the various outlets)
- ensuring safety, security and customer comfort.

Duties of Housekeeping staff

It would be clear by now that the Housekeeping Department varies enormously according to the establishment. At the five-star end of the market this department, also called the Accommodation Services Department, is very specialised, offering an enormous range of services. As with Front Office, staff are often multi-skilled and able to perform a range of duties. However, for the purpose of demonstrating the different roles in the department, these will be described separately. They are also illustrated in Fig. 9.2.

Room Attendant

A room attendant is responsible for changing linen and cleaning bedrooms and bathrooms. In luxury hotels their duties also include removing all the stock from the minibar and cleaning it, replacing toiletries, resetting video controls if necessary, and polishing mirrors, glass and furnishings to leave the room immaculate. The guest service aspect of housekeeping is most important and seldom given the acclamation it deserves. The room attendant is highly visible to guests and answers numerous questions as part of his or her daily duties.

The job requires a high level of fitness. Attendants in one hotel chain in Australia clean between 13 and 15 rooms a day, while room attendants in its Osaka operation in Japan, with their careful attention to detail, clean only seven per day. American hotels expect their staff to clean an average of 17 rooms per day. The design of the room is a great contributor to the efficiency of room attendants, for example some features, such as small tiles or windows, slow down the work considerably. The design of the buildings is another important factor as moving between buildings or individual chalets can take time. One hotel chain in the United States has the entire bathroom pressed in a mould before it is installed. This means that there are no gaps or joins where dirt can accumulate. This type of bathroom is easier to clean but is far less interesting than the beautifully restored bathroom with

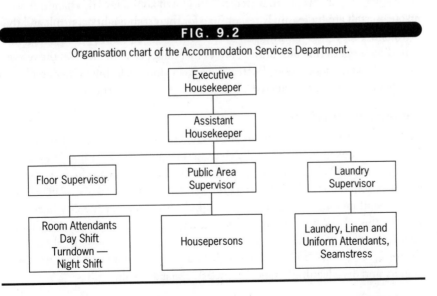

FIG. 9.2

Organisation chart of the Accommodation Services Department.

original fittings that one may find in a hotel with a long and proud history. Proximity of linen rooms containing guest-room supplies is another important factor in efficiency. The number of rooms that can be cleaned in a day also depends on how many of the guests are checking out as preparing rooms for new guests takes longer.

All hospitality establishments have their unique features. For example, Housekeeping staff at one resort complained about the mess created by cockatoos being fed by guests. Having to clean up was not appreciated by staff but the novelty for overseas visitors was understandable.

Guest Service Attendant

This is a generic title for someone who performs a variety of housekeeping tasks, including room attending. Like the Guest Service Agent in Front Office, this person is multi-skilled and takes on more responsibility. Turndown is another duty of room attendants or guest service attendants. This involves turning down the bed cover, placing chocolates and messages on the pillow, and turning on the lamps to welcome the guest when they return to the room.

Houseperson

Generally the houseperson does the heavier cleaning, particularly in the public areas. Stairwells, lifts, windows and lobbies are maintained by the houseperson. When additional beds, or cots, are required in rooms, the houseperson is the one who carries these heavy items and sets them up. Like the room attendant, the houseperson is often called a guest service attendant.

Floor Supervisor

The supervisor is responsible for checking the cleanliness of the rooms. Setting seemingly impossible standards, and being sticklers for detail, these supervisors are generally held in high regard by the staff. However, with increases in staff autonomy and changes in work practices, staff are increasingly responsible for their own quality control, and thus many of the supervisory positions of the past no longer exist. Troubleshooting, such as finding supplies that are running low or meeting special requests, is the responsibility of today's supervisors. Rosters have to be prepared, staff briefed, problems solved and shortages anticipated.

Laundry Supervisor

The Laundry Department is often one of the busiest in the hotel. At the Regent in Sydney, for example, the laundry employs 44 people in two shifts. They handle the linen from 600 bedrooms (sheets, towels, face washers, bath mats, bathrobes, etc.) and from nine food and beverage outlets (tablecloths, napkins), staff uniforms for 750 staff members and the guest laundry. This is just for the city hotel. The laundry also takes care of all linen from the airport hotel, resulting in a volume of approximately 4,500 kilograms of washing per day, which represents about 1,800 sheets, 2,700 towels, 550 uniforms and about 250 items of guest laundry. Guest laundry and dry-cleaning can be returned in about an hour.

The machine that handles the sheets is most impressive. It takes damp sheets and dries them, irons them and folds them at a rate of 400 sheets an hour.

On the *Oriana* cruise liner the volume of laundry is equally awe inspiring. The liner carries 17,000 sheets, 19,000 pillowcases and 23,000 towels. The laundry is capable of processing up to 900 kilograms of washing in an hour.

Assistant Housekeeper

As second in command of anything up to a 700-room hotel or resort, the assistant housekeeper is in charge when the executive housekeeper is not on shift. The Housekeeping office is a hive of activity, starting with an early morning allocation of duties and a staff briefing. All staff report to the Housekeeping office where they are assigned duties. All telephone calls from guests are handled in this office and reporting of clean and available rooms is managed from this location. In some establishments staff carry hand-held computer devices to update Housekeeping and Front Office, while in others the reporting is done using the guest room telephone. Front Office needs to know room status as soon as possible. All stocks are issued from Housekeeping, including bed linen, guest room supplies, uniforms and table linen. Housekeeping keys are controlled from the Housekeeping office.

One assistant housekeeper, Dianne, explained her frustration over the shortage of towels. She said that on a sunny day she could look across the main road to the beach and see all her bath towels on the sand. Guests always ignored the notices that said that beach towels were available. Running out of bath towels on the mainland is a problem, but it is a much more serious one if your hotel is on the Barrier Reef!

Executive Housekeeper

The executive housekeeper has administrative responsibilities for his or her whole department, including budgeting for supplies, controlling costs, purchasing and replacing equipment, and decorating. Sometimes employing 40–50 per cent of the hotel's or motel's staff, this is a very busy department. Recruitment, selection, induction and training of new Housekeeping staff are all aspects of this position. In addition to managing staff, often from many different backgrounds and with varied experience, the executive housekeeper is also responsible for record keeping and stock inventory, such as the bathroom towels in the above example. Linen must also be checked for stains and tears. Choosing cleaning agents and cleaning equipment is another administrative role.

Director—Rooms Division

Both Front Office and Housekeeping are part of Rooms Division. For both departments guest accommodation is their main responsibility. The director of rooms is one of the recipients of the daily report produced by the Night Audit staff in Front Office. This report gives percentage of occupancy and the average daily rate, and the figures indicate how full the hotel is and how much the average guest is spending. The director of rooms compares these figures with those of the same period in previous years. They are also responsible for the property management systems

(PMS), a combination of software packages often used in hotel administration. This software can handle:

- reservations (including central reservations for hotel chains)
- guest accounting
- point-of-sale interfaces with Front Office guest accounts
- telephone call accounting
- guest history
- yield management
- energy management
- accounting.

Services provided by Housekeeping

The Housekeeping Department is responsible for providing the following services for guests (some services only in five-star hotels):

- room cleaning
- public area cleaning
- laundry and dry-cleaning
- shoe polishing
- morning paper delivery
- unpacking and packing luggage
- babysitting
- additional towels, pillows, blankets
- cots and folding beds
- information and general assistance.

Attributes of a Housekeeping employee

One of the most important attributes of a Housekeeping employee is careful attention to detail. All establishments have standard operating procedures and these need to be followed to the letter. Punctuality is essential, especially if guests are waiting in the lobby for rooms to be cleaned! Knowledge of cleaning products and safe handling of chemicals is useful. Customer relations skills are highly prized as Housekeeping staff continually meet guests in their rooms and in the hallways. Greeting guests and asking and answering questions are all part of customer relations, so courtesy and knowledge of local history and attractions are invaluable.

Career path options

The Housekeeping Department, or Accommodation Services Department, in hotels, motels and resorts is often one of the largest departments. This means that employment opportunities are many, with entry positions mainly as room attendants and laundry staff for those who have no hospitality experience. The Laundry Department, which is generally highly automated, is a very busy area with a huge turnover of items.

Promotion to supervisory positions is very rapid, with career opportunities as Section Manager, Assistant Housekeeper and Executive Housekeeper. With huge budgets, large staff numbers and overall responsibility for the image of the establishment, the Housekeeping Department has responsibility for standards and style.

Interrelationships with other departments

A satisfied guest is the result of effective teamwork within and between departments. If, for example, the hotel is nearly full and a plane load of tourists arrives early in the morning before the previous guests have checked out, the Front Office Department will be under pressure to allocate rooms to waiting guests. This being the case, Housekeeping needs to deliver clean rooms as quickly as possible. Careful scheduling is necessary, as well as prompt advice as soon as each room is vacant and clean. The Engineering Department also contributes to this situation by making sure that rooms that require maintenance are returned to order as soon as possible.

The following departments work very closely with Housekeeping, as illustrated in Fig. 9.3 on page 116.

Front Office

Room status (such as occupied, vacant and clean, or out of order) is reported to Front Office by Housekeeping staff. In periods of high occupancy, Reservations will check when the guest is scheduled to arrive, Reception will organise room allocation to suit Housekeeping and the cashier will advise Housekeeping if a guest leaves earlier than expected.

Human Resources

As Housekeeping is a very labour-intensive department, it works very closely with Human Resources for recruitment, selection and induction of new staff. Generally, supervisors in Housekeeping conduct the training, with new staff working alongside experienced staff during their first few days.

Room Service

Checking and stocking minibars is a difficult task since there are often disputes about whose role it is. In many hotels one staff member checks all minibars each morning. Room Service is responsible for replenishing the drinks, chocolates, etc. normally found in the minibar.

Food and Beverage

The Housekeeping Department provides linen and uniforms for all food and beverage outlets and towels for sports centres, gyms and swimming pools.

Purchasing

Housekeeping has a high level of expenditure on linen and room supplies. When redecorating, the cost can run to millions of dollars. In many establishments

FIG. 9.3

Housekeeping relationships with other departments and external agencies.

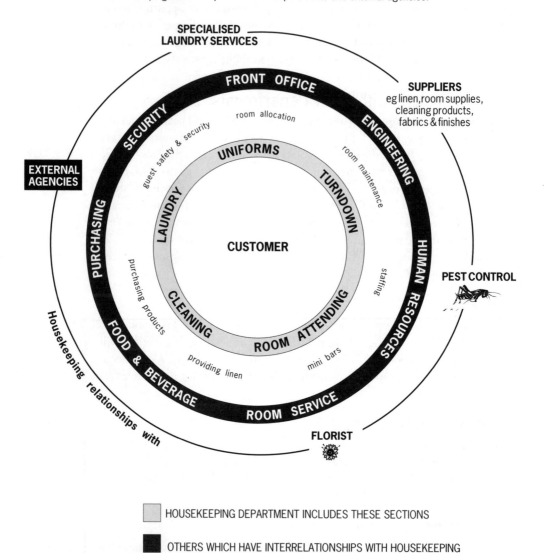

SPECIALISED
LAUNDRY SERVICES

FRONT OFFICE

SECURITY

room allocation

ENGINEERING

SUPPLIERS
eg linen, room supplies,
cleaning products,
fabrics & finishes

guest safety & security

UNIFORMS

room maintenance

EXTERNAL
AGENCIES

PURCHASING

LAUNDRY

TURNDOWN

CUSTOMER

HUMAN RESOURCES

PEST CONTROL

purchasing products

CLEANING

ROOM ATTENDING

staffing

FOOD & BEVERAGE

Housekeeping relationships with

providing linen

mini bars

ROOM SERVICE

FLORIST

HOUSEKEEPING DEPARTMENT INCLUDES THESE SECTIONS

OTHERS WHICH HAVE INTERRELATIONSHIPS WITH HOUSEKEEPING

refurbishment is done gradually, with rooms being taken out of order while painting and redecorating are done.

Engineering and Maintenance

Damage to rooms and faulty devices are reported to this department which is responsible for room maintenance and refurbishment. Guests have been known to do considerable damage to a room, with the room needing repainting before it can be used again. Fortunately this is less common than normal wear and tear.

Security

The safety of guests is paramount. Slipping on wet floors is possible if children are allowed to run in and out from the swimming pool, and an accident in the bathroom can be caused by a bath mat left on a slippery surface. Housekeeping staff play a vital role in preventative safety. For example, watching out for suspicious characters helps to avoid theft and other undesirable occurrences. Security of personal belongings is another important aspect of the work, with room attendants reporting property left behind to security staff.

Relationships with external agencies

There are several external agencies with which Housekeeping regularly liaises (see Fig. 9.3). Housekeeping deals with florists to ensure that rooms and public areas are always filled with fresh flowers and with pest control contractors to make sure that 'creepy crawlies' are not taking up quarters in guest rooms. Guests sometimes require special laundry and dry-cleaning services not available on the premises, and Housekeeping organises them. Housekeeping also deals with suppliers of linen, room stock, cleaning products, fabrics and finishes, negotiating price and delivery.

Activities

1 Consider a selection of rooms you have seen in hospitality establishments, photographs in brochures or in homes and examine their functional and design aspects from a housekeeping point of view. Take account of the following components of both bedrooms and bathrooms when analysing their suitability in guest accommodation:
   * Space—Is it sufficient and is it well used?
   * Fabrics and surfaces—How long will they last, are they easy to maintain and are they fire resistant?
   * Lighting—Is the lighting sufficient in the bathroom and the bedroom, is there a bedside light and can the lights be dimmed?
   * Furniture—Is it likely to show wear and tear in a short time, is it multi-purpose and is it attractive and comfortable?
   * Temperature—How easily can the temperature be controlled, can the windows be opened?
   * Sound—How well insulated is the room, can you hear anyone walking in the room above?
   * Theme—How well do the colours and the theme work, will the style date quickly?
   * Cleaning—How easy is it to clean the room, will bending and reaching in the bathroom be possible?
   * Allergies—Is the room likely to be a problem for allergy sufferers?
2 Investigate the differences between detergents and disinfectants. What are the differences? Develop a list of items necessary to clean a bathroom and toilet.
3 Draw an organisation chart for the different sections within the Housekeeping Department of a large establishment.

4 What are the advantages of having multi-skilled Housekeeping staff?

5 What type of information would you need to have at your fingertips to answer questions from guests.

6 Draw a diagram to illustrate the relationships between the Accommodation Services Department and other departments of an establishment offering accommodation.

7 Explain why good interdepartmental relationships are important in the industry, using Housekeeping as an example.

CASE STUDY

One rainy Sunday, David was working in the Housekeeping office taking calls from the rooms. He had received two calls during the morning from children in room 413 asking for extra towels, which were sent to the room. After the third call, David decided that he had better see to this request himself. Leaving another supervisor to answer the phone, he set off for the room. On his way down the hall he noticed that the carpets were slightly wet and that this path of water led to 413. On knocking and entering, he discovered three children in the room. Glancing into the bathroom, he realised that the children had created a swimming pool in the bath. They had also been running around the room and down the hall.

He suggested other activities to the children, including some of the games available from the Housekeeping office. He called the department right away, requesting one of the staff to come up with the games and to clean the room at the same time. He asked the children to dress and tidy up before the room attendant arrived. On leaving the room, he called Security to advise them of the situation and to ask them to keep an eye on room 413 and its occupants.

Discussion questions

1 Exactly what would you have said to the children if you had been David?

2 What would you have done if the parents had arrived shortly after you?

3 Why didn't David clean the bathroom himself while he was there?

4 What can children do in a hotel room on a rainy day?

5 Why did David contact Security?

LINKS

Omega cleaning chemicals—
http://www.omegahospitality.com.au/chemicals.htm

Visual Rota Housekeeping Scheduling—
http://www.alec.hemscott.net/hotelstaffing.htm

CHAPTER TEN

Sporting and community clubs

OBJECTIVES

This chapter provides an introduction to sporting and community clubs and the many services they provide. Most clubs are non-profit organisations. On completion of this chapter you should be able to:

- describe the different types of clubs and the roles they play within the community
- describe how the different departments within clubs interrelate to achieve a high standard of service
- outline the expectations of members and their guests
- review the duties and requirements of club employees
- describe career paths in the club industry and the training requirements for career progression.

L ily Tsoukis immigrated to Australia when she was in her early thirties. She found it *very hard to settle into her local community, finding people unfriendly compared to those in her home town. Back home people would socialise a lot more, dropping in for coffee or a drink, staying for dinner or inviting her family over. In her new neighbourhood everyone was polite but she and her family were seldom invited into other's homes. Although she made some good friends over time, she still felt that the community spirit and social intimacy of her home town were missing.*

When Lily's husband died, one of her friends suggested that she join the local club. She did this with some trepidation, going along one night with her friend to have dinner and watch a movie. When she saw the range of activities and entertainment available, and the prices of the food, she paid the membership fee of $35.00 on the spot. Bowls and Bingo became her twin passions and she could soon be found at the club almost every other day of the week. After meeting several new people, including some of her neighbours, she realised how important a part the club plays in the social life of many Australians.

While clubs offer support like this to young and old alike, they also provide a very much broader service to the community at large, as we will discover in the following pages.

Types of clubs

There are many types of clubs in Australia, all of which meet particular needs of the community in which they are located.

Sporting clubs

Football, golf, sailing and other sporting clubs are widespread. Some of these clubs focus only on one sport such as golf, tennis or sailing, while larger clubs, such as Club Banora on the Gold Coast, offer a wide variety of activities to their members. Club Banora provides golf, bowls, tennis, swimming and gym facilities. In addition the members can join up for bridge, gardening, fishing and dancing. Penrith Panthers, which supports its famous Rugby League team, the Panthers, is one of the country's largest clubs, with an enormous complex surrounded by a lake where members can fish for trout and water ski. Most sporting clubs provide venues for large functions such as birthday parties and weddings.

Returned services clubs

Many Returned Services Leagues (RSL) clubs were started after the First World War. Built on history and tradition, these clubs are proud of their older members and look towards continuing their traditions, while taking on new younger members. Recent change has seen more women employed by them and the appointment of female secretary managers. Poker machine revenue enables these clubs to maintain their premises well and to provide reasonably priced food and beverage and all types of entertainment. Their function rooms are popular for events and community activities. Some RSL clubs, such as the Redcliffe RSL and Ex-Services Club in Queensland, support local charities and provide their members with services such as financial planning and tax advice.

Business clubs

With their origins in the British gentlemen's clubs, these clubs are for business people, although some remain the preserve of businessmen. While women are now able to visit most of these clubs, few are offered full membership. No doubt this will change in time. The stuffy image of these clubs is changing through modern renovations and the introduction of upmarket food outlets. City Tattersalls in Sydney, for example, added accommodation units and billiard and snooker rooms with the aim of taking it 'to the top of the gentlemen's club tree'. Other male only clubs, such as the Australian and Union Clubs, are known as 'lunch and lavatory' clubs, offering few services and facilities other than meals. The Icebergs Club, previously a men's club in Bondi, is now open to women who wish to take a dawn dip in a freezing ocean in the middle of winter. No doubt this develops a high level of camaraderie among members.

Ethnic clubs

These clubs, which reflect the multicultural nature of Australia's population, were formed to provide support and assistance to immigrants. Today they help to retain some of the cultural traditions of their home countries, while also providing support for families in difficult times. Italian clubs, Chinese community clubs, Greek clubs and South American clubs are just a few examples.

Other clubs

Special interest groups have formed a range of clubs. An example is the Workers Club in Blacktown, which was started by a branch of the Australian Labor Party in 1955. At the time all it had was a small army hut and 26 members. It was refurbished in 1994 at a cost of $25 million and in 1999 had around 43,000 members and 500 poker machines. It also offers Keno and TAB. There are a number of food and beverage outlets, with meals available in the bistro at a very low cost.

Role of clubs in the community

Clubs play an important role in the community, providing a venue for meeting people, entertainment and, above all, many types of activities (see Fig. 10.1). Sports and games are the most popular clubs, with gymnasiums attracting the younger generation. Sponsorship is provided for sports such as football and racing. Entertainment is offered at reasonable prices, including live shows (singers, magicians, hypnotists, dancers) and movies. Meals and drinks are also affordable. In addition the clubs provide meeting places for other community groups such as Rotary and Apex. Many clubs support the community by providing services and spaces free of charge, such as rooms for community meetings and playing fields for local schools. Clubs are also well known for the support that they provide for charities. In 1995 City Tattersalls gave away $138,000 in prizes, awards and donations to mark its first 100 years. Twin Towns Services Club in New South Wales offers a $50,000 Bond University scholarship each year for a deserving hospitality management student. Poker machine revenue is largely responsible for meeting the ongoing costs of running a club and maintaining the prices at a reasonable level for members.

FIG. 10.1

Services provided by clubs to members.

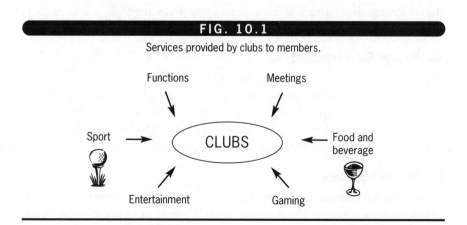

Expectations of club members and guests

Friendly service is probably the most important aspect of service in clubs. Because patrons are well known to staff, the atmosphere is quite different from many other hospitality establishments. In the words of one staff member, 'I like working with people. Getting on with customers is essential. Customers hate sour-faced, holier than thou staff. You have no idea how much they notice—first impressions are so important. People who aren't suitable are cranky and snobby. The customers come to me and say, "Who is the new one?" They want friendly, familiar faces at a club where the staff know them by name. They love it.'

Club newsletters and brochures are an important source of information for members, letting them know about changes and events. It is important to remember that a club is an association of members whose support is necessary for any changes. Members have voting rights, electing members to the board, which in turn appoints staff to senior management rolés. The staff and management must enforce club rules, such as dress codes, and membership requirements. Hygiene, safety and security are as important to club members as they are to other hospitality patrons. Another benefit enjoyed by members is subsidised holiday accommodation. Some clubs have their own holiday homes in the country or by the sea, with a ballot for booking busy times such as school holidays. Clubstay is a new concept, offering participating club members discounted accommodation at a range of resorts, inns and apartments, with such interesting sounding names as Howlong Country Golf Club and the Lobster Pot Motel and Apartments.

Departments in a club

Clubs are quite varied in their structure, some being small (as shown in Fig. 10.2) and offering limited services and facilities, while others are quite large. An organisation chart for a large club was provided in Chapter 4. In general terms the following departments are found in most clubs.

Food Service Department

Bistros and restaurants are found in most clubs. Catering is often contracted out, which means that although the operation is integrated with the club's other activities it is run independently. If the food is not up to standard, the management of the club will find a new contractor.

Beverage Department

The Beverage Department is responsible for beverage service in all food outlets and guest service bars. Sometimes the customer orders directly from the bar; at other times a dispense bar is used, with staff providing waiter service. Bottle shops are often associated with clubs, providing off-premises sales. More exclusive clubs allow sales of specially selected and labelled wines to members only.

Cellar and Stores

Supporting the Beverage Department, this section has an important part to play in ensuring that adequate stocks are maintained. Wines must be stored correctly and

FIG. 10.2

Organisation chart of a small club.

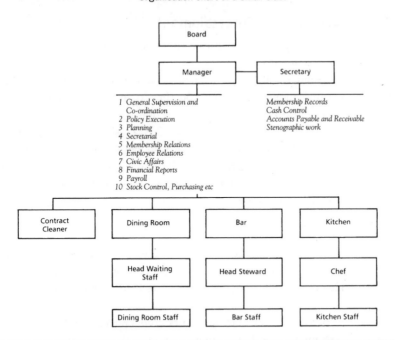

sales of bottled beer and spirits must be anticipated accurately to avoid shortages. Another important role of the Cellar is to connect the kegs and to maintain and clean the beer lines to the bars. Handling equipment in the cellar can be very dangerous.

Maintenance and Engineering

This department ensures the smooth running of all equipment, including plant and refrigeration.

Reception

Members and their guests are greeted at Reception. The receptionist must ensure that all members and guests are correctly signed in, to comply with the legal requirements of the club. Reception staff also provide information and deal with messages and enquiries.

Administration/Accounting

This department maintains all member records and accounting records, handles banking and reconciles all financial and stock reports. Liquor sales must be

Club reception.
Reproduced with permission of Forestville RSL Club.

accounted for and gaming revenue recorded. The administrative staff also ensure compliance with all legislative requirements and the smooth running of the club.

Club Activities

live shows

movies

dance classes

aerobics

darts and pool

bowls

swimming

gym

Gaming Activities

Bingo

Club TAB
(horse-racing)

Club Keno
(numbers game)

raffles

poker machines of
every variety

Gaming and Entertainment

The range of club activities is enormous and just a few are listed in the box at left.

Gaming will be covered in more detail in the next chapter. Most patrons enjoy a little flutter from time to time, sensibly taking home their winnings. One member was not so sensible. Having won a jackpot of $11,000, he was given $2,000 cash and a cheque for the rest. He took the cash to the nearby shopping centre and bought his wife a new washing machine. He then returned to the club and, using his credit, lost the remaining winnings in the poker machines over a four-hour period.

Sports Department

With the increased community interest in sport, this department plays an important role in providing sporting activities and advice. Health and safety are important issues in all member sports.

Departments in a club must work co-operatively and this is made possible by newsletters, memos and meetings to keep staff in the different departments informed and up to date. Club managers play an important co-ordinating role.

Duties of club employees

Many of the jobs available in the club industry are very similar to those in any other hospitality establishment. A person working behind the bar or in the restaurant of a club or hotel would perform the same duties in both. However, club employees must be careful to observe legislation pertinent to the operation and to provide friendly service to members.

There are many other jobs, however, including positions in catering, marketing, personnel and accounts, and these are summarised in Table 10.1. One position, 'glassie', as it is affectionately known, is an entry position. Collecting empty glasses is not as simple as it would seem—during very busy periods this person has to work very quickly and systematically. Imagine the number of glasses that would be used during a show night attended by thousands of people. Collecting glasses by stacking them up the arms, the glassie begins to looks like a deer with glass horns as the stacks grow bigger. Obviously this is not a good idea, for safety reasons, but it does demonstrate the pressures encountered by staff during busy periods. One club describes it as 'organised chaos'. By midnight their nightclub is packed, with standing room only, and from this point drinks are served in disposable glasses. By the time the club closes, the floors have to be cleared with rakes before they can be properly cleaned. Clearly a popular venue!

TABLE 10.1	
Positions available in clubs.	
Glassie	Person who clears glasses and ashtrays, and cleans tables.
Food Attendant	A food attendant serves plated food in the bistro or restaurant or assists customers at the carvery.
Bar Attendant	A bar attendant may serve customers directly (and laugh at their jokes for the hundredth time) or assist waiters who are providing drinks service.
Waiter	A person who serves customers who are seated. Waiters often carry beepers so that customers on the poker machines can call for service.
Gaming Machine Attendant	Mainly responsible for payouts and minor machine maintenance.
Accounts Clerk	Keeps records for many purposes, gaming revenue, payroll, liquor reports, etc.
Promotions Officer	Organises and promotes special events through a range of advertising material. Promotes the club and enlists members.
Entertainment Manager	Selects performers, plans and organises events, and ensures that entertainment runs according to plan.
Cook	Depending on the grade, the cook may prepare à la carte meals or provide self-service meals.
Cleaner	Responsible for all aspects of environmental hygiene.
Supervisor	Supervises a number of staff to ensure smooth service, handles problems and complaints. Trains and motivates staff.

Two of the jobs in the club industry that may not be available in other hospitality establishments, Gaming Machine Attendant and Entertainment Manager, are covered in more detail below.

Gaming Machine Attendant

This is an important club position involving the following tasks:
- paying out jackpots and completing jackpot dockets
- making minor repairs to poker machines, such as dealing with jammed coins
- accompanying mechanics who are repairing poker machines
- refilling machines with coins
- conducting meter readings of poker machines
- picking up glasses
- maintaining cleanliness of all areas, including clearing and replacing ashtrays
- assisting customers with glasses and change where appropriate
- assisting other departments where necessary
- filling change dispensers, with the assistance of the house manager.

Entertainment Manager

As entertainment is one of the main activities of some clubs this, too, is an important and varied position, involving:

- selection and employment of entertainers for various venues and events
- arranging and decorating venues for events
- planning and implementing promotions for entertainment
- designing and ordering all promotional materials, including tickets
- organising and presenting prizes
- producing newsletters, brochures and signs
- promoting and taking bookings for functions
- co-ordinating events, including light and sound
- designing in-house advertising, billboards, signs and displays.

Teamwork

As in all hospitality operations, teamwork is essential because the work flow in clubs is generally very fast and sometimes it is difficult to predict how busy it will be. In all situations where staff are working under pressure it is important that they help one another, that they communicate clearly and that assistance is sought if necessary.

Effective task management is also very important in clubs: this means managing the work flow, preparing for the shift and anticipating problems or shortages before they occur.

Rules for staff

With respect to the workplace culture, staff in the club industry are generally more friendly and less formal with members than staff in other hospitality situations are with their customers. However, there are a number of rules that may apply if you are working in a club, including:

- staff should not smoke, drink or eat while on duty
- staff should leave promptly after the shift is completed
- staff are not permitted to enter the club after duty
- staff are not permitted to play the poker machines at any time.

Staff members must, like members, adhere to a dress code. For staff it is the uniform. And general principles of health, safety and hygiene naturally apply.

The legislation relating to club membership and gaming is very specific and club employees must be careful not to breach the rules. One employee guide even spells out that employees are not allowed to bring radios or knitting into the workplace!

Career development

The club industry has been particularly proactive in its approach to training and career development. Training requirements for promotion are listed in most awards and agreements. This training can be undertaken on or off the job. Workplace assessment is widely used in the club industry to formally recognise skills. Under this system a candidate is briefed on the competency unit to be assessed and some time later a licensed assessor watches him or her on the job. Some questioning to assess the candidate's knowledge of the subject also occurs. Finally, a debriefing session is held to provide feedback and to conclude the assessment. In this way employees can achieve the required outcomes while on the job.

Activities

1 Look in your local telephone book and newspapers to develop a list of the clubs in your area.
2 Visit a large and a small club and prepare a table to illustrate the different services they offer.
3 Describe how clubs support the local community.
4 Explain how career development is encouraged in the club sector.

CASE STUDY

The Long Beach RSL Club is at a crossroads. The influx of tourists is having a big impact on the whole community. At a recent meeting of members the issue of expansion and renovation was hotly debated. Older members did not want to see any changes as they felt that modernisation and extended membership would be contrary to the history and aims of this historic club formed by ex-servicemen. Younger members were keen to increase the number of poker machines, to open a new food outlet and to provide for the needs of tourists. This, they argued, would bring more revenue into the club and create more jobs for locals.

There is no doubt that the club is presently doing well: it is supported by a good local membership and certainly has the potential for expansion, even without the tourists. One of the key issues appears to be the value to the community in making changes to meet the needs of the tourists.

Discussion questions

1 What is the history of the RSL clubs in your area?
2 If you were a returned serviceman and a founding father of the club, how would you feel about these changes?
3 If you were a younger club member and the owner of the local souvenir shop, how would you feel about these changes?
4 Can you think of any compromises in this situation?

LINKS

Club Managers Association Australia—
http://www.cmaa.asn.au/Info/About_CMAA.htm

Registered Clubs Association NSW—http://www.clubsnsw.com.au/

Returned Services League Australia—http://www.rsl.org.au/

CHAPTER ELEVEN

Gaming and RGS

OBJECTIVES

This chapter introduces gaming—an activity that is very popular in clubs, hotels and casinos. On completion of this chapter you should be able to:

- describe the gaming sector within the hospitality industry
- outline the attributes of staff working in gaming
- describe employment opportunities and career paths in gaming
- outline responsible gambling service (RGS) guidlelines.

Gaming is growing in popularity worldwide, with extraordinary new casino developments in Las Vegas, which cannot fail to capture the imagination. Some of these unusual adult theme parks will be described later in the chapter. On a slightly smaller scale, the gaming industry has had a major impact on the Australian hospitality sector with the opening of several large casinos in the capital cities. These casinos provide accommodation and entertainment, and attract many tourists and local customers.

Gaming has had a long history in Australia: the first gaming machines were introduced into clubs in the 1950s. The hotels objected to the legalisation that allowed gaming machines in clubs, with accusations that clubs were using gaming machine profits to subsidise sales of alcohol. The government of the day decided that profits from gaming would be taxed and that the revenue would be used for hospital funding. Today, state governments across Australia are becoming increasingly reliant on revenue generated from gaming.

Gaming activities (from Bingo to Keno) continue to be popular in many clubs, and numerous hotels offer gaming machines as well. The TAB, with its focus on horse racing, has expanded into hotels with the introduction of Pub TAB and into clubs with the introduction of Club TAB. Gaming is any activity which involves having a bet with the prospect of winning money. Some betting games are particularly Australian in their origins and one favourite, two-up, has now been introduced in many casinos. Gambling is certainly part of our culture. It is said that Australians will bet on two flies crawling up a wall and tourists can even enjoy cane toad racing when visiting Queensland!

One of Australia's most famous gamblers is Kerry Packer, described by Las Vegas operators as one of the most formidable gamblers in the world. It is reported that

Packer has a $US20 million credit line at several casinos in the United States and that on one visit to the MGM Grand in Las Vegas he won $US26 million after betting $200,000 on each hand of blackjack.

Casino Department of Wrest Point Hotel Casino.

Scale of gaming operations

Developments in Las Vegas have been on such a large scale that they are quite difficult to comprehend. The first of these was the MGM Grand, mentioned above, which has 5,034 rooms, making it the largest hotel in the world. The second, the Luxor, is an Egyptian extravaganza, with a ten-storey sphinx and a Nile cruise in the basement. The hotel of the Luxor is a 30-storey, 400-room glass pyramid. The third extravagant hotel in Vegas is the Excalibur, a medieval castle. The themes and entertainment provided by Las Vegas casinos attract over 30 million tourists a year and keep the hotels at a 90 per cent occupancy level. In total, the city of Las Vegas has over 100,000 hotel rooms.

In Australia, the following casinos opened during the last decade: Conrad International and Treasury in Brisbane, the Reef Hotel Casino in Cairns, the Crown Casino in Melbourne and Star City in Sydney. The first casino in Australia was Wrest Point in Hobart, which opened in 1973 and made $1.75 million in its first year. In South Australia $156 million was spent on poker machines in the first five months of their introduction. The Burswood International Resort Casino in Perth now employs 3,000 people. Since opening on 30 December 1985, more than 30 million people have visited this casino, an average of 8,000 people per day. It is the most popular tourist attraction in Western Australia. Crown Casino in Melbourne is one of the largest gaming facilities in the southern hemisphere. The formidable gaming area, 350 gaming tables and 2,500 'pokies', is half a kilometre in length, representing only 12 per cent of the total 500,000 square metre property, which is dominated by an extensive entertainment precinct and world-class hotel.

The gamblers with the most money to spend are called 'high rollers' and they often visit Australian casinos on junket tours, bringing the minimum gambling stake of $50,000 with them. Gaming generates revenue for governments, for hospitality and gaming establishments, for clubs and hotels. In addition, it attracts tourists to other facilities, services and local attractions. Gaming provides employment for many hospitality staff, with Star City, for example, employing approximately 4,500 people in the complex, which includes seven restaurants, seven bars, two theatres and a retail shopping centre.

Types of gaming venues

It is claimed that up to 80 per cent of hotels rely on gaming machines to maintain their businesses. And apart from hotels, there are many other gaming venues, including:

- pubs
- clubs
- casinos
- TAB
- newsagencies.

Games and gaming machines

In just the past few years the legalisation of gaming machines and table games in all states and territories has seen an explosion in the availability of these facilities. The pros and cons of issuing gaming licences have been discussed at length and these discussions have mirrored the prohibition (of alcohol) debate. Governments have now accepted that the revenue generated from gaming is very useful for funding other projects, while the boost given to tourism and the job creation that implies are other factors that have influenced a positive attitude to gaming. Gaming is still highly regulated, with strict controls over margins, licences issued to operators and individuals working in the industry.

Outlined below are some of the games offered by gaming establishments.

Gaming machines

These machines have become more and more complex. Computer hardware and software are required to run the machines, many of which now have animation, sound and video. The variety of game options and strategies is growing as a sophisticated group of young players hits the market, used as they are to computer and hand-held games. It must be remembered that a machine is a gaming machine when the player has the opportunity to gamble.

The most common type of gaming machine is a poker machine and it has several rows of 'cards' which spin, hopefully with a lucky combination to produce a winning result. The name 'poker machine' derives from the early machines which all involved the game of poker as the basis of play. In some cases there are items of fruit on the spinning wheels. A winning combination on a 'fruit machine' is three cherries. Some gaming machines are referred to as 'slot machines'—the slot is the part of the machine into which the token or money is inserted. The hollow tray, into which the winning coins fall, is designed to make a loud noise. When the gambler wins a large jackpot, bells ring to call an attendant to pay out. The noise level generates a high level of excitement on the floor.

Hospitality establishments that offer gaming need to keep abreast with change, continually providing new and exciting machines. This need to stimulate gamblers has to be carefully balanced with the need to keep some games simple enough for first-time users who would be put off by too many options.

Raffles

These remain very popular in all clubs, especially in sporting clubs where a meat or chicken raffle is often used to raise funds. There are many types of raffle and the larger establishments offer large prizes, such as cars, as incentives for people to visit.

Bingo

Bingo is a simple game in which players place tokens or marks on the Bingo card when their numbers are called. The first player to complete a line wins 'Bingo'. In longer games the player might need to fill the corners, more than one line, or the entire card for a 'full house'.

Big wheel

In this game players bet on the wheel stopping at a certain point. A bet is made by placing value chips on the appropriate areas on the layout. The wheel is illustrated in Fig. 11.1

FIG. 11.1

The big wheel.

Blackjack

This is one of the most popular card games in which the player attempts to make 21 with the cards dealt. If the cards total more than 21, the player is 'bust'; if far under 21, the player may be beaten by the dealer. The object of the game is to get closer to 21 than the dealer.

Roulette

Roulette is a well-known game in which the object is to guess where the spinning ball will rest. The odds are high, 35 to one, for guessing the correct number. The odds are one to one for guessing red or black. Thus if you placed your chip on a number (this is called 'straight up') you would win 35 chips if the number came up, but you would have to be very lucky since there are 36 numbers. If you placed your chip on red and a red number came up, you would win one additional chip. With an almost 50 per cent chance of choosing correctly, this is a very conservative way to play. If the zero comes up, every player loses.

Two-up

In this game players bet on 'heads' or 'tails'. One player is the spinner and this player places the coins on a kip, with one coin head up and the other coin tail up. The spinner tosses the coins and bets are paid if both coins land with heads up or tails up. If there is one head up and one tail up, bets are frozen until the spinner throws two heads or two tails.

Caribbean stud poker

In this game, which is based on the well-known five-card stud poker, each player plays individually against the house. The best hand between the player and the dealer wins. There are also various jackpot prizes for combinations, such as $500 for four of a kind.

Craps

This is a suspense-filled game. There are a number of bets and the payouts are based on the throw of the dice. Each player has a chance to 'shoot' (throw the dice).

Baccarat

The object of this game is to reach a total of nine with the cards. The player with nine points, or closest to nine, wins. You can bet either on the player's hand or the banker's hand.

Sic bo

This is an ancient Chinese dice game played with three dice.

Pai gow

Originating in China some thousands of years ago, this game is played with 32 tiles (dominoes). The direct translation of 'pai gow' is 'make nine'. To win, both your hands must be of a higher value than the banker's hands.

Keno

This is a game of chance in which the player bets on the probability of matching the winning numbers. First introduced to Australia at Wrest Point, this game has a long history. Apparently it was used to finance the building of the Great Wall of China 3,000 years ago.

TAB

Betting in this case is on races (horses, greyhounds, etc.). Bets can be placed for a win, place, each way, trifecta and many other combinations.

Gaming industry issues

There are a number of controversial issues in the area of gaming that are often raised by interested groups in the community. The supposition is that gaming increases crime and thus is socially unacceptable. This concern has been shown to be ill-founded, with many gaming venues providing gaming as just one of many types of entertainment. The average gambler is happy to lose a small amount of money while playing the odds. The payout levels are quite high and it is possible for careful players to leave with substantial winnings. There is, however, understandable concern about gambling addiction. Gambling addiction can have a very serious impact on individuals and families. Most casinos encourage players to 'bet with your head not over it' and counselling services are available for people with gambling problems. It is certainly a cause for concern when pensioners lose their money on pension day and when younger players' entire pay packets find their way into gaming machines. In some cases suicide has been attributed to gambling addiction.

Smoking in gaming areas is also a point of concern for many operators. The customers appear to be clearly divided in their expectations: some want a smoke-free environment and others are equally adamant that you can't gamble without smoking. It certainly isn't the sort of activity that lends itself to a break outside if you're on a winning streak. Equally, if you're losing, you might hope that a break might change your luck. For the moment, the issue remains highly controversial for both customers and staff.

Security is an issue for gaming establishments and customers. There are large amounts of cash, which need to be accounted for and kept safe, and customers must be able to leave the venue in safety. For these reasons security is a priority for establishments that offer gaming.

There are strict legislative guidelines for the operation of gaming establishments. Table games and machines are closely monitored by the establishment and the relevant authority. Revenue must be accounted for, statistics submitted to the appropriate bodies (usually the liquor, gaming and racing authorities) and taxes paid. Croupiers and employees who work on gaming machines are individually licensed after demonstrating probity. Penalties apply for permitting a minor into a restricted area or permitting a minor to operate a gaming device, and these infringements can result in loss of licence.

Responsible gambling service (RGS)

There are state and territory legislative requirements and codes of practice to encourage responsible gambling. Their aim is to provide responsible gambling services, as well as information and assistance to customers. In some states and territories this is referred to as responsible conduct of gambling (RCG).

Staff working in a gaming environment are expected to:

- follow procedures in accordance with the relevant legislation and organisational policy
- communicate with appropriate personnel on gambling-related incidents or situations in compliance with relevant legislation and organisational policy
- maintain accurate records of gambling-related incidents and related staff action in accordance with organisational policy and procedures
- ensure gambling environmental features support responsible gambling policies
- provide accurate player information to customers
- respond appropriately to requests for information
- follow procedures for self-exclusion requests in accordance with legislation, organisational policy and confidentiality requirements
- display signage and information related to responsible gambling in appropriate places visible to players according to organisational and legislative requirements
- provide information on available support services in accordance with confidentiality requirements, organisational policy and legislative requirements.

Working in the gaming sector

Customers visiting gaming venues perceive gaming as a form of entertainment. Win or lose, they want to enjoy themselves and the role of the staff is to ensure that they do so. Some customers are regulars and want to be recognised and acknowledged, while others are first-timers who might not understand the rules. The service ethic is just as important in gaming as it is in any other hospitality sector.

Gaming legislation is very specific and staff need to adhere strictly to the regulations such as not permitting minors to gamble. Diplomacy is essential when customers complain about payouts or other issues. Honesty in dealing with large sums of money is expected, with serious penalties applying if money cannot be accounted for. Since staff work closely together, sometimes taking over from one another on the tables, teamwork is also essential. Clear communication with the pit boss, for example, is a crucial part of the job of a croupier as placement of a chip can sometimes be disputed. Patience, good humour, speed and problem-solving skills are important requirements for work in this area.

Attributes of gaming employees

Staff working in gaming establishments must be enthusiastic. The customers are there for fun and they want to enjoy themselves, even if they lose money! Personal service, an interest in the needs of particular customers and an ability to explain games carefully without sounding patronising are all important. As we have mentioned, diplomacy is essential when there is a dispute, either over a

payout or between two patrons. Speed and accuracy are imperative.

A detailed knowledge of a range of games is necessary for all casino staff working the tables. Numeracy and manual dexterity are essential attributes for dealers. Most gaming staff spend several months in training and many, many hours practising their skills. Seasoned gamblers are generally very acute observers and are able to make instantaneous calculations and decisions. Gaming staff must be able to do the same. They also need to manage their games, being patient with new players while not disturbing the flow of the game for others.

Courtesy to customers and managing work efficiently are thus essential aspects of employment in this sector. Gaming industry employees also need to keep up to date with information relating to gaming and this can be done by reading professional journals or by joining professional associations. The Department of Gaming and Racing in each state and territory produces a range of publications and important gaming statistics.

Staff positions in the gaming sector

The organisation chart of Wrest Point Hotel Casino in Hobart in Fig. 11.2 shows the range of positions available in the gaming sector. Job descriptions for some of the casino staff, including Inspector (Fig. 11.3), Electronic Gaming Operator (Fig. 11.4) and Coin Cashier (Fig. 11.5), have also been provided by Wrest Point (see pages 136–138).

FIG. 11.2

Organisation chart of Casino Department of Wrest Point Hotel Casino.

Wrest Point Hotel Casino

CASINO DEPARTMENT

Casino Manager

Special Tours Manager

Table Gaming Manager

Management

Electronic Gaming Manager

Chief Cashier

Pit Bosses

Training & Compliance Officer

TAS Keno Manager

Assistant Chief Cashier

Electronic Gaming Supervisors

Cashier Supervisors

Representatives

Inspectors

Trainers

Electronic Gaming Inspectors

Cashiers & Coin Change

Dealers

Attendants/ Writers

Helpline Operators

Source: Casino Department of Wrest Point Hotel Casino.

FIG. 11.3

Example of job description for position of Inspector.

POSITION DESCRIPTION & SPECIFICATION

Position	Inspector
Classification	Inspector
Department	Casino
Section	Table Gaming
Sub-Section	n/a
Reports	To Pit Boss

RESPONSIBILITY AND AUTHORITY

- Supervision and control of Casino games in accordance with the rules, procedures, Company policies and procedures.
- Compliance with Company policies and procedures including the Occupational Health & Safety standards as set down by the Company.
- Participate in training as required for this position.

SCOPE OF DUTIES

- Supervision of Dealers, with instruction, direction and assist new/inexperienced dealers.
- Inform management of abnormal/sensitive situations.
- Respond professionally to customer queries and direct as required.
- Perform management representative duties where qualified, as directed by Management.
- Be motivated in applying and maintaining the knowledge and application of the Inspector's duties pertaining to the game/s supervised as outlined in the Inspector's duties (red box) Training Manual.
- Be motivated in applying and maintaining the knowledge the current Rules and Procedures involved for each table game dealt, rosters, time sheets, staff notices, Company Staff Policy Manual and Handbook, forward Program, user friendly attitude and communication required for guests and other staff/management.
- Initiate the required duties in the security of chip stock, government issued equipment, table equipment, cash, forms and clips and other Casino property.
- Respond when required to be a medium by which the Marketing Mission/s can be communicated to customers or other staff. Offer assistance to Patrons in need.
- Other duties as required by the Management Representative.
- Initiate customer contact with positive body language and appropriate greetings.
- Efficient use and management of table float, gaming equipment, the game and public.
- Upselling of other Wrest Point and Federal services.
- Maintenance of correct uniform and grooming.
- Maintenance of customer and Company confidentiality.
- Monitor notice boards and table action.
- Be aware of the needs of players as well as your own performance and effectiveness.
- Notify supervisors and/or management representatives of any circumstance which is unusual and has not come to their attention.
- Perform other duties as required.

Source: Casino Department of Wrest Point Hotel Casino.

FIG. 11.4

Example of job description for position of Electronic Gaming Operator.

POSITION DESCRIPTION & SPECIFICATION

Position	Electronic Gaming Operator
Classification	Electronic Gaming Attendant
Department	Electronic Gaming
Section	Casino
Sub-Section	n/a
Reports To	Electronic Gaming Inspectors

RESPONSIBILITY AND AUTHORITY

- Perform duties on a particular shift in the Keno game or Video Gaming Machines in accordance with the rules and procedures as required by the rules and directions, Internal Control and Accounting Manual and Company policy.
- Compliance with Company policies and procedures including the Occupational Health & Safety standards as set down by the Company.
- Participate in training as required for this position.

SCOPE OF DUTIES

- Follow the procedures specified in the Internal Control and Accounting Manual.
- Issue Keno tickets, process wins, voids and replay.
- Call and verify Keno games as required.
- Stock up and tidy as required.
- Assist public in playing Keno.
- May be required to process TAB transactions.
- Ensure no persons under the age of 18 years play Keno or Video Gaming Machines.
- Ensure no person under the age of 18 years is in the vicinity of Video Gaming Machines even when in the company of a parent or adult.
- Assist the public in playing Video Gaming Machines.
- Request fills for Video Gaming Machines and ensure fill slips are completed correctly and signed.
- Ensure fill register is completed correctly.
- Bring hand pays to the attention of Electronic Gaming Inspector and complete the appropriate form.
- Cancel accrued credits.
- Attend to minor machine malfunctions.
- Bring major Video Gaming Machine malfunctions to the attention of Electronic Gaming Inspectors.
- Ensure Master door opening log is kept up to date and accurate.
- Ensure room neatness. Collect discarded coin cups, glasses, ashtrays.
- Attend to enquiries about Federal Casino Club.
- Perform other duties as required.

Source: Casino Department of Wrest Point Hotel Casino.

FIG. 11.5

Example of job description for position of Coin Cashier.

POSITION DESCRIPTION & SPECIFICATION

Position	Coin Cashier
Classification	Coin Cashier
Department	Casino
Section Cash	Desk
Sub-Section	n/a
Reports To	Chief Cashier, Assistant Chief Cashier

RESPONSIBILITY AND AUTHORITY

- Act in accordance with the internal control/accounting manual and the directions as they apply to coin operations incorporated within the Casino Cash Desk responsibilities.
- Compliance with Company policies and procedures including the Occupational Health & Safety standards as set down by the Company.
- Participate in training as required for this position.

SCOPE OF DUTIES

- Attend to normal daily running of coin booth from counter i.e. coin sales and redemption, completion and computer processing of fills and handpays.
- Check and take over float from previous shift.
- Set up of counter, incorporating of machinery testing and adequate coin supply for day's trading.
- Prepare cash exchanges when required.
- Balance till prior to next shift starting.
- Perform hard counts when required.
- Maintain the automatic teller machine.
- Check all cupboards and safe are locked at close of shift.
- Comply with all existing security procedures.
- Perform other duties as required.

Source: Casino Department of Wrest Point Hotel Casino.

Following are some brief descriptions of other positions available in the gaming sector.

Croupier

The role of the croupier is to deal for various games such as blackjack and baccarat. The croupier or dealer must ensure the security of chip stock, government-issued equipment, and cash forms and slips. The croupier should promote the game and the patrons' enjoyment of the game, reporting any unusual circumstances to the pit boss or inspector (see job description in Fig. 11.3 on page 136).

Keno Writer

The role of the Keno Writer is to validate Keno tickets for patrons, pay out prize winners and answer queries regarding how the game is played. They are responsible for assisting with the running of the games and promoting the game to patrons.

Video Attendant

The video attendant assists guests playing on the video machines to understand the various games. They also assist with payouts when customers win jackpots.

Surveillance Operator

The responsibility of the Surveillance Department is to provide protection and security of the facilities and operations, the patrons and the employees. Operators are trained to detect illegal activities to protect the guests and the casino. Surveillance staff establish emergency and evacuation procedures, supervise the removal of table boxes and escort cash. They ensure adherence to gaming and other legislation by, for example, checking that staff comply with gaming directions and that liquor outlets close at the scheduled time.

Activities

1 Investigate three establishments from the following categories that offer gaming and list the types of games/gaming machines available:
   - hotel
   - club
   - casino.
2 What other types of entertainment are offered by these establishments?
3 Find out the name of the body that implements gaming legislation in your state or territory.
4 What are the main regulations with respect to gaming that employees must remember?

CASE STUDY

Warren, 24, started gambling at 16 but it 'took over his life' when he won $23,000 at the Canberra Casino aged 18. He lives in Sydney's south with his parents and finds 'the adrenalin rush' difficult to refuse when he plays blackjack. Although he wrongly sees himself as a successful gambler, he has no assets and owes money. His mother now controls his money and he is also considering a self-exclusion order. (Sunday Telegraph, 25 February 1996)

Discussion questions

1 Are establishments within their rights when they refuse entry to some patrons?
2 How do you think someone becomes addicted to gambling?
3 The Sydney Harbour Casino Act requires the casino to pay 2 per cent of its turnover to fund programs for addicted gamblers. What do you think about this idea?

4 Whose responsibility is it to ensure that a person behaves sensibly, i.e. 'to gamble with your head, not over it'?

5 What percentage of patrons do you think are at a casino for the entertainment, and what percentage do you think are driven by an addiction to gambling?

6 Do you think the article above is sensationalist or does it describe a serious problem?

LINKS

Department of Racing, Gaming and Liquor WA—
http://www.orgl.wa.gov.au/gaming/gambling.php

Tasmanian Gaming Commission—
http://www.treasury.tas.gov.au/domino/dtf/dtf.nsf/main-v/gaming

CHAPTER TWELVE

Hospitality laws

OBJECTIVES

The aim of this chapter is to introduce you to the legal aspects of running a hospitality establishment. On completion of this chapter you should be able to:

- differentiate between different types of legislation
- describe enterprises in terms of their legal structures of ownership and control
- list and briefly describe the acts and regulations applying to the hospitality industry
- outline the obligations of staff in the hospitality industry
- investigate state and federal legislation relevant to the industry.

Some time ago two policemen were shot after being called to a domestic dispute. The man involved had been drinking at the local club, he had then returned home, threatened his wife with a gun and turned on the two policemen, killing them both. This was a great shock to the local community and a source of grave concern. The causes of these events were investigated, leading to prosecution of the club and two of its employees for not complying with relevant legislation. This legislation refers to responsible service of alcohol under liquor licensing law.

The complexity of this issue is immediately apparent. Staff in the industry must question whether they can be held responsible for the actions of people who are intoxicated. This was the inference in the above case and it caused concern among beverage service staff across the country.

At least two issues emerge from this situation. Firstly, there could be a number of staff serving the same customer and, secondly, people respond in different ways to different amounts of alcohol.

The case has led to an evaluation of what is meant by 'responsible service of alcohol'. By no means a simple issue, it is nevertheless clear that staff working in the industry should be appropriately trained to make them aware of their obligations under liquor laws. If a club can show that the question of responsible service of alcohol has been addressed in the development of operating procedures and staff training, the directors are in a far better position when their licence is up for review.

Meeting legal obligations

The above example is particularly interesting because liquor law is the only area of the law other than, of course, criminal law under which staff can be held personally liable for their actions in the workplace. Under liquor licensing law both the hospitality establishment and the employee can be fined. This occurs mainly for service of alcohol to patrons who are under the legal age or for service outside the permitted hours. In most other situations the employer assumes responsibility for the employee's actions. If, for example, a customer slipped in a puddle in a bar, the employer would be liable for any damages sought. This is not to say that the employee who left the puddle on the marble should be allowed to carelessly display such lack of concern for guest safety! Depending on the severity of the mistake, such carelessness could lead to warnings and dismissal. A similar situation exists with fines for traffic offences while driving company vehicles. The employer is liable, but the employee would not last long in the job!

The employer has responsibility for supervision of staff, ensuring that they work safely and competently to meet the establishment's legal obligations. The employer has a duty of care for the customers. The employer is also responsible for any damages. Employees must be trained and encouraged to work safely and competently. If they fail to do so over a period of time, their employment can be terminated.

The aim of this chapter is to illustrate the employer's obligations under the law so that employees are able to act as the employer's agents in upholding the law. In many cases the legal aspects of work are not clear cut. Responsible service of alcohol in the first example is a grey area, very difficult to define and implement, and this makes the guidelines even more important. Balancing customer safety and security of staff employment is another complex area. Dismissal of a staff member could occur for one instance of reckless behaviour that endangered the safety of guests. However, this same behaviour could be described as a 'mistake' and lead to a claim for unfair dismissal. All of these issues which relate to the law and to its implementation make this a most interesting field.

In this chapter only the general principles of the laws listed will be described as laws often differ in the various states and territories. However, in most cases, the general principles remain the same. An awareness of pertinent laws and their general principles is essential for all staff. This leads to a better understanding of why standard operating procedures have been developed and why they are so important.

Source of law in Australia

Describing the sources of law can provide some insight into how laws and regulations have come into being. Australia has three levels of government, the commonwealth government, state and territory government, and local government. These are shown in Fig. 12.1. In the century since Federation, federal government has increased its power, mainly owing to the need to develop national consistency. As a result there are many areas of the law in which there is some overlap between state and federal legislation. Unfair dismissal legislation exists at both federal and state level. In the past people who wanted to claim unfair dismissal often sought advice from their union as to whether to make a claim under state legislation or federal legislation, depending on which was most favourable. This is now impossible as the federal unfair dismissal laws now state, in accordance with recent changes, that the Industrial Relations Court will refuse to hear claims protected by state laws.

Laws relating to business ownership

The most common forms of business ownership in the hospitality industry are companies, partnerships, sole traders, co-operatives and public authorities which are discussed in more detail below.

Company

The majority of large hospitality operations are companies. Two companies may establish a joint venture with different levels of investment and control over operations.

FIG. 12.1

Levels of government and sources of law.

Commonwealth Government
(Federal law)

State Government
(Laws of states and territories)

Local Government
(Regulations)
• cities
• municipalities
• shires

Franchising is one of the most common arrangements for business operators who have the investment dollars but not the expertise. The benefits of running a franchise operation are the established plans for building and decorating, national advertising, sharing of group discounts, and tried and tested standard operating procedures. Franchising began in the hotel industry in the USA with the Ritz-Carlton, which is one of the world's most prestigious hotel groups. Holiday Inn is another well-known franchise company, which sells its franchises to hotel operators in the mid-price range.

To establish a franchise business, the franchisee must pay fees for starting up and for ongoing trade, and must meet all standards set by the franchise company. Under this arrangement there are thus two companies involved, the franchisor and the franchisee. Many fast food operations are run on a franchise basis, paying fees to franchise companies for the use of their systems and advertising. McDonalds is one example of a franchise company with very high standards of quality control.

Another arrangement is leasing whereby a hotel, for example, may be leased by a management company. The hotel operator manages the property and pays a lease, based on a percentage of the profits, to the company that owns the property. The lessor owns the property and the lessee manages the operation. The hotel operator is responsible for all aspects of administration and financial control. With this arrangement there is a high degree of control of the operation by the management company.

Management contracts enable investors to make arrangements with management companies to run their hospitality operations for a fixed period (normally 10 to 20 years) at a fee based on a percentage of the profits. The benefits of using an established management company include the use of a well-known name, standard operating practices and a worldwide reservations system. Under this type of arrangement the management company earns fees based on profit, while the investor has a substantial ownership and financial investment in the operation.

Partnership

Partnership operations are common in the motel business, with some operations divided 50–50 between the investors and the operators. This means that each party contributes 50 per cent of the cost and obtains 50 per cent of the profits.

Sole trader

Many small hospitality operations, such as cafes, coffee shops and snack bars, are run by sole traders. The trader generally owns the business and invests in the operation. Premises are usually leased at a fixed rate, although some sole traders own their own premises. Sole traders can lose everything in the event of the collapse of their business because they are not an incorporated company.

Co-operative

Co-operative arrangements are also common in the motel industry and a central reservation system is pivotal to the arrangement. The name, such as Flag Inn, may be associated with each of the operations but, apart from this, each of the establishments is run more or less autonomously. All members of the co-operative share common benefits through combined marketing efforts.

Public authority

Non-commercial hospitality operations were mentioned in Chapters 1 and 7. Accommodation and food services provided in institutions, hospitals, jails, some retirement villages, schools, universities and the armed services all fall under the hospitality banner.

Common law and duty of care

The Australian legal system is based on the English model whereby common law developed through custom, from the decisions of the courts—the judge is the law-maker, judging each case on its merits. This practice is particularly evident in claims of negligence. All business operations and enterprises have a duty of care. If it can be shown in the courts that there was a breach of duty of care and the plaintiff (the one who brings the action) suffered damages because of this, the judge would make a decision in favour of the plaintiff. This decision would clearly be made after all the circumstances had been described and evaluated. For example, a claim of negligence (and thus a claim for damages) might be made against a restaurant if a customer, having described his or her particular food allergy, was served a dish containing the allergic substance, which resulted in illness and disability.

Laws and regulations relating to hospitality establishments

Legislation that is passed by federal and state and territory governments is 'black and white' not 'grey', as with common law, and there are many such laws applicable to hospitality operations. Under federal law, taxes must be paid, while gaming, for example, is covered by state legislation, the different laws having a big impact on gaming profits in the various states and territories, which has been the subject of much heated debate. At the local level, setting up tables on the footpath would have to comply with local council regulations. Fig. 12.2 shows some of the laws that protect the hospitality customer.

Forgetting for a moment about whether laws are federal or state in origin, the main principles of the laws affecting the hospitality industry in most states are described below.

FIG. 12.2

Some types of legislation which protect the customer.

Food hygiene laws — Liquor laws — Trade practices → CUSTOMER ← Gaming laws — Anti-discrimination laws — Building & safety laws

Anti-discrimination legislation

Hotels and restaurants have the right to refuse entry to a customer if they breach the dress code or are drunk, for example. However, staff cannot refuse entry on the basis of race, sex or physical or mental disability. It is also illegal to discriminate against customers or employees on the basis of marital status, pregnancy or sexual preference. In many states discrimination on the basis of age is also illegal (except, of course, where alcohol cannot be sold to minors). Two notable cases in the hospitality industry concerned a mother who was feeding her baby in a hospitality establishment and was asked to leave, and a Sikh who wanted to join an RSL club but was not admitted because he refused to remove his turban.

There is one exception to this legislation, which is particularly relevant to the hospitality industry. Employers in ethnic restaurants can employ staff of the appropriate nationality or appearance if to do so would be reasonable for reasons of authenticity.

The Human Rights and Equal Opportunity Commission site is listed at the end of the chapter and this contains more detailed information on anti-discrimination legislation.

Liquor licensing legislation

This legislation generally covers the age of drinkers, the venues and situations (for example, with meals) in which alcoholic drinks can be served, and the legal hours of alcohol service. Liquor must be correctly labelled and sold in legal measures. A sign must be displayed to say that it is an offence to sell or supply or obtain liquor on behalf of a person under the age of 18 years. The licensee must show that reasonable steps have been taken, including requests for identification, to ensure that minors are not served alcohol. Noise or indecorous behaviour complaints can be made to the Licensing Board.

In general terms, the purpose of the legislation is to:
- encourage responsible attitudes towards drinking
- minimise the harm associated with drinking
- show regard for the welfare of the community
- respond to the varied demands of the consumer in relation to alcohol service.

Ultimately it is essential that the licensee (and his or her employees) ensure that the intoxicated person is not a danger to him or herself or to others.

There are different liquor licences for all of the following:

- hotels, restaurants, etc. (these are called on-licences)
- caterers
- nightclubs
- communities
- special events
- vignerons.

Health and safety legislation

While the main purpose for developing this legislation (and associated workers compensation legislation) is the prevention of employee accidents and illness, the employer also has a responsibility under the various acts for people at a place of work, whether or not they are employees. This legislation will be covered in more detail in Chapters 13 and 22.

Food hygiene and related legislation

This legislation covers the preparation and storage of food, the composition of food and food handling practices generally. It also covers the places where food can be prepared and sold. Under this legislation adulteration of food (where it is filthy, decomposed, deteriorated or perished) is a criminal offence. The guidelines are very detailed and very strict covering, for example, personal hygiene of food handlers, recommended temperatures for washing glasses and plates, the necessity for discarding chipped or cracked crockery and the provision of appropriate serving utensils for salad bars.

Food safety systems are an important component of recent legislation in this area. HACCP (hazard analysis critical control points) is the name given to the guidelines, under this legislation, for storing, preparing and handling food (see also Chapter 24).

Food is adulterated or falsely described if it:

- is mixed or diluted with substances that diminish the food value or commercial value
- contains substances that are prohibited
- is displayed so as to conceal damage or inferiority
- consists of decayed food matter.

These issues are closely linked to consumer protection as described in the next section.

Consumer protection legislation

This legislation ensures that goods sold or services provided are those advertised. For example, accommodation must be of the standard advertised, ocean views must match those featured on the hotel's brochure, and services, such as tours and entertainment promised as part of a package, must be provided.

On a trip to a very small Barrier Reef island many years ago, a couple was astonished to find that the activities advertised were unobtainable. With 30 guests on the island, and one small boat, a consensus had to be reached about the activity for each day. Once decided, a lottery would be held to determine who would participate. If, after all this decision-making, the tides had changed, the activity would be cancelled anyway. So, too, on the day of the activities co-ordinator's birthday— he was too drunk to drive the boat! Technically this is a breach of trade practices legislation. The establishment must meet its promises.

Forming monopoly groups to influence prices is also illegal under trade practices legislation. For example, if a hotel calls to find out the current room rate and occupancy of another and uses this information to reach agreement between operators on pricing, this is in conflict with trade practices legislation. It is known as price fixing. Under trade practices the following are not acceptable:

- merging companies to form monopolies and restrict trade
- restriction of competition through agreements on pricing
- false and misleading advertising
- deceptive selling
- misleading or deceptive conduct or statements.

Sale of Goods Acts in each state and territory also protect the consumer. They define a number of 'unfair practices', including:

- misleading information about the nature, purpose, quality or quantity of goods and services
- accepting payment with no intention of supplying
- pyramid selling
- coercion or harassment in relation to the sale and supply of goods and services.

Innkeepers' acts

There are various state acts covering businesses providing accommodation, and these generally require a register of persons to be kept by the establishment. An important component of the legislation relates to duty of care for guest safety. It also limits liability for property lost or damaged on the premises unless it is handed in for safekeeping or the damage is due to the negligence of the hotel or motel staff. A notice to this effect must be prominently displayed at reception and in guest rooms. Some of the acts are archaic, however, and it is said that one requires the proprietor of a hotel to find accommodation for a horse if a guest arrives on one!

Building and safety regulations

Fire exits must be kept clear to comply with this legislation. Nightclubs that admit more patrons than permitted are in breach of this legislation. When these regulations are not complied with, there is an increased danger of accident or fire, which can lead to death or injury. Parking requirements, toilet facilities and signs are covered by local council regulations.

Gaming legislation

Gaming laws deal mainly with fair returns on gamblers' investments, access to gambling facilities (customers must be over 18) and propriety of management and staff in gambling establishments. All gaming staff have to apply for licences and these will not be issued if the person has a criminal record.

Rights to refuse entry

A proprietor has the right to refuse entry to, or ask a customer to leave, an establishment. This is generally in the interests of other customers. Dress codes are often the basis for refusal of entry to sports clubs and nightclubs. There is clearly a potential conflict between right of refusal and discrimination. For discrimination to be claimed, the claimant would have to show grounds for discrimination such as those listed in the section on 'Anti-discrimination legislation' earlier in this chapter.

Licences

Licences are required to play recorded music (from, for example, the Australian Performing Arts Association), to sell cigarettes (state government) and to sell small-goods (local council). This clearly illustrates how businesses can be affected by laws and regulations created at the three levels of government.

There are offices and agencies that advise businesses on their legal obligations (see below). In turn, employers must make staff aware of requirements to comply with the legislation.

All businesses are obliged to deduct PAYE tax from their employees' earnings. 'Black' cash money is illegal, though it is more common in the hospitality industry than in most others. All businesses are also required to take out workers compensation and vehicle third party/transcover insurance. Other insurances, such as fire, burglary, cash and public liability, are sensible precautions for any business. In fact, the increased cost of public liability insurance is having a big impact on many small tourism operators, particularly in the area of adventure tourism, forcing some to close. Risk management is also a topical issue, with legislative changes occurring in some states. This will be covered in more detail in Chapter 22.

A number of other laws are relevant to the employment of staff, such as equal employment, which is covered in the next chapter, and occupational health and safety legislation, which is covered in Chapters 13 and 22.

Employer associations

Employer associations are a useful source of legal advice. Associations such as the Registered Clubs Association, Restaurant and Catering Australia and the Australian Hotels Association provide advice to businesses that are members of their associations. These associations keep up to date with legal requirements and changes to legislation, and keep members informed through newsletters. If you were operating a hospitality business and needed an answer to a question, such as whether it was legal to add a tip to a credit card voucher if the guest did not fill in the total, you could ask your association for advice. (The answer, by the way, would be 'No'— it is neither legal nor ethical.)

Powers of police and inspectors

Police have the power to arrest and charge anyone who breaks the law. They work closely with staff in hospitality establishments where customers sometimes behave in inappropriate ways, such as being under the influence of drugs or alcohol. Police have the right to enter premises if they have a search warrant.

Inspectors are also appointed to uphold the law and they, too, have the right to enter premises. There are health inspectors (who could forget the Siberian hamster episode of *Fawlty Towers?*) and building, food and occupational health and safety inspectors. In some cases the business is forced to stop trading until a health or building matter has been resolved.

Obligations

All employees are obliged to uphold the law, despite any instructions to the contrary. Being asked to get to the airport in a hurry to pick up VIPs is no excuse for speeding. If an employee received a fine for speeding, the employer would pay it, but the employee would get a warning at the very least. A parking attendant who careered around the basement in a new Ferrari, leaving tyre marks all over the concrete and half the car attached to a pillar, would be dismissed instantly. If an employee's action is intentional or reckless, the employer may have the right to seek damages.

In the interests of all concerned—employer, employee, customer and supplier—it is important that all obligations under the law are met.

Ethics

In addition to running a business legally, there is also the issue of ethics. Ethics are a code of conduct, a way of doing things. It is both illegal and unethical to substitute flathead for barramundi if that is what is advertised on the menu. It is also illegal and unethical to pour a spirit into the wrong bottle and pretend to customers that it is the labelled variety. Although not illegal, it could be argued that putting up room prices when all other hotels are full is unethical. (This is also known as extortion.) Others say it is simply good business practice—the upside of discounting. Employees in the hospitality industry are expected to behave in an ethical manner in their relationships with customers, suppliers and other employees. Some of these issues will be discussed in more detail in Chapter 14.

Activity

Find out the names and dates of the following legislation in your state or territory:
- food handling
- health and hygiene
- liquor sales and service
- sale of goods
- trade practices
- anti-discrimination.

CASE STUDY

This was a wedding turned riot. After a quiet start, the party that followed the speeches became increasingly noisy. The bride appeared to be enjoying herself more than anyone else, having had more than her fair share of the champagne. A brilliant redhead, and very tall, she was the centre of attention on the dance floor. The duty manager, Kevin, had received a number of complaints from regular customers in the bar about the noise and arrived at the reception room to find the bride beginning a striptease. This, he decided, was not acceptable behaviour, and walked over to caution her and her husband. The guests booed Kevin as he crossed the dance floor, her husband grabbed him, holding his arms behind his back, and she took off a stiletto shoe and hit Kevin in the face with it, causing a gash over his eye. By this stage most of the guests had joined the fracas and the commotion had come to the attention of other staff who called the police and went to Kevin's assistance. The bridegroom had become very violent and was being restrained by two staff who tied his hands and feet to await the arrival of the police. The bride proved to be even more difficult to restrain. She picked up a table knife and accused Kevin of assaulting her. Fortunately the police arrived before any further physical damage could be done. However, claims and counter claims of assault were made.

Discussion questions

1 How could this situation have been prevented?
2 Would the police have been allowed to enter the premises in this situation?
3 What charges would be brought as a result of this incident?
4 What were Kevin's general obligations and rights under the law?

LINKS

Department of Employment and Workplace Relations— http://www.dewrsb.gov.au/links/default.asp

Human Rights and Equal Opportunity Commission—http://hreoc.gov.au

Lawsearch Online—http://www.lawsearch.gov.au/

CHAPTER THIRTEEN

Working conditions

OBJECTIVES

The aim of this chapter is to introduce you to your rights and obligations as an employee under industrial relations legislation. On completion of this chapter you should be able to:

- list and illustrate the rights and obligations of employers and employees under common law
- describe major industrial relations legislation which covers all employees
- describe the awards system, giving examples of the terms and conditions of employment under an award
- describe the system of workplace agreements, giving examples of the terms and conditions of employment under a workplace agreement.

Joanne had heard all about the wonderful opportunities available in the hospitality industry. She had been looking for a job for a week and was becoming quite despondent. She had tried to find a job as a waitress in some of the restaurants in the city and had been told by a few managers that she needed training and experience. Training she could understand, but experience she could not acquire unless someone gave her a break! The manager who upset her most told her that he employed only blondes, maximum size ten since the remaining uniforms were all small sizes.

Joanne was finally given the opportunity to try out for a job. The manager of the restaurant advised her that she would be given four hours work per day for three days as a trial. During the trial period her duties entailed polishing glasses and cutlery, setting tables and cleaning the carpet. At the end of her third day she was told that her services would not be required in the short term but that her name would be added to the list of casuals for any future work.

Under industrial relations legislation, which covers the legal relationship between employer and employee, several legal issues arise from Joanne's work trial. Firstly, while a skills test for employment is quite acceptable, this should not have taken three days! Indeed, a short skills test would have been a far more appropriate selection method. Secondly is the question of whether or not Joanne should have been employed for the three days as a casual staff member. If Joanne had burned herself while working on trial, this would have presented a very interesting legal situation. Technically she is not an employee unless she is earning money, but in this case she should have been paid and her employment contract (despite its brevity) would have entitled her to workers compensation. She would have been likely to win this test case. Thirdly, if the employer did not have workers compensation insurance, he would have been acting illegally and would have been liable for large fines. Joanne, if found to be an employee, would have been entitled to workers compensation from a special fund set up for employees caught up in situations where the employer is not insured. Workers compensation legislation covers all employees, including employees who are paid (illegally) in cash without tax deductions, for work-related injuries, illnesses and worsening of pre-existing conditions.

And there are some further issues. The manager who told Joanne that she was unsuitable on the basis of her size and appearance was in breach of equal employment opportunity legislation, which allows for employment and promotion on merit.

Secondly, Joanne would be wise to undertake some formal training and receive formal recognition for her skills. Performance standards (in the form of Competency Units) have been established in the hospitality industry and these have been used as the basis for training. The training can be completed on or off the job, at a private college or a public institution. In addition, the units are portable and widely recognised in the industry.

Finally, if Joanne were paid for her three days work, she would most likely have been paid a rate negotiated as part of an industry award covering restaurant employees. Such awards state the terms and conditions of employment, including pay rates, meal breaks, normal hours of work, overtime, minimum hours for casuals, and so on.

In the example of Joanne, two acts have been discussed, equal employment opportunity and workers compensation. These acts and several others described in this chapter apply to all employees.

Statute laws (acts) relevant to employment

Statute laws are laws made in parliament at a state or federal level. They include the following acts, described here in general terms as they may differ marginally from state to state.

Workers compensation

This law requires all employers to insure their staff against work-related accidents or illnesses. Staff are entitled to know the name of the insurer. Any staff member should report work-related accidents immediately, even if no medical attention is required, as workers compensation insurance covers absence from work and medical expenses. The highest risks for hospitality employees are back injury, falls, burns and scalds, cuts and Hepatitis B. Clearly it is preferable to avoid such occurrences and it is prevention which is the aim of occupational health and safety legislation.

Occupational health and safety

Prevention of workplace accidents and workplace-related illnesses is essential. The various acts require that employers:

- provide a safe place of work
- provide a safe method of work
- ensure that equipment meets the required safety standards.

The obligations of employees under this legislation are to:

- take reasonable care with their own safety and the safety of others
- comply with instructions on safety issues
- report all accidents
- render all necessary aid to others who may be injured.

Occupational health and safety will be discussed further in Chapter 22.

Equal employment opportunity

Equal employment opportunity (EEO) aims to ensure that the workplace is free from discrimination and harassment so that employees can get on with their work in a harmonious and productive environment. EEO requires that people should be treated equally without consideration of irrelevant factors such as age, marital status, sex, race or disability. Discrimination based on these factors is illegal. Selection, training and promotion should be based on merit.

Sexual harassment involves unwelcome behaviour that causes offence. If you should find yourself in such a situation, you should tell the person that their behaviour is unacceptable and that they should not do it again. The incident should be reported to your supervisor or manager, or to the Human Resources Department. You also have the right to make a complaint to the relevant state or territory board or to the Human Rights and Equal Opportunity Commission.

In addition to equal employment opportunity legislation there are laws which require employers to keep statistics on the composition of their workforce and address imbalances. This is called affirmative action legislation.

All of these are employment-related laws, which have been passed in parliament at a state or federal level.

Common law

Besides laws that have been agreed in parliament, there is also common law, which we have described in Chapter 12 and will discuss further in Chapter 23 in relation to customer safety and security. Common law is not as black and white as statute (parliament-made) law and decisions have to be made in court, based on precedent (previous cases). If, for example, a Front Office manager were in breach of contract for not fulfilling his or her duties, the case could be argued in court. Both sides would be represented and the judge would make a decision. This is why common law is called 'judge-made' law as opposed to parliament-made law.

Under common law both employer and employee have specific responsibilities. The employer's responsibilities are to:

- pay agreed wages
- pay full-time **and** part-time employees for times when business is slow
- provide a statement of service to the employee on termination
- comply with all statutory legislation relating to the employment of staff.

The employee's responsibilities are to:

- work in a safe and competent manner (consider safety, service and other staff)
- obey lawful instructions (comply with reasonable requests, providing they are legal)
- hand over moneys owed to the employer (all day's takings, excluding tips)
- maintain trade secrets (such as recipes, sales projections, marketing strategies)
- make over inventions to the employer (a new recipe, for example, which is developed as part of the job)
- disclose information relevant to the employer (such as illness, criminal record, theft).

Awards

For many employees the terms and conditions of their employment are covered by awards. As part of award negotiation, items such as the following are agreed:

- hourly rates of pay for various levels
- overtime rates
- penalty rates for working late at night or at weekends (rapidly disappearing in a 24-hour service environment)
- meal breaks
- rostered days off
- termination
- uniforms
- definitions of casual, part-time and full-time employment.

Staff at higher levels—senior managers, for example—are not covered by awards. They are governed only by common law and statute law. They have a contract covered by common law, which spells out their responsibilities and pay, and they are covered by statute law, such as workers compensation, equal employment and annual leave legislation, which applies to all employees. The terms and conditions for senior managers are thus very vague compared with those for employees covered by an award. Senior managers do not generally negotiate specific hours of work or meal breaks, nor do they get overtime. In the hospitality industry a 14-hour day is quite common for managers.

Negotiation of an award

An award is generally negotiated between a union (representing workers) and an industry association (representing management) (see Figs 13.1, 13.2 and 13.3). The *Hospitality Industry— Accommodation, Hotels, Resorts and Gaming Award*, 1998, for example, applies to the Australian Hotels Association (and its

FIG. 13.1

Award negotiation.

Australian Hotels Association (AHA)

Australian Liquor, Hospitality and Miscellaneous Workers Union (LHMU)

Hospitality Industry — Accommodation, Hotels, Resorts and Gaming Award, 1998

members) in New South Wales, Victoria, Tasmania and the South-Eastern Division of Queensland. The union involved in the negotiation of this award (and many others in the hospitality industry) is the Australian Liquor, Hospitality and Miscellaneous Workers Union (LHMU). This award is known as the 'hotels award'.

The *Motels, Accommodation and Resorts Award*, 1998 applies to the same area and covers employees working for establishments belonging to the Motor Inn, Motel and Accommodation Association. This award is commonly known as the 'motels award'. The wage rates for the 'motels award' are shown in Table 13.1 on page 156. Information relating to federal awards can be accessed on the Internet at the addresses listed at the end of this chapter.

Some awards are negotiated at state level. For example, the *Restaurant etc. Employees State Award (NSW)* covers employees working in the restaurant sector in New South Wales. The wage rates, including part-time and casual, are shown in Table 13.2 on page 157. In this award there are seven grades of employees, including waiters and chefs, with a range of different weekly wage rates. Other states and territories have similar awards covering this sector.

In all three examples of awards, the union involved has been the LHMU. Fifty thousand hospitality workers belong to this union which spans all sectors of the hospitality industry, including hotels, motels, resorts, restaurants and casinos. The other union relevant to the hospitality industry is the Australian Workers Union.

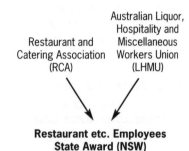

FIG. 13.2

Award negotiation.

Motor Inn, Motel and Accommodation Association → Australian Liquor, Hospitality and Miscellaneous Workers Union (LHMU) →

Motels, Accommodation and Resorts Award, 1998

FIG. 13.3

Award negotiation.

Restaurant and Catering Association (RCA) → Australian Liquor, Hospitality and Miscellaneous Workers Union (LHMU) →

Restaurant etc. Employees State Award (NSW)

Workplace agreements

While awards are negotiated at an industry level, for hotels, motels and restaurants, as in the previous examples, it is possible to negotiate a workplace agreement at a much lower level. Such an agreement can be reached by the staff and management of a single restaurant or restaurant chain. The purpose of these more localised agreements is to develop greater flexibility, to encourage higher productivity and to bring benefits to both employers and employees. The aim is to run more productive operations, with better service and more satisfied staff. This, at any rate, is the rhetoric. And quite a contentious issue it is too. Careful consideration is necessary to compare conditions negotiated under an agreement with those under an award.

Another significant benefit for employers is that workplace agreements can sometimes bring in a range of employees who were previously covered by different awards. At an island resort, for example, there could be staff covered by a number of awards such as storemen and packers, carpenters, metal workers, electrical trades, shop workers and so on. With an agreement, all can work under the same conditions. This is often preferable for staff of an island resort because they prefer to take

Wage rates under the *Motels, Accommodation and Resorts Award*, 1998.

Level and Classification	Minimum Award Rate Per Week $
Introductory Level	413.40
LEVEL 1 Hospitality Services Grade 1	430.10
LEVEL 2 Hospitality Services Grade 2 Leisure Attendant Grade 1 Hospitality Administration and Front Office Grade 1 (excluding South-Eastern Queensland)	455.20
LEVEL 3 Hospitality Services Grade 3 Hospitality Administration and Front Office Grade 2 (excluding South-Eastern Queensland) Leisure Attendant Grade 2	473.50
LEVEL 4 Hospitality Services Grade 4 Hospitality Administration and Front Office Grade 3 (excluding South-Eastern Queensland) Leisure Attendant Grade 3	507.20
LEVEL 5 Hospitality Services Grade 5 Hospitality Administration and Front Office Supervisor (excluding South-Eastern Queensland)	548.90
LEVEL 6 Hospitality Services Grade 6	567.80

FIG. 13.4

Workplace agreement negotiation.

Management
(optional: employer
association)   Staff
(optional: union)

Workplace agreement

several days off to return to the mainland. Although the agreement is reached between the management and staff of an enterprise, both groups can seek assistance from their association and union respectively to assist them with the negotiation. This is illustrated in Fig. 13.4. The types of terms and conditions negotiated in an agreement are the same as those negotiated in an award, for example hourly pay, overtime, meal breaks, uniforms and days off. If required, the agreement can cover only limited conditions, with all others falling to the award.

Australia Asia Pacific Hotels negotiated an agreement with their staff (who sought the assistance of the LHMU), which

TABLE 13.2

Wage rates under the *Restaurant etc. Employees State Award (NSW)*.

Classification	Full-time $	Part-time (per hour $)			Casual (per hour $)			
		M–F	Sat	Sun	M–F	Sat	Sun	Hol. pay
Grade 1: Kitchen hand, cleaner, useful, general hand, pantry hand, basic gardening duties	420.30	11.06	13.83	16.59	13.28	16.59	19.91	1.11
Grade 2: Basic waiting, basic bar attending, cashier, laundry attendant, sandwich hand, storeperson	437.30	11.51	14.39	17.27	13.81	17.27	20.72	1.15
Grade 3: Specialised waiter/bar attendant, cook alone, grill cook, senior storeperson, security guard (licensed)	462.90	12.19	15.23	18.28	14.62	18.28	21.93	1.22
Grade 4: Unqualified a la carte cook, head waiter, supervisor, head bar attendant, head storeperson	481.60	12.68	15.85	19.01	15.21	19.01	22.82	1.27
Grade 5: Cook/waiter, tradesperson	516.00	13.58	16.98	20.37	16.30	20.37	24.45	1.36
Grade 6: Demi chef, maitre d'	556.60	14.65	18.31	21.98	17.58	21.98	26.37	1.47
Grade 7: Chef de Partie	577.90	15.21	19.01	22.82	18.25	22.82	27.38	1.52

Source: Restaurant etc. Employees State Award (NSW), Award Code 577, Serial B9292.

allowed them to have the day off on their birthday instead of the union picnic day. The agreement led to a higher proportion of permanent part-time staff. Annualised salaries (which absorb penalty rates) created more flexibility in rostering, so there were benefits to both parties.

This agreement provides a further example of the potential benefits of workplace agreements. Previously, staff working for the company had been covered by a number of awards.

The objectives for the single agreement reached between management and staff (with union involvement) are illustrated in Fig. 13.5 on page 158. The advantages for employees under the agreement were:

• greater job security with the introduction of more permanent positions

FIG. 13.5

Enterprise (workplace) agreement negotiated between management
and staff of Australia Asia Pacific Hotels.

ENTERPRISE AGREEMENT

OBJECTIVES:

■ To achieve best practice, in the domestic and international
hospitality arena, for all aspects of its operation.

■ The recruitment and retention of an effective, flexible and
motivated team of employees.

■ To utilise the available workforce in the most productive manner
consistent with principles of equity.

■ To provide a satisfying working environment that encourages
employees to offer a consistent level of high quality service.

■ To provide challenging work and career opportunities for staff; and
a satisfying working environment where all employees will have
enhanced opportunities for developing their skills across a broader
range of functions than in the past.

■ To optimise return on investment.

By permission of ACCOR Asia Pacific.

- multi-skilling, which necessitated increased employer commitment to training
- enhanced career-oriented training, which necessitated greater attention to the design and direction of training programs
- clear career pathing
- challenging career opportunities
- national recognition of competency level, facilitating transfer between companies
- more staff receiving paid annual leave because more staff were permanent
- hospitality rate of pay (which incorporates penalty rates for night and weekend work)
- leave and overtime based on the higher annualised rate

- effective communication through joint consultative representatives
- structured grievance resolution procedures
- greater flexibility of rostered hours or days off
- incentive bonuses available when sick leave was not used
- birthday (or day after!) off.

A shared vision

In a speech to the Tourism Training Conference, The Joint National Secretary of the Australian Liquor, Hospitality and Miscellaneous Workers Union, Christine Huxtable, shares her vision for expanding excellence together:

In developing an ideal picture of the future, LHMU recognises that our role as the industry union must be to look not only at a single industrial issue, but to look to the health and long term viability of the industry, and only in doing this will our members' and future members' jobs and livelihoods be protected and advanced.

- *In that light then we see an ideal industry as one that is profitable and attractive to both consumers and workers.*
- *Such an industry must necessarily be characterised by a customer focus and by quality service provision.*
- *We see the achievement of both underpinned by a large, stable workforce— multi-skilled and flexible.*
- *We see that stability and skilling arise out of rewarding jobs (both in terms of job satisfaction and pay), career structures and training.*

Working Toward a Common Vision: Expanding Excellence Together, Tourism Training Conference, May 1995.

What should I do when I get a job?

Staff in the tourism and hospitality industry often begin work without knowing how or when they will be paid. They have little idea of their obligations for their own safety and the safety of others, their rights and their responsibilities. A job description and an employee handbook are frequently provided by larger employers, but staff working in small businesses are often left in the dark. The following guidelines from the LHMU may assist you in this respect:

1 Find out about the award or agreement you will be working under (dependent on your employer's type of business—restaurant, hotel or motel—the appropriate award being different for all of these).

2 Find out what employment category you are to be employed in (are you full-time, part-time, casual or seasonal?).

3 Find out what your pay rate will be (per hour for casual, per week for a full-time permanent).

4 Ensure that you have access to basic information about your company's human resources policies (the company will have policies in many areas, such as occupational health and safety, employee conduct, handling of complaints, sexual harassment, etc.).

The union can be contacted to provide advice on points 1 and 3. It also provides protection and strength in the areas of pay, conditions and job security, and offers a variety of other services. Your employer should advise you on points 2 and 4. It is important that you have all this information before you start your job so that you know your rights and obligations.

Activities

1 Find an example of a letter offering employment to see which aspects of the employment contract are covered in the wording.

2 Investigate whether staff working in fast food outlets are covered by the same award as staff working in restaurants in your area.

3 Look for workplace signs that refer to any of the acts mentioned in this chapter.

4 Develop a list of the conditions of employment covered by a specific award.

5 Develop a list of the conditions of employment covered by a specific agreement.

CASE STUDY

Frieda had only been working in Housekeeping for three days when she was involved in an accident. She was overcome with fumes from the cleaning agent she was using in the shower. Because she was new to the job, she did not tell anyone about it. She was particularly concerned as she suffered badly from asthma, but had not disclosed this on the application form. Her parents were furious with her for not being honest. They said that correct training in the use of chemicals was the responsibility of the employer and that she had a right to demand training and compensation for her medical expenses.

Discussion questions

1 Could the employer have rejected Frieda's application for this job on the basis of her health?

2 What obligations does Frieda have to her employer?

3 What obligations does the employer have to Frieda?

4 What would you suggest Frieda do?

LINKS

Australian Workplace (federal government site)—http://www.workplace.gov.au/

Liquor, Hospitality and Miscellaneous Workers Union—http://www.lhmu.org.au/

National Occupational Health and Safety Commission—http://www.nohsc.gov.au/

NSW Awards—http://www.dir.nsw.gov.au/awards/

OSIRIS (database of federal awards and agreements)—http://www.osiris.gov.au/

CHAPTER FOURTEEN

Trends and issues in the industry

OBJECTIVES

This chapter introduces some of the ethical issues that have an impact on the hospitality industry and its staff as well as some of the emerging trends in the industry. On completion of this chapter you should be able to:

- obtain information on legal and ethical issues to assist effective work performance
- conduct day-to-day hospitality industry activities in accordance with legal obligations and ethical industry practices
- monitor current issues of concern to the industry
- identify trends for the future of the industry and utilise them in decision-making.

One hundred million hamburgers—one for every two adults in the US—were withdrawn from the market in the biggest panic in the history of modern fast foods. The millions of kilos of beef were recalled by the Hudson Food Company as it indefinitely closed down its plant in Columbus, Nebraska, following evidence found by government inspectors that an E.coli outbreak was more widespread than had been recognised.

ASSOCIATED PRESS, 25 AUGUST 1997

Using leftover food in the next day's buffet is not uncommon in the hotel industry. The large hamburger manufacturing company mentioned above was investigated for contamination following a similar practice.

Food hygiene is just one of many issues, both legal and ethical, for staff working in restaurants and catering. While fatal cases of food poisoning are rare, consumers must be protected against even the mildest case of food poisoning.

The two preceding chapters provided some broad information on the various laws and regulations that are relevant to the hospitality industry. While many hospitality organisations adhere to those laws and also treat both customers and employees in an ethical manner, there are some that don't. For example, a fast food operation which repeatedly hires new employees in the youngest age bracket (thus paying the lowest rates) and does not offer work to casuals who reach the higher age bracket (effectively dismissing them) is following the relevant employment award but acting in an unethical way. And sometimes employers ask employees to behave in unethical ways, for example in substituting cheaper brands of alcohol for more expensive brands to increase the profit margin. This is not only unethical, but also illegal.

Tensions in the business environment

Business is often described as 'cut-throat', and indeed it is. Imagine for a moment that you are operating a beachside restaurant and paying all your staff the correct wages, deducting tax, paying superannuation, payroll tax, and so on. At the same time, your competitors on the restaurant mile are paying most employees in cash, thus avoiding many of their legal obligations. In this cash culture they can afford to offer menu items at a lower price than yours. Their conduct is both illegal and unethical. However many would say that they have to do this to stay in business. As you can see, it is extremely difficult to run a business in this type of competitive environment.

Another tension exists between stopping service to a patron who is intoxicated, in accordance with the liquor laws, and accurately assessing the point when this condition is reached. Early intervention might send all pub patrons home sober and send the business bankrupt in a very short period of time.

Smoking in hospitality environments is another good example. Most hospitality managers acknowledged some years ago that smoky environments had an impact on the health of employees. However, they also knew that if they were to act alone to ban smoking, they would soon find many of their customers visiting one of their competitors. It was only after many years of lobbying by employees and unions, as well as the outcomes of a few landmark test cases, that laws were passed regarding smoking in some hospitality establishments, particularly restaurants. This is also a good illustration of changing attitudes in society. Practices that were once commonplace are now being regulated. While smoking has been banned on most international airlines for quite a long time, there are still some which allow passengers to smoke on board. The number of countries in which smoking in dining areas is banned is very limited. In fact, some of these countries would view such a suggestion as absurd.

It is essential for hospitality employees to keep up to date with such issues. Professional associations, such as the Australian Hotels Association and Restaurant and Catering Australia, help to keep their members informed on legal and other issues, and changes to legislation are usually discussed in the press in the lead-up to legislation being passed by the respective parliamentary or regulatory body.

Legal issues

As soon as a customer becomes a paying client the hospitality business is subject to laws, such as contract and tort law (common law) and statutory law (legislation such as food and liquor acts).

Under common law, actions must be deemed reasonable by a court and a business must demonstrate that it has not been negligent. Duty of care must be shown to all customers, employees and other individuals on site, such as visiting workers or contractors. Statutory law is more 'black and white', as we have mentioned, with clear penalties such as fines for specific actions. Service of alcohol to a minor, for example, attracts a specific fine and can result in the loss of a liquor licence.

The following statutory laws (some of which we have already discussed) are most relevant to the hospitality industry.

Consumer protection

Under consumer protection legislation, the customer must receive the advertised products and services. If the quality of the food and service provided is not as advertised, the customer can seek redress under consumer protection legislation. Tourists taking holidays on cruise ships where the advertised activities and services have not been available have been known to take a class action. Breakdowns in electrical services and plumbing on a cruise would also provide ample ammunition for complaint.

Customers have high expectations, which must be fulfilled.

Employee protection

Employees are covered by a wide range of laws, including anti-discrimination and occupational health and safety, as discussed in Chapters 12 and 13.

Environmental protection

Laws under the environmental protection acts are particularly relevant to resorts situated in World Heritage listed areas. Coral reefs, for example, can be adversely affected by run-off from fertilisers and other nutrients added to soil and for this reason careful planning by a resort in such a location is needed to minimise its impact on the environment. Plans for wide expanses of green lawn may have to give way to natural bush with raised walkways. All employees of eco-resorts work towards educating their guests and protecting the surrounding, sometimes fragile, environment.

Community interest

Community interest must also be served, and laws and regulatory bodies work towards its protection. For example, government may declare a site containing historic buildings a heritage site under law, thus preventing major redevelopment. All new developments must be passed through local government, in fact, and many require environmental impact statements. Other measures that may have an impact on local communities include the introduction of gaming machines in hotels and the development of casinos and large hotels. While improving the local economy and providing employment, not all hospitality developments work in the long-term interest of the community.

Ethical issues

In addition to legal issues in the tourism and hospitality industry, there is also the issue of ethical practice. Although there is much overlap between the two, in some situations it is only the ethical, or unethical, approach of an individual or organisation that affects staff and customers. For example, while it is technically illegal to fill a teapot with beer and serve it in the staff canteen after hours, few people would regard this as theft. Serving alcohol to staff is, however, an ethical issue, particularly if the practice gets out of hand. While some would argue that this is not responsible service of alcohol, others would question the harm done by a few staff drinks after work.

Below are a number of issues relevant to the tourism and hospitality industry, some of which are purely ethical, others having both a legal and ethical component.

> By day he was reception supervisor. But at shift's end he secretly retired to his third floor room to become Aaron Boyd, the mysterious, big spending hotel guest. With a tap of his computer keyboard the receptionist checked into his own hotel under an assumed identity and lived there, undetected by fellow staff, for two months. Using service elevators and rear entrances to avoid detection, he racked up bills of almost $10,000 on accommodation, room service and telephones during his stay.
>
> DAILY TELEGRAPH, 4 MAY 2001

Pricing collusion

Restaurants that work co-operatively to increase prices are working unethically. So too are hotels when they compare occupancy and room rates and change their room rates accordingly. Pricing is always a contentious issue when large events are being held and city hotels have reached their capacity. At such a time room rates can double. While many customers complain that this is unethical, business operators argue that it is simply a response to market environment. Airline tickets, too, are sold in various different price ranges to maximise yield.

Cash payments

Paying employees in cash is both illegal and unethical. Australia's taxation system is designed so that all employees contribute to the upkeep of the country and the services provided by governments and other bodies. Employees should be given all entitlements, including superannuation and leave.

Confidentiality

Privacy legislation protects the personal details of individuals. In a hotel, privacy goes further, with guests provided full protection from unsolicited visitors. If a visitor or person telephoning asks for a guest they will be put through to the room but never told the room number. The concierge in every hotel is also required to be the master of discretion, particularly when reporters are trying to weasel out information about celebrities and other important guests.

Commissions and kickbacks

Some hotel staff, particularly receptionists and concierges, enjoy commissions for bookings they make on behalf of guests. This practice, though quite widespread, is unethical as it narrows the range of recommendations given to guests.

Overbooking

Airlines and hotels are known to overbook based on historical 'no show' figures. This puts them in a very difficult situation when all customers arrive—some have to be 'bumped' to other hotels.

Familiarisations

Familiarisations are visits to hotels by travel agency staff who may at some future time sell the destination to travel customers. This practice is unethical when the particular destination is singled out from other good choices simply because of the prospect of more familiarisations or commission. In this case, the booking agent is prompted by self-interest rather than by the interest of the client.

Tipping

Some 'high rollers' in Las Vegas casinos tip thousands of dollars to casino staff. On a smaller scale, trendy city types tip heavily to ensure that their new sports cars are left in the hotel driveway in order to impress their clients. Preferential treatment for high tipping customers should not occur.

Free gifts and services

High spending casino patrons are sometimes accommodated free of charge in the best suites of the accompanying hotel, based on the premise that they will lose enough money in the casino to offset the cost. A purchasing officer being personally rewarded for selecting a certain wine is acting unethically, too. Free gifts and services are inappropriate when they affect objective decision-making.

Product recommendations

Whenever making a recommendation to a hotel guest or other hospitality client on tours to attractions, restaurants and retail outlets, for example, the information provided should be objective and in the interest of the client.

Issues of concern to the industry

The sustainability of tourism and hospitality is very important, and the industry must be managed well for this to occur. Laws and regulations are in place to protect individuals, organisations and the industry as a whole. Fires in backpacker lodges, tourists left out on the Barrier Reef and food poisoning by airline food all damage the country's tourism profile. Australia needs to be able to be sold as a safe, friendly, eco-sensitive and culturally sensitive holiday destination. To do this the industry must work towards these objectives.

There are a range of concerns of government and industry bodies and these have prompted a number of positive moves to protect the industry.

Government initiatives

Both federal and state governments fully understand the importance of tourism to the Australian economy. For example, while the decision to host the Sydney 2000 Olympic Games was a difficult one owing to the enormous cost, government knew that the long-term benefits to tourism would make it worthwhile. The various tourism commissions maintain outstanding websites and stage widespread international and local advertising campaigns using themes, such as the outback, aimed at increasing regional tourism and providing a boost to regional economies. Government is also cognisant of the fact that political relations between Australia and other countries have an impact on in-bound tourism and attempt to smooth any ripples through visits by government representatives and other measures.

Industry research on emerging markets

The Bureau of Tourism Research is one of the bodies that closely monitors emerging markets in Australia. The advice it provides is valuable to tourism operators, enabling them to prepare their long-term strategic plans. Industry research is also essential for ensuring that advertising campaigns are directed at the appropriate target markets and for providing the right mix of tourism products (accommodation, meals and tours) for the targeted clientele. The tourism industry is very competitive and Australia has to work harder than most. The attractiveness (and cost) of a visit to Australia has to outweigh the disadvantage of the distance that international visitors, particularly Americans and Europeans, need to travel.

Management of environmental and social impact

Eco-tourism is a very popular sector of the tourism industry but at the same time it is very hard to manage. In the words of one operator, the impact of 500 managed visitors can be less than the impact of 50 unmanaged visitors. Australia's World Heritage Sites have endeavoured to develop ecologically sensitive areas in such a way that the impact on the environment is minimal. The construction of aerial walkways over forests and the introduction of carefully managed river and reef tours are examples of such measures.

Social issues, such as immigration, refugee management and reconciliation are of interest to international visitors and affect tourist numbers. Governments must therefore be mindful of all publicity on these issues, since tourism is a key component of the economy. Gambling is another social issue, widely discussed in the press, which also has the potential to impact upon tourist numbers unless it is managed in a balanced way by state and federal governments. The construction of new nightclubs, hotels, resorts and entertainment venues comes under intense scrutiny by government because of the social impact on local residents. If government does not allow their construction this action, in turn, has an economic impact on local residents and tourism.

Waste management

Another environmental issue for the industry is that of waste management. If the hotels, cafes, restaurants and other retail food outlets in Sydney's CBD recycled their paper and cardboard, instead of throwing it out, and followed best practice in waste minimisation, they would save 110,000 trees, 21,000 barrels of oil, 33,000 cubic metres of landfill space and 255 million litres of water in a year. Food waste generated in Sydney's kitchens in one year would fill 3,800 buses. According to one audit, an average of $15.25 worth of cutlery, crockery and cloth tableware is accidentally disposed of by hospitality businesses every day. ('Eating into Waste', Training Manual, Tourism Training Australia, 2000) Figures like these illuminate the importance of best practice in waste management by the hospitality industry.

Waste management can be improved by industry taking care with the following: menu planning, purchasing, receipt and storage of products, meal preparation, serving and cleaning.

In some restaurants each menu item is analysed in terms of waste produced (such as vegetable and meat offcuts) and any excess food is used in other dishes. Careful planning such as this also means increased profit to the establishment.

In line with all other industries, the hospitality industry needs to monitor and manage waste in order to reduce its environmental impact. Hotel Inter-Continental Sydney, for example, has a well-recognised program for waste management, which involves all staff:

> To improve its environmental performance and save nearly $300,000 per year, the Hotel Inter-Continental Sydney changed some practices that seemed insignificant in themselves but which, collectively, wasted massive resources. The changes cost around $275,000 and had no adverse affect on guest amenity. They included lowering the power of lights that were too bright, lowering the temperature of unnecessarily hot water and better control of air-conditioning.
>
> (http://www.ea.gov.au/industry/eecp/case-studies/intercont.html)

Employment issues

The significant expansion of part-time and casual employment is especially evident in the tourism and hospitality industry, and this has led to less job security for some. On the other hand, the industry is attractive to students and others who wish to work part time, and labour is readily available to the industry. The end result, however, is high staff turnover for many hospitality operations, some cities being described as washing machines tumbling staff around from one job to another as employees become unhappy in their jobs.

Linked to the issue of part-time and casual work in the industry is the issue of expansion and contraction of the industry workforce. As many hospitality operations are seasonal, expansion and contraction are unfortunately inevitable consequences of the nature of the industry.

Staff turnover is a tricky problem for hospitality businesses as investment in staff training is unlikely to be realised. And high turnover of staff has an impact on productivity and job satisfaction, creating a vicious cycle for all concerned. Sadly, programs designed to retain staff are too often unsuccessful.

Making ethical decisions

Employees face daily ethical dilemmas in the tourism and hospitality industry. Asking the questions below helps employees make the right decision on issues as they come up:

- **Is it legal?** Having studied in this field you will know better than most which laws and regulations apply.
- **Is it ethical?** While there may be no legal issue at stake, the practice you have observed or have been asked to carry out, such as punching the time card for another employee or covering for their absence, may be unethical.
- **What is the impact of your action?** Sometimes this can be quite severe.
- **How does the action affect others?**
- **Are there alternative approaches?**
- **What is best practice?** Looking at standards of best practice may result in a more reasonable approach to the situation.
- **Can we develop a code of conduct on this issue?** Larger companies, in particular, generally have a code of conduct, which covers topics such as commissions and client confidentiality.

Activities

1 Investigate one major political event reported overseas that you think had a negative impact on the number of international visitors to Australia. Discuss the reasons why this and other similar negative factors influence tourist attitudes to Australia and decisions not to visit our country.

2 Discuss your reasons for dissatisfaction with an experience in a restaurant with two of your friends or colleagues. Decide whether the issues related to legal or ethical practice on the part of the restaurant or its staff.

3 List five actions (such as excessive use of company telephone/Internet) that could be regarded as unethical and put these actions to the test using the questions suggested above.

CASE STUDY

As a kitchen hand working for a catering company, you are on the lowest rung of the ladder. The chef does not allow you to forget this, dealing with you in an autocratic manner and criticising you severely if you do something wrong—sometimes you find it difficult to read his mind!

Last night he asked you to take out a five-kilogram box of prawns to defrost. When you left you asked him if he wanted you to put it in the fridge. He replied that he would do it. When you arrived this morning (a very hot day!) you found the box of prawns sitting in a puddle on the kitchen bench—they had clearly been left out all night. You don't know whether to put them in the fridge right away, to leave them out and wait for the chef to arrive, or to bring this situation to the attention of the maitre d'. You know full well that the chef will blame you for the spoiled prawns. If you put them in the fridge now you can avoid the conflict entirely.

Discussion questions

1 Is this an ethical decision?
2 Are there any laws or regulations to consider?
3 What are the potential outcomes of the actions you have considered?
4 What would you do in this situation?

LINKS

Australian Hotels Association—
http://www.midcoast.com.au/cmsm/entert/hotels/aha.html

Hospitality Magazine—Isubscribe.com.au
http://www.isubscribe.com.au/title_info.cfm?prodid=1004

Restaurant and Catering Australia—http://www.restaurantcater.asn.au

PART 2

Working with Others

The hospitality industry is a people industry. This section of the book will encourage you to develop interpersonal skills with both colleagues and customers. Good service is the result of effective planning, collaborative teamwork and outstanding communication at all levels. Most hospitality employees work in a socially and culturally diverse environment and, for this reason, information on cross-cultural communication and tradition and religion is also included. Indeed, this is an industry where you will meet the world in your workplace.

COMPETENCY UNITS

WORK WITH COLLEAGUES AND CUSTOMERS (THHCOR01B)

Elements

- Communicate in the workplace
- Maintain personal presentation standards
- Provide service to colleagues and customers
- Work in a team

WORK IN A SOCIALLY DIVERSE ENVIRONMENT (THHCOR02B)

Elements

- Communicate with customers and colleagues from diverse backgrounds
- Deal with cross-cultural misunderstandings

DEAL WITH CONFLICT SITUATIONS (THHGCS03B)

Elements

- Identify conflict situations
- Resolve conflict situations
- Respond to customer complaints

CHAPTER FIFTEEN

Communicating in the workplace

OBJECTIVES

This chapter deals with verbal, non-verbal and written communication. On completion of this chapter you will be able to:

- describe differences in verbal, non-verbal and written communication, giving workplace examples
- provide assistance to internal and external customers
- maintain personal presentation standards
- communicate effectively in the workplace.

Sometimes mistakes can have positive results. I once made a booking for an elderly couple and their friends at a very expensive hotel in the Dandenongs. The deal that I negotiated was better than even I had expected. In fact, the hotel reservations agent made a mistake but she was unable to change the rate she had charged as we had it in writing. I never told my client, who came back into the office in raptures about his holiday and what good value it had been. He has since booked some very expensive tours through our office and has told all his friends about the amazing deals that I can negotiate! In the end it has led to thousands of dollars worth of bookings and an impressive client list.

TRAVEL AGENT

This travel agent was lucky that she could build her reputation on someone else's mistake. All forms of communication are important, but in this case the verbal discussion about rates with the reservations agent and the written confirmation of the rate quoted prevented her having to go back to the client to change arrangements because of someone else's error.

In this chapter and the chapters that follow, the principles of effective communication discussed can be applied to both external customers and internal customers. External customers include guests, clients and suppliers. Internal customers include colleagues, team members, managers and employees from other departments.

Non-verbal communication is particularly relevant in the hospitality industry where customers expect prompt attention. Questioning and listening are other key elements of effective communication.

Verbal communication

Slang and jargon can lead to misunderstandings with both customers and colleagues. Slang changes from generation to generation and this can lead to problems in the workplace where staff are often quite disparate in age. Misunderstandings can also occur with other employees for whom English is not their first language.

Following are examples of slang that could be encountered in the hospitality industry.

Australian slang

Places	People
Back of beyond	Cabbie
Back water	Dag
Banana land	Dingbat
Oz	Galah
Tassie	Grease monkey
	Hostie
Food	Kiwi
Brekkie	Knucklehead
Bush tucker	Muso
Chew and spew (takeaway food!)	Yobbo
Chook	
Damper	
Junk food	**Children**
	Ankle-biter
	Carpet grub
Alcohol	Nipper
Amber	Rug rat
Brew	Tyke
Brownie	
Snort	

Any of these terms used in conversation with customers or colleagues could lead to confusion and, at times, distress. 'Will you be taking the nippers with you on holiday?' could be quite puzzling for someone who didn't know what 'nipper' meant. Likewise if they were told that there was a lot of 'junk food' for sale in the vicinity of their motel!

The expressions (idioms) below might also cause confusion if used in the workplace when there are problems:

> What a kafuffle!
> Don't do your nut.
> Don't pull a fast one on me.
> Stop frothing at the mouth.
> Don't come the raw prawn with me.

Don't get your knickers in a knot.
You're a slow poke.
Pull the other leg.
You can do it standing on your head.
Nothing to it.
Don't chuck a wobbly.
Catch you later.

And of course the question, 'Are you right?', confuses many people who are looking for service. Interpreted literally by a non-Australian, this phrase could be confusing, almost as confusing as the one that follows: 'The sweat is that duffers who don't know the lingo have a devil of a job coming to grips with something that really is a piece of cake for Aussies'. This would require quite careful translation.

Jargon is another form of speech that can cause difficulty for both employees and guests. People who start new jobs in the industry say that they have to learn a whole new language. Below are some of the terms that you might encounter:

Guaranteed booking	Room guaranteed due to advance payment received from customer or room guaranteed by credit card even if guest fails to arrive
Confirmed booking	Hotel reservation confirmed verbally or in writing
Adjoining rooms	Rooms that abut along the corridor but do not connect through a private door
Connecting rooms	Rooms that connect through a private door
Cut-off time	Time at which room is released for sale owing to non-arrival of guest
Check-out time	Time by which guests must check out or be charged an extra day
Posting	Adding expense items to a guest account
Skipper	A person who departs leaving an unpaid bill
Overstay	A guest who stays beyond the date reserved

An awareness that these terms are commonly used in the workplace but are seldom understood by those who have not been through induction and training is essential. These terms are useful only when communicating with others in the hospitality workplace who understand their meaning.

Common verbal misunderstandings

Verbal misunderstanding often occurs when asking someone of a different culture to do something. In Australia we usually end a request with 'please' and a higher tone of voice. An opener, such as 'Would you mind' or 'I wonder if', is also commonly used. This is not necessarily the case in other cultures. Many languages do not include a word for 'please' or it is not customary to use it in many situations.

In addition to using the word 'please', the English language includes numerous ways of making requests without sounding overbearing. A request is often expressed with a 'could' or with a raised tone at the end of the question. Several possibilities are given below:

> Would you carry my bags **downstairs**?
> Do you think you **could** carry my bags downstairs?
> **Please** could you carry my bags downstairs?
> Would you **mind** carrying my bags downstairs **please**?

There are varying degrees of politeness in these phrases and it is easy to see how difficult the English language is for those accustomed to communicating in another language and learning to communicate in English. The words used, together with tone of voice and emphasis, communicate a great deal if you understand the language well. If you don't, misunderstandings can easily occur.

Non-verbal communication

There are various forms of non-verbal communication. The term 'body language' is sometimes used to describe non-verbal communication; however non-verbal communication is a much broader concept. If someone keeps you waiting while they talk on the phone, this 'timing' is a form of non-verbal communication. 'Timing' conveys that their conversation is too important to interrupt in order to serve you. If they turn their back on you, this too is a form of body language.

Non-verbal communication can be broadly divided into the following categories.

Head movements and facial expression

Smiles, eye contact and head movements are among the most important aspects of non-verbal communication in the services sector. Although some cultures, such as the Japanese, are less accustomed to eye contact, most others expect it. If a salesperson does not make eye contact, they appear inattentive, as if they are concentrating on something other than you. Bowing and nodding to others in passing is another form of non-verbal communication and the natural thing to do is to respond accordingly.

Voice qualities

Voice qualities such as loudness, emphasis, pitch and speed are important aspects of non-verbal communication and can convey quite different meanings.

Loudness

In most cultures, if someone speaks very softly, it can be interpreted as a lack of confidence. At the opposite end of the scale, someone who speaks very loudly is generally seen as overbearing. The volume of the voice needs to be tempered by the level of noise in the environment and the volume of the voice of the listener. In conversation most people follow one another's lead in managing the loudness of their voice.

Emphasis

If particular words are important they are usually given emphasis. Emphasis can also be linked to inflection. If a request such as 'You'll remember the special requirements for Mr Johann?' were said with no inflection at the end it would sound very flat and would indicate that it was not very important. If, on the other hand, the emphasis were placed on 'remember', with a slightly sarcastic tone, you would possibly be quite offended by the inference that you might have forgotten. If the emphasis were placed on 'you', the supervisor would sound very domineering.

Pitch

People with high-pitched voices are often regarded as unsure of themselves because a high pitch is commonly associated with young children. Low pitch, when used continuously, indicates boredom or lack of interest. Moderation in pitch keeps the listener's attention. To show that you are interested and enthusiastic, you need to vary your pitch.

Speed

People who speak very quickly are hard to follow if you are not familiar with the language or the jargon they are using. Speaking rapidly can communicate impatience; speaking slowly can indicate that you are unsure and grappling for the right information. However, if the customer is not familiar with the language, or the context of the communication, the service provider should slow down their pace of speaking.

Gestures

Hand and arm movements can be used to reinforce messages and to close the distance between individuals. Gestures can be used both to emphasise and to demonstrate. One of the most effective strategies for breaking down interpersonal barriers is to hand the customer something and to take it back. This physical interaction reinforces the verbal interaction. You might have noticed that door-to-door salespeople often hand you something as soon as you open the door. By accepting it you are already far more committed to the conversation than you would have been if you had not.

Posture

Good posture is regarded as an indicator of confidence and poise. It is one of the selection criteria for many positions in the tourism and hospitality industry, including airline, hotel, restaurant and tour guide positions.

Orientation of the body

The position of the body in relation to the other person's is another form of non-verbal communication. If your body were turned slightly away, this would indicate that you were not fully attentive. Turning away is generally regarded in our culture as a 'flight' position and conveys that you have other things you need to do (or would rather do). However, other cultures may use this as a gesture of politeness.

Touching

Touching includes handshaking and patting on the back or arm. There is some debate about the acceptability of shaking hands with customers and this is further complicated by the fact that hospitality staff deal with many different people across many different ages and many different cultures. Patting could also be seen as too intimate a gesture in many service situations. However, many overseas customers say that they enjoy the friendly spontaneity of Australian service, which more than likely includes a friendly pat on the back or a warm handshake.

Use of space

Space also communicates messages. If you are an executive, you are likely to have a larger desk and a larger office. The smaller and more cramped the office, the less prestigious is the image. A large, spacious office implies substantial rent, amongst other things. Likewise, more expensive restaurants tend to have more open areas and larger spaces between tables. With hotel rooms, the more spacious the room, the higher the price.

Human space, or the distance between people, is another form of non-verbal communication. The degree of distance that is acceptable varies between cultures.

Use of time

Punctuality is handled very differently by different cultures. Some countries value punctuality and their people are highly offended if you are late. In others, time is not as important and not as much attention is paid to punctuality.

Timing, however, is very important in the service context and keeping customers waiting is a common cause of dissatisfaction. Acknowledging waiting customers is essential. Finding ways to keep them busy, such as providing menus or brochures, is also essential. You do not want them to turn around and walk out!

Clothing

Uniforms are designed with messages in mind. The most formal are in dark colours with gold braid while the least formal are brightly coloured. Covering of the arms and legs is another aspect of uniform design, which takes into account the image desired by the establishment.

Uniforms in the tropics tend to be lighter and less formal.

Dirty, crumpled uniforms are not uncommon in young staff who are untrained in the domestic skills of bleaching, soaking and ironing. Indeed, many young people who have recently left home forget to wash and iron until it is too late. Dirty, scruffy collars, torn hems and unmatched socks are further examples of slovenly uniform standards. Shoes need to be well maintained. If black shoes are required, they should be made of leather. Sneakers, even if black, do not meet safety regulations in the kitchen and their smell makes them inappropriate in the food and beverage department. Cotton or cotton blend shirts are more comfortable to wear in the heat; polyester should be avoided as it makes one perspire.

Industry standards for clothing describe the minimum expectations of all employees in the industry. Enterprise standards describe the specific expectations of particular establishments. The most critical aspects of personal presentation relate to hygiene.

Personal hygiene and grooming

Not only does it look dreadful to see a chef or waiter rub his or her nose or touch his or her hair while working, but there are health reasons why this is not a good idea. Hair should be clean and tied back neatly, or a chef's hat should be worn. Hands should be washed often, very thoroughly after going to the toilet, after blowing the nose or after touching the face. Hands should also be washed after handling raw meat or poultry and after peeling vegetables that may still have soil on them. Clean skin, minimal make-up, perfect nails without polish and clean breath are all important aspects of professional presentation.

Since smell is such an important aspect of taste, heavy perfume or lavish use of deodorant (a little is recommended) can interfere with the food smells that should start the mouth watering.

Personal presentation differs from one enterprise to another based on:
- enterprise requirements (each hospitality workplace has a different style and decor that is enhanced by matching staff uniforms that need to be worn consistently)
- work location (for example, uniforms designed for working in the tropics tend to be lighter in weight and colour and less formal)
- occupational health and safety issues (chefs must wear closed-toe shoes with steel caps for safety reasons)
- impact on different types of customers (customers from some countries expect formality and find it offensive if staff are underdressed)
- specific requirements for particular work functions (for example, staff working in departments such as the outdoor pool area would be expected to wear hats and long sleeves for sun protection).

Environment and decor

Decor also communicates messages. A gold and marble foyer in a hotel indicates luxury and you would expect to pay top rates for the rooms. Lighting is an aspect of the environment that has an influence on how comfortable people feel. In restaurants and banquet rooms where the lights are too bright everyone feels uncomfortable, even though this may be unconscious. When the lights are dimmed, people relax and interact more freely. Again, this is culturally based.

Etiquette

Knowledge of etiquette is essential for staff working in this industry, especially as eating at home becomes less and less formal. These customs come into play when

FIG. 15.1

Table setting.

2.5 cm

formal meals are served, for example in fine dining restaurants and at banquets. Fig. 15.1 shows the correct way to set a table.

As traditions change, and the roles of men and women as hosts change with them, understanding etiquette becomes quite a challenge. In earlier times it was unheard of for a woman to choose and taste the wine, or pay the bill. Today, waiting staff need to be aware of, and sensitive to, these changes. As a female host, it can be quite embarrassing if the bill is presented to your guest when you thought you had made it clear to the waiter (by placing the order yourself) that you were the host.

Written communication

Expressing yourself in writing is easy if three important rules are followed: your writing should be clear, correct and concise. These days people no longer write formal letters but write the way they speak. To be clear about what you are trying to say, you need to adopt a logical structure and to use everyday words. When you have finished writing, check the message to make sure it will be clear to the person reading it. The information should be accurate and the spelling and grammar should be correct. Finally, it is important to be concise. People are more receptive if you express your ideas or requests briefly. The three rules for effective writing are summarised in Fig. 15.2 and illustrated in a memo from a chef to a restaurant manager in Fig. 15.3.

FIG. 15.2

Effective written communication.

CLEAR

CONCISE

CORRECT

The different media for communicating in the hospitality workplace include:

- Internet (bookings and reservations are increasingly made using the Internet as a communications device)
- Email (usually used by customers to ask more complex questions or by staff to communicate with each other)
- Fax (orders for lunch takeaway food are often sent by fax)
- Telephone (Housekeeping is the invisible department contacted by telephone by guests who have special requests such as towels and pillows)
- Two-way communication systems (radio type systems are common in large resorts where, for example, staff may travel around on buggies)
- Face-to-face (the most common form of communication among staff members in busy areas)
- Simple written messages (restaurant bookings and phone messages)
- Standard forms and pro formas (a standard form, called a requisition form, is used when ordering supplies—it is only one of many forms used and is an important control system).

The selection of the appropriate medium is based on a variety of factors including the urgency, degree of formality required and access to the necessary equipment. For example, a staff member involved in an emergency situation at a resort may use a two-way radio and would follow emergency protocols to the letter.

FIG. 15.3

Sample memo written in concise, clear language.

MEMO

Date: 20 October 2002

To: Helen Harley

From: Frank Vermeuelen

Re: Orders to the kitchen

Dear Helen

We need to improve the ordering process. Last week one order went missing. I am not blaming anyone in your department for this, only asking that all staff (including mine) take greater care with orders.

Also, some orders are very hard to read and this can lead to mistakes. In your next staff meeting please ask your staff to write clearly and explain what can happen if the chef makes a mistake because she can't read the order.

Thanks

Frank

Accessing and organising information

Knowing where to find information is a valuable skill for hospitality employees. The telephone directories for all states and territories are now on the Internet and reservations systems for airlines and hotels are all linked for instant access. Australian and overseas newspapers are also available on the Internet these days. If someone asked you for the average daily temperature for February in Jakarta you should be able to answer the question.

Once information has been found, it needs to be organised and summarised. This involves note taking or highlighting key points. The data then needs to be categorised and filed alphabetically. This chapter includes an activity that requires research and organising skills, and an ability to respond to queries regarding some aspect of the research. An index, with summaries, will assist you in answering promptly.

To respond quickly to queries you must be either very knowledgeable or very organised. For both activities at the end of this chapter you will be required to be both knowledgeable and organised so that you can respond appropriately, courteously and quickly to questions.

Checking information

Information needs to be accurate and to achieve this the best thing to do is to check everything. When completing workplace documents, it is essential to check all the information carefully. When taking down details, key information should be repeated, or summarised at the end. This helps to ensure that misunderstandings do not occur. Taking the birthday party reservation at the end of this chapter as an example, a check would need to be done on the number of guests just before the night to ensure that catering was accurate, otherwise the event might be unprofitable for management, and to ensure that all seats at the table were filled for the convenience of the guests. Check, check and check again is the motto of many catering companies which work off site and cannot afford to forget anything. Check lists are often developed for this purpose.

Confidentiality

One final and important point about handling verbal and written information is confidentiality. When Michael Jackson visited Australia, the press was unable to obtain even one interesting fact about him from the hotel staff who had been sworn to secrecy. In both the tourism and hospitality sectors, discretion is very important and is highly valued by customers.

Listening

Listening is arguably the most important communication skill for anyone in a sales or service position. Careful listening can cut down the amount of information you need to find. In fact, much time can be saved by asking questions and listening attentively.

The technique of asking open questions has already been discussed in Chapter 3. Another useful technique is paraphrasing. By repeating parts of the message you are receiving, you show the customer that you are being attentive and fully understanding what they are saying. This encourages the person to continue. You might say something like, 'You want to go on a tour to see natural environments but you want to be comfortable? You would like something leisurely, interesting and linked to the natural environment?' Finally, the use of mm's and uh ha's, combined with attentive body language such as nodding, will also encourage the speaker. This is called giving feedback or back channelling.

To sum up, listening can become more active by:
• using attentive body language
• making positive noises and giving feedback
• repeating parts of the sender's message
• asking open questions.

Activities

1 Assemble a range of information about attractions in your local area for tourists. This should include information on natural attractions, fun parks, zoos, museums, entertainment, dining out, and any other information you would need at your fingertips if you were the concierge of a hotel, such as information about shopping, banking, medical assistance and child care. If available, historical material on your local area and any notable landmarks should also be collected. This information should be drawn from a range of sources (information centres, newspapers, libraries, the Internet, etc.). Once collected, it should be categorised and indexed. Then, using your assembled information, act out the role of a concierge in a five-star hotel answering a range of queries from guests.

2 The following reservation form is provided for large bookings in your restaurant. Use the form to make a reservation for a 21st birthday party, with the following special requests:

Restaurant Luccio

295 Beach Road Sandy Hills 4096
Telephone (02) 9928 6129 **Fax** (02) 9928 6190

Reservations Form

Guest name _____

Address _____

Telephone number _____

Fax number _____

Number of guests _____

Table number _____

Arrival time _____

Confirmation _____

Special requests _____

_____

_____

- One long table seating 14 guests is needed.
- Specific seating for guests is required, with names on the table.
- A three-course meal (entree, main and dessert) is expected for the standard price of $35 per head (you need to negotiate the menu details).
- A pink colour scheme has been planned (which could be taken through to the food too).
- Wine and beer (you need to discuss brands) will be provided, but guests must pay for spirits.
- The cake will be served after coffee and there needs to be a microphone for the speeches.
- The host will pay by credit card and you need a $500 deposit.

Having finalised the reservation, send a confirmation to the host in writing. This should be accurate and should enhance the establishment's image. If you wish, you could also reinforce the party theme.

Discussion questions

1 What is the difference between slang and jargon?
2 Give your own examples of Australian slang that tourists might not understand.
3 Find your own examples of industry jargon that customers or employees might find hard to understand.
4 Discuss the different types of non-verbal communication.
5 Discuss a range of sources from which you could find out about the weather in all Australian capital cities.

CHAPTER SIXTEEN

Providing service to colleagues and customers

OBJECTIVES

This chapter focuses on the important issue of customer relations. On completion of this significant chapter you should be able to:

- identify the elements of good customer service
- compare the different expectations of a range of customers
- describe customer relations techniques that ensure customer satisfaction
- make recommendations for improved customer relations in specific situations
- describe methods for dealing with customer complaints.

This chapter features a job description for an entry position at the Hyatt Hotel in Canberra. This is a particularly good job description because it reinforces many of the points made in the last chapter about communication. It also mentions 'exceeding guest expectations' which is the focal point of this chapter.

Dealing with the tricky issue of customer complaints will also be covered, together with the all-important need to seek feedback so that the quality of services can be improved. We will also deal in greater depth with a couple of international tourist groups, and their customs and interests.

Reading the job description below, we can see many of the points mentioned earlier reinforced, such as uniform and personal presentation. And there is emphasis on policies relating to fire, hygiene, health and safety, which is timely as these are the topics of chapters that follow. However, in this chapter we will again focus on the customer even though much has already been said. The customer cannot be emphasised enough as hospitality is, above all, a service industry.

JOB DESCRIPTION

Job Title	Waiter/ess
Areas of Work	The Promenade Cafe
Division	Food and Beverage
Division Head	Director of Food and Beverage

Basic Function	To follow all directions regarding the operation of the Promenade Cafe and to maintain all standards of food and beverage service consistent with established outlet operation policies and procedures
Responsible To	Manager/Assistant Manager/Team Leader/Host
Responsible For	None

Main Duties and Accountabilities

1 Have a sound knowledge of all menu and beverage items and ensure prompt and efficient service following standard operating procedures.
2 Maintain flexible and willing attitude, service guests using friendly, polite and courteous manner at all times. Exceed guest expectations.
3 Constantly check that assigned section is clean and all tables are set up correctly.
4 To attend all training sessions and Department meetings.
5 To attend to all guests' requests and to immediately refer any problems that they cannot deal with back to their immediate supervisor.
6 To report for duty punctually wearing the correct uniform and name badge at all times.
7 To maintain good working relationships with your own colleagues, Management and all other Departments.
8 To maintain a high standard of personal appearance and hygiene at all times.
9 To have a complete understanding of the Employees Handbook and adhere to the regulations contained within.
10 To have a complete understanding of and adhere to the Hotel's Policy relating to Fire, Hygiene, Health and Safety.
11 To ensure service stations are fully stocked and kept clean during service.
12 Remember you are part of a team, so take pride in your team's performance.
13 To prepare all necessary mise-en-place.
14 If in doubt, do not guess, ask the Supervisor.
15 If leaving your section, inform your Supervisor.
16 To carry out any other reasonable duties and responsibilities as assigned.

Reproduced with the permission of The Hyatt Hotel, Canberra.

Understanding customer needs

Many, many books have been written about customer service. It is such an intangible thing, mainly because customers differ in two major ways—they have different expectations and they have different perceptions. Developing a better understanding of the customer is essential and this can be done by studying their

- activities and interests (golf, art, music, wildlife) (see Figs 16.1 and 16.2)
- cultural factors (diet, etiquette, customs)
- socio-economic factors (wealth, disposable income, status, place of origin)
- health (ranging from totally unfit to ready for any challenge)
- available time (short weekend break, week-long visit to take in the whole of Australia, extended visit, e.g. backpacking)

- age (babies, young children, teenagers, young adults, adults, mature adults)
- personality (extrovert, introvert, lazy, energetic).

With all of these different profiles, customers have different needs. They select their hospitality destinations based on their needs, and their expectations are developed according to the advertising and other promotions they have seen. Even if an establishment has been portrayed accurately, all customers will have different perceptions of it, depending on their cultural or social backgrounds. By communicating effectively, through observing, listening and questioning, staff are able to accurately identify the needs and expectations of their customers. Staff must then ensure that these needs are met, even if they are not within their own area of responsibility, by exceeding expectations wherever possible. Providing information and promoting other services that are available are excellent ways to meet unrecognised needs. Customers can become very frustrated if they have to actively seek out information. Most prefer the information to be offered to them by attentive staff. However, selling the services of your establishment must be matched to customer needs: some prefer a passive approach, while others prefer suggestive selling where advice is given on what they should do and how to do it.

In addition to selling the particular enterprise, staff in the tourism and hospitality industry should sell their country to international visitors who want an insight into Australian culture and history, as well as an understanding of the history and culture of the local area. Guests often praise employees who take pride in their country and initiate conversations that are interesting and informative on satisfaction cards requesting feedback, which they complete at the end of their stay.

Although not showing it in the best light, the following article describes the area called The Rocks (which is situated under the Sydney Harbour Bridge and is visited by nearly every overseas visitor to Australia) in 1858, many, many years before it became a popular tourist attraction. Information such as this is of great interest to many tourists.

FIG. 16.1

Top ten leisure activities of international visitors to Australia 1997.

Type of activity	No. of Visitors
Going to the beach	1510
Visiting national parks	1351
Visiting wildlife parks and zoos	1232
Guided tours or excursions	1232
Visiting botanical/public gardens	1192
Visiting historical/heritage sites, buildings, monuments	1152
Visiting casinos	755
Visiting amusement/theme parks	675
Visiting museums/art galleries	556
Going to discos/other night life	397

Source: *International Visitor Survey*, 1997, Bureau of Tourism Research. Reproduced with permission.

FIG. 16.2

Selected leisure activities of domestic travellers 1997–1998.

Leisure activity	No. of Travellers
Visiting friends or relatives	7983
Driving and sightseeing	6388
Attending special events	3294
Participating in sport/recreational activity	3019
Visiting theatre, opera, ballet, concert, cinema	2874
Visiting animal parks, wildlife reserves, zoos	2238
Visiting entertainment and theme parks	1828
Visiting museums/art galleries	1436

Source: *National Visitor Survey*, 1998, Bureau of Tourism Research. Reproduced with permission.

These streets are at least not roads, being scarcely traversable by vehicles, and destitute of all signs of forming, metalling or guttering. The houses which line them are small and comparatively ancient stone cottages, so unevenly and irregularly built that the doorstep of one residence sometimes approximates the eaves of another. Where the erections are of wood their dilapidated, filthy appearance is all the more striking. The interior of these abodes normally consists of two dirty bare rusty-coloured chambers, of small size, and yet too large for the scanty articles which constitute their furniture. Of the inhabitants I will not say much: in some cases misfortune may have led and may keep them there; but in others the unhappy, debauched, wicked face, the slovenly, dirtily clothed person, tell too plain a tale.

But what chiefly requires remedy in this ill-favoured locality, is the utter absence of all means of drainage or of removing filthy matter, which consequently lies where it is and poisons the ground beneath and the air above. It is a positive fact that in many cases the foul drainage of one cottage trickles down the hill till it encounters, as the case may be, the back or front wall of the house next below; here it accumulates, soaking down into the foundations, or sometimes actually running in at the door. (*Sydney Morning Herald*, 7 October 1858)

Providing service to customers

In providing service to customers (and to colleagues—internal customers—for that matter) the following guidelines are most useful.

Identify customer needs

Identify customer needs and expectations correctly, including those with special needs, and provide appropriate products, services and information. Products are things such as meals and tours, while services are things such as babysitting or making reservations. Customers with special needs might include those with a disability, those with specific cultural and language needs, unaccompanied children, parents with young children or customers who are unwell.

Meet time frames

Meet all reasonable needs and requests of customers within acceptable enterprise time frames. Every customer sees his or her needs as the most urgent. In practice customers' needs have to be prioritised to some extent so that, for example, the guest who has inadvertently soaked his bath towel is provided with another straightaway while the guest who needs a softer pillow can wait just a little longer. Emergency and risk situations (such as gas smells) need to be investigated immediately. This may involve escalating the issue to a higher level and involving other people.

Enhance the quality of service

Identify and take all opportunities to enhance the quality of service. Customers are pleasantly surprised if additional and unexpected services, or information, are provided. 'You asked for the *Financial Review* yesterday and it is already on your breakfast table, Sir', or 'I have telephoned the restaurant and they have faxed the specials for the day'.

Recognise dissatisfaction

Recognise customer problems and dissatisfaction promptly and take action to resolve the situation according to your level of responsibility and enterprise procedures.

Customers often have problems, so problem-solving skills are essential for hospitality staff. Here is a list of problems commonly expressed by customers:

The air-conditioning is too cold.
My meal is overcooked.
It is too noisy in here.
The water in the bathroom is not hot enough.
I can't open the window.
There is nothing I like on the menu.
I am running late, I will miss the flight.
This is not what I expected.
There are not enough beds in the room for the children.
Your prices are too high.
The people at the next table are annoying.
Someone took my place after I had reserved that poker machine.

All these statements represent problems, and most of them can be easily resolved. For the most part, customers are not complaining, they are indicating that there is a problem. Taking a problem-solving approach is a positive way to resolve issues of this type. To refer to 90 per cent of the problems experienced by customers as complaints, or indeed to refer to them as conflict situations, is unnecessary. The hospitality industry is a service industry, and staff should notice non-verbal clues and listen carefully to what customers are saying in order to resolve problems early. Positive steps to solve problems should be a standard part of quality service.

Handle complaints sensitively

Handle customer complaints sensitively and politely in consultation with the customer. Finding out what is wrong is the most effective way of improving the quality of the products or services provided to customers. Complaints and suggestions should be welcomed: 'Thank you for bringing that to my attention'. Complaint handling will be covered in more detail later in the chapter.

Refer difficult problems and complaints

Sometimes the complaint is sufficiently serious for it to be referred to a more senior staff member. A mistake on a restaurant booking for a large party might create a serious situation unless handled creatively by, for example, opening one of the function rooms after negotiating with the functions department.

Document issue and action

For legal and other reasons, including quality management, it is important to document issues and the steps taken to resolve them. A follow-up process of checking that all matters have been satisfactorily resolved is a valuable final step.

Throughout the process of problem-solving (see Fig. 16.3 on page 190), it is essential to maintain a positive and helpful attitude, rather than a defensive one. It is your aim to please, and problem-solving is a core part of any hospitality employee's duties.

FIG. 16.3

Problem-solving process.

> Listen (sensitively, with discretion)
> Acknowledge (establish details)
> Respond (take action)
> Report (refer if needed)
> Follow up (documentation and checking)

Understanding international visitors' needs

In Chapter 2 a few market segments (customers who display similar characteristics) were introduced. Now, two groups of international tourists, and their needs and expectations, will be explored in some depth to illustrate how widely different the interests of groups can be. This is done, however, with some caution as there is the risk of stereotyping, which was mentioned earlier. Too rigid stereotyping of customers into defined groups can be limiting. This knowledge is helpful, but a flexible attitude in dealing with customers from all walks of life is essential. There are many who do not fit the mould!

Japanese visitors

Because the Japanese value hard work, they take very short holidays. Many try to visit the capital cities on the east coast of Australia and the major attractions. This is hard to achieve, given the distances involved. Japan is approximately half the size of New South Wales and has a population of 124 million (Australia, 20 million). There is a strong sense of group cohesion but, although tour groups are common, Japanese tourists are increasingly travelling independently. Punctuality and formality are highly regarded. Japanese use first names with family and friends, in all other cases using the family name for address. This can lead to confusion over which is the first name and which is the family name and needs to be clarified for reasons of courtesy and accurate recording of reservations. Japanese find prolonged eye-contact uncomfortable, as we have mentioned. Greeting by means of a small bow and brief eye contact is advised. They will seldom say 'No' or complain formally.

Malaysian visitors

Malaysia's economy has grown rapidly. It is a country with 13 states and several ethnic groups, the Malays, Chinese and Indians. Each group has its own culture and customs. Most Malays are Muslims. They do not eat pork or drink alcohol. The fasting month of Ramadan is strictly adhered to, with fasting from sunrise to sunset. Muslims eat with the right hand and with spoons. Public displays of intimacy are taboo. The head is sacred and must not be touched. For Chinese Malays pointing is also unacceptable, and so too are public displays of affection. When near the opposite sex it is customary to stand at least a metre away.

From these two examples we can see how useful a study of the cultures of visitors can be. The next step is to decide how the needs of these tourists can be met. Too determined an effort to match the language and customs of the visitor group would eclipse the friendly, relaxed atmosphere that is part of the Australian culture and has such appeal for visitors. Japanese visitors to the Gold Coast have been known to complain that it is too Japanese!

Providing appropriate service

There are many special needs expressed by customers and it is necessary that these are attended to efficiently by hospitality staff. For example, careful attention to the special diets of customers is vital as allergic reactions to foods such as MSG (monosodium glutamate), wheat and dairy products can be severe for some people. Needs are sometimes expressed non-verbally, by looking at a watch, for instance, or trying to catch someone's eye, so understanding customer needs can require a high degree of insight and sensitivity. The following factors distinguish good service personnel:

- effective non-verbal and verbal communication
- sensitivity to special needs and anticipation of unexpressed needs
- offering courteous service, advice and information
- promoting the establishment and its products and services
- promoting the local area and its attractions
- promoting the country and its history.

The profile of Joy from Hamilton Island Resort illustrates what good service is all about.

Joy has worked at Hamilton Island Resort for nearly two years. The activities she co-ordinates generally attract a wide range of people of different age groups, interests and nationalities. On some occasions she has been known to run two activities simultaneously. Joy has the most extraordinary ability to quickly develop rapport with guests and to build relationships with and between them. One of her skills is a capacity to remember names, an attribute appreciated by guests when she greets them by name several days after meeting them. This is a significant and important part of her job. Her ability to meet at least 50 new people each day—and remember them—makes her an asset to her employer and to the hospitality industry.

The role of hospitality employees is to find out as much as possible about their customers' needs and then to obtain feedback (verbal and non-verbal) about their level of satisfaction. The key steps are to:

- establish the client's name and its correct pronunciation
- observe carefully, watching for non-verbal and other cues
- ask questions

- provide appropriate information
- speak clearly and more slowly than usual if necessary
- repeat if necessary (not loudly—the customer is not deaf!)
- ask more questions, seeking feedback on whether you are on the right track
- guess meanings from the context
- obtain information from written documents the customer may have (brochures or tickets)
- give one piece of information at a time (don't give unnecessary or confusing information)
- show the customer what you mean by using pictures or maps
- confirm details
- provide the required service or product
- seek feedback on whether expectations have been met
- continue to observe carefully, watching for non-verbal cues
- follow up to see whether your customer is satisfied.

A final suggestion for improved communication is to offer choices in order to narrow down the possibilities: 'Would you like . . . or . . .?' is a good strategy when dealing with customers who are unfamiliar with the options, and then to ask which the customer prefers, ideally while showing them a brochure.

As already mentioned, in many cultures around the world the word 'no' is not often used. For example, in some countries, if you explained something and then asked the person if they understood you they would always answer 'Yes'. To say 'No' would mean that you had not communicated clearly. Therefore to be polite or to avoid embarrassment the person would say 'Yes'. In many cultures it is also rude to refuse food and, once again, offering a choice would enable the person to select as much or as little as they pleased. For this reason buffets have proved very popular with international tourists.

Some other tips for effective cross-cultural communication include:
- Avoid double negatives ('You can't go on the tour if you haven't booked a ticket in advance').
- Use simple English words.
- Be logical in your explanations.
- Use short sentences and simple sentence structures.
- Use pictures or symbols.
- Show or demonstrate what you are trying to convey.
- Give only the key information.
- Avoid jargon and idioms.

If you were to visit a foreign country and you weren't fluent in the language, you would expect that people would assist you in this way.

Handling complaints

The following case study provides a good example of unexpected reactions from customers. It illustrates the value of customer relations experience and exposure to situations in which quick decisions have to be made.

Denz was working for a seaside hotel as a car parking valet. On a particularly busy day a guest arrived to pick up her car, and he was the staff member who arrived with the car in the front driveway, following a request to the garage to bring it upstairs. The customer had several complaints, the most serious being that there was a scratch on the passenger door. Unfortunately this type of complaint is not uncommon as drivers seldom see their passenger doors (they usually get into the car on the driver's side) unless standing waiting in a hotel driveway.

The hotel's standard operating procedure for car parking involved checking the car and noting any damage on the rear of the parking ticket before taking it down to the garage. Fortunately, on this occasion, the person who had parked the car had done his job properly (staff often forgot to do this when in a hurry). Denz was most relieved to be able to point out the diagram on the back and quickly scotch the complaint. The guest snatched the keys and marched around to the driver's seat, getting out again almost as soon as she got in. This time the complaint was that the car showed many more kilometres than when she left it, and smelt of pizza. She accused Denz of using her car to buy pizza. With no evidence to the contrary, all Denz could do was calmly explain to the guest that her car had not been used for any other purpose and had been parked directly after she had handed over the keys. This had to be restated several times while other cars banked up behind. The Duty Manager quietly intervened to assure the customer that staff were obliged to follow standard operating procedures. He said he hoped that she would visit the hotel again and asked if she would mind moving her car as there were several others waiting and the traffic was becoming congested.

In every job in this industry complaints will occur. Sometimes they are the customer's fault, sometimes the establishment does not meet the customer's expectations, sometimes a staff member makes a mistake, and sometimes another guest causes a problem. There are as many reasons for complaint as there are complaints. The point is if the complaint is aired, something can be done about it. Complaints are an important source of feedback on how services can be improved.

The following are standard steps for handling difficult situations (see also Fig. 16.4):

1 Focus on the customer and listen carefully and attentively. Sometimes a small problem is a symptom of a larger one. Listening is the most effective way to diffuse a situation and interrupting, the most likely way to exacerbate it. Questions and prompts can help the customer get the complaint off their chest. In some cases this is all that is required as the customer just wants to let off steam about an unexpected delay or something similar.

2 Be courteous, using the customer's name, and be discreet. Where possible, take the customer away from others and handle embarrassing or noisy problems with discretion.

FIG. 16.4

Handling complaints.

Focus on customer
↓
Listen attentively
↓
Be courteous and discreet
↓
Suggest alternatives
↓
Refer if necessary
↓
Implement solution
↓
Follow up
↓
Record the situation

3 Suggest alternative steps that can be taken to resolve the problem. Even if there is nothing that can be done for this customer, thank them for bringing the problem to your attention to ensure that it will not happen to others.

4 If necessary, take the problem to someone who can better handle it. However, this does not mean passing the buck. You should continue to stand by and see it through to a resolution.

5 Finding a solution and implementing a solution are two different things. If Housekeeping has been asked to provide pillows 'because no-one should be expected to sleep on the concrete bags you call pillows', then check to ensure that the pillows have been delivered.

6 Follow up the customer to make sure that they are satisfied. Thank them again for bringing it to your attention.

7 Record the situation. Most hospitality establishments have logbooks, which are used to record incidents that have occurred. Any incident could be taken further at a later time and an accurate record of events is vitally important for legal reasons. The data in the logbook can also be used as the basis for improving operations.

Benefits of good service

The recurring theme throughout this chapter has been how to understand customer needs and perceptions and how they make decisions. Rather than trying to speculate about customers who may walk in the door, staff need to learn instead from the ones who are there, or who have been there.

Seeking feedback, with open-ended questions, is the most effective way to improve and modify service to meet customers' expectations and unanticipated needs. An organisation that encourages staff to request feedback, and which harnesses the feedback for the dynamic process of change, is an organisation that has the competitive edge. According to the General Manager of the Anchorage Port Stephens, a winner of the Australian Customer Service Award in the medium business category, 'Our personalised service includes speaking with at least 30 per cent of our guests and going through their experiences to see if we can make improvements'. This boutique hotel and marina resort offers unique services such as houseboat hire with room service, daily cleaning and fully equipped kitchens, as well as video and television. Like many hotels, the Anchorage keeps a detailed record of guests' likes and dislikes to assist with personalised service.

In fact, some of the simplest and most original ideas come from guests, and it is important that staff do not overlook them. In one resort, for example, a guest commented that when the information desk was closed late at night guests were unable to reach the brochures on display at the back of the booth. The guest suggested that a display rack be built in the hotel lobby to which guests could have access at all hours.

A number of benefits, as outlined below, result from good communication in the tourism and hospitality workplace, not the least of which is the achievement of a more satisfying experience for the guests and for the staff who serve them.

Time saved

When guests are given specific information, rather than huge amounts of unnecessary information, everyone saves time. Selling should not produce information overload; selling should provide exactly what the customer is looking for. Questioning is a key communication skill, as we have learnt, and it should be utilised to establish this.

Fewer mistakes

If careful listening is part of the interaction with the client, and the information is checked, fewer mistakes are likely to occur. In the travel industry, in particular, one small mistake can have dreadful repercussions.

Accurate expectations

If clients or guests are given accurate information, they will have accurate expectations. If, for example, January is the wet season in the tropical north, they should be informed of this and told what to expect.

Increased customer satisfaction

If customers' needs are fulfilled, they are likely to be satisfied with their experiences. If value is added to good, positive and professional service throughout the whole process, this will lead to even higher levels of customer satisfaction.

Increased employee morale

Working in an environment where things go smoothly (most of the time) and where both staff and customers are enjoying themselves is a decided pleasure and immensely rewarding. This is the attraction that the industry has for its employees. One hospitality employee commented that his job was more fun than work. This attitude, combined with a professional approach to communication, leads to high employee morale.

Growth in tourism and hospitality

The tourism industry is growing worldwide. However, it is also very competitive. Hawaii, for example, is a competitor for the Japanese market. New Zealand has some of the most scenic eco-tourism destinations in the world. South Africa is working hard to offer some of the most luxurious but inexpensive holidays available. It is essential that staff in the tourism industry in Australia do not become complacent and instead work towards providing the best service possible. At the moment Australia is one of the world's favourite destinations. We need to keep it that way.

Providing good service to local hospitality customers is equally important, as local hospitality establishments rely heavily on repeat business. Word of mouth travels very quickly, more so in the case of complaints than compliments. Alienating one customer can lead to alienating a whole street or a group of mothers who meet nearly every morning for coffee. Customers who enjoy personal and attentive service are far more likely to be loyal, and are quite forgiving of the occasional mistake.

In a competitive environment, retaining customers is very important as the customer has a lot of choices.

Activities

1 Visit a restaurant, coffee shop or fast food operation and closely observe some of the scenarios around you. Write up a case study similar to the one below.
2 Analyse the scenario in the following case study in terms of your knowledge of the industry and your knowledge of customer relations.
3 Visit a tourist attraction and list the various categories of visitors to the attraction. Speculate about the needs of these groups of visitors.
4 Negotiate an itinerary with a guest who is being unrealistic in wanting to see all of Australia's capital cities in five days. Remember that the customer is always right, but ensure that the information they are given leads to accurate expectations.

CASE STUDY
Filling up the spider

'I'll have a chocolate milkshake.'
'I want an alcohol-free Pina Colada.'
'Coke'.
'Banana smoothie'.
'Do you do alcohol-free cocktails?'
'Fanta'.
'What sort of alcohol-free cocktails do you do?'

The six children lounging around the hotel pool were shouting out their orders all at once, not a 'please' among them. Greg, the Room Service waiter, was attempting to write down the orders, the perspiration running down between his shoulder-blades, wishing that his shift was over.

The clamour continued, 'Do you do spiders?'
'Do you mean Coke with ice-cream float?' Greg asked.
'I'll have a spider.'
'I'll have a spider.'
'I'll have a spider.'
'I'll have a spider with Fanta.'

'And what would you like?' Greg asked the smallest girl, aged about seven, while he ripped out his original order and wrote up the latest requests.

'She'll have a milkshake, strawberry', replied her brother, the biggest child, with a strident voice, 'and we want a plate of chips'.

'With tomato sauce'.
'Barbecue sauce'.
'Do you have chilli sauce?'

'A plate of chips, sauce, three Coke spiders, one Fanta spider and a strawberry milkshake', Greg confirmed, but already the children had lost interest in him and had started arguing among themselves about the choice of bikes for the afternoon ride.

Running up the stairs to the kitchen, past the glorious blue of the swimming pool, and past the lounging guests, Greg could not help compare his level of discomfort, dressed as he was in long-sleeved shirt and black trousers, with that of the guests lazing under umbrellas. It had not been a good day. Room Service had been behind in its orders since breakfast and every customer was annoyed at the delays, many complaining to him on his rounds to deliver earlier orders. One such complaint came from the table of children, the eldest of whom beckoned to him, 'We've been waiting 20 minutes and people have been served before us'. This complaint was reiterated by his siblings and cousins who demanded their food, shouting and yelling, 'We're starving, how come it's so slow?' and 'What are you doing?'

Diplomatically suggesting that he would check on the order, Greg was fully aware that the other customers, whose orders had just been delivered, had been waiting even longer, but refrained from saying so.

The order was finally delivered, 40 minutes later, by Huong Min, who had just started his shift. Smiling broadly, he carried the tray to the table. Ignoring the remarks about the slow service, made around the table in loud voices, Huong Min placed the drinks in front of the children and offered an extra glass of Coke, saying, 'I brought this so that you could top up your spiders as the ice-cream bubbles so much'.

Turning from the table after asking the eldest to sign the room charge, he was brought to a standstill by a loud yell, 'Where's the extra Fanta to top up my spider?' Turning back to the table, he found that all the children were arguing about the chips so he shrugged his shoulders at the ten-year-old and raced off to get another order that he knew was waiting up in the kitchen.

Clearly the child's mother was able to hold a conversation with her sister-in-law and listen to the children simultaneously, as mothers are prone to do. She interrupted her speculation about the shaky marriage of a relative to deal with her child's problem. 'Ring Room Service on the pool phone and ask for more Fanta', she instructed the ten-year-old and resumed her conversation.

By the time the Fanta arrived, the ice-cream spider had long melted and the children had run off to play in the pool.

Discussion questions

1 Have you any suggestions for Greg?
2 Have you any suggestions for Huong Min?
3 Have you any suggestions for the management of this hotel?
4 The customers are all children. Develop a profile of the needs and interests of several age groups of children who visit hospitality establishments.
5 How can hospitality establishments meet the needs of these age groups?
6 Parents ultimately pay for hospitality products and reach decisions about future patronage. How should this affect the service provided for children and the interactions of staff with parents?

CHAPTER SEVENTEEN

Working in teams

OBJECTIVES

In this chapter we will give particular emphasis to working in teams in a culturally diverse workplace. Supportive, efficient, effective and courteous work team interactions are the key to job satisfaction. On completion of this chapter you will be able to:

- participate in small work teams
- accommodate individual and cultural differences
- discuss workplace issues and reach conclusions
- identify tasks and time frames
- achieve group goals.

O*ne of the staff turned on a colleague in the kitchen and shouted at him. It was just a coincidence that he was holding a knife at the time. However, this was interpreted as a physical threat and a fight broke out. A fight in a kitchen with knives and hot oil is a frightening experience. During busy periods tempers do get frayed but this was the worst misunderstanding I have ever seen. Although other staff intervened to break up the fight there was never any action taken to fully resolve the issue, and factions developed in the kitchen as a result. The situation was ripe for another confrontation when we least expected it. I couldn't work there any longer. My chef said, 'If you can't take the heat get out of the kitchen'. He insisted that this type of aggressive behaviour was found in every kitchen and that staff should adapt to the culture.*

COOKERY APPRENTICE

Teamwork is essential for effective workplace performance and customer service, especially in the tourism and hospitality industry. However, there are two factors that mitigate against group co-operation. The first of these is the mobility of the workforce. This is particularly pertinent to the hospitality industry, as staff turnover rates are high in some departments. When members of a team change frequently, it makes it difficult to establish a positive team environment. The second challenge relates to individual rewards. Where one person achieves a goal at someone else's expense, co-operative teamwork is not easy to achieve. In travel agencies, for example, staff are rewarded individually with prizes such as trips to locations which they have sold successfully. In such offices, sales by staff members are closely monitored and individual performance is measured in dollars. This can lead to minimal co-operation as each agent wants to keep clients and bookings as part of their own territory. The same applies in hospitality situations where guests tip the staff. Where this is the case, staff often work as individuals, seldom helping others during busy periods. Some restaurants solve this problem by pooling tips and sharing them amongst the waiting staff. The next question, of course, is whether kitchen staff should share the tips, too, as they are part of the team that provided the food and the service.

Where teams work towards mutually rewarding goals a spirit of co-operation will develop. In such situations communication is far more effective.

Teamwork in the hospitality industry is illustrated in Fig. 17.1. This illustration shows the number of people involved in the team that puts a beer in front of a customer in a bar. The purchasing officer orders the keg from the supplier. The keg is delivered to the stores officer and then to the cellar where it is sent through beer lines under the building to the tap at the bar. These lines and the refrigeration of the beer are the responsibility of the cellarperson and the refrigeration mechanic. The beer is then poured and sold to the customer, and the day's takings are sent to

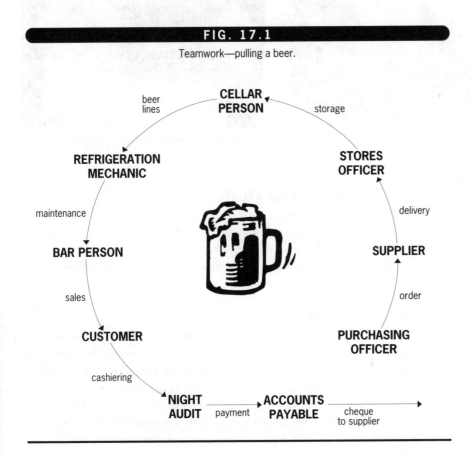

FIG. 17.1

Teamwork—pulling a beer.

the night auditor for reconciliation, then to Accounts Receivable for banking. The Accounts Payable Department, on the advice of the Stores Department, arranges for a cheque to be sent to the supplier.

Clearly customer satisfaction is the result of teamwork by all departments, and teamwork within departments. Features of effective teams are:

- demonstrating trust, support and respect towards team members
- identifying work goals for the team
- prioritising and completing work goals within deadlines
- recognising and accommodating cultural differences
- seeking and providing assistance to team members
- responding to feedback from team members
- building on quality service through continuous improvement.

A strong service ethic is essential in any hospitality enterprise. It contributes to positive attitudes and a 'can do' approach. Team spirit contributes enormously to camaraderie and the resulting friendly atmosphere of a hospitality operation.

Working co-operatively in groups benefits everyone—the employer, the employee and the customer.

Working towards group goals

In the following example, a supervisor found a solution to a situation in which one staff member had become isolated from the rest of the team because he was quite different from them. In this Housekeeping Department, staff were required to clean 12 guest rooms each day. The supervisor's aim was to develop a more cohesive work group with common goals. This is how she achieved this.

What was the problem?

There were incredible communication problems in the team. Some of the staff had been there a long time and socialised together in their spare time. They were very close and covered for each other when there was a problem. When Taig started he was treated as an outcast from day one. He started by performing really well but this didn't last long. His work rate dropped and every time there was a problem I was told that it was his fault. I had the feeling that the group was using him as a scapegoat and that they were anxious that he would show them up by working so quickly. Initially he had been finishing his rooms at least an hour before the rest of the staff.

What did you need to know?
I needed to know more about the reasons why this problem had started. I needed to know how the older members of staff felt about the situation as well as how Taig felt. I needed to know something about cultural differences, about job satisfaction and about conflict resolution. I was actually very worried that investigating this problem might make it worse and I was tempted to leave it alone.

What were the alternatives?
Well, as I have said, my strongest temptation was to leave the situation to sort itself out, hoping that eventually they would work out their differences. Alternatively, I could talk first to Taig and then to the rest of the team. Of course, I could do that the other way round. I could run a meeting with all the staff and make some general remarks, hoping that that would make a difference. Finally, I could look at the potential reasons for the problem myself and work out a way to resolve it.

Looking more carefully at the situation I realised that Taig did not fit in because he was young, male and from a different cultural and language background. When he had started he had worked incredibly quickly, cleaning more rooms than any of the older staff and finishing early. No doubt this did not make the rest of the staff very happy because they thought it could lead to a directive that they should all do an additional room each day. I understood that most of them were not as fit as Taig. They also had homes and families to go home to—and more cleaning. I understood why they would want to pace their work and was quite satisfied with current room cleaning rates.

What did you do and why?
At first I was going to have a meeting. I thought that telling them that I was happy with their current level of productivity might solve the problem, but then I had an excellent idea. I decided that we should move away from individual goals to team goals. Rather than allocate rooms to individuals I would allocate them to a group. Anyone having Taig in the group would finish early. I had read about superordinate goals, and having looked up this incredible word in the dictionary, I realised that this might be the solution to the problem.

What happened and what did you learn from this?
Well, as you can imagine, Taig became the most popular person in the department. Everyone wanted him in their group. He also proved to be good at doing the heavy work because he was so fit. His differences were turned to advantage. Taig appeared to be much happier when he was included in the

groups and after a few weeks I noticed him sitting with the others in the canteen. I resolved that I should employ more men for the job and avoid developing cohesive groups that were not working towards my goals for the department.

The approach taken by this supervisor is consistent with the concept of 'utilization' suggested by Julie Shaw (1995). She recommends that the skills and knowledge of immigrant staff should be utilised, that adjustment to a multicultural workforce is not enough, and that utilisation of a multicultural workforce can be achieved through team development. Some of the concepts she introduces are consistent with the themes of this chapter: goal setting for teams; awareness of change and adaptation to change (quality management); consultation; sharing of information and problems; communicating clearly; and recognition for achievement of team goals.

Contrast these observations with an unpublished observation of the hospitality workplace:

> The industry is characterised by a large female labour workforce. However, this dominance is restricted to part-time and casual employment. Most of the part-time jobs available involve lower skilled tasks and less secure jobs which indicates a marginalisation of female employees. Many properties claim that these flexible working hours allow employees to meet family commitments. Women are constantly underrepresented in management positions and rarely occupy levels above supervisor except in the areas of Human Resource Management and Housekeeping. Executive Housekeeper is an interesting position in that it does not have a direct career pathway after this position—there tends to be a concrete rather than a glass ceiling.
>
> Even more marginalised are the employees from non-English speaking backgrounds. They are restricted in employment opportunities and promotion by stereotyping—they are often seen as suitable only to do lowest skill jobs due to inability to communicate 'well' in English. Quite often the level of English is not the problem—rather strong accents are considered detrimental and many lack confidence in expressing themselves in English. Many non-English speaking employees are well educated in their home countries, with relevant and transferable skills. They also tend to be very loyal to the company and become long-term employees.
>
> Appearance could also play a part in this restriction of opportunities by non-English speaking employees. The hospitality industry places a strong emphasis on appearance and employees interacting with the public tend to fit the company image. Symmetrical, Anglo-Saxon looks dominate the industry. Those from different ethnic backgrounds don't necessarily fit the 'image'.
>
> This systemic discrimination leads to the stagnation of women and non-English speaking employees particularly at the less skilled end of the industry. Skills, enthusiasm, experience and loyalty are wasted and any potential is ignored. (Cassidy, 1997)

The researcher, Geert Hofstede (1983), well known for his work in cross-cultural communication, has suggested a cultural dimension of collectivism and individualism. This dimension can be expressed in the form of a continuum such as that shown in Fig. 17.2.

The differences between cultures that emphasise group orientation as opposed to individual orientation are summarised in Table 17.1.

Clearly, cultures are seldom at one or other end of the collectivism-individualism continuum. However, most cultures have an orientation towards one or other end. Hofstede described Australian culture as individualistic while many Asian cultures were described as collectivist. This is one of the reasons for the success of quality team concepts in Japan.

Building effective work teams

In the activity provided at the end of this chapter you will be given the opportunity to work in a team to develop common goals in regard to an important issue. The management of your workplace has suggested that an agreement should be negotiated for your pay and working conditions. Federal legislation suggests that a

FIG. 17.2

Cultural factors in work teams.

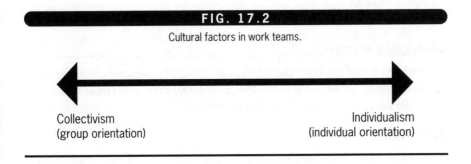

| Collectivism (group orientation) | Individualism (individual orientation) |

TABLE 17.1

Collectivist and individualist cultures.

Collectivist	Individualist
Emphasis on the needs of the group	Emphasis on own needs
'We' important	'I' important
Concern for group goals	Concern for individual goals
Emphasis on harmony	Confrontation, directness acceptable
Prefer long-term relationships	Accept short-term relationships
Like to work together	Like to work individually

'no disadvantage' test be applied to ensure that employees are not paid less than award wages. However, management is hoping for more flexibility in work hours. As a team you will have to decide whether to enter into the negotiation with management and also to reach agreement on your team goals. This is not an uncommon situation for employees to find themselves in and the information available on this issue is quite complex. However, since it has an impact on employee wages, it is a very important issue. Having looked at agreements, awards and working conditions in Chapter 13, you will be well prepared for the final section on job seeking in the tourism and hospitality industry.

For work teams to be effective they require full participation of members and agreement on common goals. In the activity provided you will be expected to demonstrate the following work team skills:

- contribute ideas
- help others
- give feedback
- check understanding
- ask questions
- respect differences
- follow procedures
- share leadership
- agree on goals.

Contribute ideas

Feedback from staff has been identified as an essential component of any quality improvement program. To achieve this, individual employees must be able to contribute ideas and communicate them clearly.

Help others

In any work team, some members will be more experienced than others, some members will be more knowledgeable and some members will be more skilled. Working co-operatively means assisting one another to develop and harness your individual strengths.

Give feedback

People respond well to positive feedback. As a team member, one role is to provide feedback to colleagues. Positive feedback is most useful when it is specific. It says what the person did that was helpful and why it was helpful. Positive feedback sounds something like 'When you . . ., it was good because . . .'.

When conflict develops in a group, it is sometimes difficult to confront the person concerned. Like positive feedback, negative feedback should be specific. If it is vague ('You're useless') it will not be effective. Negative feedback can be given in the following way: 'When you . . . then . . . If you could . . . then . . .'. As an example you might say, 'When you interrupt me, then I feel that my view is not important and I get annoyed. If you could wait until I have finished speaking, then I would feel that the group respects my opinion.'

Check understanding

Paraphrasing is a useful tool for checking understanding. It involves repeating the gist of what someone has said, for example 'You are saying that management have lawyers working on this and that we should be looking for some expert help?' In this way you show that you are listening attentively and at the same time you are checking your understanding. This is one of the most powerful communication strategies that can be used with other staff and with customers.

Ask questions

Questions can help to clarify goals. 'Why do we need to talk about that issue at the first meeting? Surely we would need more information first?' is a helpful question to keep the group on track. Questions can be closed (looking for 'yes' and 'no' answers) or open, such as the one above where a full answer is required.

Respect differences

Much of this text has been about differences, differences between individuals and differences between groups. In a work context, a full consensus may not be reached in all situations. Where this is the case, differences need to be respected and worked through to achieve mutually agreed goals.

Follow procedures

Structure is useful in any group discussion. Timing should be agreed beforehand, as should the topics to be discussed. Decisions should be recorded so that the individuals in the group can check their understanding.

Share leadership

In work teams with shared leadership each person should have the opportunity to 'manage' the discussion. This ensures that everyone has the chance to express their views.

Agree on goals

The final characteristic of an effective work team is the ability to reach agreement on team goals. Teams that achieve their goals become very cohesive (consider, for example, the sporting team that wins games). For this reason, goals have to be realistic and achievable, taking into account the skills of the members.

Communication in the cross-cultural workplace

The model for successful communication presented in this book is based on a deep understanding of individual differences and a positive attitude towards communicating effectively. This is illustrated in Fig. 17.3 on page 206, which summarises the following key points:

- Attentive and responsive customer service is good customer service in any environment.
- Cohesive work teams are groups that work towards shared goals.

- Checking for understanding and obtaining feedback are the core skills required for effective communication.
- An open-minded attitude towards people, their individual differences and their needs underpins the above three points.

FIG. 17.3

A positive approach to teamwork and service.

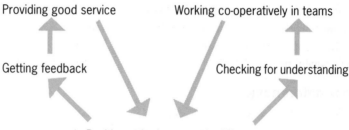

Providing good service   Working co-operatively in teams

Getting feedback   Checking for understanding

Positive attitudes towards differences

Dealing with conflict

When a conflict situation develops, it needs to be dealt with promptly and effectively, and the following guidelines are useful in resolving conflict in the workplace.

Identify the conflict situation

Early identification of conflict developing can lead to a quick resolution. Being sensitive to this possibility is also helpful in maintaining team spirit. Situations in which the personal safety of customers or colleagues is threatened need particularly urgent attention.

Understand the causes of the conflict

As mentioned earlier, listening is one of the most effective ways of fully understanding a conflict situation and the causes underpinning it, but it is also essential to take a neutral position until the investigation has been concluded. All parties need to be treated with respect and asked for their ideas on potential solutions.

Take charge of the conflict situation

When a situation is serious it needs to be handled confidentially and discreetly, and this might involve moving to a quiet area to discuss it. Recommending a positive outcome as the goal is usually appreciated by everyone involved in the situation. Successful resolution of a conflict or a complaint can lead to closer working relationships and more satisfied customers.

Escalate the situation

In serious situations the conflict must be escalated, the Human Resources Department having detailed procedures in place for this reason. For example, a breach of the anti-discrimination or sexual harassment policy would need to be referred to that department. A situation involving a drug-affected or violent person is another example of a problem that would be beyond your capacity to resolve. Recognising such situations and following correct procedures is essential.

Activity

You are a small work team of different ages and cultural backgrounds with different needs in terms of conditions of employment. Some of you can afford to be more flexible than others. Management has approached you with a proposal to increase your hourly rate of pay in exchange for more flexible working arrangements. Currently you are paid $12.19 per hour, Monday to Friday, $15.23 per hour on Saturday and $18.28 per hour on Sunday. You are also paid double time for any hours worked in excess of eight hours per day.

The variations on the award conditions that management proposes include abolishing higher penalty rates for working on weekends and requiring you to work for between six and ten hours per day, at a standard rate of $14.50 per hour. When you work ten hours in a day, you will not be paid overtime unless you have worked more than 38 hours in the week. Thus if you worked six hours on a Monday and ten hours on a Sunday you would not receive penalty rates or overtime unless you had worked more than 38 hours in that week. For example, you might work the following hours:

Monday	Tuesday	Thursday	Friday	Sunday
6	6	6	10	10

Meet as a group and discuss the approach you wish to take with management in relation to this agreement. If you wish to obtain more information about Australian Workplace Agreements you may wish to visit the Department of Employment Workplace Relations on the Internet at http://www.osiris.gov.au

Keep in mind that an Australian Workplace Agreement will only meet the no-disadvantage test if your overall wages and conditions under a workplace agreement are not less than the overall wages and conditions you would get under any relevant awards and laws.

During a series of group discussions, you need to reach agreement on group goals. You also need to decide whether you will be better or worse off with this new pay rate. In participating in the group, you should demonstrate that you are able to:

- contribute ideas
- help others
- give feedback
- check understanding
- ask questions.

Discussion questions

1 Is an 'Employee of the Month' award the type of goal which would encourage team work?

2 Do you agree that the key skills for effective team development are appropriate regardless of the cultural composition of the group? Explain why.

3 Do you have any suggestions for solving the situation that developed in the case study at the start of the chapter? Did cultural differences give rise to the dispute or was this a simple misunderstanding?

4 What do you think about the chef's comment in the above-mentioned case study, 'If you can't stand the heat get out of the kitchen'?

CASE STUDY

The problem resulted from a guest being sent to a room that had not been cleaned by Housekeeping. The guest was tired and exceptionally angry because the receptionist had already kept him waiting for half an hour and then the room was not a smoking room, as he had requested. He met the room attendant in the corridor and took her to task about the whole situation. Apart from being kept waiting, he was particularly angry about being shown to a non-smoking room when he had specifically requested smoking. The room attendant called the receptionist who said that there was no record of a smoking request and that Housekeeping should 'get their act together' as they were always behind schedule and guests were frequently waiting in the lobby for their rooms. This conflict came to the attention of the Rooms Division Manager who realised that it was symptomatic of many of the problems occurring between the two departments. He asked that it form the basis of a meeting between the staff involved in the situation.

Use the steps suggested in this chapter to recommend ways in which this, and future conflicts of this nature, could be resolved.

LINKS

Australian Dispute Resolution—http://www.ausdispute.unisa.edu.au/home.htm

Conflict Management Research Group—
http://www.humanities.unisa.edu.au/cmrg/

Results through training—
http://www.resultsthroughtraining.com/downloads/TipsFacil.HTML

Team management systems on-line—http://www.tms.com.au/tms12-2c.html

CHAPTER EIGHTEEN

Communication and social diversity

OBJECTIVES

This chapter looks at the concept of culture and how perceptions, attitudes and values are often determined by our culture. On completion of this chapter you will be able to:

- explain the concept of culture
- describe how cultural factors lead to different needs and expectations
- briefly describe Australia's history and unique features
- use research information to inform tourists about Australia and Australians
- identify Australia's major cultural and social groups.

When I applied for a job with Captain Cook Cruises I asked my father to help me prepare for the interview. He asked me a number of questions about Sydney Harbour, such as when Cook had arrived, why the Quarantine Station was necessary and who had designed the Opera House. He also asked whether any Aboriginal settlements had been in the Sydney Harbour area when Cook arrived on the scene. I'm afraid that I could not answer the questions as well as I should. It became obvious that I had a lot of homework to do before the interview, and before I would be able to help tourists visiting Sydney.

JOB APPLICANT

Many visitors to Australia and to its attractions are interested in our culture. For many tourism and hospitality staff this concept is difficult to understand, as culture tends to be invisible to most of those who live with it. However, an awareness of our own culture is a prerequisite for an understanding and appreciation of other cultures. To help you understand Australian culture we have included a brief history of Australia later in this chapter.

What is culture?

Culture determines how people think and feel; it defines their outlook on life. It is so much a part of the fabric of life that it is taken for granted.

Culture can be defined as the framework for accepted modes of behaviour among members of a particular society. These members tend to share similar value systems, they have common attitudes and they perceive things in like ways. Have a look at this Japanese man's observations:

> I can remember so clearly the first time I saw someone use a handkerchief. First he blew his nose in a white cloth during a meal in a restaurant. Then he rolled it up and put it in his pocket. I was horrified that someone would carry this around in a pocket all day! In our culture it is very bad manners to do this while eating. We think sniffing is more acceptable and hygienic, otherwise we go to the bathroom. Until I saw this I had no idea that there were other ways to deal with a running nose.

The concept of culture is difficult to grasp, and the concept of our own culture is even more difficult to come to terms with. This is because living in our own culture makes us take it for granted. It is a bit like the air around us: it is something we rely on and use for many different purposes (including breathing) but seldom notice. Until you move away from your own culture and try to live in another, you are often unaware of the many facets of your own.

A culture is dynamic; it is constantly changing. The Internet has had a major impact on cultures worldwide, in turn developing its own sub-culture. There are people on the Internet looking for facts, others looking for opinions, some for conversation, others for romance. Each of these sub-cultures also develops different jargon and different habits.

Perception

Perception can best be described as a person's way of looking at the world.

Firstly, people pay attention to different things. When walking through a shopping centre, for example, people are most likely to look at other people of the same age. A couple in a restaurant with children tend to look at their own children and other people's children (possibly to compare their behaviour). On the other hand, it is unlikely that a group of teenagers would pay any attention to small children at all. Secondly, perceptions of the world are processed in the brain according to a person's frame of reference. Our concepts help us to organise information in our brains ready for processing. Perceptions are structured and ordered in this way.

Perception can therefore be defined as the active process of selection and categorisation of input. Each person's version of reality is different. Our senses, our culture and our social environment act as filters between what **is** 'out there' and what we **think** is 'out there'.

Attitudes and values

While perceptions can be 'one off' occurrences, attitudes are regularities in an individual's feelings and thoughts, and lead to a tendency to behave in a certain way. An attitude can therefore be defined as a way of thinking, feeling and behaving towards a particular person, situation, thing or idea.

Values are more general, central and resistant to change than attitudes.

Your perceptions and your attitudes influence communication with other people. You pay attention to some communication; you filter out other communication. The way you deal with communication is influenced by your attitudes. If you were willing to try to help someone from another country, you might try different ways of communicating with them to develop a better understanding of their needs.

In the following section we will discuss various aspects of communication that are influenced by your perceptions and your attitudes.

Cross-cultural verbal communication

Language is the 'code' used for communication. Even where two people speak the same language there is room for interpretation and misunderstanding. Americans, for example, use different words from Australians. For Americans 'biscuits' are what we call 'scones', and they are eaten at several different mealtimes. Imagine the consternation of an Australian who was asked to serve biscuits with a meal! As far as Americans are concerned the correct word for 'biscuits' is 'cookies'. Similar confusion might exist with tomato sauce, which for Americans is something they would serve on spaghetti. An American would be quite confused if you offered tomato sauce with a pie and chips—she would be expecting tomato ketchup instead. You may also encounter customers who order hard boiled eggs and expect them to be served in a cup, having been scraped out of the shell!

Greetings are particularly important, especially the pronunciation of the client's name and the correct order of first and family names. Many travel agents and reservations staff write down the phonetic pronunciation of the person's name so that the next time it occurs it is said correctly. Accurate spelling is also essential. Foreign family names are often the hardest to spell and to remember. Different cultural groups have different forms of greeting and this makes it extremely difficult to decide how to respond. However, as already mentioned, a survey of Japanese visitors revealed that they were disappointed that the areas they visited in Australia were 'too Japanese'. From this we might conclude that an Australian style is generally appreciated provided that expectations of politeness are met. Politeness is most often expressed non-verbally.

In the second exercise at the end of this chapter you are required to work in a group to find out the verbal forms of greeting and farewell in a range of languages. As you will discover, there are many variations in phrasing. It is important to note that the tone used to pronounce certain words in some languages can completely change the meaning of those words. In addition, many English expressions do not have literal translations into other languages.

Cross-cultural non-verbal communication

Numerous studies have shown that people are very attentive to non-verbal communication. In fact, where there is difficulty in understanding the verbal message, listeners are even more attentive to non-verbal communication, listening to the tone of voice and watching facial expressions and gestures. Mehrabian (1971) suggests that under 10 per cent of the message is communicated through words, 20 per cent through pitch and tone of voice and 70 per cent via posture, gesture and facial expression. Roger Axtell (1991) has described over 200 gestures used in 82 countries. Clearly it is impossible to learn all of these or to understand all their meanings. For a start it would be necessary to know where the person comes from, and this is not always easy to ascertain. His book also illustrates that body language can lead to misunderstandings. In his discussion about gestures for signalling a waiter, Axtell explains that in some parts of Mexico customers call the waiter by pursing the lips and making kissing noises. In other countries this could easily be interpreted quite differently!

For your interest Table 18.1 lists just a few observations he and other authors have made in relation to body language around the world.

These examples of verbal and non-verbal behaviour illustrate how people from different backgrounds have different expectations of language and body language. The role of the tourism and hospitality employee is to be sensitive to

TABLE 18.1

Body language gestures from around the world.

China	Sucking air through the teeth occurs when something is surprising or difficult. In China it is best to change the request to avoid the embarrassment of having to say 'No'. The host always has his back to the door while the chief guest faces the door. To beckon someone, the palm faces downward and the fingers are moved in a scratching motion. Bones are often left alongside the dish. When finished eating the custom is to place the chopsticks parallel across the bowl.
Germany	When signalling thanks Germans clasp their hands together and hold them over their heads. Guests do not drink until the host begins (don't forget to fill the host's glass). Where the table is large, rapping the knuckles on the table is a form of greeting and farewell.
Indonesia	Indonesians rarely disagree in public and will laugh to mask embarrassment. Eating while walking in the street is impolite. Sunglasses should be removed when talking to someone. A clean plate is often a signal for more food. In crowded restaurants people may share tables.
Japan	It is customary to remove the shoes before entering houses and restaurants. Direct eye contact can be seen as intimidating. Bowing in greeting is customary. Waving the hand (palm outwards) in front of the face signals 'I don't know' or 'I don't understand'. A waiter's attention is attracted by catching his eye and dipping the head. Listening without interruption is polite. A Japanese person wearing a mask in public probably has a cold.
Korea	The Western gesture for 'come here' is only used for dogs. To beckon someone in Korea the arm is extended, palm down and a scratching motion is used. Drunkenness is quickly forgiven.
Thailand	Showing the soles of the feet or pointing with a foot is insulting as the foot is seen as the dirtiest part of the body. The head is the most sacred part of the body, and children should not be patted on the head. The left hand is 'unclean' and is not used to pass objects or food.

these differences and to provide information in a clear and positive manner. External organisations that can provide support include:

- interpreter services
- diplomatic services
- local cultural organisations
- appropriate government agencies
- educational institutions.

What is discrimination?

Discrimination occurs when a person or a group of people are treated less favourably than another person or group because of race, colour, national or ethnic origin; gender or marital status; disability; religious or political beliefs; sexual preference; or some other central characteristic.

Discrimination occurs when a person is denied the opportunity to participate freely and fully in normal day-to-day activities. It might include harassment in the workplace; being denied a job or a promotion; being denied entry to public places and other facilities; or being denied goods and services.

Discrimination can either be direct or indirect. Direct discrimination takes place when an individual is disadvantaged or treated less favourably than another person. An example of direct discrimination is failing to employ someone because he or she is in a wheelchair. Indirect discrimination occurs where a practice or policy appears to be fair and to treat everyone the same way but actually disadvantages people from a particular group. An example of indirect discrimination is requiring all people who apply for a certain job to pass an English test, even though English is not necessary for the job. Such a test would probably exclude more people whose first language is not English than those for whom it is.

When Australia entered into international agreements about human rights, it made commitments to **all** its people to respect individual human rights and fundamental freedoms and to ensure that **everyone** under its jurisdiction could exercise these rights. (Only very few rights are for citizens only.) And Australia promised to provide an effective remedy if an individual's right were breached or his or her freedom violated. This obligation operates regardless of who the violator is, and even when it is the government itself.

Human rights legislation imposes obligations, or responsibilities, on everyone—governments, private organisations, community groups and individuals. We all share the responsibility for respecting and protecting the human rights of all other people. All human rights must be exercised in ways that do not impinge on the rights and freedoms of others. (http://www.hreoc.gov.au/faqs/general.html)

A brief history of Australia

In this chapter we have talked about culture in general and the difficulties that can be encountered in communicating with people from different cultures. As an employee in the hospitality industry, you will sometimes be called upon to discuss our culture with your customers. For this reason, we have provided a brief overview of Australia's history, which we hope will motivate you to learn more about what makes us Australian.

The original Australians

Two separate groups of people make up the original Australians. These are the Aboriginal people and the Torres Strait Islanders. 'Aborigine' was not the name these people used to describe themselves. The name 'Aborigines' was given to the first Australians by the Europeans because it means 'the original inhabitants of a country'. Today's Aboriginal peoples are more likely to call themselves by the name of the language or territory group to which they belong.

Gradually, archaeological research is unveiling the story of the earliest Australians. It is reasonable to claim that Aboriginal people have made Australia their home for at least 60,000 years.

As in the past, Aboriginal clans today hold deep religious links with their lands, which were formed in the Dreamtime. The great ancestral creative beings, which journeyed across the continent at the beginning of time, established the land boundaries between Aboriginal groups and the sacred sites. Carrying out ritual obligations at these sacred sites and performing religious ceremonies are the ways by which the Aboriginal peoples feel bound to their lands and protective towards it.

On arriving in Australia, the British declared the continent *terra nullius*, or 'nobody's land'. It is estimated that 20,000 Aborigines were violently killed during the period of colonisation.

Non-verbal communication
Aboriginal and Torres Strait Islander peoples

Handshakes	Aboriginal and Torres Strait Islander peoples may prefer to give soft handshakes which are polite and do not intrude on personal space.
Silence	Silence may mean that they are unwilling to discuss the topic or are thinking deeply in order to give the appropriate response.
Eye contact	Respect for age or authority is given by lowering the eyes.
Questioning	Aboriginal and Torres Strait Islander peoples are more likely to respond to indirect, as opposed to blunt or direct, questions.

Adapted from Australian Indigenous Cross-cultural Awareness Program, Tourism Training Australia.

Below, Peter Smith describes the origins of Native Title legislation following a move to recognise the Aborigines' long-standing cultural links with the land.

On 3 June 1992 the doctrine of *terra nullius* was overturned in the High Court of Australia. *Terra nullius* was a legal fiction, which argued that Australia at the time of colonisation was a land belonging to nobody and that it could therefore be taken and owned by the British. The High Court decision is popularly known as the 'Mabo' decision after Eddie Mabo. Mabo was one of five Torres Strait Islanders who went to court in 1982 arguing that colonial annexation had not extinguished existing land rights. Their case was to become a crucial test, which led to the 1992 High Court decision to overturn *terra nullius* and recognise that native title had always existed under common law, albeit unrecognised. The High Court argued that a group was entitled to claim native title so long as they had an abiding connection with the land in question through laws, customs, beliefs and ceremonies. (Smith, 1994, pp. 656–7)

Colonisation

The second major migration to Australia took place in 1788 when the First Fleet arrived at Port Jackson from Britain. Between 1788 and 1852 about 170,000 convicts were despatched from England, Ireland and Scotland to Australia. From 1850 to 1868, 10,000 convicts were sent to Western Australia. Most of these migrants were from Britain. The first free settlers arrived in New South Wales in 1793 and by 1836 the number of free settlers had outstripped the number of convicts.

When gold was discovered in the 1850s Australia's population trebled. For the first time, many of the newcomers were non-British—they came from Germany, China (for gold mining) and the Pacific Islands (for sugar cane farming). In the early 1900s many southern European migrants arrived from Italy and Greece. Many more arrived after World War II. Since the 1970s, when multicultural policies were put in place, the number of migrants from all over the world has increased.

Demographics

By 1991, 19 per cent of Australians had been born in Australia and had at least one overseas born parent. The birthplaces of major settler arrivals in Australia from 1970 to 2000 are shown in Table 18.2 on page 216.

All migrant groups have brought some of the culture of their birth countries to Australia. One of their most important contributions is to the culinary development of Australia's restaurant industry which is rapidly becoming world renowned.

Developments in Australian culture

Culture was defined in Chapter 16 in terms of 'modes of behaviour'. The following will now help you to define contemporary Australian culture, particularly as it relates to tourism and hospitality. Remember that in many respects culture is dynamic, responding to changes in the economy and to fashion trends.

TABLE 18.2

Country of birth of major settler arrivals 1970–2000.

Country	'000	%	Country	'000	%
1970			**1990**		
United Kingdom and Ireland	369.1	47.3	United Kingdom*	107.0	17.4
Yugoslavia	63.5	8.1	New Zealand	82.5	13.4
Italy	62.7	8.0	Vietnam	38.9	6.3
Greece	56.0	7.2	Philippines	36.3	5.9
Germany	18.7	2.4	Hong Kong (SAR of China)	27.5	4.5
United States of America	13.7	1.8	Malaysia	26.6	4.3
All birthplaces	781.0		All birthplaces	616.1	
1980			**2000**		
United Kingdom*	86.2	25.0	New Zealand	80.6	18.4
New Zealand	39.8	11.6	United Kingdom*	48.1	11.0
Vietnam	30.6	8.9	China (excluding SARs and Taiwan)	36.3	8.3
Lebanon	18.4	5.3	Former Yugoslav Republics	28.3	6.5
South Africa	10.2	3.0	South Africa	21.4	4.9
Malaysia	8.4	2.4	India	16.4	3.7
All birthplaces	344.7		All birthplaces	438.6	

* Excludes Ireland

Source: Australian Bureau of Statistics, www.abs.gov.au. Reproduced with permission.

Cuisine

Australia's cuisine is attracting increasing attention from the world's food media, with Australia now an attractive destination for food and wine lovers from around the globe.

Eating out is very popular with Australians of all income levels, with the average household spending almost 27 per cent of their weekly food budget on eating outside the home. Ethnic restaurants and takeaway shops serving food from many different countries abound. The influence of other cultures is also felt in contemporary Australian restaurants where ingredients from a variety of countries are combined in innovative ways.

This is in sharp contrast to the Depression years of the 1930s. In the earlier part of this century, Australian cooking was based on English traditions, with a few Australian adaptations. Wood-burning stoves were used for cooking and heating, with a constant supply of hot water and stock (or soup) kept simmering on the stove. Early dishes would have included such things as mutton broth and kangaroo tail soup. Making kangaroo tail soup involves boiling the tail with some cloves, bay leaves and mace, and adding some port wine and currant jelly towards the end of the cooking time. Axiom Publishers have produced a small cookery book, edited by Brian Cooper, called *Early Australian Recipes* (1996), which includes dishes and sweets, such as fish pie, curried sardines, liver and bacon, sheep's brains, rissoles, rabbit casserole, baked lamb shanks, damper, scones, Anzac biscuits, bread and butter pudding, lamingtons and pavlova. Most of these recipes are very different from those used in our kitchens today. One of the areas which is specially resistant to change is the traditional Christmas dinner with roast turkey, baked ham, Christmas pudding and other rich foods which are served hot in mid-summer. Many Australians are now changing, however, electing instead to serve a banquet of cold seafood on Christmas Day.

Patterns of eating are also changing. Traditional mealtimes included breakfast (porridge or eggs and bacon), lunch (sandwiches) and dinner (roast or stew with vegetables) as well as morning and afternoon tea at 10.00 a.m. and 4.00 p.m. These traditions are evolving rapidly to a snack food and takeaway mentality. Fixed mealtimes are also less common as family members often eat at different times owing to a range of commitments outside the home.

Nowadays Australian cuisine portrays many cultural influences and includes dairy, soy and olive oil based cooking. Ingredients are more varied, with items such

Glossary of Australian native ingredients

Native ingredient	Source	Characteristics
Bunya nuts	Southern Queensland highlands	Chestnut-like; use in toffees
Bush apple	New South Wales to North Queensland rainforests	Rainforest fruit with apple, plum and custard character
Bush tomato	Desert areas	Solanaceae family; can be used for chutney
Davidson plum	Northern New South Wales and Queensland rainforests	Used in salad dressings, sauces and jams
Kangaroo meat	Many areas of Australia	Rich, lean meat (Venison-like) which is low in cholesterol
Lemon aspen	East coast rainforests	Tangy, yellow, citrus flavour
Lemon myrtle	East coast rainforests	Taste and aroma of lime, lemon and lemongrass
Lillipilli	Rainforests and woodlands	Berries of various colours, ranging in flavour from sour to cinnamon; used in vinegar and sauces
Macadamia nut	North Queensland	The only indigenous nut exported overseas; high in fat and cholesterol free
Munthari	Desert areas	Use for sauces, especially with veal
Native thyme	Central Queensland desert	Flavour of thyme, tarragon and gum leaf
Pepperleaf	Alpine regions	Can be used as a substitute for bay leaves
Quandong	Desert areas	Acid fruit, with the texture of peaches, used in stews
Riberry	Rainforest areas	Most widely grown rainforest tree, riberry (or cherry alder) has small pink berries with a cinnamon clove taste
Warrigal greens	All over Australia, except Northern Territory	Native equivalent of English spinach; seasonal
Wattleseed	Dry areas	From dryland wattles; the seeds have a coffee/chocolate/hazelnut taste
Wild limes	East coast	Used for drinks and marmalade

Source: Tourism Training Australia.

as coconut milk, red curry paste, fish sauce, five spice powder, sesame oil, lemongrass and vegetables suitable for stir frying now widely available. Australian native ingredients are also increasingly being used, particularly in restaurants.

Leisure and interests

To help us define Australia's culture let us look at some of the information produced by the Australian Bureau of Statistics. The most popular sporting and physical activities in 1997–98 were swimming, aerobics and fitness, golf, tennis, fishing, cycling and ten-pin bowling. Participation is summarised in Table 18.3. Watching sport was also found to be popular, with over 2.5 million people paying to watch an average of one sporting event a month. Australians' enthusiasm for participating in sport, and watching it, is illustrated in these figures.

This type of information is very interesting to overseas visitors, some of whom find one of our favourite sports (golf) very expensive in their home countries.

The most popular leisure-time activities in 1997–98 are summarised in Table 18.4. Apparently, Australians do not spend a great deal of time thinking!

TABLE 18.3

Most popular sports and physical activities 1997–98.

Sport	Players ('000)
Swimming	1628
Aerobics & Fitness	1379
Golf	1116
Tennis	937
Fishing	641
Cycling	628
Ten-pin bowling	438

Source: Australian Bureau of Statistics, Participation in Sport and Physical Activities Australia 1997–98, Cat No 4177.0. Reproduced with permission.

TABLE 18.4

Leisure-time activities of Australians 1997–98.

Activity	Time spent daily (minutes)
TV/Video/Radio	257
Reading	37
Relaxing	16
Thinking	2

Source: Australian Bureau of Statistics, Leisure Time Activities Australia 1997–98, Cat No 4153.0. Reproduced with permission.

Australians on holiday

A survey of the leisure activities of domestic travellers reveals that swimming and surfing are the most popular activities for Australians while on holiday, followed by fishing and boating. Bush activities and visiting national parks and heritage sites come a reasonably close third and fourth. These are followed by attendance at sporting events and having fun in theme parks. Visiting art galleries, attending live theatre and attending musicals/operas complete the list of ten favourite cultural activities for holiday periods. (ABS, Australian Social Trends, 1995)

Australia's unique features

Many tourists are attracted to the unique animals that inhabit this large continent and are generally keen to learn more about them.

Fauna

Australia is home to the only two monotremes left in the world: the echidna and the platypus. Monotremes are egg-laying mammals: they lay eggs but raise their young on their own milk. Native Australian birds include the emu, cockatoo, galah, lorikeet, kookaburra and the lyrebird, which can imitate sounds (including car alarms).

Some of Australia's most interesting animals are marsupials. These are animals that keep their young in a pouch. Australia has 119 different species of marsupial, and 40 of these species are very rare. The best known marsupials are:

- kangaroos (five species, largest living marsupial)
- wallabies (27 species)
- koalas (only eat certain eucalypt leaves and do not drink)
- possums (22 species, adapted to tree living, hang by their tails)
- wombats (large burrows up to 15 metres)
- bandicoots (look like rats, nocturnal, eat insects)
- Tasmanian devils (rare carnivorous marsupials, ferocious).

The inaccurate portrayal below of Australia's favourite marsupial, the koala, illustrates how important it is to develop knowledge of local fauna:

> In the ski resort of Park City, Utah, Stuart Hutton, of Lilyfield, found a little bit of Australia. Well, almost. In a shop, he and some other Australians found a quart bottle of something called Kiwi Bear. The label: 'Doin' Down Under'. 'In its native Australia, some say the kiwi bear (many call it a koala) presides over the kiwi fruit harvest. And guava picking too. These fruits, plus a few from heartier climes, give our Kiwi Bear Juice Brand special zzzzip . . . Too bad the Kiwi Bear can't enjoy our Kiwi Bear like we do. It doesn't drink anything.'
>
> It's made by After the Fall Products of Battleboro, Vermont. 'No wonder Americans are so confused about Australia', says Stuart. And the drink? 'Sickly sweet, but popular.'

'Column 8', *Sydney Morning Herald*, 6 April 1997

219

Many visitors call the koala a bear, which of course it is not. An explanation of the diet and other interesting habits of these unique and endangered animals would be welcomed by visitors from any country.

Flora

The spring flowers in the deserts of Western Australia are a magnificent attraction for both domestic and international tourists. The following flowers are the floral emblems of the different states and territories:

Waratah	New South Wales
Cooktown orchid	Queensland
Common heath	Victoria
Sturt's desert pea	South Australia
Tasmanian blue gum	Tasmania
Kangaroo paw	Western Australia
Royal bluebell	Australian Capital Territory
Sturt's desert rose	Northern Territory

The wattle is the floral emblem of Australia. Banksias are well-known bushy trees named after Sir Joseph Banks, the botanist who sailed with Captain Cook. Interestingly, some very Australian symbols have come from our migrant heritage. For example, the Australian Coat of Arms was designed by a Croatian grape grower for use on a wine bottle label (Cope & Kalantzis, 1997).

Activities

1 A restaurant chain in Australia trains its staff to sit down at the table with guests when taking orders. Try this out with a group of 'customers' and see how each of them feels about this new approach. Compare the reactions of the people closest to and farthest away from the super-friendly waiter.

2 Using the table on the next page, work in teams to find out as much as you can about the different forms of greeting used in those countries.

3 Try to find some statistics on another country (for example, sporting interests) similar to those provided in this chapter.

4 Look at the *Yellow Pages* for the capital city in your state. How many different types of ethnic restaurant are listed?

5 Former Australians of the Year include Fred Hollows, Eddie Mabo, Victor Chang, Elizabeth Evatt and Patrick White. Provide a short description of the contribution made by each of them.

6 Interview five Australians to find out how they would describe their own culture. Collate your information with a group and write a summary of your findings.

7 Use the factual information provided in this chapter (and any other factual information you can find from sources such as the *Australian Year Book*) as the basis for a description of Australians and their interests. Compare this to the earlier summary in terms of its value to you as a tourism professional selling Australia to international tourists.

	Good Morning	Good Afternoon	Good Evening
Cantonese			
Indonesian			
Japanese			
Korean			

	Goodbye	Yes	No
Cantonese			
Indonesian			
Japanese			
Korean			

	Excuse me	Please	Thank you
Cantonese			
Indonesian			
Japanese			
Korean			

Discussion questions

1 What is the Native Title Act?
2 What are the most popular at-home leisure activities of Australians?
3 Explain why sport is viewed as part of Australian culture.
4 Prime Minister John Howard made the following observation of Australian qualities in an Australia Day speech: 'Defiance against the odds, down-to-earth practicality, courage, commitment, mateship and love of country are all examples of the characteristics we love and applaud'. Comment on his observations.

LINKS

Australian Bureau of Statistics, Australia Now—
http://www.abs.gov.au/ausstats/abs%40.nsf/94713ad445ff1425ca25682000192af2!OpenView

Australian Tourist Commission (Australia)—
http://www.australia.com/index.aust

Murdoch Reading Room, Culture and Communication—
http://wwwmcc.murdoch.edu.au/ReadingRoom/

CHAPTER NINETEEN

Tradition and religion

OBJECTIVES

In this chapter we will cover some of the traditions and religious beliefs you will encounter in the workplace in your interaction with colleagues and with domestic and international tourists. On completion of this chapter you will be able to:

- describe the traditional and religious beliefs of Australia's domestic and international tourists, as well as those of hospitality workers
- explain how traditional and religious beliefs can lead to specific customer demands
- explain the role of hospitality employees in meeting the traditional and religious needs and expectations of customers.

The hotel guest was accompanied by several men who were clearly very respectful of his status. As it turned out, the guest was a prince from Saudi Arabia. One of the first requests the group made was for a detailed list of the ingredients included in each of the items on the room service menu. The second was a request for a meal to be delivered to the room before dawn each morning. The timing of the meal was crucial because Muslims who are fasting during Ramadan are not allowed to eat or drink from sunrise (when one can tell a black thread from a white one) to sunset. For this reason it was imperative that the meal be delivered on time. On the night before his departure, the prince made a more difficult final request—he wanted to buy the diamond ring on display in the jeweller's window and he also wanted an identical copy. This had to be manufactured overnight before his departure the next morning. Curious staff discovered that the rings were for his two wives. According to Muslim custom it is possible for a man to have up to four wives, though this is very rare. Islamic law requires that if a man has more than one wife each wife must be treated equally in every way.

GUEST SERVICE AGENT

With increasing numbers of international visitors coming to Australia, an awareness of their needs is most important, particularly in relation to their religious beliefs. Many overseas visitors, as well as local customers, are restricted in their eating habits: abstinence from pork or pork by-products, for example, is common to several cultures and religions. Religious affiliations also have important implications for workers, who need to be sensitive to the different religious needs of their co-workers. For example, you need to be aware that some staff members will wish to take time off at particular times of the year to attend festivals associated with their religious practices.

This chapter provides a brief description of the world's major religions and therefore the religions of many international visitors, Australian tourists and hospitality employees.

In the hospitality workplace a number of cultural variances are encountered with regard to the following:

- customer expectations
- forms of address and greeting
- formality and informality
- appropriate non-verbal behaviour
- sincere communication
- humour
- food preferences and restrictions
- work ethic
- days of prayer
- dress and appearance.

Many of these factors will be discussed in this section, including the food and eating habits of Australians and visitors from other countries. Religious and cultural factors are particularly important in the food and beverage sector of the hospitality industry.

The major religions of Australians are shown in Table 19.1 on page 224 and some of them are discussed below.

Buddhism

Originating in northern India around 500 BCE, Buddhism spread to South East Asia, China, Korea, Japan and Tibet between the second and seventh centuries CE. More recently Buddhism has made its way to Europe and North America. It is now one of the most widespread religions in the world.

Religion

Historically, Gautama Buddha was the founder of the Buddhist movement. However, a more general concept of the 'Buddha' has evolved over time, by which there are other Buddhas in addition to Gautama. A Buddha is one who has realised the four noble truths as a result of fulfilling the ten special precepts for thousands and thousands of years over many, many lives.

Buddhism presents a way of living which focuses on the cessation of suffering (Nirvana). The Path to Nirvana is based on three virtues: morality, concentration (meditation) and wisdom. Wisdom (Prajna) is the insight that frees a person from suffering and from the cycle of rebirth.

Festivals

Uposatha days are observed by many Buddhists. These four holy days correspond with the new and full moons of each lunar month and the eighth day following

TABLE 19.1

Major religions of Australians.

Religion	1981		1996		Growth 1981–1996
	'000	%	'000	%	%
Christian	**11133.3**	**76.4**	**12582.7**	**70.3**	**13.0**
Anglican	3801.5	26.1	3903.3	22.0	2.6
Baptist	190.3	1.3	295.1	1.6	55.0
Catholic	3786.5	26.0	4798.9	27.0	26.7
Church of Christ	89.4	0.6	75.2	0.4	−15.8
Jehovah's Witness	51.8	0.4	83.4	0.5	61.0
Lutheran	199.8	1.4	249.9	1.4	25.0
Orthodox	421.3	2.9	497.0	2.8	17.9
Pentecostal	72.1	0.5	174.7	1.0	142.3
Presbyterian	637.8	4.4	675.5	3.8	5.9
Salvation Army	71.6	0.5	74.1	0.4	3.4
Uniting Church	1203.4	8.2	1334.9	7.5	10.9
Other Christian	607.8	4.1	219.1	1.2	−63.9
Non-Christian	**197.6**	**1.4**	**616.4**	**3.4**	**211.9**
Buddhism	35.1	0.2	199.8	1.1	469.2
Islam	76.8	0.5	200.8	1.1	161.4
Judaism	62.1	0.4	79.8	0.4	28.5
Other Non-Christian	23.6	0.2	68.6	0.4	190.6
Inadequately described	**73.6**	**0.5**	**54.1**	**0.3**	**−26.4**
No religion	**1576.7**	**10.8**	**2948.8**	**16.5**	**87.0**
Not stated	**1595.2**	**10.9**	**1550.5**	**8.7**	**−2.8**
Total	14576.3	100.0	17892.4	100.0	22.7

Source: Australian Bureau of Statistics, 1981 Census, 1996 Census. Reproduced with permission.

each of these. On Uposatha days lay people observe the eight or ten precepts with the help of Buddhist monks. This provides very useful training for lay people in gaining the self-control that leads to happiness and liberation from suffering.

Buddhists celebrate Buddha's Birth, Enlightenment and Parinibbana (entry to final Nirvana) on the same day, which is called Vesak. Most Buddhists celebrate Vesak on the day of the full moon in May. However, Vesak is not celebrated on the same day in all countries.

On special occasions Buddhists always give pride of place to Buddhist practices.

Eating and drinking customs

Traditional precepts outline the conduct that the lay follower must observe. These prohibit killing, stealing, engaging in sexual misconduct, lying and drinking intoxicating liquor. Novice Buddhist monks follow five additional precepts: they do not eat during prohibited hours; they do not take part in festivals and amusements; they do not use garlands, perfumes or ointments; they do not use a bed or chair that is too luxurious and they do not accept money for their own use. Ordained monks are required to follow 220 disciplinary rules of moral conduct.

Because Buddhists should not kill or harm any living creature, most Buddhists are vegetarian. Some practise vegan principles, which means that they eat neither meat nor dairy products.

Christianity

Christians number nearly two billion worldwide. Christians are part of the 'the Church' which has various denominations including Catholic, Anglican and Uniting, among others.

Religion

Christians believe in God, Jesus the Messiah, and the Holy Spirit, which guides the Church. The Bible, which has two parts, the Old Testament and the New Testament, is the Christian holy book. Jesus was born in Bethlehem near Jerusalem. Jesus preached the word of God and Christians see him as God incarnate. Many Christians have great reverence for Mary, 'the mother of God'.

Festivals

The major Christian festivals are Christmas, Jesus' birthday, and Easter, the time of Jesus' death and resurrection. Christmas is a celebration of Jesus' birth and Christians traditionally attend church on Christmas Day. This is followed by gift giving and a traditional dinner. Owing to commercial influences Christmas is now celebrated in many countries by the giving of gifts to family and friends. Easter, too, is an important time in the Christian calendar, many people attending church, many more spending time with family and friends.

Eating and drinking customs

Many Christians say Grace before meals, asking God for his blessing and giving thanks for the food provided. Lent is the period leading up to Easter when some Christians give up certain luxuries to remind them of the importance of sacrifice. Some Roman Catholics do not eat meat on Fridays in memory of the Friday on which Christ died on the Cross. At Easter Christians eat hot cross buns in memory of His death.

Confucianism

Confucianism is more a philosophy than a religion. Confucius, a great early Chinese philosopher, taught the importance of respectful behaviour, especially in regard to one's elders, as well as the importance of service to others.

Elderly Asians are revered and would therefore have the following expectations with regard to service (Engholm, 1991):

- constant attention
- standing up when they enter
- greeting in a formal manner before younger people
- avoiding smoking and drinking, without asking permission
- not reclining or crossing the legs
- removing sunglasses when speaking to an elder, even when outside
- never raising the voice.

Hinduism

Hinduism is one of the oldest religions of the world. It began in India where many of its followers still live. There are now many Hindus in neighbouring countries, including Nepal, Bhutan, Sri Lanka, Bangladesh and Burma, as well as in Malaysia and Fiji. Hinduism spread to South East Asia, to Malaysia and Indonesia in particular, about 1,000 years ago. Although most Indonesians are now Muslims, Hinduism is an important religion of the Balinese. Today there are about 700 million Hindus in the world and, apart from India and Asia, they can be found in the United Kingdom, the United States, central and southern Africa and, of course, Australia.

Religion

Hindus have a code of beliefs called Sanatana Dharma, which means eternal law. This involves working hard, telling the truth and recognising obligations to family. Hindus believe in reincarnation, and the cycle of birth and death is called Samsara. The aim of a Hindu's life is to break out of this cycle and to reach Moksha, or salvation. Only by leading a good life can a person be reborn as a more evolved being and move closer to salvation. Bathing plays an important part in Hinduism, and Hindus believe that bathing in the River Ganges and drinking its water will wash away their sins and lead them closer to Moksha. Karma, a cause and effect principle, plays an important part in whether one's actions will lead to salvation.

Hinduism allows its followers to worship in many different ways, although they believe in one divine principle. The many gods and goddesses are only aspects of this divine principle. The three main gods are Brahma (creator), Vishnu (sustainer) and Shiva (destroyer). Hindus worship daily, often setting up a shrine or image in one corner of the house.

There are four paths to Moksha: the path of devotion (Bhakti Yoga); the path of knowledge (Griana Yoga); the path of right action or acting selflessly (Karma Yoga) and the path of exercise (Hatha Yoga). A sadhu, or Hindu holy man, lives a life of prayer and meditation. He relies on other people for food as he is supposed to have renounced all material things.

Festivals

Diwali, also known as the festival of lights, is celebrated at the end of October or at the beginning of November. People light small oil lamps and place them by their doors and windows to celebrate the victory of good over evil. This festival derives from the story of an evil, tyrannical King who was tricked and killed by Krishna, one of the incarnations of Vishnu. Upon his death the people rejoiced and were no longer afraid to light up their houses. Diwali is also a time for worshipping the goddess of good fortune. The celebrations last for five days, with people exchanging gifts and sharing special food.

Other festivals include Holi, the spring festival, Janmashtami, the birthday of Krishna, and Shivaratri, the festival of Shiva (destroyer and re-creator of the universe).

Eating and drinking customs

Many Hindus are vegetarians as they have great respect for living things. Cows are sacred and Hindus will not eat beef. People eat with their fingers, using the right hand only because the left hand is considered 'unclean'. For this reason, Hindus would be offended if served food or handed anything with the left hand. Food is often offered to the gods in both the home and the temple and this offering is called Prasad. It is seen as an expression of respect and affection for the gods.

Islam

Islam is a religion based on the will of God as revealed to humanity by prophets sent since the beginning of time. A follower of this religion is a Muslim, a person who submits to God's will (Islam means 'submitting'). Muslims are united in their belief that the Koran, the holy book of Islam, is the word of God.

Today, the largest number of Muslims is found in South Asia and South East Asia. Islam is, in fact, the major religion of Indonesia, one of Australia's growing source countries for international visitors. There are also many Muslims in Australia and they have come from a variety of countries throughout the world.

Religion

Muhammad is the Prophet who was born in Mecca in Arabia. The word of God was revealed to Muhammad and forms the basis for the poetic writing of the Koran. Muhammad said that God was the creator of the world and that there would be a day of judgement when men and women would be sent to Heaven or Hell. Muslims believe that Jesus was also a Prophet but not that he was divine.

The five pillars of the Islamic religion are:

- Shahadah (to confess belief in one God, Allah, and that Muhammad is the Prophet of Allah)
- Salat (to pray five times a day)
- Zakat (to give alms to the needy)
- Saum (to fast in the month of Ramadan)
- Hajj (to make pilgrimages to Mecca).

Islam also means 'peace'. Muslims believe that when people submit to Allah's will and live by the teachings of the Koran peace will come to everyone. They also believe that Muhammad was the man through whom God chose to speak to mankind and that the Koran is the word of God. The Koran is written in Arabic and is thought to be the most perfect use of the Arabic language.

Muslims have great respect for the elderly and older Muslims expect to be treated with similar levels of respect when they travel.

Festivals

Ramadan occurs in the ninth month of the Muslim calendar and coincides with the month in which the Prophet first began to receive revelations from God. Muslims are supposed to fast from dawn to dusk for the 30 days of Ramadan. At the end of Ramadan is the festival of Eid ul-Fitr during which gifts are given and elaborate meals are prepared.

The other main festival is Eid ul-Adha, the festival of sacrifice, which marks the completion of the revelations to Muhammad. Animals are sacrificed and shared with family, friends and the poor.

Eating and drinking customs

Muslims are not allowed to eat pork, nor to drink alcohol or to gamble. Pork in any form is prohibited and this includes pork by-products, such as lard, which are sometimes included in ice-cream, cakes and biscuits. For this reason Muslims need to be told about the ingredients in menu items.

Meat has to be prepared in a special way when the animal is slaughtered. Meat that is prepared properly is called halal (permitted) meat (see Table 19.2). The

TABLE 19.2

Religion and food.

Type of food	Christian	Jewish	Hindu	Muslim	Buddhist
Vegetables, fruit and nuts	Yes	Yes	Yes	Yes	Yes
Alcohol	Most	Yes	No	No	No
Lamb	Yes	Kosher	Some	Halal	No
Beef	Yes	Kosher	No	Halal	No
Pork	Yes	No	Some	No	No
Animal fats, e.g. lard	Yes	No	Some	Halal, no pork fat	No
Fish	Yes	With scales, fins and backbone	With fins and scales	Halal	Some
Shellfish	Yes	No	Some	Halal	No
Chicken	Yes	Kosher	Some	Halal	No
Eggs	Yes	Yes	Some	Yes	Some
Milk products	Yes	No rennet (used for curdling milk for cheese); no milk products with meat	No rennet (used for curdling milk for cheese), e.g. parmesan	No rennet (used for curdling milk for cheese), e.g. parmesan	Yes

meat is killed in a similar way to kosher meat and if halal meat is not available Muslims will often buy from a kosher butcher.

Muslims fast during the month of Ramadan to show that they follow the will of Allah and appreciate what it is like to be without food and water. As mentioned earlier, the timing of meals served during Ramadan, especially those served before dawn, is most important.

Judaism

The Jewish people trace their history back to Abraham who left the area now known as Iraq to settle in the Promised Land, now known as Palestine or Israel. The descendants of Abraham, the Hebrews, were led out of slavery in Egypt by Moses. During this journey God parted the sea for the Israelites and this is celebrated at Passover. The Ten Commandments were revealed to Moses on Mount Sinai. The 'law of Moses' is the most important part of the Torah, the Jewish Bible.

Religion

Jewish people can worship in a synagogue or at home individually where the reading of the Torah plays an important part. The Torah is the teaching of God and should be obeyed by Jews. There are 613 Commandments in the Torah.

The Sabbath, on Saturday, is a day of rest. It begins at sunset on Friday evening and ends at sunset on Saturday evening. On Friday evening and Saturday morning Jews gather at the synagogue for Sabbath services.

Festivals

Passover lasts for eight days in spring and celebrates the exodus of the Hebrews from slavery in Egypt. During Passover Jews eat matzo, an unleavened bread, to remember the haste with which they left Egypt (the bread they had baked had no time to rise). A special meal called Seder is prepared on the first two nights to commemorate the story of the Passover.

At Rosh Hashanah (Jewish New Year) a ram's horn is blown to call Jewish people to repent. This begins the ten days leading up to Yom Kippur, a day of fasting and repentance, and the holiest day of the Jewish New Year.

Eating and drinking customs

Many Jews eat food that is kosher. This means that the animal has been slaughtered to the accompaniment of a ceremony called Schechitah during which a prayer is said as the animal is killed. It is a particular way of slaughtering an animal to ensure as painless a death as possible. As much blood as possible is then drained from the meat. Meat and dairy foods are not used as ingredients in the same dish or at the same meal. Jews allow several hours between eating the two types of food. Kosher kitchens therefore contain two sets of equipment, one for meat products and another for dairy products.

During the day of Yom Kippur, Jews do not eat or drink anything for approximately 25 hours (from one hour prior to sunset to the following evening when the first star is sighted). On this day, also known as the day of atonement, Jews think about their sins and make resolutions to live better lives.

Taoism

Taoists believe in the way of nature and view water as the most powerful of substances. Living in harmony is most important, with balance in life and longevity desirable blessings. The followers of Tao use ritual ceremonies to harness Te (power) in the hope of becoming immortal. The Yin and Yang symbol represents opposites: the Yin (dark, female, passive and soft) and the Yang (light, male, active and hard). In China, Confucianism, Buddhism and Taoism have merged. They are regarded as the 'Three Ways': order and respect, compassion and devotion, and mystical understanding.

Hot chips—universally popular.

Multicultural Australia

The definition of multiculturalism is a broad one. It means that members of all groups are accepted as equals in society, with the right to maintain and share aspects of their cultures, while at the same time respecting the institutions of the society in which they live, for example, its language, laws and parliamentary system. In Australia multiculturalism has meant that people may celebrate their own culture and religion.

Asian cuisine and eating habits

People coming from Asian countries such as China, Malaysia, Indonesia, Japan and Vietnam to live in Australia have had an enormous influence on Australian cuisine and eating habits. For hospitality employees, an understanding of the customs and eating habits of Asian visitors can contribute to a better understanding of their needs. Australia's culinary trends have ensured that many of the dishes and ingredients mentioned below are readily available in our restaurants and stores. This has contributed enormously to an understanding of customer expectations. Additionally, the multicultural menu enjoyed by Australians today has led to a shared vocabulary. For example, the use of chopsticks is popular, especially in our cities. If you turn back to Chapter 18, in which the eating habits and meals served in Australia in the early part of this century were described, and compare some of them with current eating trends, the changes are more obvious.

Chinese

Chinese food has some special features. Food is usually cut into small pieces in the kitchen and eaten at the table with chopsticks, which the Chinese have been using since 1600 BCE. If you were a visitor from China, you might find it odd to see people cutting up a steak at the table.

In Chinese cooking many different ingredients are included in the one dish, their tastes and textures being retained by very fast cooking methods, such as stir frying. This allows for vegetables such as bamboo shoots to retain their crispness. China has the world's biggest population (one-fifth of the world total) and foods vary from region to region. In the north beef and lamb are popular; in the south people prefer vegetables and rice; on the coast fish and seafood are favoured. In the western provinces the food is hot and spicy.

Rice is a staple part of the diet and is served with most meals. Bread dough is steamed rather than baked and this is illustrated in the following recipe for cha shiu bao (steamed pork buns). To make these buns, barbecued pork is diced very small and added to garlic, soy sauce, sesame oil and oyster sauce. This is thickened with cornflour, and hoi sin sauce, sugar and red colouring are added. The mixture is then placed in a ball of dough and steamed until the dough is light and fluffy.

Noodles, including both egg and rice varieties, are served at any time of the day. Soy sauce is one of the most popular seasonings used in Chinese cooking. Peking duck is a popular Chinese dish, particularly for banquets, which takes hours to prepare. The duck is cooked and basted carefully to produce a delicious crackling skin. Apparently the secret to this is blowing air between the skin and the flesh and hanging the duck in a special barrel before cooking. It is then carved and served in small pancakes, spread with plum sauce and wrapped up with spring onions and cucumber.

Chinese meals do not feature a main dish: dishes are placed on the table, usually one after the other, for everyone to share. Seasoned restaurant goers often smile at novices who each order an item from the menu and eat the whole thing. The Chinese tradition is to share all the dishes around and to enjoy the variety of cooking methods and ingredients used.

Yum cha, where customers choose individual servings from selections arranged on trolleys, is now widely enjoyed by Australians. Dim sums are always a popular choice at yum cha and are generally served with Chinese tea. Small prepared parcels, normally containing seafood, vegetables or pork, they are often steamed in bamboo baskets.

Indonesian

Food in Indonesia differs widely, depending on the area, though rice is served with most Indonesian meals. It is cooked by the absorption method or by steaming. This produces a better flavour than boiled rice, which tends to become flavourless and mushy. Rice should be pearly in colour and the grains should separate easily. Several curries are usually served at the same time, accompanied by sambals. Sambals are side dishes, which include lots of chillies. A meal would normally include a fish, poultry and meat curry served with rice and sambals. Curries are traditionally eaten at any meal with the fingers of the right hand. A favourite curry is beef rendang, which is flavoured with many spices and cooked in coconut milk. Tamarind liquid is added towards the end of the cooking process and the curry is cooked until it is quite dry but full of flavour.

Rice is also cooked with coconut milk and flavoured with tumeric, cumin, coriander, shrimp paste and lemon grass. Fruits and sweets (very different from our traditional sweets) are popular in Indonesia.

Japanese

Freshness and flawless presentation distinguish Japanese food. Oil is seldom used in cooking, with most dishes served raw or steamed. Flavours are very subtle, bringing out the tastes and textures of all ingredients. Sushi is very popular in Japan and increasingly in Australia. Rice is served in very small portions with raw fish and small amounts of vegetables or omelette. Sushi is often flavoured with horse-radish, which is quite strong. At one Australian school Japanese children were reportedly exchanging their painstakingly prepared selection of sushi for packets of Twisties—their contribution to multiculturalism! Miso shiru is a staple part of the diet. This soup, the basis of which is dashi (made with water, seaweed and dried fish) is flavoured with soy bean paste. Bean curd, onions and mushrooms are added to the broth. Instant miso is now often found in hotel room minibars to meet the needs of Japanese and Korean tourists.

Japanese meals are served individually, arranged with great care and attention to detail. Small bowls on trays are given to each guest. Particular attention is paid to colour in the presentation of all aspects of the meal. Bowls and plates are usually of the highest quality. A Japanese customer would therefore find food served on chipped or damaged crockery unacceptable. The quality of the rice (which should be cooked by the absorption method) is most important. Australian rice growers have spent many years achieving the required standards of the discriminating Japanese export market.

The chopsticks used for most dishes are more pointed than Chinese chopsticks. Sake, a kind of rice wine, is served with Japanese meals. Green tea, hot or iced, is also popular and of course it is not served with milk in the European style. It is impolite to fill one's own glass or cup so it is essential to ensure that the Japanese customer's or guest's glass is kept filled. Slurping is quite acceptable and is a sign of enjoyment.

Korean

Rice is served at every meal and again the quality of the rice is most important to the Korean visitor. Kim chi (pickled cabbage) is a favourite dish. The cabbage is finely sliced and pickled with onions, garlic, chillies and ginger. It is generally flavoured with light soy sauce. Koreans use a variety of cooking methods including steaming, stir frying, boiling and char grilling. Steamboat is another well-known dish, served on ceremonial occasions: the ingredients are arranged in a steamboat and broth is poured over them. Everyone helps themselves to the meat and vegetables until only a soup is left. This is then served at the end of the meal.

Malaysian

Malaysian cooking is very similar to Indonesian cooking. Many different peoples live in Malaysia and this is reflected in their diet. Muslims do not eat pork and would be most offended if offered it. Hindus do not eat beef. Aside from these limitations, the foods served are extremely varied. Fruits are abundant in this tropical climate and include such exotics as rambutan and star fruit, which are now available in many Australian fruit markets. Many desserts are coconut based. Gula melaka is a favourite and is made of chilled and moulded sago served with palm sugar syrup (gula melaka) and coconut milk.

Thai

Thailand is very well known for its curries and these have become so popular in restaurants in Australia that they are also available in supermarkets. Red curry paste, which is made from a wide variety of ingredients (including chillies, shrimp paste, fresh herbs and several spices) is now sold pre-prepared. It has a superb flavour and forms the basis for a quick meal. Small chicken pieces are browned with onion and to this red curry paste is added, followed by coconut milk and a little fish sauce. Green curry paste is also available. Fish and seafood are the main ingredients for many other curries. Rice is a staple part of the diet and provides the background for the many dishes served and shared at mealtimes.

Thai cooks are very skilled at carving vegetables and their dishes are superbly decorated with small flowers and leaves made from vegetables.

Other Asian customs

Following are some very general observations by writers who have visited eastern Asia. However, it is important to note that these vary between the various countries of this region.

Eating

In parts of Asia, people may:
- politely deny that they are hungry
- slurp their food in appreciation
- pick up the bowls from which they are eating
- use chopsticks.

Gift giving

Generally people will:
- find something unique, authentic or special to their culture
- wrap gifts with care
- use both hands when giving
- open gifts in private and not in the presence of the giver
- refer to the gift later
- take a gift when invited to a home
- sometimes give fruit or drink as a gift
- send thank-you notes.

Giving flowers to Asian peoples is not recommended as it is linked to illness. Writing in red ink should also be avoided as it is reminiscent of funeral notices.

Luck

Superstitions include:

- three is lucky in Thailand
- in Japan and Korea four is unlucky for room numbers and floors (the word is linked with death)
- in China eight is lucky, and nine is particularly auspicious.

Saving face

Generally people will:

- avoid public statements of blame or reprimand
- avoid open conflict and confrontation
- resolve conflicts privately without placing blame
- allow for a safe retreat.

Respecting the elderly

Respect for the elderly was mentioned in Chapter 2 and earlier in this chapter, but it needs to be stressed again because it is relevant to all market segments in the older age group (Australians included). Codes of behaviour have become more relaxed in most cultures and elderly people can find the resulting familiarity offensive. They expect to be treated with respect. The perceptions of this market are most important.

In Australia the number of people over 65 is expected to double by 2051. This projection is exactly the same for Japan, Germany, New Zealand and Canada, while in Korea, China, Indonesia, Singapore, Malaysia, Vietnam and Papua New Guinea the number is expected to triple. This has significant implications for the hospitality industry in Australia as these people are important customers.

Stereotyping

Cultural and other stereotyping is a complex issue. In some cases, stereotypes can help us to anticipate customer needs; in other cases, they can be completely inaccurate and quite harmful. There will be customers who do not fit the stereotype. For example, many elderly people like 'old-fashioned' plain food. However, selling only those items that fit the stereotype could result in loss of trade if the elderly people in the situation were more adventurous than anticipated. Likewise, hard selling of a coach tour to an elderly customer who has had a bad experience on such a tour would not be advisable. It is therefore essential to treat customers as individuals and to use a variety of strategies to establish and confirm their needs and expectations.

Activities

1 Visit a cultural, historical or religious museum. There are a number listed in the *Yellow Pages*. When you visit the museum of your choice, investigate the factors

that would most strongly influence customers' expectations of the tourism and hospitality industry.

2 Find appropriate recipes for foods that meet the religious requirements of one of the major religions discussed in this chapter.

3 Visit some Internet sites relating to the religions listed in this chapter. Remember that information on the Internet is uncensored and in some cases inaccurate.

Discussion questions

1 Where would you find the information you would need to advise a customer who asked about the times for church services?

2 How would you find the location of a temple or a mosque?

3 Which days of the week have religious significance for the various cultural groups discussed?

4 Which of the religious groups described in this chapter have particular needs in regard to food?

5 Which of the religious groups described have particular observances relating to alcohol?

LINKS

Asian cuisine—http://asiarecipe.com/

Ethnic foods and customs—http://www.eatethnic.com/

World religions—http://www.geocities.com/Athens/Forum/1699/

World Religions Index—http://wri.leaderu.com/

PART 3

Quality Service

After completing this section, you will be able to use your communication skills to promote products and services to customers. Using customer feedback, which is the basis for any quality service, you will be able to fine tune your service skills to effectively meet the needs of a wide range of customers.

COMPETENCY UNITS

PROMOTE PRODUCTS AND SERVICES TO CUSTOMERS (THHGCS02B)

Elements

- Develop product/service and market knowledge
- Encourage customers to use and buy products and services

COMMUNICATE ON THE TELEPHONE (THHGGA01B)

Elements

- Respond to incoming telephone calls
- Make telephone calls

CHAPTER TWENTY

Promoting quality products and services

OBJECTIVES

This chapter provides an introduction to the concepts and practices of sales and promotion and quality assurance in the hospitality industry. On completion you will be able to:

- encourage customers to buy products and services
- use advanced selling techniques
- describe the key concepts of quality management
- develop skills in open questioning.

We visited an Indian restaurant in Crows Nest the other evening. I don't usually choose Indian food because I have a preconceived idea that the food is too hot and spicy. My perception was turned upside down—it was the most exotic food I had eaten for years, the flavours were very subtle and the dishes I chose were not too hot at all. Above all, they were quite unlike anything I had ever prepared at home or anything I had tasted before. My husband was equally delighted with the very hot curry he had requested. The food was presented extremely well in small stainless steel bowls with several accompaniments. The plate-sized rice pancake roll (dosai) was perfectly browned and filled with a mildly spiced potato mixture that was pure heaven. The turbanned waiting staff were absolutely charming, assisting us with our choices and explaining ingredients. The service times were excellent, fast at first and slower towards the end of the meal. The pistachio ice cream (koulfi) was creamy and rich, full in flavour and quite unlike anything I had ever tasted. The dinner was an unqualified success, the quality of the food and the service being quite beyond our expectations.

RESTAURANT CUSTOMER

At the end of the above meal a small feedback card (see Fig. 20.1 on page 240) was presented to each customer to evaluate their perceptions of the food and the service. This feedback, combined with the reactions of customers to the owner and manager's questions about their meals, had clearly led to the development of menus and service approaches which best met the needs of the clientele. The fact that a very high percentage of their business was return business was another indication that for this restaurant quality management principles were being applied successfully. Other adjacent restaurants were practically empty.

FIG. 20.1

Sample customer feedback card.

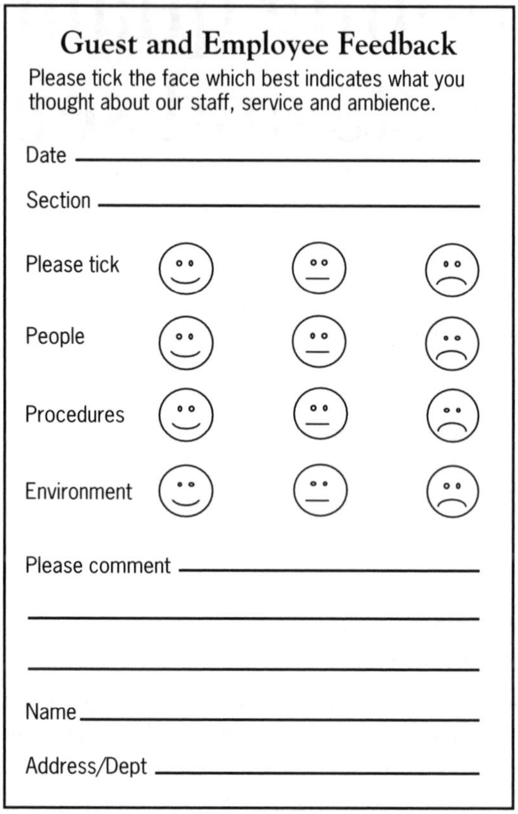

Guest and Employee Feedback

Please tick the face which best indicates what you thought about our staff, service and ambience.

Date _____

Section _____

Please tick	☺	☻	☹
People	☺	☻	☹
Procedures	☺	☻	☹
Environment	☺	☻	☹

Please comment _____

_____

_____

Name _____

Address/Dept _____

The selling quality loop

In this chapter we will look closely at the topic of promoting products and services to customers. This will be linked to the feedback and quality assurance processes that are used to monitor the success of an operation. Good promotional work is wasted if products and services are not up to standard. Quality products and services are wasted if they cannot be sold effectively. Most hospitality organisations work hard to achieve a balance between these two aims, selling effectively and monitoring success in order to meet customer needs. This is illustrated in Fig. 20.2.

Your role is to promote products and services and to monitor the quality of those products and services to ensure that customers are satisfied.

Developing product/service knowledge

Having completed the earlier chapters on the various departments (and the services they offer) in most large hospitality organisations, you should be in a good position to promote the products and services that your enterprise offers.

FIG. 20.2

Promoting quality products and services.

```
   Promoting products        Managing quality
      and services
```

To be effective in promoting products and services, you need to develop your knowledge of the products and services available from:

- your department (such as ironing service)
- other departments (such as room service)
- within the organisation (such as meeting facilities).

For example, although your hotel might not be big enough to host a large conference, you might be able to put a client in touch with the Sales and Marketing Department of another hotel within your chain.

As an ambassador of the hospitality industry in Australia, you also need to be able to promote products and services that are:

- provided by external agencies (such as transport or childminding)
- available in your local area (such as museums, galleries or shopping)
- available within Australia (such as attractions, tours and transport).

A product is generally something tangible, such as a comfortable bed or a delicious meal. Service is intangible: it is the help, support and cheerfulness that staff offer customers and other staff, which is particularly important in the hospitality industry. Most people will leave home for a meal in order to enjoy the intangible elements of the dining-out experience, even if they are very good cooks.

To extend your knowledge of products and services, it would be useful to refer back to Chapter 3, which covered the topic of research, and to find time to:

- make opportunities to develop product/service knowledge (for example, visiting exhibitions)
- monitor the media (including the press and industry journals) for up-to-date information
- use formal and informal research skills to update your knowledge
- observe industry practices in the promotional area
- share your knowledge with colleagues and develop a team approach to selling
- monitor changes in customer preferences
- take a proactive approach to seeking customer feedback

- suggest ideas for improvements to the products and services offered by your organisation.

The last two suggestions form the basis of the section below on quality management.

Legal issues that impact on selling

As an employee in the hospitality industry, you need to be aware of legislation that protects consumers. Trade Practices legislation (at federal level) and Sale of Goods Acts (at state and territory level) are designed to ensure that consumers receive what they expect. This means that your selling efforts must be tempered with caution. It is unwise to encourage customers to have unrealistic expectations of your products and services. By providing clear, correct information about your products and services to customers, you will ensure that they have realistic expectations of what is available.

Promotional efforts include advertising, and this is one strategy undertaken by the Marketing Department or business owner to sell their products and services to the customer. Promotional material (such as an advertisement in the *Yellow Pages* or on the Internet) includes, for example, images of the location and some of the products available. Generally speaking, promotional material includes information on the level and diversity of the services available, which must be accurate to comply with the legislation mentioned above.

Quality management

Quality management is a philosophy of continuous evaluation and improvement and this concept is illustrated in Fig. 20.3. This philosophy has proved extremely successful in a world of changing customer expectations. Some hospitality organisations take on quality management as a major approach to the way they do business, formalising many of their systems and procedures for quality management. Other smaller hospitality businesses achieve the same goals by managing quality issues unconsciously. Anyone running a small business who listens closely to customers and adapts to meet changing customer requirements is managing quality, even if there is no formal label attached to the process.

FIG. 20.3

Feedback cycle for continuous improvement.

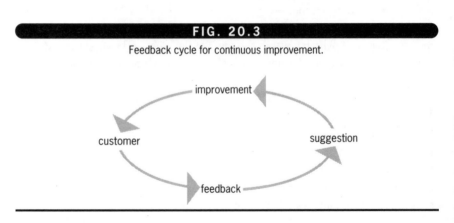

Selling products and services

Some service staff are very reluctant to sell. What they don't realise is that customers want to be given information, as they want to try new things. For example, a customer in a bar might welcome a suggestion to try a new cocktail, especially if it were described in an interesting way. Believe it or not, most customers are very shy.

There are several types of selling, and these are described below.

A team approach to selling.
Manly Pacific Parkroyal, located on central Manly beach.

Top down selling

In this type of selling you offer the highest price and quality first, moving down the scale until you establish the customer's needs.

Bottom up selling

Once the customer has been told the lowest prices available and what they will provide, you can work your way up the scale, offering better products and services. Views, larger rooms and butler service may be some of the more expensive options when selling accommodation in a hotel.

Suggestive selling

With this method the product and service features are sold to the customer. Flavours and textures, freshness and preparation method, colour and presentation of food items are some of the features that would help a customer to choose an item on a menu. Outlook, price, convenience and spaciousness would assist in selling a motel room.

Cross-selling

In addition to the basic service or product being sold, there may be other associated products of interest to the customer. Travel insurance is a good example, likewise tickets for entertainment and tours, and vouchers for car rental. This is also known as lateral selling.

Benefit selling

This approach involves selling benefits to the customer. For example, an early check-in might allow for a full day's sightseeing but it could also involve an earlier, more expensive flight.

Informational selling

Where the sales person is very knowledgeable, they are likely to be viewed by the customer as highly credible. A customer would take the advice of a wine waiter who clearly knew which wine would best suit the chosen meal. Likewise a travel agent who has visited a large number of tourist destinations would find it easy to sell those destinations to a client.

FIG. 20.4

Steps for successful selling.

1 Manage all incoming customers promptly.

2 Keep all waiting customers interested by, for example, giving them brochures on the establishment's products and services.

3 Introduce yourself and use the customer's name.

4 Use open questions to build a relationship.

5 Offer recommendations and sell benefits.

6 Acknowledge and overcome objections.

7 Cross sell associated products and services and promote add-ons.

8 Complete a sales proposal form, agree on a plan of action and follow up.

9 Always obtain a commitment by using open questions.

10 Thank every customer for choosing the company.

Guidelines for successful selling are provided in Fig. 20.4.

The practice of providing extras, or add-ons, is quite commonplace, and has the benefit of enhancing the customer's perception of value for money. Examples of add-ons are a free cooked breakfast and a liqueur and chocolates after dinner.

Feedback ensures improvement

From a management point of view, one form of feedback is falling revenue, but waiting for a business to go bad is not good management and poor financial results seldom show reasons for falling trade or provide ideas as to how to turn the situation around.

In research at a higher level, Mok, Armstrong and Go (1995) investigated the perceptions of Taiwanese travellers with regard to the importance of various features of holiday destinations. Interestingly, they rated safety as the most important destination attribute, followed by scenic beauty, cultural interests and friendliness of the local people. These findings are summarised in Table 20.1.

Surveys like this one often produce quite surprising results. However, knowing that safety is one of the most important features for Taiwanese tourists, hotels and tour operators can make a special effort to ensure that this aspect is highlighted in their promotional material and that safety issues are addressed when these travellers arrive. In some countries the chances of being attacked are high so when visiting those countries tourists would be keen to know where they could walk safely at night. Local residents tend to take the safety of their environment for granted.

TABLE 20.1	
Ranking of destination attributes by Taiwanese travellers.	
Attributes (destination features)	**Ranking (order of importance)**
Safety	1
Scenic beauty	2
Cultural interests	3
Friendliness of local people	4
Price of trip	5
Services in hotels and restaurants	6
Quality and variety of foods	7
Shopping facilities and services	8
Climate	9
Entertainment (night life)	10
Recreational and sports activities	11
Destination distances from place of residence	12
Friends and relatives at destination	13

Source: C. Mok, R. Armstrong and F. Go, 'Taiwanese Travellers' Perception of Leisure Destination Attributes', *Australian Journal of Hospitality Management*, vol. 2, Jan. 1995.

For international visitors who can't swim, emergency procedures would be an important consideration for management of, say, a Great Barrier Reef cruise. Adequate translations would also be an important issue. Safety of valuables can be fairly simply addressed by providing room safes, though this is not always done. One person we have heard about had his watch stolen from his room. On reporting this to the staff at the hotel, they showed him a videotape of someone coming in through the window and removing the watch from behind his bed while he was asleep. He was not sure whether to be more upset about the theft or about the fact that his room had been under surveillance without his knowledge! In comparison, Australia is generally regarded as a reasonably safe destination and this feature can be used to advantage to market Australia to overseas countries.

While the research mentioned above was quite general in its findings, it is clear that it also has quite wide-ranging implications.

Role of staff in obtaining customer feedback

It is the role of most hospitality staff to obtain feedback. This type of feedback is more specific than the above.

Employees can help both their organisation and their customers through a number of actions. They can:

- watch procedures and suggest better ways of doing things
- watch customers and see how they react, noting particular trends
- ask customers for specific feedback
- make suggestions and check responses

- brainstorm new ideas
- visit competitors and compare operations.

One company sends its employees out for dinner so they can review the operations of their competitors. Other companies send travel agents on 'educational' visits to experience destinations first hand. Feedback from knowledgeable operators is invaluable. Some organisations have mystery shoppers, mystery tourists and mystery guests.

Quality standards and audit procedures

Many organisations have quality standards. KFC has provided us with the set of standards they have compiled for their operations (see Fig. 20.5). They show staff

FIG. 20.5

KFC key quality measures.

FLAVOUR AND TEXTURE

If you don't . . .
1 Have the right ingredients
2 Use fresh shortening
3 Follow correct cooking procedures
4 Hold the product to standard
5 Select fresh products
You won't get . . .   GOOD TASTING FOOD

APPEARANCE

If you don't . . .
1 Have the right ingredients
2 Cook with fresh shortening
3 Use the right breading procedures
4 Choose raw products at the right temperature
5 Use fresh products
6 Handle and package it right
You won't get . . .   APPETISING APPEARANCE

TEMPERATURE

If you don't . . .
1 Cook with shortening at the right temperature
2 Use the right holding procedures and times
3 Follow KFC's cooking procedures
4 Set equipment correctly
You won't get . . .   RIGHT TEMPERATURE

AVAILABILITY

If you don't . . .
1 Update and follow the MP&C
2 Have equipment on to cook enough product
3 Prevent mispacks
4 Have a productive team
You won't get . . .   ENOUGH READY TO SELL

Courtesy of Kentucky Fried Chicken.

how the four key quality measures can be achieved effectively. If you read these carefully, you will see where things can go wrong. If fresh products aren't used, the flavour and texture won't be right. Limp lettuce, for example, is not the best ingredient. If food is not cooked at the right temperature, it will be colder than the customer would expect and will also increase the risk of food poisoning. Chips that have been standing for too long will become mushy. For all these reasons, quality standards are essential for an effective fast food operation. To audit these quality measures, the temperature of cooking equipment can be checked, holding times for cooked food can be observed, quantities of ingredients can be measured and food can be tasted for flavour and texture.

A booking agent would also follow standard procedures, though different from those above. One of these would be to obtain the customer's name and contact number for follow-up calls. Another would be the repetition of key information such as credit card numbers and dates. Any errors here would have serious consequences. An audit of these procedures would involve checking the time it took to answer the call, whether the person identified themselves correctly, whether the tone of voice was helpful and how readily questions were answered.

Implementing quality procedures

There are a number of ways in which staff can make a valuable contribution to quality control. The first of these is to obtain feedback from customers, and the second is to obtain feedback from work teams, as already discussed in Chapter 17. Quality is also an issue in relationships with suppliers and, as Fig. 20.6 shows, a purchase specification will ensure that the right product has been ordered and delivered.

FIG. 20.6

Order/purchase specification.

Tenderloin (centre cut)

Portion weight:	120–130 grams
Portion size:	Thickness 25–35 mm
Trim:	No butt or tail, centre only, uniform thickness
Description:	Moderate marbling, light red in colour or slightly dark red; free from odour, deterioration and evidence of freezing or defrosting
Delivery:	Chilled

Statistics can also be used to analyse performance. Customer preferences for certain tours, particular meals and special activities provide important guidelines for better planning. In most computerised hospitality operations a range of reports assists with this process of analysis. In a bar, for example, preferences for cocktails or other trends on certain nights provide guidelines for ordering fresh ingredients and having them ready for rush periods.

Preparing for a day's trading is one 'critical control point'. In kitchens this is known as mise-en-place. When all ingredients are ready, and each item is in its correct place, service will flow smoothly. If, on the other hand, not enough potatoes have been peeled, or if the cream has not been ordered, chaos will occur during the busy period. Receiving the food for the kitchen and checking that the quantity and quality of the food is in line with written specifications is a quality assurance measure.

Checking the temperature of food at critical control points is also very important in order to avoid the growth of bacteria, which can cause food poisoning. Another simple, but important, procedure in the hospitality environment is checking that there is enough change. Based on previous trading the business should be able to predict the amount of money needed in the cash register and the denominations required for giving change.

All of these procedures are in place for good reason and work teams need to ensure that they are followed correctly. It is very easy, for example, to lose a note recording a request for a customer (such as a change to booking details) and this would have serious outcomes. Clear communication during training and between team members will help to avoid such problems. However, not all problems can be anticipated and complaints are another valuable form of feedback (even though they are negative), which assist in the smooth running of an operation.

Handling complaints

Complaints are, in fact, one of the most important forms of customer feedback. They should be discussed openly, so that the reasons for them can be avoided in the future. Customers should be thanked for bringing problems to your attention.

The steps for handling complaints have been covered in Chapter 16. However, not all of them can be followed all the time, and sometimes they should not be followed in the specific order mentioned. For example, if you were particularly busy, you would need to make a snap decision without consulting the client in detail. This is the judgement required in communication that we have talked about in Part 2. Some complaint situations are unusual and need to be handled individually and as promptly as possible, and analysed later.

Open questioning

The last topic to be covered—and possibly the most important—is that of questioning. One of the most valuable skills a person in this industry can have is the ability to ask open questions. In fact it could be argued that being able to ask open questions is one of the most important keys to building all successful relationships!

Closed questions are questions that can be answered with a 'yes' or a 'no'. Some examples are: 'Are you enjoying your meal?', 'Did you like the trip?' and 'Are you just looking?'

Open questions, on the other hand, demand a full answer. They would be something like 'Which galleries would you like to visit on your trip overseas?' or 'Which parts of Australia have you visited so far?' or 'How is the food here different from your food at home?'

By practising the art of questioning, hospitality staff can ascertain customer needs, make conversation and obtain the all-important feedback necessary for quality improvement in products and services.

Activities

1 I would never tell my manager about a problem or a complaint. It would be admitting that I had made a mistake. He would be furious and it would cost me my job. Develop a short talk to persuade this manager to change his approach to negative feedback.

2 Use the check list below to evaluate the quality control in two takeaway shops. Rate the items from 1 (poor) to 5 (excellent).

Cleanliness of windows and floors	[ ]	[ ]	[ ]	[ ]	[ ]
Cleanliness of food preparation areas	[ ]	[ ]	[ ]	[ ]	[ ]
Tidiness/organisation of food preparation areas	[ ]	[ ]	[ ]	[ ]	[ ]
Lighting	[ ]	[ ]	[ ]	[ ]	[ ]
Staff uniforms	[ ]	[ ]	[ ]	[ ]	[ ]
Cleanliness and professional presentation of staff	[ ]	[ ]	[ ]	[ ]	[ ]
Name badges	[ ]	[ ]	[ ]	[ ]	[ ]
Food advertising/menu	[ ]	[ ]	[ ]	[ ]	[ ]
Food displayed	[ ]	[ ]	[ ]	[ ]	[ ]
Temperature, taste and texture of food	[ ]	[ ]	[ ]	[ ]	[ ]
Speed of service	[ ]	[ ]	[ ]	[ ]	[ ]
Friendliness of staff	[ ]	[ ]	[ ]	[ ]	[ ]

3 Assume that you are a very anxious elderly traveller on a plane. Role play this situation to show how staff could make this trip less traumatic for you?

4 Looking at the survey results for the Taiwanese tourists in Table 20.1, rate the attributes (destination features) and list them in order of importance (from most to least important) for your own overseas holiday. You can choose any destination.

Discussion questions

1 Explain why customer feedback is useful.

2 Some fast food outlets would throw out up to ten kilograms of hot chips per day. Chips prepared during rush periods cannot be kept indefinitely. How long do you think that hot chips should be left standing before they lose their quality?

3 Give some examples of open questions which would encourage feedback from a client or customer.

CASE STUDY

Trevor was a customer desperate for information. He kept asking questions when attempting to make a reservation but the person on the telephone seemed to have limited knowledge of the resort. In fact, it became evident that she had not worked at the resort for long and had not become familiar with the facilities and services provided. She could not answer questions like whether or not there was a bath in the room, whether ironing boards were available or if room service was open for late arrivals. When Trevor finally discovered that she was an Irish backpacker who had been working at the resort for only three days, he gave up completely and decided to book elsewhere.

Discussion questions

- When a person is booking into a resort, what information might they ask for?
- How would a new employee become familiar with the facilities and services of their resort?
- Who is responsible for the training for this role?
- In addition to providing all the information that customers might require, what other selling suggestions would you give to new staff working in this role?

LINKS

Hotel Resource (successful upselling)—
http://www.hotelresource.com/newsletter/magazine/stories/article0205.html

Restaurants and institutions (suggestive selling)—
http://www.rimag.com/022/Togo.htm

CHAPTER TWENTY-ONE

Communicating on the telephone

OBJECTIVES

This chapter deals with the skills and knowledge required for communicating on the telephone. On completion of this chapter you will be able to:
- respond to incoming calls from internal and external customers
- use telephone calls to enhance communication with internal customers
- handle emergencies
- promote products and services
- handle complaints.

Helloooo!
Good morning, is that the Broadway Bed and Breakfast?
Yeah it is. Can I help you?
I would like to find out about your accommodation.
It is $110 per night and it includes a cooked breakfast.
I am a vegetarian and I would prefer cereal, toast and fruit.
No worries, we have fresh and canned fruit.
Do you allow children?
Yeah, we have two teenagers so that's not a problem. The kids can sleep in your room or in the rumpus room.
Are you close to transport?
Yeah.
Well, that's fine. I will ring back when I want to make a booking.
No worries, see you then. Bye.
Goodbye.

This conversation illustrates the importance of effective telephone communication when dealing with customers, particularly prospective customers like this one. While the language used by the bed and breakfast operator—let's call her Dawn—is quite colloquial, this is not the major concern as there are many customers who would enjoy the authenticity and informality of her approach. However, if you look at the conversation closely, there are a number of things that Dawn forgot to do:
- She did not identify herself or her bed and breakfast operation by name.

- She did not find out the customer's name, nor did she use it during the conversation.
- She talked first about price and did not sell the features of her bed and breakfast.
- She did not offer any information about the location, transport or attractions in the area.
- In response to the question about children, she assumed that the caller had children she wanted to bring with her whereas the caller might have wanted to avoid children (some bed and breakfast operations do not accommodate children).
- Finally and most importantly, Dawn did not try to close the sale.

Closing the sale would have involved asking some open-ended questions such as 'When would you like to stay?' If Dawn had sought this information, she could have offered to make a provisional booking for the dates given and could have closed by asking for a telephone contact number. This would have avoided asking a direct, closed question such as 'Would you like to make a booking?' which might have produced a negative response. In summary, Dawn did not ask enough questions nor did she offer enough information to appear interested, friendly and professional.

In this chapter we will look at telephone communication from a number of perspectives (see Fig. 21.1). First, we will review how you should respond to incoming calls, provide information and take messages. Then we will look at making telephone calls to internal and external customers, using the telephone in an emergency, which is particularly important, and finally, the skills required to promote products and services over the telephone. Some revision of the principles of handling complaints will reinforce information covered in Chapters 16 and 20.

Responding to incoming telephone calls

When you hear an incoming telephone call, you should respond promptly and speak clearly and politely. You should follow the standards set by your organisation, which usually include the name of your organisation or department and your name. You should then find out how you can be of assistance.

Be prepared, with paper, pen, telephone message pad and internal telephone directory handy. You should know how to put a caller on hold and how to transfer a call. The caller should get your full attention. Dividing your time between the call and another task is inappropriate because the caller may tune into your non-verbal communication and sense that you are not paying attention. If you are asked to do something, make sure that you are clear about what is required and check your understanding with the caller.

Recording information

Recording information is essential. You should write down the caller's name immediately so that you can use it during the conversation. In addition, if you have to take a message, you won't have to ask for the person's name again, which is

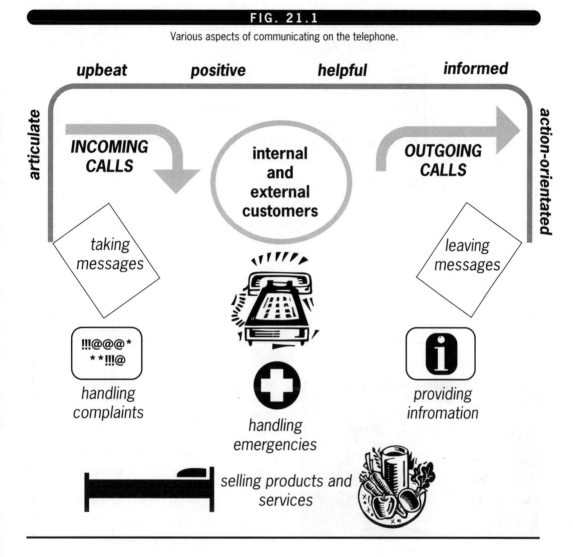

FIG. 21.1

Various aspects of communicating on the telephone.

embarrassing if you have forgotten it. Repeating information as you write it down will ensure accuracy, especially if you are dealing with numbers and the spelling of people's names. Record the date and time of the call, how and when the caller can be contacted and the message (see Fig. 21.2 on page 254).

Ensuring 'one-stop' service

One of the most frustrating things that can happen to a caller is to be transferred from department to department. Where possible, you should investigate the issue yourself, find out the information and call the customer back. This involves taking ownership of the problem and solving it for the customer. 'One-stop' service is a good example of quality service in a business environment in which many

FIG. 21.2

Recording telephone messages

Date	Time
Caller	Telephone number

Please call back ☐   Will call again ☐   Returned your call ☐

Message

Manly Pacific Parkroyal, located on central Manly beach.

callers have no other option but to choose numbers on the telephone after listening to a recorded message.

When you say, 'May I help you?' you should place the emphasis on 'I' and really mean it.

In a hospitality organisation information on the following products and services may be required:

- tours and transport
- conferences and conventions
- restaurant facilities and menus
- function facilities
- entertainment
- special events
- shopping services
- food and beverage facilities, including bars
- gaming facilities
- add-on facilities (such as health and business centres).

Leaving a message

When leaving a message on an answering machine, always identify yourself and give your telephone number and the time you called. When giving the telephone number, say it slowly enough for the person to be able to write it down. In addition, explain why you are calling and when you will be available.

Handling telephone complaints

Although this topic has already been covered, some of the key points are relevant to handling telephone complaints. Finding out the customer's name and the full details of the complaint is essential. You should write down everything the customer says. If you find that you can't handle the situation yourself, you will then be able to explain it fully to the appropriate person. Customers who complain should not have to repeat themselves. Once you understand the nature of the complaint, you should look at the options and make a decision on the course of action. Finally, you should make sure that the customer agrees with the next steps to be taken. Following through to complaint resolution and advising the customer of the result generally leads to loyalty from your customer who, by issuing the complaint, is helping you to improve your products and services. If complaints are seen in this positive light, the approach you take to solve them will satisfy the customer.

Making emergency calls

When dealing with an emergency, it is extremely important that you stay calm so that you can find out what the emergency entails. If you have all the details, you will be able to arrange the appropriate emergency service and ensure that it goes to the right place. It is always helpful to arrange for someone to meet the emergency crew at the gate or the entrance.

The three key things you need to know are:
- the exact nature of the emergency
- the exact location of the emergency
- who the caller is and what they or anyone else has done.

There will be specific procedures for emergencies in your organisation. Usually the Communications Department is the emergency command centre. Their role is to call emergency services and advise the appropriate people in your organisation, for example, the duty manager and the security officer. In the case of a bomb threat it is vital that you write down everything that is said by the people involved. This information will help investigators.

The importance of voice quality

Using a positive, upbeat tone of voice is one of the golden rules of effective telephone communication. You will also find these additional guidelines useful:
- Speak clearly.
- Don't use slang or colloquial expressions.
- Avoid using industry jargon that the customer might not understand.
- Pitch your voice at the right level: too high is irritating and too low sounds as though you are almost asleep.
- Pace your speech. If you speak too quickly, the customer will think that you are too busy to help them; if you speak too slowly, the customer will think that you are bored or unhelpful.

- Use questions to check understanding.
- Adopt a positive approach and positive expressions.

This final suggestion is the most important one. By using expressions such as 'Certainly', 'Of course', 'Yes, I understand' and 'Right away', you will quickly build rapport with your client.

The importance of open questions

If you ask open questions (what, when, why, how) you will be able to gain more information from your customer. These questions will also enable you to tailor the information you provide to meet your customer's needs. If you paraphrase what they say to you, you will not only be able to check your understanding, but you will also offer encouragement to the customer by indicating that you are attentive to them.

In summary, the performance standards usually associated with good telephone technique are as follows:

- calls are answered promptly, clearly and politely
- friendly assistance is provided to the caller
- the purpose of the call is established
- details are repeated for confirmation
- callers are transferred to appropriate people
- requests are recorded and passed on
- opportunities for promotion of products and services are utilised or followed up.

Activity

Read the following excerpt from the brochure on Puffing Billy, one of Australia's last remaining steam railways. Then, you and a partner role play a customer and the receptionist discussing details of a proposed trip on the telephone.

Puffing Billy is a genuine relic of our more leisurely days. An historic steam train still running regularly in the mountain district, it was built to serve at the turn of the century. The railway is the sole survivor of four experimental narrow gauge lines used to develop rural areas in the early 1900s. Puffing Billy runs every day of the year, except Christmas Day, so why not take yourself and your family or friends on a sentimental journey along this 25 kilometre operating museum. Enjoy the mountain scenery and panoramic views which pass your carriage window. Why not stop over at Lakeside and enjoy a few hours in beautiful Emerald Lake Reserve or travel to Gembrook, the terminus of the railway and explore this picturesque little township.

HOW TO GET THERE

All Puffing Billy trips depart from and return to Belgrave in the Dandenong Ranges, only 40 kilometres from Melbourne. However, when the timetable permits, a round trip may also be commenced at Menzies Creek, Emerald or Lakeside.

TAKE THE TRAIN Suburban trains run frequently from Flinders Street direct to Belgrave in 70 minutes. For train times, phone the Transport Information Centre on 131 638. The Puffing Billy station is a short walk from Belgrave 'Met' station.

DRIVE YOUR CAR Belgrave is located on Melway Map 75, reference F10. Alternatively, take Wellington Road to Clematis, then turn left towards Menzies Creek or right towards Emerald and Lakeside. Car parking is available near these stations.

CAR PARKING AT BELGRAVE There is no parking area or road access at Puffing Billy's Belgrave station. Park your car in the 'Met' carpark near the suburban railway station, then follow the walkway under the main road bridge, or park in the Bayview Road parking area.

GROUP BOOKINGS A trip on Puffing Billy is the ideal outing for your school, club, social or church group. Except in the month of January, discounts are available for pre-booked groups of 20 or more mid-week and on Saturdays.

CONCESSIONS Concessions for travel between Belgrave and Lakeside are available to bearers of a health care, student, transport concession or seniors card. Children under four years of age, not occupying a seat, are carried FREE. 'Family' tickets are available for two adults (aged 17 and over) plus three children (aged 4–6) OR one adult plus four children.

DAY TOURS Day tours which include a trip on Puffing Billy are operated by AAT Kings, Australian Pacific and Gray Line Melbourne.

DISABLED PASSENGERS Specially designed carriages accommodate a limited number of passengers in wheelchairs.

REFRESHMENTS Refreshment rooms at Belgrave, Menzies Creek, Emerald and Lakeside stock a wide range of snacks, confectionery, drinks, ice-creams and Puffing Billy souvenirs.

PRAMS Due to the narrow carriage doors, only folding type pushers can be accommodated on Puffing Billy.

DOGS Dogs are prohibited on the train (guide dogs are an exception).

TIMETABLE

Refer to our website:
www.puffingbilly.com.au

Note: Information is correct at the time of publication. Confirm events and timetables by contacting (03) 9754 6800 or email us on info@pbr.org.au

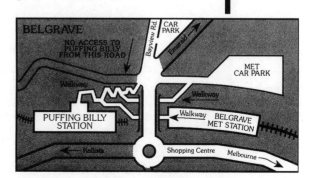

Courtesy of Puffing Billy Railway.

PART 4

Health, Safety and Hygiene Systems

This section deals with the systems that support service. These include health, safety and security procedures and workplace hygiene procedures. This section also includes information on waste management, an important issue for the hospitality industry as it relates to cleaning and maintaining premises.

COMPETENCY UNITS

FOLLOW HEALTH, SAFETY AND SECURITY PROCEDURES (THHCOR03B)

Elements

- Follow workplace procedures on health, safety and security
- Deal with emergency situations
- Maintain safe personal presentation standards
- Provide feedback on health, safety and security

FOLLOW WORKPLACE HYGIENE PROCEDURES (THHGHS01B)

Elements

- Follow hygiene procedures
- Identify and prevent risks

CLEAN PREMISES AND EQUIPMENT (THHGHS02B)

Elements

- Select and set up equipment
- Clean wet and dry areas
- Maintain and store cleaning equipment and chemicals

CHAPTER TWENTY-TWO

Occupational health and safety

OBJECTIVES

This chapter takes the topic of workplace health and safety further to discuss risks to the health and safety of staff, and suggests steps that can be taken to avoid workplace accidents. On completion of this chapter you will be able to:

- describe the most common workplace accidents in the hospitality industry
- describe unsafe working conditions and practices
- list effective accident prevention practices for the workplace
- state the responsibilities and obligations of employers and employees under current occupational health and safety (OHS) legislation
- review employment-related health risks such as stress, alcoholism and drug dependence
- describe measures to prevent the contraction of blood-borne diseases such as Hepatitis B and AIDS
- use appropriate lifting techniques.

A first year apprentice, scraping melted sugar off a spoon, flicked some of the sugar onto her bare arm causing terrible burns. She spent many weeks in hospital having skin grafts, all of which was covered by workers compensation insurance. However, although she did not lose financially, the pain and suffering were unforgettable. The scars will last a lifetime.

Safe work practices are absolutely essential in an industry in which burns, cuts and back injuries are reported every day. If the apprentice had been wearing the required long-sleeved cotton uniform, her injury would have been prevented, and that is why prevention is the main focus of this chapter.

A risk management approach to occupational health and safety identifies current and potential risks, their potential severity and the measures that can be taken to minimise or eliminate them. This involves an ongoing process of improvement, and is the recommended path to health and safety in the workplace.

Workplace accidents in the hospitality industry

The most common injuries to workers in the hospitality industry are burns, cuts, falls, strains, chemical accidents and electric shocks.

Burns and heat-related illness

Burns can be caused by carelessness such as:

- taking the lid off a pot and leaning over the steam
- brushing against an open flame
- picking up a pot or holding the handle of a pot without a towel
- knocking over saucepans containing boiling water or soup
- touching hot elements, such as froth-makers on cappuccino machines
- leaving hot oil unattended
- using flammable liquids carelessly
- leaving spills.

Preventative measures include:

- wearing the correct uniform, including long sleeves and safety shoes
- wearing cotton clothing
- working carefully
- avoiding filling saucepans too high
- checking the pan handle before picking up a pan
- turning pan handles inwards to avoid bumping against them
- using a towel to pick up hot items (but not a wet towel—steam burns)
- watching other people and warning them when carrying hot or heavy items
- avoiding tiredness and preoccupation.

If burns occur:

- do not touch the injured areas or burst any blisters
- do not remove anything sticking to the burn
- cool the burnt area
- hold the burnt area under cold running water for at least 10 minutes.
- if it is a chemical burn, run cold water over the burnt area for at least 20 minutes
- if the burn is to the eye, flush the eye with water for 20 minutes.

Many chefs and their assistants work in hot environments and this can lead to heat-related illness. The symptoms of heat illness include dizziness, fainting, nausea and headache. Treatment includes drinking water and resting in a cooler area. Prevention involves drinking sufficient water, wearing appropriate clothing and taking breaks as needed, particularly in conditions of extreme heat as sometimes occur in kitchens.

Cuts

The second most common injury in the kitchen is cuts. These are caused by:

- using the wrong knife
- using a blunt knife
- not handling items for cutting correctly
- not using a wet cloth under a chopping board
- inattention.

There are a number of chefs around the country with tips of their fingers missing. This might have been avoided by taking the following precautions:

- using the correct knife for the job (not too small, nor too big)
- using a sharp, well-maintained knife

- stabilising the items being cut (e.g. flat side down)
- using an appropriate cutting board with a wet cloth underneath to steady it
- keeping the fingertips out of the way and using the knuckles to guide the knife (this takes practice)
- using guards on equipment
- paying attention.

Falls and strains

Slipping and falling are not uncommon in this busy industry. During mealtimes kitchen floors can become very slippery from oily substances, scraps and dropped napkins, all of which can cause falls, particularly when service staff are rushing with heavy trays.

Accidents can happen in the following ways:
- bumping into items when vision is obscured
- slipping on wet or slippery floors
- losing one's balance when locating items stored incorrectly or on unsafe shelves.

Preventative measures include:
- correct storage with proper shelving
- good lighting
- non-slip floors (clean and dry)
- cleaning spills and removing obstructions
- keeping the work area tidy
- wearing rubber-soled shoes.

Signs are essential to prevent customers and staff slipping on wet floors.

Manual handling injuries

Manual handling is a common cause of workplace injuries in hospitality, particularly for housekeepers (moving beds), porters (moving bags and boxes), cellarmen (moving kegs) and banquet attendants (moving tables). Fig. 22.1 on page 264 details the common causes of manual handling injuries and recommended preventative measures.

Employees should be given advice on safe handling techniques. These are:

1 Squat close to the load and keep your back straight. Do not stoop over the load to get a grip to pick it up.
2 Test the weight of the object before attempting to lift it.
3 Lift using your knees and legs (not your back) as leverage.
4 Keep your back straight, not bent forwards or backwards. Do not twist or turn the body while carrying the object or putting it down.

Fig. 22.2 on page 264 provides an illustration of safe lifting, which should be practised by employees in the hospitality industry to avoid back injury.

Chemical-related injuries

There are many different cleaning agents, some of which are very toxic, thus increasing the risk to staff. The most serious accidents are caused when chemicals are not mixed correctly or are kept in the wrong containers and used for the wrong purpose.

FIG. 22.1

Guide to manual handling.

Common causes of injury	Preventative measures
Lifting boxes from the floor	Do not store items on the floor. Use correct lifting technique.
Moving beds, tables, kegs and suitcases	Test item before lifting or moving. Get help if needed. Use a trolley. Avoid twisting.
Carrying boxes or equipment	Use proper lifting techniques. Get help or use a lifting aid. Use a cart. Avoid over-reaching, twisting or lifting over head.
Pushing carts	Maintain casters in clean, operating condition. Match the casters to the floor type.

FIG. 22.2

Safe lifting.

Mixing incompatible chemicals can be extremely dangerous. Chemicals should be stored and labelled correctly. They should be used in well-ventilated areas or, if this is not possible, masks should be worn. Chemicals should not be used near a naked flame or cigarette. Care and concentration are most important when dealing with chemicals.

Equipment-related injuries

Manufacturers' instructions should be followed. Careful attention should be paid to safety features to avoid, for example, getting fingers or hair caught in machines. Appliances should be turned off before disconnecting, and cords and plugs should be kept in good condition.

The three most important contributions employees can make to safety in the workplace are good housekeeping (keeping the workplace tidy), wearing the correct uniform and shoes, and avoiding tiredness caused by too many late nights, too many shifts or too few breaks.

Other workplace risks

In addition to workplace accidents, the following can cause discomfort, serious illness and even death if not properly managed.

Sunburn

Hospitality employees working at resorts and outdoor locations should be provided with appropriate uniforms (including hats and sunglasses) and sunscreen, which should be applied regularly, as too much exposure to sun has been shown to be a major cause of skin cancer.

Passive smoking

Increasing numbers of hospitality enterprises are banning smoking, in some cases in response to new legislation, in other cases based on commonsense. In New South Wales the *Smoke Free Environment Act* 2000 aims to promote public health by reducing exposure to tobacco and other smoke in enclosed public places.

Noise

Noise (including music) above peak levels, which are measured in decibels, can be damaging to your hearing, and ear protection must be used by employees in the industry. High levels of noise may be reached in laundries, bars, nightclubs, machine rooms, and even in some kitchens.

Personal security

Violence may occur in the form of verbal abuse by inebriated customers or irate staff. Harassment and physical assault are other workplace risks, particularly in nightclubs and bars, while armed hold-up is one of the most serious threats of all to the personal safety of staff.

Such risks can be contained by:
• undertaking training in how to deal with violence
• being familiar with correct procedures (e.g. calling for security)
• avoiding being alone
• becoming familiar with emergency systems
• avoiding dark areas when leaving work late
• reporting incidents of harassment.

Occupational health and safety legislation

Occupational health and safety legislation aims to prevent workplace accidents and injury. Under the various acts employers are obliged to:
• provide a safe place of work
• provide a safe method of work

- ensure that equipment meets the required safety standards.

The obligations of employees under this legislation are to:
- take reasonable care with their own safety and the safety of others
- comply with instructions on safety issues
- report all accidents.

The importance of reporting accidents cannot be stressed enough. To make a claim for workers compensation at a later date the injury must have been reported, even if no time had been lost or medical expenses incurred. The log of accidents is also a valuable source of information for the Occupational Health and Safety Committee. This committee regularly inspects workplaces and investigates all reported accidents.

The new Occupational Health and Safety Act in New South Wales sets out requirements for workplaces to put in place systems to identify, assess, control and/or eliminate health or safety risks. This process is called risk management. It also details the employer's duty to consult with employees about health and safety in order to comply with the act. These requirements are common to the acts in all other states and territories.

Risk management

The concept of risk management mirrors that of quality management—a continuous process of improvement. The risk management regulation provides broad coverage for all workplaces, along with specified control measures for particular hazards and industry activities. Risk management involves assessing such hazards and activities in accordance with the stipulated process:

1 Identify any possible hazard (anything in the workplace that has potential to harm anyone at the workplace, e.g. moving parts in machinery, toxic chemicals, manual handling tasks).

2 Assess the risk from the hazard (establish how significant is the risk, e.g. could it cause a serious injury, illness or death and how likely would be the possibility of any of these occurring).

3 Eliminate the hazard or, if this is not possible, control the risk from the hazard (implement strategies to eliminate or control the hazard, e.g. designing equipment differently, adding machine guards, using safer chemicals, providing lifting devices to minimise manual handling, or using personal protective equipment).

Employers must consult with employees about any OHS matter that affects them, including the risk management process. Involving employees in risk management can be done through the consultative arrangements that have been agreed at the workplace. Consulting with employees about hazards and how to eliminate or control them will help to:
- comply with the legislation
- get the whole team involved in the process
- obtain many different points of view
- encourage safe thinking.

A number of procedures can be implemented in the hospitality establishment to enable workplace hazards to be identified:

- observation
- consultation
- workplace inspections
- health and environment monitoring
- safety audits
- monitoring complaints
- monitoring injury and illness records.

Once the hazard has been assessed, control options for eliminating or reducing the risk of exposure to the hazard must be considered. Occupational health and safety legislation generally requires the following hierarchy of control options to be established, particularly in relation to plant, noise, manual handling and hazardous substances:

ELIMINATION	Modify the design of the workplace
DESIGN OR SUBSTITUTION	Use less hazardous chemical materials
ENGINEERING CONTROLS	Enclose or isolate the hazard; introduce mechanical aids or machine guards
ADMINISTRATION	Modify work procedure and work organisation
TRAINING	Ensure that staff are following safe procedures
PROTECTIVE EQUIPMENT	Provide personal protection by introducing protective equipment.

The following case study illustrates the types of control measures that might be needed in the hospitality industry to reduce risks to health and safety.

We were working in a temporary kitchen in a marquee and by the third day the floor was so slippery with oil that it was just like a skating rink. The apprentices were skylarking around, having races and doing spins. The temporary flooring was some sort of vinyl and despite being cleaned at night had developed a residue of oil.

Our safety team met after work and we decided to implement a range of ideas since two chefs had already taken a tumble carrying hot food. We hired some safety mats for the main areas of the kitchen. As it was not possible to deliver these mats to some of the other areas, we cleaned these areas thoroughly with a powerful detergent and then roughed up the floor with equipment provided by the site manager. Fortunately it was temporary flooring because, after this, it was not very attractive. All staff were advised to take extra care, and correct footwear in the kitchen (even for visitors) was obligatory.

The OHS Committee

Occupational Health and Safety Committee members are elected by the employees at a workplace. To ensure that all views and groups are represented, members should be drawn from all sections, levels, cultures and trades within the workplace. Committee members must receive accredited training in risk management and the effective running of a committee.

Functions of the OHS Committee

Occupational Health and Safety Committees can:
- help to resolve any health and safety issues
- carry out regular safety inspections
- develop a system to record accidents and incidents
- make recommendations to management about improving health and safety
- access any information about risks to health and safety from any equipment or substance or occupational disease.

Reporting of accident, injury or illness

The *Occupational Health and Safety (First-Aid) Regulation* 1989 requires that a Register of Injuries and Illnesses (in which all injuries and illnesses are recorded) is kept at each place of work. Accurate reporting and recording of workplace accidents and illnesses helps in identifying workplace hazards and is therefore an important tool in risk management.

Workers compensation

In the event of a work-related injury or illness, these are the steps you must take:
- Report the injury or illness to your employer (or supervisor) as soon as possible.
- Enter details in your employer's Register of Injuries and Illnesses (if there is one), or ask your employer or supervisor to do so.
- Obtain a medical certificate from your treating doctor and give the certificate to your employer.
- If you are going to be off work for more than seven days, ask your doctor and employer about suitable duties and participate in the injury management plan to help you get back to work. You must make all reasonable efforts to return to work as soon as possible.
- Keep in contact with your employer and your employer's insurance company while you are recovering from your injury or illness.
- Keep a copy of any documents relating to your injury or illness.

Employment-related health risks

Alcoholism, drug dependence, stress, AIDS and Hepatitis B are health risks in most industries, but there are reasons why some of them might be more prevalent in the hospitality industry than in others, and these are outlined below.

Alcoholism, drug dependence and stress

This is an industry in which customers enjoy themselves and staff often leave work on a high, continuing on to other hospitality establishments to socialise in the early hours of the morning. This can lead to a hospitality lifestyle, both at and after work. And a very expensive lifestyle it is. Although staff should not be permitted to drink alcohol while on duty, many do, and management silently condones it. In the worst scenario a staff member might finish a shift behind the bar, change out of uniform and immediately appear on the other side of the bar. This is not appropriate for the organisation or its customers, nor is it in the interests of good employee relations to have inebriated employees on any side of the bar. Fortunately, it is not permitted in most establishments. Poor control systems might fail to show up free drinks for staff members but, in any event, this sort of conduct should not be condoned.

Stress levels are high in the hospitality industry because many operations keep their staff levels to the bare minimum (labour is generally the highest overhead), which leaves the staff on duty under pressure when there is an influx of customers. Alcohol and drugs are sometimes used for stress relief and then become lifetime habits. The degree of alcoholism among hospitality staff has not been investigated, but anecdotal evidence points to it being higher than in many other industries. The temptation for such stress release is understandable, given the presence of shift work and long hours. Such health-related issues often go unnoticed until something serious occurs.

There are other remedies for stress, such as regular exercise, and this should be encouraged among hospitality staff.

AIDS and Hepatitis B

Contagious blood-borne diseases are a small risk to hospitality industry employees. However, needle injuries sometimes do occur when customers leave needles in garbage bins, curtain linings or cushions. Contamination can also occur when dealing with cuts in the kitchen. Broken glass is a danger for staff, particularly for those working in Food and Beverage. Blood-borne pathogens can be transmitted in vomit and through open wounds. Any opening on the skin surface should be covered as these pathogens can enter through breaks in the skin caused by acne or dermatitis.

Risk of infection from AIDS is very slight but use of protective gloves is recommended when assisting colleagues or guests with injuries. You cannot develop AIDS from any other means than by direct route of entry of infected bodily fluids. Hepatitis B is a far more serious health risk. Apparently more people in the world die in one day from Hepatitis B than die in a year from AIDS. There are approximately five to ten AIDS viral particles in a teaspoon of infected blood while there are approximately 500 million Hepatitis B viral particles in a teaspoon of blood infected with that disease. The risk of infection by Hepatitis B is thus much higher. However, you can be vaccinated against Hepatitis B, either before or immediately after exposure.

Activities

1 Two acts of parliament deal with workplace injury and illness. Find out the names of these acts in your state or territory and their main provisions. Hint: one has to do with workplace safety (prevention) and the other has to do with compensation and rehabilitation.

2 Interview several hospitality employees to find out about risks to health and safety in the industry.

3 Design a staff uniform with safety as the main consideration.

4 Investigate the issue of alcoholism, its definition and its possible causes.

CASE STUDY

The chef was looking after his apprentice who had cut his finger. The first aid officer walked into the kitchen to see the chef holding the apprentice's arm in the air, with blood running down both their arms. The apprentice was in shock, having seen so much blood. His knife had slipped when dicing carrots. As it turned out, he only needed a few stitches and he was back at work a week later.

Discussion questions

1 What could the chef have done to avoid the apprentice seeing so much blood and going into shock?

2 What could the chef have done to avoid contagion?

3 What steps should the chef take next?

4 How do you think the accident might have happened?

5 What could have been done to avoid it?

6 Can an apprentice return to work with stitches in his finger?

7 Who would pay the medical expenses?

LINKS

National Occupational Health and Safety Commission—
http://www.nohsc.gov.au/

Northern Territory Work Health Authority—
http://www.nt.gov.au/dbird/dib/wha/

Safety Institute of Australia—http://www.sia.org.au/index.jsp

Victorian Workcover Authority—
http://www.workcover.vic.gov.au/dir090/vwa/home.nsf

Workcover NSW—http://www.workcover.nsw.gov.au/

Workcover Queensland—http://www.workcover.qld.gov.au/

Workplace Standards Tasmania—http://www.wsa.tas.gov.au/

Worksafe Western Australia—http://www1.safetyline.wa.gov.au/

CHAPTER TWENTY-THREE

Safety, security and emergency

OBJECTIVES

This chapter deals with the very important issues of safety and security. On completion of this chapter you will be able to:

- follow workplace procedures for health, safety and security
- deal with emergency situations
- maintain safe personal presentation standards
- provide feedback on health, safety and security, including breaches of security.

The history of fires in hotels is not a happy one. In 1980 a fire swept through the MGM Grand Hotel in Las Vegas destroying the 26-storey hotel. Of the 3,500 guests staying at the hotel, nearly 100 were killed. Only a short time later, in 1981, the Las Vegas Hilton fire resulted in the death of eight guests. A serious fire in a small Kings Cross hotel in Sydney in 1989 caused the death of six backpackers who were staying at the hotel.

The Hilton bombing in 1978 was the first serious international security incident in Australia. A bomb, targeting a visiting group of dignitaries, went off in a rubbish bin outside the Hilton Hotel, killing two garbage collectors and a policeman, and injuring several bystanders.

> Yesterday, the whole block between Market and Park Streets looked like a set from a doomsday movie. Hardly a shopfront or a window was left intact, there was glass everywhere, and only a few disconsolate shopkeepers moved in the deserted shops.
>
> Directly outside the Hilton, the mute traces of the night tragedy remained. Bloodstains were everywhere, on the pavement, high on the pillars. (*Sydney Morning Herald*, 14 February 1978)

With the influx of tourists from all over the world and the increased risk of terrorism, security is a serious issue. Australia, nevertheless, is perceived as one of the safest countries in the world, and our national airline Qantas has an enviable safety record. It is hoped that this will continue.

In this chapter, we will discuss all aspects of safety and security in the industry, including the very important issue of dealing effectively with emergencies.

Legal aspects of safety and security

In Chapter 12 we introduced some of the laws which are relevant to the hospitality industry. All those discussed were laws made in parliament, such as the Food Hygiene Act and the Liquor Licensing Act. Common law was briefly introduced in Chapters 12 and 13, but now we will talk about it in relation to customer safety.

As we have learnt, common law is 'judge-made' law under which decisions are based on precedent. In the area of guest safety and security, a business must be able to show that all reasonable care has been taken to avoid injury to guests. If a proprietor were taken to court over an injury claim, he or she would have to demonstrate that reasonable care had been taken to avoid such an accident. Having heard all submissions, the judge would make a decision based on the judgements of previous cases. Business has a duty of care under common law, meaning that management must ensure that:

- premises are reasonably safe
- patrons are warned about dangers (such as slippery floors)
- staff do not take any action which might cause injury or accident
- premises are inspected regularly for safety risks.

One of the most serious safety risks, in fact, is blocked stairways. It is not uncommon for hospitality operations to use fire stairs for storing equipment (there is never enough storage space). This is extremely dangerous, as these areas cannot be cleared fast enough in the event of a fire. Regular inspections will ensure that access to stairways is available and that they are clear of any stores or equipment.

As another example, if a customer were to slip on a floor that had just been cleaned and was still wet, this would be judged negligent if warning signs had not been displayed. If, on the other hand, the customer were to slip on a foil wrapper dropped by a passing child, management would not be held responsible, providing it could be shown that regular cleaning programs and inspections by Housekeeping staff had been undertaken. Reasonable care is hard to define and this is why this area of litigation is so complex.

There are a number of ways that staff can ensure customer safety:

- Observe all safety rules.
- Follow standard operating procedures, which are designed with customer and staff safety in mind.
- Be observant of safety risks and report them.
- Keep work and public areas clean and tidy.
- Report all safety incidents.
- Follow instructions for mixing chemicals carefully.
- Avoid leaving chemicals or dangerous equipment within the reach of children.
- Report for duty well rested and fully fit.
- Avoid being careless or silly.

The following example illustrates the importance of standard operating procedures in the hospitality industry. A customer received a deep cut in the foot after treading on glass near the hotel swimming pool. A few minutes earlier a child had dropped a glass and a staff member had attempted to clean up the broken pieces. However, standard operating procedures stipulated the use of plastic glasses in pool areas so negligence could be shown in this case.

The first few minutes after an accident are the most important. Apart from calling for medical assistance (first aid is covered later in the chapter), the guest should be treated with care and courtesy. This goes a long way towards ensuring that the guest will feel that sufficient care has been provided. Follow-up after the incident will let the organisation know whether the situation was resolved in a satisfactory way or not.

Safe personal presentation standards

There are many ways in which the safety of employees can be protected, and these include wearing uniforms and appropriate footwear and using safety equipment. For example, a chef should wear a uniform, generally made of cotton, with a draw-string waist for the trousers (which allows for quick removal in case of a hot spill, especially oil) and long-sleeved shirt (to protect the arms from serious burns). Working in a t-shirt is not safe, even if it is very hot. Steel-tipped shoes are an important personal protection item for many hospitality staff, including those working in engineering or in the grounds of a resort. Gloves should be worn to protect the hands from toxic chemicals, as we will discuss in Chapter 25, and earmuffs are sometimes required in machine rooms.

Common safety and security precautions

Apart from following standard procedures, staff should be observant of what is happening in their establishment and report all incidents (however minor) so that they can be followed through and prevented from occurring again. Employees should also treat any information about guests with the strictest confidence. Why this is so will be discussed in more detail below.

Observation

Staff who are observant are an asset to any type of hospitality establishment. They are the ones who identify people who should not be on the premises or who are acting suspiciously. Noticing valuables left lying around and recommending safe deposit boxes or better security measures can be very helpful preventative measures against theft. Valuable items found in odd places should be picked up immediately and handed in to Lost and Found (usually managed by Security). Children need to be watched carefully, as they can be quite reckless, jumping off rocks into pools and sliding on wet floors. So too customers who have lost their inhibitions as a result of too much alcohol. They can do dangerous things or intrude on the comfort of other patrons. Destruction of expensive fittings while staff wait for the police to arrive will not help the establishment's reputation in the eyes of other customers.

Theft is a major problem for large establishments and all too often valuable cutlery, crockery, linen, and even televisions disappear. Some guests seem to be quite compulsive, despite their obvious wealth. The story of the lady in Sydney's best fine dining restaurant who put the silverware in her handbag revealed an interesting aspect of human nature. Staff who had observed the silver salt and pepper set disappearing into her handbag told the manager and asked him what to do. The manager billed the host for the silverware, with a small note suggesting that the bill would be reduced if the items were returned. The host chose to pay the bill, and thanked the staff for their discretion.

Observation and following standard procedures are the best ways to thwart theft.

More subtle observation includes noticing equipment left unattended, electrical wiring snaking through a puddle or smoke emerging from a rubbish bin.

Any observation of an incident, accident or safety risk should be reported using the enterprise system for risk management. In most cases, this involves completing a form called an 'Incident Report Form' on which are described the full details of the incident and any witness to the incident. Many minor accidents and incidents can provide early warning of a systemic problem, the resolution of which can prevent more serious occurrences.

Care with keys

Room locking systems are becoming increasingly sophisticated, with many guests and staff using credit card style keys to access rooms. With individual codes which are changed each time a guest checks out, these keys have increased security of guest property. Nevertheless, care of keys is essential. Front Office staff should always check the identity of anyone unfamiliar who asks for a room key. 'May I have the key to my room, 45 please' should be followed by 'Your name please, sir?'.

Confidentiality

Likewise, it is not appropriate to divulge the identity or room number of anyone staying on the premises. Although most guests appreciate this security precaution, one woman's husband was not amused when, arriving two days after his wife, he could not get access to the room until she would vouch for him. His imagination ran riot while he waited for her in the lobby!

Safety and security in emergencies

Emergency situations in hospitality establishments can be caused by any of the following:

- fire
- bomb threats
- robbery or armed hold-up
- accidents
- floods, earthquakes or hurricanes (especially on island resorts)
- power failure.

We will now deal in more detail with fire, bomb threats and hold-ups, as well as evacuation, which is sometimes necessary as a result of these threats to the safety and security of staff and customers.

Hold-ups

In the case of a hold-up, staff are advised to stay calm and hand over the money, as the safety of staff and customers is paramount. A tragedy such as the Pizza Hut hold-up incident in which a young man lost his life should be prevented at all costs. Staff should also observe carefully so that they can identify thieves if necessary.

Fig. 23.1 contains the rules recommended for minimising danger and aiding apprehension in the event of a hold-up.

Bomb threats

It is known that two rival nightclubs in Melbourne ring each other with bomb hoaxes on Friday and Saturday evenings. The resulting evacuation from one sends most customers across the street to the other! Unfortunately this practice makes it

FIG. 23.1

Recommended rules for managing a hold-up.

1. Do not be heroic and turn a hold-up into a murder; no amount of money or property is worth a life.
2. Stay as calm as possible. Control fear by concentrating on observing and making mental notes of exactly what is happening.
3. Obey the offender's instructions, but **do only what you are told**, nothing more, nothing less. Do not volunteer any information.
4. Stay out of danger if you are not directly involved and activate the hold-up alarm if one is available and it can be done with safety. If you can leave the building, do so, and then raise the alarm.
5. Be deliberate in your actions. If you are ordered to hand money to the bandit, put as much coin into the bag as possible, followed by smaller denomination notes.
6. Phone the Police emergency number, 000, if you or some other responsible member of your staff is able to do so without danger. Keep the line open. (Police can, if necessary, contact Ambulance, etc.)
7. Carefully observe any vehicle used by the bandit, taking particular note of its registration number, type and colour.
8. Observe as much as possible. In particular, note speech, mannerisms, clothing, scars, or any other distinguishing features.
9. The Police want individual impressions of what happened. Don't be influenced by other staff members.
10. Audible local alarms (bells, sirens, etc.) are not favoured for hold-up use as the sudden warning sound may force the bandit into a panic situation where a firearm may be accidentally discharged as a reflex action.

Source: http://www.safetyline.wa.gov.au/PageBin/workhazd0003.htm. Courtesy of WA Police Service.

very hard to discern a genuine threat. This can also be a problem for large hotels, particularly in countries where bomb threats are fairly common.

A bomb threat check list should be kept near the switchboard telephone, outlining the questions to ask and the information to secure about the caller. Keeping the caller talking, while alerting another staff member, can help the operator to identify whether the call is a hoax and to find out the location of the bomb.

Fire

There are various types of fire and various types of extinguishers to deal with them. A tour of any building will reveal the location and type of extinguisher (read the instructions on the spot) and fire exits.

In the event of a fire, the switchboard should be immediately notified of the exact location of the fire and doors should be closed to avoid the fire spreading. Lifts should not be used, as the buttons are heat sensitive, the lift shaft becomes a smoke chimney and the lift could get stuck between floors. Staff should be well drilled so that they can advise customers calmly and organise evacuation if necessary.

Fire emergency procedures are provided in Fig. 23.2.

Evacuation

The law requires that all workplaces provide for the safe and rapid evacuation of people in the event of an emergency, such as fire, gas leaks, leakage of hazardous material (for example, dangerous chemicals) and bomb threats. If a building, because of its construction, offers some internal protection against the threat to safety, initial evacuation may only require the removal of occupants away from the immediate danger (room or floor) to adjacent safe areas (rooms or floors).

As we have mentioned, the switchboard is generally the emergency centre for a hotel and activities are co-ordinated from there. All staff should be aware of their duties and procedures and these should be carried out calmly. After a hotel fire in Potts Point, Sydney, staff were praised for the manner in which they evacuated all guests in the early hours of the morning without any injuries.

FIG. 23.2

Emergency fire procedures.

- Alert others of the fire.
- Ensure the immediate safety of anyone near the fire.
- Call the Fire Brigade on 000.*
- Fight the fire if safe to do so.
- Evacuate the area.

* Even if an automatic alarm has been instigated, a 000 emergency telephone call should still be made to confirm receipt of alarm and to give further details.

Source: http://www.samfs.sa.gov.au/fire_safety_information.htm

Emergency planning and procedures

Emergency planning is based on Australian and international standards. A summary of the guidelines is provided in 'DR00180—Emergency control organisation and procedures for buildings' (Standards Australia). A committee called the Emergency Planning Committee (EPC) is responsible for emergency planning. This committee should:

- establish the emergency response plan
- ensure that appropriate people are assigned to specific roles, such as Chief Warden, and clarify their responsibilities in the Emergency Control Organisation (ECO), the team responsible for responding to the emergency
- arrange for training for all members of the ECO team
- arrange for evacuation drills
- review procedures
- ensure that ECO staff are indemnified against civil liability where they act in good faith in the course of their emergency control duties.

When developing the emergency response plan, specialist advice from, for example, consultant security organisations, is recommended. The plan should take into account:

- peak number of people in the hotel, resort or other venue
- evacuation routes and signage
- people with disabilities
- lifts and escalators (assume that these are not used, except by fire authorities)
- checking people in the building (making sure everyone has left)
- marshalling points (especially for very large operations)
- routes for evacuation and assembly
- safeguarding cash and valuables
- communication systems (emergency warning and emergency intercom systems, as well as public address systems)
- emergency equipment
- control and co-ordination point(s) or locations(s) for the emergency response by the Chief Warden, and liaison with emergency services
- co-ordination with other agencies such as local council and emergency services.

The Emergency Control Organisation includes the following team members:

- Chief Warden
- Deputy Chief Warden
- Communications Officer
- Floor or Deputy Wardens.

During an emergency, instructions given by ECO wardens should override those given by any other person in the organisation structure.

The structure of the ECO is illustrated in Fig. 23.3 on page 278.

The public address system is used by the Chief Warden using the tone BEEP . . . BEEP . . . BEEP for alert and WHOOP . . . WHOOP . . . WHOOP for evacuation.

The warden intercommunication phone (WIP) is used to advise the Chief Warden of danger in specific areas. All staff should be trained in their specific roles in such a situation.

FIG. 23.3

Structure of the Emergency Control Operation (ECO).

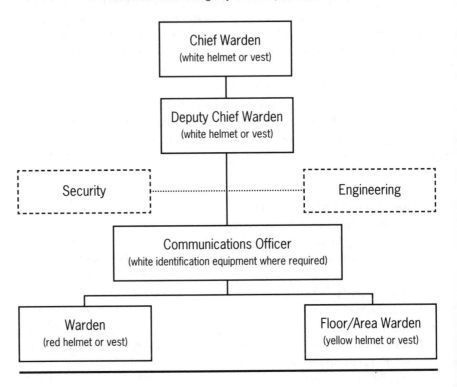

In the event of an evacuation it is important for staff to:

- remain calm
- be observant
- listen to and follow instructions
- provide information and instructions to staff and customers when advised to do so
- follow all safety precautions (such as not using lifts in case of fire).

First aid

A first aid certificate is highly regarded by employers in the hospitality industry as it indicates that you have the skills and knowledge to deal with emergency situations such as choking and drowning. St John's Ambulance now offers part of the course on CD ROM, effectively reducing the course to a practical component. Knowledge of CPR (cardio-pulmonary resuscitation) and other first aid procedures is most valuable.

In all such situations the key steps are:

- Evaluate the situation and administer first aid or CPR if necessary.
- Call for help, ensuring that you give accurate details and directions.
- Check to see if there are any remaining hazards.

• Do not move the victim unless absolutely necessary.

Many lives have been saved because hospitality staff have been well trained. Only when you have a certificate are you adequately equipped to deal with some of the situations described below. However, in any emergency, you can be of help by checking for further danger, calling for assistance and remaining calm.

Choking

You may be able to tell if someone is choking if they are clutching at their throat, coughing violently, turning blue in the face or on the neck, lips, ears or fingers, or are unconscious and not breathing. If the person is able to cough, they should be encouraged to continue coughing to dislodge the object. If they are not breathing, lay them on the ground with the head low and give four sharp blows between the shoulder blades. There are other approaches, too, which are taught as part of first aid training. In food service operations it is most important to be on the alert for signs of choking.

DRABC Action Plan

DANGER ✓ Check for danger to you, to others and to casualty. ✓ Call for help. **EMERGENCY PHONE 000** ▼	
RESPONSE NO REPONSE ——→ RESPONDS ▼ ✓ Reassure, make comfortable. ✓ Treat bleeding and other injuries.	**AIRWAY** ✓ Turn casualty on side. ✓ Turn face slightly down. ✓ Clear airway.
BREATHING NO BREATH ——→ BREATHING ▼ ✓ Leave on side, in stable position. ✓ Observe: Airway, Breathing and Circulation.	✓ Roll casualty on to the back. ✓ Tilt head backwards. ✓ Seal casualty's mouth. ✓ Give up to five full breaths in ten seconds.
CIRCULATION NO PULSE ——→ PULSE ▼ ✓ Continue mouth-to-mouth. ✓ Check neck pulse and breathing after one minute, then every two minutes.	✓ Place heel of hand on lower half of the breastbone. ✓ Compress chest 4–5 centimetres 15 times and give two breaths. ✓ Repeat four times per minute.

Courtesy of Zee Medical, © Zee Medical 1999.

Wounds

If left untreated, wounds can become infected. This can result in the patient developing tetanus, which is a very serious disease. Any wound should be washed, antiseptic cream or lotion should be applied and the wound should be covered. This is important, even if the wound is very small. For food hygiene reasons, gloves should be worn if there is a cut on the hand.

Poisoning

The Poisons Information Centre (13 11 26 in all states and territories) can assist with advice if the nature of the poison is known. If the poison is corrosive (burning), the patient should not be made to vomit, otherwise the corrosive action will burn the oesophagus again during vomiting. This is applicable, for example, where someone swallows dishwasher liquid or petrol, as sometimes happens when poisonous fluids are put in unidentified containers. In other cases it is appropriate to encourage vomiting and a syrup may be available in the first aid kit for this purpose. Poisonous liquids and substances should never be left within reach of young customers who might try them.

If poisons (such as strong chemicals) have been inhaled, move the person into the fresh air and loosen their clothing. If poisons have been absorbed by the skin, the person should be washed immediately.

Burns

Burns should be held under cold water for 10 minutes. Clothing or any other items stuck to the skin should be left alone. The burn should not be covered with a dressing because it might stick to the skin. Only non-stick sterile dressings should be used. Do not apply ointments. Medical assistance is necessary if the burn is bigger than a 20-cent piece or if it is deep.

Bleeding

To stop bleeding a dressing or pad of material should be applied to the wound. You should wear gloves or encourage the person to hold the dressing. They should lie down and medical attention should be sought if stitches are required.

Electric shock

Switch off the power supply. Do not touch the victim if the power is still on. Call for help, but stay with the person until help arrives. Alert someone who knows how to do EAR (expired air resuscitation) or CPR if the patient is not breathing or has no pulse.

General security

Security departments assist staff in protecting the safety of customers, other employees, contractors who are on the premises, and property and other assets. Security looks after people and goods. In order to do so effectively, there are a number of control measures that should be implemented:

- access control points (such as specified staff entry areas)
- key control systems (usually swipe cards)
- security patrols and cameras
- room safes for guest property
- lost property procedures
- money handling procedures (for daily takings, floats and banking)
- audits and stocktakes of equipment and stores
- checking and reconciliation of incoming goods against orders
- point of sale reconciliation and links to inventory control systems.

Activities

1 Investigate the options available in your area for completing a first aid course.
2 Find out as much as you can about the various classes of fires and the extinguishers used to put them out.
3 Go on a tour of any building and note any risks to safety.

CASE STUDY

Swimming pools, spas, saunas and gyms are high safety risk areas for guests, especially younger ones. After a number of incidents relating to pool chlorine had been reported at Franjipani Lodge, it was decided that new procedures should be adopted and followed to the letter. These incidents included a child being overcome by chlorine fumes after floating around the pool clinging to the 'pool pill' container. In another incident a child had been severely burned when playing with chlorine left behind the benches. Two letters of complaint had been received from parents whose children had developed 'tropical ear', a middle-ear infection, sometimes caused by germs in pools.

The new procedures included safekeeping of pool chemicals, regular checking of water for chlorine and pH levels, and monitoring of pool safety for children.

Discussion questions

1 What are some of the other risks associated with pools, spas and gyms?
2 Which department do you suppose would be responsible for pool maintenance?
3 Why is chlorine dangerous?
4 What are some of the general issues of children's safety while they are on the premises of a hospitality establishment such as a fast food outlet, restaurant, club or resort?
5 How would you approach a situation in which a child was behaving in a way that was potentially unsafe?

LINKS

Is your hotel safe?—http://seniors.tcnet.org/articles/article03.html

Lockteck—http://www.plicards.com/home/

St John First Aid Training—http://www.stjohn.org.au/firstaid/index.html

CHAPTER TWENTY-FOUR

Following hygiene procedures

OBJECTIVES

This chapter deals with the topic of workplace hygiene. On completion of this chapter you will be able to:

- follow workplace hygiene procedures in accordance with enterprise standards and legal requirements
- handle and store food items according to the above guidelines
- identify hygiene risks
- take action to minimise hygiene risks
- report hygiene risks for follow-up.

John was a third year apprentice chef, completing his final year at TAFE, with only one year to go before becoming fully qualified. He had just started in a new position, working with a chef who had developed an outstanding reputation in the trade for his imaginative treatment of Australian ingredients. The job had been organised by his group employer. It was John's third placement and he was delighted with his new position at the Mataranka restaurant.

John had just recovered from a bad bout of the flu before starting work at the Mataranka and was still not feeling well some weeks later. He therefore went back to his doctor, who told him that he might have Hepatitis A and that he would send some samples for testing. Although John was told to stay in bed for a few days and then ring for the results, he returned to work because he knew that the restaurant was understaffed.

While John's commitment to his work was commendable, there are some serious health and food hygiene considerations in this scenario. Food hygiene legislation mentioned in Chapter 12, specifically precludes anyone with an infectious disease from working with food. If they do so, they could be breaking the law. John should have checked this with his doctor and advised his supervisor.

The health of customers and other staff in the hospitality industry is at risk if poor hygiene practices are condoned as they encourage the transmission of bacteria and viruses. There are 200 known bacteria that are pathogenic for humans. In the old days it was thought that all infectious diseases were caused by bacteria; now it is known that viruses, too, are disease producing. Bacteria can cause food poisoning if food is warmed for long periods or if staff do not follow correct handling procedures such as using different chopping boards for raw and cooked meats. In the right conditions food-based bacteria can multiply at an alarming rate.

Viruses were discovered only in 1892. Well-known viruses include the common cold, measles, chicken pox, hepatitis and influenza. In John's case there was a strong possibility that he would pass on his infectious disease to customers and other staff. Viruses are transmitted through droplet infection, by coughing, sneezing and drinking from glassware that has not been washed at the right temperature. Practices such as rinsing a glass and stacking it on the shelf without drying it put the customer at risk of catching a virus from the person who last used the glass. Too few food and beverage outlets follow the correct procedure for washing cutlery and crockery. Under the relevant legislation all such items should be washed at a minimum of 77°C to avoid cross-infection.

Food safety

A generally accepted definition of potentially unsafe food is provided in the Food Safety Standards of the Australian and New Zealand Food Authority (ANZFA) (Part 3.2): '**potentially hazardous food** means food that has to be kept at certain temperatures to minimise the growth of any pathogenic micro-organisms that may be present in the food or to prevent the formation of toxins in the food'. Food is unsuitable for human consumption if it is damaged, decomposed, contaminated, deteriorated or perished.

Hygiene procedures are important in many departments of the hospitality establishment, not just in the Kitchen. In addition to sections in which food is prepared and served, the Housekeeping Department must also pay special attention to hygienic work practices, as should the Beverage Department.

Safe hygiene procedures include:
- safe and hygienic handling of food and beverage, including beer lines
- regular hand washing (between, say, handling poultry and peeling vegetables)
- use of gloves when appropriate
- appropriate and clean clothing (a damp apron is a perfect place for bacterial reproduction)
- correct food storage (not on the floor)
- checking manufacturers' labels for storage instructions (e.g. length of time permitted under refrigeration)
- use of suitable containers for storage
- correct labelling of items, including expiry dates
- correct stock rotation (first in, first out)
- avoidance of cross-contamination (e.g. avoid using the same preparation areas for fish and salads)
- safe disposal of linen and laundry (especially when contaminated with bodily fluids)
- appropriate handling and disposal of garbage (watch out for needles)

- cleaning and sanitising surfaces (sanitising kills germs too)
- cleaning and sanitising floors, etc. (environmental hygiene)
- personal hygiene (including clean hair and wearing hair covering in the kitchen).

Correct storage of food and utensils prior to use.

Hygienic storage for prepared food—food is plated in a refrigerated area and kept there until served.

Perishable foods are most prone to physical damage and contamination by bacteria. Perishable foods also decay quickly. Semi-perishable foods last in storage (including cold storage) for a short time. Non-perishable foods (such as spices) have a long shelf life if stored correctly.

Potential risk to the health of customers and staff who consume food prepared in hospitality establishments can be caused by:

- bacterial contamination (contamination of fish or poultry is potentially very dangerous)
- inappropriate storage (wrong temperature, uncovered)
- poor personal hygiene
- poor work practices (food preparation areas should be thoroughly cleaned and sanitised daily)
- vermin
- air-borne dust and other pollutants (people sneezing and coughing)
- incorrect disposal of contaminated waste.

Cleaning and sanitising

There is a big difference between cleaning and sanitising. Cleaning is the process of removing dirt, dust and food from surfaces. Sanitising is a sterilising process, which kills bacteria. This can be done by using heat—dishwashers in commercial kitchens usually wash at temperatures high enough to sterilise glassware, cutlery and crockery—or by using chemicals, such as diluted bleach, which would be used daily for sanitising kitchen surfaces. Commercial cleaning agents provide this information on the label.

Food laws and regulations

In 1975 a conference of commonwealth and state ministers for health, working with their New Zealand counterparts, agreed to prepare a model food act for adoption by all states and territories. The reason behind this was to ensure uniform guidelines for food hygiene. Although this law was not passed at federal level but was passed by state and territory governments (food hygiene is a state responsibility), there are few significant differences in the various food laws. Queensland's was the first statute to be based on the model food act.

Ensuring appropriate food storage.

A joint Food Standards Code for Australia and New Zealand will be introduced in both countries in the near future and implemented over a two-year period.

Food handling legislation allows inspectors to enter premises during working hours and take samples or seize foodstuffs for analysis. Inspectors can give warnings to the owner of a business selling food to the public and set times for re-inspections. They also have the power to fine the owner and ultimately to close down the business.

In the wake of the contamination of smallgoods at the Garibaldi meatworks in 1994, and the resulting death of one child and illness of several others, the authorities are more concerned than ever about food handling procedures. Poor hygiene practices by staff at the meatworks led to an outbreak of haemolytic uraemic syndrome, which caused the child's death.

Hygiene laws cover:
- food handling and food service
- food storage
- cleanliness of storage areas and equipment
- temperatures for washing cutlery, crockery and kitchen equipment
- personal hygiene
- uniforms and hair coverings
- rights of inspection
- rights to remove samples.

Types of food contamination

Viruses and bacteria were discussed at the beginning of this chapter; now it is important to look at the different types of food poisoning and infection they can cause.

Viral food-borne infection

There are different ways food can be contaminated. In the example of John in the case study, the virus could have travelled on the food to the customer. Viral gastro-enteritis can also be transmitted in the same way—in fact, it is estimated that in 80 per cent of cases of viral gastroenteritis it is. This is known as viral food-borne infection.

Bacterial food poisoning

In contrast to viral food-borne infection, bacterial food poisoning is caused by bacteria in the food multiplying in the right conditions of heat and moisture, in some cases developing toxins, which then cause food poisoning. The human involvement in this situation is ignorance or carelessness.

Bacteria, in the right conditions, grow at a most alarming rate. They double their numbers every 20 minutes, as illustrated in Fig. 24.1. To multiply, these bacteria need moisture and warmth. The danger zone for heating and reheating food is between 5°C and 60°C, as illustrated in Fig. 24.2. Below 5°C the bacteria cannot grow and temperatures above 60°C will kill the bacteria.

The most common types of bacterial food poisoning are described below.

Salmonella

This is the most common form of food poisoning and causes vomiting, fever and stomach pain. Bacteria from raw meat and poultry, for example, can be transferred by using the same surface for raw foods and cooked foods. The cooked food would be contaminated and the bacteria would grow if the cooked food were heated at low temperatures. As long as the temperature is high enough, cooking will kill salmonella. In brief, cooking kills it, heating breeds it.

If a chopping board used for cutting raw chicken were not properly sanitised before being used to make sandwiches, the bacteria transmitted to the sandwiches would multiply if the sandwich were left at room temperature for a few hours.

In addition to exercising care to guard against cross-contamination, personal hygiene is most important as faecal contamination with the salmonella bacteria can occur if hands have not been adequately washed.

Staphylococcus aureus

This bacterium is found in many parts of the healthy body, including the nose, throat, hair and ears. It is also found in pimples, cuts and abrasions. Once transferred to food, this bacterium will multiply rapidly (see Fig. 24.1), producing toxins which cause food poisoning. This is a major reason why staff are not permitted to touch the nose, the face or the hair when preparing and handling food. As mentioned, temperatures above 60°C will kill the bacteria, but the toxins can be heat stable.

FIG. 24.1

Bacteria multiplying.

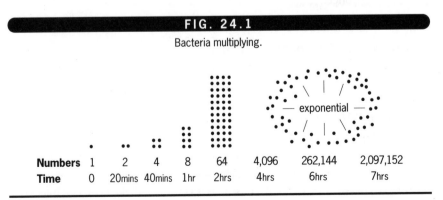

Numbers	1	2	4	8	64	4,096	262,144	2,097,152
Time	0	20mins	40mins	1hr	2hrs	4hrs	6hrs	7hrs

Outbreaks of food poisoning in Australia, 1995–2000

1995   E.coli contamination of mettwurst made 150 people ill and killed one child in South Australia. The direct costs of this incident to health authorities and the industry have been conservatively put at $20 million.

1996   Salmonella contamination of peanut butter affected 60 people, many children.

1996   Salmonella infection in a chocolate sauce served by an airline on one flight affected more than 100 people.

1997   Hepatitis A infected 440 people who ate oysters from Wallis Lakes in New South Wales. One person died.

1999   Faecal contamination of South Australian orange juice affected nearly 500 people.

A food handler pushing hair away from his face could transmit the bacteria from his hair to a potato salad in which the bacteria would multiply rapidly to produce toxins in only a few hours. Food should be kept at temperatures above 60°C and below 5°C (see Fig. 24.2). Use of utensils and gloves also helps to avoid contamination.

Clostridium perfingens

These bacteria produce spores that are heat resistant and survive boiling. They produce a toxin in the intestine after ingestion. Food is often contaminated by faeces of insects or rodents, or by spores in dust. The best preventative measure is to cook food at 60°C, or above, just prior to serving. Covering food is another important preventative measure for controlling all bacteria that cause food poisoning.

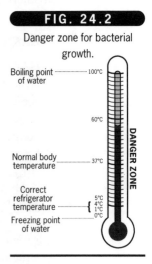

FIG. 24.2

Danger zone for bacterial growth.

Boiling point of water — 100°C

60°C

DANGER ZONE

Normal body temperature — 37°C

Correct refrigerator temperature — 5°C / 4°C / 1°C

Freezing point of water — 0°C

Food hazards

Biological concerns, such as:
- bacterial, parasitic or viral contamination
- bacterial growth
- bacterial, parasitic or viral survival
- bacterial toxin production
- bacterial, parasitic or viral cross-contamination

Physical objects
- stones
- glass
- metal fragments
- packaging materials

Chemical contamination
- non-food-grade lubricants
- cleaning compounds
- food additives
- insecticides

Infection by pathogens

Many foods contain nutrients, making them a place where micro-organisms can live and even grow. Some of these organisms are pathogens, which means that under the right conditions and in the right numbers, they can make someone who eats them ill. Raw animal foods such as meat, poultry, fish and eggs often carry bacteria, viruses or parasites that can be harmful to humans.

Soil and other contamination

Because foods are from the environment, they sometimes contain objects such as stones, and these can cause injury. And food may be contaminated naturally, for example from the soil in which it is grown, or during harvest, storage or transportation. Some foods undergo further processing and, even despite best efforts, become contaminated. These hazards, along with hazards that may occur in a hospitality establishment, such as metal fragments finding their way into food, can lead to injury, illness or death.

Hazard Analysis Critical Control Point

HACCP (Hazard Analysis Critical Control Point) is a system that records critical control points throughout the process of food production. It can be applied to any food service operation.

A critical control point (CCP) within a HACCP plan is defined as 'any point, step or procedure at which control can be applied and a food safety hazard can be prevented, eliminated or reduced to acceptable levels' (National Advisory Committee on the Microbiological Criteria for Foods, 1992).

HACCP helps an organisation to plan and monitor its food safety program by:
- analysing its food production processes
- determining where hazards could occur
- monitoring the control points that are critical to product safety
- maintaining food safety records
- evaluating the system to ensure it is working effectively.

One of the control points could be delivery of produce at the loading dock. You might check the temperature of food when it is delivered and monitor how long it takes to reach the stores, or more importantly how long it takes before it is refrigerated. You might also monitor the temperature at which it is stored. With hot food, your food service organisation might determine that hot foods must be held at a temperature above 60°C to reduce the risk of microbiological hazards. All food handlers would record the temperature of the food being held on a check sheet.

A HACCP food safety policy manual is generally developed for a food safety program. It contains all the food safety instructions for staff and suppliers, as well as all audit documents. This enables your organisation to demonstrate that it is complying with food safety legislation.

Prevention of bacterial food poisoning

Inadequate cooking is the biggest cause of food poisoning, closely followed by incorrect holding temperatures and contaminated equipment, all of which have been discussed earlier in this chapter. Poor hygiene is also a contributor, and recommended personal hygiene procedures are outlined below, followed by other preventative measures such as cleaning and pest control.

Personal hygiene

Bacteria need the following conditions to reproduce:

- moderate temperatures
- moisture
- food
- time.

Personal hygiene is an important preventative measure against food contamination and the following procedures should be strictly adhered to:

1 Wash hands thoroughly with a rich lather after:
   - using the toilet
   - handling raw meat, chicken or fish
   - handling vegetables
   - handling waste
   - smoking or eating
   - blowing the nose.
2 Keep nails short and clean.
3 Dry hands with disposable towels or hot air (towels can soon become contaminated).
4 Don't wear jewellery, as bacteria can survive in crevices and under rings.
5 Cover minor cuts and abrasions and wear gloves.
6 Don't touch the body, hair, nose or ears as bacteria can be transmitted from them to food.
7 When tasting food, use a new spoon or a tasting dish.

The importance of the above measures is illustrated in this article which appeared in the *Sydney Morning Herald* on 11 December 1993 (reproduced by permission).

POISONING SCARE AT HOTEL

The NSW Health Department is investigating one of Sydney's most exclusive hotels, the Park Lane, to determine whether a number of patrons contracted food poisoning after dining there last week. Park Lane public relations manager Katrina Stormon confirmed yesterday the hotel had contacted health authorities immediately after prominent Sydney law firm Mallesons Stephen Jaques informed them a large number of employees were too sick to attend work on Monday.

Mallesons celebrated its Christmas party at the hotel on December 3. 'As soon as we had a call from Mallesons we jumped on the line to the Health Department and the Sydney City Council health inspectors and asked them to jump on the case,' said Stormon.

'We are expecting to get the results next week.'

Peter Doyle, managing partner at Mallesons, declined to comment 'because the whole matter is under investigation'.

But after about 300 people—almost half the staff—were absent from their desks on Monday, a message to employees has asked them to volunteer 'stool samples' to assist the investigation.

Stormon also confirmed the Park Lane had received phone calls from corporations other than Mallesons which had functions at the hotel on December 3.

She said those corporations had also notified the hotel that some diners had suffered illness this week.

Dr Mark Ferson, director of the Eastern Sydney Area Health Service's Public Health Unit, has confirmed the service is investigating 'a Sydney hotel' following claims that a number of people suffered food poisoning.

Cleaning

In addition to personal hygiene, food handlers need to know about the different types of cleaning agents. Detergents, including most soaps and dishwashing liquids, help to remove grease and dirt. They do not kill bacteria. After removing most of the dirt with detergent, high-risk areas and hands need to be cleaned with disinfectants, such as bleach, to destroy bacteria. To be effective bleach should be diluted correctly and left on the item for a short time. Sanitisers are chemicals that are a combination of detergent and disinfectant. They must also be handled carefully and diluted correctly.

Disinfectants usually take a little time to work when used on surfaces and in toilets. Hot water or steam over 80°C, used in industrial dishwashers, is most effective as a disinfectant as it prevents chemical residue on pots, cutlery and crockery.

Abrasives should be used for scouring, while solvents are necessary for surface cleaning. Caustic cleaners should be used for removing grease and spills from ovens.

The cleaning process involves removing food scraps (without throwing out cutlery at the same time), washing in hot water with detergent, rinsing and drying. In establishments without dishwashers one sink should be used for washing and the other for rinsing. The rinsing water should be hot enough for disinfecting. Finally, items should be stacked to dry and packed away only when they are dry. Moisture is ideal for bacterial growth and wet towels are one of the biggest sources of bacteria in a kitchen.

Cleaning in Housekeeping involves chemical disinfection of toilets and cleaning of all tiled surfaces and floors. Glasses and cups should be returned to the kitchen to be washed properly. A used guest towel (full of bacteria) should not be used to dry cups or polish surfaces! Cracked and chipped crockery should be thrown away as it harbours germs.

Colour coding of bins and utensils

Some commercial kitchens use large rubbish bins for storage of, say, peeled potatoes. This is quite harmless provided the bins are clean and are not used for garbage. Use of different coloured bins for different purposes is recommended to avoid confusion. Colour coding of chopping boards in the kitchen and cleaning rags in the Housekeeping Department is also recommended for avoiding cross-contamination.

Pest control

In addition to the normal pests—flies, cockroaches and mice—Australia has a few rather more exotic pests. A hotel restaurant in the tropical north opens onto a seating area where guests can dine under the stars, which creates a wonderful ambiance. However, the design of the restaurant has created enormous problems for the staff in controlling pests: unbeknown to the guests, the fruit display on the buffet attracts fruit flies and bats, while bush roaches run across the floor and geckos hang in the rafters, defecating on the food. Small marsupials, which look just like rats to the uninitiated, rush under the tables to pick up scraps. Many of these animals are protected species, so the staff have created feeding areas outside the back of the hotel to keep the animals and insects out of the restaurant. One resort, situated on a picturesque swampland turned lake, sprays the bugs at sunset every day. Staff travel around the perimeter of the resort in a buggy and spray tons of insecticide into the air. This is for guest comfort as well as for reasons of food hygiene. Not good, however, for the environment!

While on the subject of guest comfort, an American guest staying at a rainforest lodge reached down for her handbag and, feeling it more slippery than she had expected, bent down to look. Her reaction to meeting a cane toad the size of a dinner plate is still enacted by staff to this day! She returned to the States with an amazing tale and a most interesting gift from the management—an exquisite handmade leather box with an inset of toad skin on the lid.

Flies are the most common pest, responsible for most cross-contamination. This legendary advertisement sums it up:

> Flies can't eat solid food, so to soften it up they vomit on it. Then they stamp the vomit in until it's a liquid, usually stamping in a few germs for good measure. Then when it's good and runny, they suck it all back again, probably dropping some excrement at the same time. And then, when they have finished eating, it's your turn.

Cockroaches also cause cross-contamination as they live in dark, moist areas and feed on waste—and even in ears:

ROACH IN THE EAR

Overseas visitors usually fear crocodiles and poisonous spiders, but a Swedish backpacker is recovering from an encounter with a four-centimetre Kings Cross cockroach. Mr Magnus Carlstedt, 19, received a rude awakening when the cockroach crawled into his ear and refused to budge. Ambulance officers eventually removed the bug with tweezers. (*Sydney Morning Herald*, 29 February 1996)

Rats and mice carry food poisoning bacteria in their droppings, which they leave on surfaces and on uncovered food. Rats and mice will gnaw their way into bags and packets.

Pest control companies can assist with control methods, but several practices can help to eliminate pests:

- disposing of garbage before leaving work
- cleaning floors and surfaces regularly and before leaving work
- covering food
- storing food in plastic or metal containers
- preventing access to the premises
- sealing off pipes and crevices
- using baits, traps and insect killers (do not use sprays in kitchens).

Activities

1 Physically demonstrate bacteria multiplying, using polystyrene balls, matches or something similar. Take photographs of your model and design a poster for staff on safe food hygiene practices.

2 Having just started a vegetarian cafe, you need to select some cleaning agents from the local supermarket. Develop a list of what you need and go shopping. Try to find cleaning agents that are multipurpose, non-toxic and biodegradable.

3 Develop an advertisement for home delivery based on the 'spotless kitchen' idea.

4 A number of resorts and guesthouses have indigenous birds and animals which are very popular with guests. One has kangaroos, which help themselves to scones on the verandah, another has cockatoos which drink the milk. Do they pose a health risk?

5 Visit the following Internet sites for useful information on food handling and workplace hygiene:

- The NSW Health Department—http://www.health.nsw.gov.au
- 'Pest—Facts on Rats'—http://www.public.health.wa.gov.au/ehs45.htm
- Commonwealth Department of Health, 'Communicable Disease Intelligence Bulletin'—http://www.health.gov.au
- US Food Code Standards—http://www.ntis.gov

CASE STUDY

Vikram, who owned a small takeaway and home delivery operation, was about to renovate when he struck upon a brilliant idea. It was prompted by a trip with his family to a theme park where he looked into the kitchen of one of the food stands and was appalled by the standards of cleanliness. He knew that his own kitchens were immaculate, but realised that his customers were unaware of this. If his customers knew about the standards of food hygiene in his operation, this could give him a marketing edge.

Vikram contacted several suppliers and designed his new business with a state of the art kitchen which was open to the public. Customers waiting for takeaway food could watch it being prepared. The kitchen was designed with moulded stainless steel from ceiling to floor; the walls, bench tops and sinks were all part of the same mould, with rounded edges for easy cleaning and safety.

Customers were fascinated to watch the staff working so efficiently in such a small space and were entertained by the goings on in the kitchen while they waited for their food. Business skyrocketed. By the end of the year Vikram was in charge of a franchise operation with six outlets.

Discussion questions

1 Some restaurants have developed networks so that you can order dishes from two or more restaurants for a home-delivered meal. This involves a driver picking up from various locations and delivering to your home. What concerns would you have about food hygiene?

2 How would you ensure that you would not get food poisoning if you decided to eat the leftovers the next day?

3 What sort of uniform would you suggest the staff wear at Vikram's fast food operations?

LINKS

Australia New Zealand Food Authority—http://www.anzfa.gov.au/

Australia New Zealand Food Authority, Food Safety Standards—
http://www.anzfa.gov.au/foodstandardscodecontents/standard32.cfm

CHAPTER TWENTY-FIVE

Maintaining clean and green premises

OBJECTIVES

The hospitality industry and its employees can make a significant contribution to environmental initiatives. On completion of this chapter you will be aware of your responsibilities in relation to environmental protection and you will be able to:
- select and set up cleaning equipment
- clean wet and dry areas
- maintain and store cleaning equipment and chemicals
- follow OHS guidelines
- use protective clothing where required
- take appropriate care with hazardous materials
- use environmentally friendly cleaning practices
- use the appropriate methods to recycle materials
- reduce landfill by minimising waste.

Kim was carrying a container of cleaning fluid into the kitchen when she dropped it on the footpath. Some of the liquid splashed her arm, leaving her with minor burns. The rest spread quickly over the whole goods receiving area. Since it was slippery, one of her colleagues used a hose to wash the chemical down the drain to ensure that nobody would be injured on the slippery spill.

Although Kim's colleague was appropriately concerned about the possibility of an accident, washing the chemical down the drain was not a good idea. Anything washed into a stormwater drain reaches our waterways and oceans, and contributes to pollution levels. A spill clean-up kit should be used to deal with chemical and oil spills and every effort should be made to avoid polluting the stormwater system.

Takeaway outlets should be mindful of providing sufficient bins for the disposal of cartons, napkins and drinking cups (many of them polystyrene) so that litter does not find its way into the stormwater system through the carelessness of customers and the incorrect cleaning procedures of staff.

Restaurants are one of the biggest culprits when it comes to disposing of oils through the waste water system. They are required by law to use a grease arrestor to avoid pollutants being discharged into this system. If you work in a kitchen, there are a number of steps that you can take to avoid pollution and generally act in an environmentally friendly way. These will be discussed below.

Preventing stormwater pollution

Do not use a hose to clean areas around your establishment as this will result in litter, grease, oil, leaves and other matter entering the stormwater system (see Fig. 25.1). When cleaning outdoor areas, you should sweep up the litter and dispose of it appropriately. Use a composting bin for leaf litter and place paper and drink containers in the appropriate bins. Plastic drink bottles should not be sent down the drains to the ocean.

Preventing waste water pollution

As mentioned previously, all commercial kitchens should have a grease arrestor. This stores waste water, allowing oils and grease to rise to the top and scraps to settle on the bottom. A waste contractor is employed to remove the grease and food scraps, and the treated water is discharged into the system. All food scraps should be removed by scraping them into the bin before washing plates. A basket arrestor should be installed in all floor drains. This needs to be cleaned regularly.

Waste management

For most commercial kitchens, up to 22 per cent of the total waste generated is food. Of this 60 per cent is plate scrapings and 40 per cent is preparation waste such as peelings. (Tourism Training Australia, 2001) The pie chart in Fig. 25.2 on page 296 indicates how the balance of waste produced in most commercial kitchens is generated. From these figures, we can see the importance of reducing waste, so we will now look at how this can be achieved.

Adopting correct recycling practices will certainly help in the reduction of waste and resulting landfill. These involve disposal of paper, cardboard, plastic and glass bottles in the correct recycling bins. Since cork is in short supply worldwide, the corks from wine bottles should also be recycled. You can make a valuable contribution by making sure that contaminants don't find their way into recycling bins. For example, a sandwich in a paper-recycling bin will contaminate the paper and make the recycling process more expensive.

Waste audits carried out by hotels discover the most extraordinary things in the waste system, including silver cutlery, towels, unused stationery and bathroom supplies. All contribute unnecessarily to landfill and cost companies significant amounts of money. As we learnt in Chapter 14, an average of $15.25 worth of undamaged cutlery, crockery and table linen is accidentally disposed of by every hotel business every day.

FIG. 25.1

Contamination of rivers and oceans.

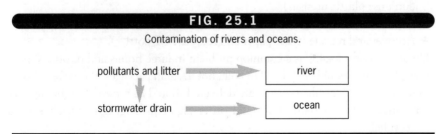

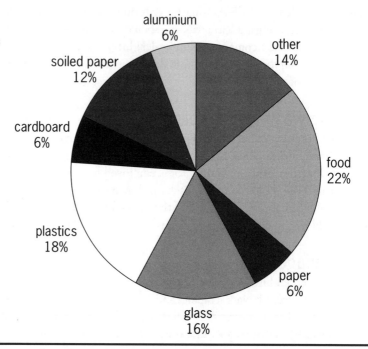

FIG. 25.2
Estimate of commercial kitchen waste.

aluminium 6%

other 14%

soiled paper 12%

cardboard 6%

food 22%

plastics 18%

paper 6%

glass 16%

Source: 'Eating into Waste', Training Manual, Tourism Training Australia, Sydney, 2000.

The waste generated in the kitchen occurs at various stages of the food preparation process:
- menu planning (overestimating)
- purchasing (buying large quantities of perishable goods)
- receipt and storage (poor handling and storage)
- meal preparation (food scraps and wasted food)
- serving (excessive quantities)
- cleaning (lack of care in recycling).

In any waste management strategy, the four main rules are:
1 Avoid using too much of anything or unnecessary products
2 Recover and reuse (cutlery and plates, for example, can be washed and reused—don't use plastic utensils)
3 Reprocess (for example, use leftover items from one recipe in another)
4 Recover and recycle (reuse paper and recycle PET bottles).

Unnecessary packaging is a common problem in large hotels and resorts. Where possible, items should be ordered in bulk, not in small packages. Polystyrene boxes in which vegetables like broccoli are delivered should be returned to the supplier for reuse, and cardboard boxes and other paper packaging materials should be recycled.

Using hazardous materials safely

If storing hazardous chemicals, they should be kept in a safe container in a safe place. Too many of these liquids and powders are left with lids open in unsafe areas. Many of these chemicals are toxic and should be treated with respect.

If working in the Kitchen or Housekeeping Department, you will no doubt be required to mix cleaning chemicals on a regular basis. It is essential that you take care to read and follow the instructions, as workplace accidents such as burns and severe allergic reactions can be caused by mixing the wrong items. Many hospitality employees use such chemicals with too high a concentrate, hoping that this will make their work easier. It does not. All it does is release larger quantities of potential pollutants.

Wherever possible, hospitality establishments should use less toxic materials, such as chlorine-free bleaches and bicarbonate of soda, for cleaning.

Employees who work in Housekeeping need to be particularly aware of the risks associated with needle disposal, since these and other contagious materials are sometimes left in guest bins or under mattresses. Gloves and appropriate yellow bins should be provided. When cleaning up vomit (a ghastly task that someone has to do), proper precautions, such as wearing gloves, should be taken, as the risk of contracting hepatitis is high.

Cleaning procedures and precautions

Cleaning procedures are summarised in Table 25.1 on page 298, starting with the selection of equipment and following through to cleaning and maintenance.

Protective clothing includes overalls, masks, gloves and safety footwear. Hazards identified might include broken glass, needles, fumes, blood, broken furniture, damaged electrical wires, hot utensils and surfaces, sharp knives or other sharp objects. Remember that any item contaminated with human bodily fluids is a risk to health.

Cleaning products and chemicals might include:
* general purpose and spot cleaning agents
* specialised cleaning agents (e.g. for window cleaning)
* disinfectants for sanitising
* deodorisers
* furniture and floor polishes
* pesticides
* pool-cleaning agents.

When using chemicals, safety dictates that employees check the manufacturer's instructions for correct dilution, use and disposal.

When dealing with the inhalation or ingestion of chemicals check for:
* abdominal pain
* drowsiness

Specialised equipment has been developed for the safe use of chemicals and other substances.

TABLE 25.1

Correct cleaning procedures.

Set up cleaning equipment and materials.	• Select correct equipment. • Check for safety. • Select chemical or cleaning agent. • Check manufacturer's instructions. • Select correct protective equipment and clothing.
Clean wet and dry areas.	• Schedule cleaning to avoid inconveniencing customers. • Identify hazards. • Use warning signs. • Use correct cleaning products, following instructions and safety procedures. • Use equipment safely. • Dispose of garbage in accordance with hygiene, safety and environmental guidelines.
Maintain and store equipment.	• Clean equipment after use. • Carry out routine maintenance. • Identify faults and report them to appropriate department. • Store equipment in correct area. • Store chemicals correctly.

- nausea or vomiting
- burning pains from mouth to stomach
- difficulty in breathing
- tight chest
- blurred vision
- odours on breath
- change of skin colour and blueness around the lips
- sudden collapse.

It is also important to take one or more of the following steps, depending on the accident that has occurred:

- If the casualty is conscious, try to determine the type of poison.
- Call 13 11 26 for Poisons Information Centre.
- Call Fire Brigade on 000 if the area is contaminated with smoke, gases or fumes.
- Monitor airway and breathing of casualty (follow the steps given in the St John DRABC Action Plan, outlined in Chapter 23).
- Call 000 for an ambulance.

Air quality management

If systems are kept in good condition, and filters cleaned or replaced regularly, fumes and odours leaving the premises can be avoided. In the case of air-conditioning systems, this is particularly important as they can harbour disease.

Reducing energy and water usage

Some of the ways in which you can help to minimise energy and water usage include:

- checking the seals on cool rooms, refrigerators and freezers
- turning off appliances and lights when not in use
- using energy-efficient cooking methods
- sweeping instead of using a hose
- fixing leaking taps.

Safe use of ozone-depleting substances

Most organisations are now aware of their obligations in relation to the use of CFCs, halons and other ozone-depleting substances.

Legal responsibilities

An environmentally friendly business can improve its image as well as operate more cost effectively. It will also avoid environmental fines or prosecutions.

Laws such as the Environmental Protection Act carry penalties for both companies and individuals. In addition, there are council regulations covering this area.

For further information you can visit the website of your state or territory environmental agency (these addresses can be found at the end of the chapter) or contact your local council to find out about their regulations.

The main environmental issues are:

- noise pollution (especially if you trade late at night)
- air quality
- water quality
- waste management
- disposal of hazardous materials.

Local councils carry the main responsibility for policing environmental issues and they hold the power to enter premises and issue clean-up notices.

Activity

Visit the following websites for information about environmental management and develop a list of ways in which work practices can support environmental initiatives:

- Department of Industry, Tourism and Resources—http://www.industry.gov.au
- NSW Environmental Protection Authority—http://www.epa.nsw.gov.au
- NT Department of Lands—http://www.nt.gov.au
- Queensland Department of Environment—http://www.env.qld.gov.au
- SA Department for Environment—http://www.denr.sa.gov.au
- Tasmanian Department of Lands—http://www.delm.tas.gov.au
- Victorian Environment Protection Authority—http://www.epa.vic.gov.au
- WA Department of Environmental Protection—http://www.environ.wa.gov.au

PART 5

Your Career

This final section will help you to research and plan for a career in tourism and hospitality. It covers preparing for interviews and developing interpersonal skills appropriate to the tourism and hospitality workplace, and includes sample letters of application and résumés. Strategies for successful job seeking are also covered. The necessity for developing effective communication skills and improving your knowledge to support interaction with colleagues and customers is reinforced in the following chapters. Once you have completed all the activities in this book, you should be more prepared, when applying for a job in tourism and hospitality, than most applicants. You should also be able to demonstrate that knowledge and skills are crucial to any successful career.

CHAPTER TWENTY-SIX

Preparing job applications

OBJECTIVES

This chapter links to Chapter 3 as research skills are essential for investigating job opportunities and current trends in the industry. On completion of this chapter you will be able to:

- use a variety of information sources to research current trends and issues in the industry
- use a variety of information sources to research information on jobs
- evaluate employment-related information
- make enquiries by telephone
- prepare a letter of application
- prepare a résumé
- maintain a portfolio of industry-related information.

After waiting two hours, we file into the seminar room for a three-hour first-stage interview. Sitting at tables of five and joined by a Qantas staff member we do the obligatory, 'Hi, my name is Sarah'. Everyone at my table works in the ubiquitous customer service and one woman admits to dreaming of being an air hostess ever since she was a little girl. At this, our friend from Qantas gasps. You don't say 'air hostess'. I know this because I had used the term 'stewardess' in an earlier meeting with Qantas and haven't quite recovered from the look of shock on their faces. 'Flight attendant pleeeaaase.' I wonder what would have happened if I had said 'trolley dolly'.

AUSTRALIAN MAGAZINE, 22 JUNE 1996

In this investigative article the journalist posed as an applicant for the job of flight attendant at Qantas. She found that the waiting time was used to evaluate people's energy level and that the three-hour-long interview was followed by group exercises in which applicants were pitted one against the other. In this part of the selection process, the applicants were asked to assume that they were crewing a flight between Darwin and Sydney and that the six Aboriginal artists on board had asked for advice on planning an itinerary for the couple of days they were to be in Sydney. The group of applicants had to come up with suggestions.

It is evident from the above just how important the role of research is in preparing for a rigorous selection process. It also illustrates the importance of keeping up to date with trends and issues in the tourism and hospitality industry.

The article goes on to describe how one successful applicant had applied 17 times—every year since he was 21. 'I told them on my 17th interview that I had been 16 times before and if they didn't give me the job this time around then I would only come back next year and start to get resentful. When I got the job I cried. I think I hold the record because Qantas didn't believe me when I told them.'

The recommendations that follow will help you in your preparation for that all-important task of finding—and getting—the right job for you in the industry.

Research tourism and hospitality trends

Changing trends in tourism and hospitality have important implications for anyone seeking employment in this field. Current interest in careers in this industry has surged in recent years and as the industry continues to expand it will provide

more and more professional career opportunities. As explained in earlier chapters, growth in leisure activities and travel is occurring worldwide, and Australia is uniquely placed to meet the needs of international tourists, including those from the rapidly developing Asian nations, which are closer than traditional markets such as the United States and Europe. As domestic tourism is growing at an average rate of around 1 per cent and international tourism is predicted to grow at 7–8 per cent, the importance of cross-cultural awareness and the advantage to tourism and hospitality employees of speaking more than one language are clear.

Career opportunities for chefs are increasing all the time.

Throughout this book we have emphasised the importance of developing a sound knowledge of such trends in order to plan effectively for a career in the industry. The convention business, for example, is worth an enormous amount to the Australian economy, with several major conventions bringing thousands of visitors into the country every year. Research into trends such as this can be very productive when planning a career and this is why we have suggested, as an activity at the end of the chapter, compiling a portfolio of press clippings on the industry.

Collect information on hospitality jobs

In addition to collecting information about the industry, it is useful to maintain a collection of advertisements for jobs in the industry. These describe the jobs available, the duties that have to be performed and the skills required. This information is very useful for preparing job applications.

In general terms, there are many sources of information about jobs and career paths. These include:

- hospitality establishments and organisations
- personal contacts in the industry
- government employment service
- private employment agencies
- *Yellow Pages*
- hospitality publications
- newspapers.

One very useful document for preparing your letter and résumé is the job description for the position. Employers will seldom provide these for they are confidential company documents given only to employees. However, there are many relevant job descriptions in tourism and hospitality texts, and a collection of these will prove very valuable when writing letters, modifying résumés or anticipating interview questions.

Develop telephone skills

Good telephone skills are essential, as most advertisements will ask you to call to obtain an application form. Such conversations are used to evaluate your communication skills on the telephone. Some useful guidelines have been included in Chapter 21.

All of these skills are necessary in securing an interview since they are also requirements of the job. It is just as important to plan for the telephone call as it is to plan for the interview. If information is required and you are unsure or ill prepared this will be noted by the potential employer. In particular, if you are applying for a role which involves telephone sales (which includes many tourism and hospitality jobs), you can be sure that your telephone skills are being evaluated, even at this early stage.

Writing the letter of application

The next step is generally to complete an application form and to send it in with an accompanying letter and résumé. The letter should be presented in the standard way as illustrated in Figs 26.1 and 26.2 on pages 306 and 307. This presentation is known as 'full-block' and you will notice that there is no punctuation in any part of the letter except in the main body—the sender's address, date, receiver's name (always find out who this is) and address, the salutation and the closing lines all have no punctuation. In the body of the letter a number of things need to be clear. Which position you are applying for, what you have to offer, why the position would suit you and how you can be contacted all need to be clearly stated (see Figs 26.1, 26.2 and 26.3 on page 309).

The presentation of the letter is critical. If an employer is faced with hundreds of applications for a single position, the easiest way to cull them is to throw out the messy letters written on torn scraps of paper. Flawless presentation on quality paper

FIG. 26.1

Sample job application letter.

23 Burell Street
McRAE VIC 3076
(03) 9756 5757

4 October 2002

Ms P Parkinson
Human Resources Director
Continental Hotel
110 Park Street
PARKTOWN VIC 3007

Dear Ms Parkinson

Re: Position of Trainee

I am very keen to apply for the position you advertised for a trainee. As you can see from my enclosed résumé, I have a keen interest in cross-cultural communication. I am sure that numerous foreign visitors are attracted to the Continental Hotel and this would give me an opportunity to develop my language skills. I have studied several countries at school and have looked at their culture, traditions and religion as part of subjects such as Geography and Hospitality Studies. I would like to continue this interest with the aim of developing fluency in Mandarin and Japanese, although I think this will take some time.

As you can see, I have had some experience in food preparation and service which should be very valuable since I had to work with a team to deliver fast service during very busy periods. I also have a good range of communication skills, which I feel sure will develop further in the job you have advertised. I can type reasonably quickly and can use several types of computer software.

Having worked at a popular tourist destination, I have a good understanding of the range of customers one can expect and how their needs differ. I know a little about tourist attractions in Victoria and am eager to learn more. I have studied history at school for three years and I think that I am a good ambassador for Australia.

If you would like to contact me for an interview I am available at the above number late in the afternoon, or if you wish to leave a message I will call you back.

Yours sincerely

Patricia Lee

FIG. 26.2
Sample job application letter.

BRIAN DESSAIX
116 FRENCHS FOREST RD FRENCHS FOREST
NSW 2086

11 November 2002

Ms Fiona Calabrese
Human Resources Department
Marriott Hotel
515 Queen Street
Brisbane Qld 4000

Dear Ms Calabrese

Re: Banquet Supervisor/Waitperson

As a current student studying Hospitality Management at Brookvale TAFE and having had three years experience working in the industry, I wish to respond to your advertisement in the *Sydney Morning Herald*, Saturday, 10 November.

Included in the above qualification is a study of Food and Beverage operations. I have covered and will soon complete the following modules:

• Patron Care (Responsible Service of Alcohol)
• Bars and Service of Drinks
• Wine and Wine Service
• Cellar Operations
• Advanced Cocktail Knowledge
• Restaurant Prep for Service
• Restaurant Service
• Silver Service.

Upon completion of these subjects at the end of the current semester, I will have a good idea of Food and Beverage operations, and I would only require minimal training to join your team. My completion of One-to-One Job Instruction has also taught me how to train people in all environments and about all aspects of a particular task.

(continues)

FIG. 26.2 (continued)

Sample job application letter.

In the year of 1998 I was nominated as the Year 12 College Captain of St Augustine's College, Brookvale. My duties as Captain included dealing with people of all ages, ranks and types. It was in this same year that I was head organiser of my Year 12 formal. Whilst organising, my interest in the hospitality industry began to focus on the banqueting department. It was my responsibility to interact with such people as banquet supervisors. Organising my formal was hard work but most enjoyable. Not only was I dealing with people with similar career ambitions as myself, but people with similar personalities.

During my time as College Captain I learnt many skills, such as the importance of good leadership, the advantages of successful teamwork and how to use communication skills as well as to develop them.

Hospitality is a large industry and can only get bigger, according to trends and current statistics. This thought excites me and provides a challenge that I am not afraid to attempt.

Through working in a cafe kitchen in Manly at the age of 16 I realised the thrill of the hospitality industry. My training prior to this was at McDonalds, as a casual kitchen hand. The cafe I was working in closed down due to ownership disputes, and it was then that I began work at Shakespeare's Pies, Manly. After one year I have extensive knowledge of espresso machine techniques and can operate the machine under high pressure.

Through studying and working, especially through successfully working shifts, I have learnt good organisational skills. I am able to fit in work, recreation and study—all necessary for achieving maximum results.

I believe that through hard work, dedication, an energetic approach and a constant positive attitude I can find a successful career in a banquet department. I have been to your hotel and was highly impressed with its features, and would be more than happy for this to be my place of employment and future career. If a successful applicant, I offer you my flexibility and availability.

I can be contacted at home on (02) 9452 2259 or by fax on (02) 9975 5229.

I look forward to hearing from you.

Yours sincerely

Brian Dessaix

FIG. 26.3

Match between applicant and position.

Job suits you   You suit the job

reflects an understanding of the importance of personal presentation in any service industry. The wording of your letter can be simple and informal. Spelling must be correct.

Below are guidelines for preparing job application letters:

- Address the letter to a specific person.
- Include the name of the position under the greeting/salutation.
- Explain how your skills and knowledge are appropriate for this position.
- Explain how the job would meet your needs for career development.
- Allay the employer's concern about your ability to work shift or weekend work.
- Close strongly with an action ending.

Preparing the résumé

The résumé is similar to the letter in that it needs to be flawlessly presented and tailored to meet the specific requirements of the job advertised. With the word processor this is very easy to achieve since your basic résumé can be modified to closely match the advertised criteria. As in most communication situations, it is useful to try to anticipate the receiver's expectations and to modify the information accordingly. There are a number of standard features in the résumé and, in addition, we recommend the inclusion of an additional page that lists skills and knowledge appropriate to the position advertised. This is, after all, what will interest the receiver most.

Personal details

Your contact number is the most essential item on the résumé and it is surprising how many people forget this important detail. For those applying for jobs in beverage departments age is also important as alcohol cannot be served by anyone under 18 years of age. Marital status and other personal details are not relevant.

Skills and knowledge

As illustrated in the résumé in Fig. 26.4 on page 310, a skills and knowledge list developed to match the position advertised is most useful for the potential employer. If you were applying to work as a waiter in a restaurant, for example, this would include food, wine and beverage knowledge, and waiting, cash register and espresso

FIG. 26.4
Sample résumé.

Patricia Lee
23 Burell St, McRae Vic 3076 Tel 03 9756 5757

Skills and Knowledge

Communication

Effective communication with customers and fellow staff members using the skills of:

- Speaking
- Letter and memo writing
- Questioning
- Listening
- Interpreting and using non-verbal communication
- Telephone skills.

Personal Presentation

Ability to meet industry and enterprise standards of personal presentation:

- Uniform requirements
- Etiquette
- Poise and deportment.

Cross-Cultural Awareness

Knowledge of:

- Tourism trends
- Culture, tradition and religion of Japan, China, Korea and Indonesia
- Japanese, Chinese, Korean and Indonesian countries and tourist expectations
- Food requirements and general expectations in accordance with religious beliefs
- Strategies for managing cross-cultural and language issues
- Individual perceptions and special needs of the above tourists
- Basic conversational skills in Japanese and Mandarin.

Quality Assurance

- Standards and procedures
- Maintaining service standards
- Seeking feedback for continuous improvement.

(continues)

FIG. 26.4 (continued)

Sample résumé.

Work Team Communication
- Recording and conveying routine information
- Giving routine instructions
- Checking for understanding
- Team building and goal setting.

Educational Background

St Joseph's High School

Subjects	English	Mandarin
	Maths	Hospitality Communication
	Geography	Computer Studies
	Biology	

St John's Ambulance   First Aid Certificate

Work Experience

Red Hill Community Market   January 2002—Present (Sundays),
                                            Selling handmade souvenirs

Arthur's Seat Chairlift Tea Room   September 2002—Present
                                            (weekends and school holidays)
                                            Waiter, cashier and breakfast cook

Skills include greeting and seating guests, taking orders, processing payment, as well as basic cooking skills during busy breakfast periods.

Other Activities
- Establishment of St Joseph's Web page for the Internet with a team of four computer students.
- Weekly scanning of school magazine for digital storage.
- A grade netball player.
- Participation in a Toastmaster's public speaking group.
- Computer software: word processing, spread sheets and desktop publishing.
- Typing: 45 wpm, 97 per cent accuracy.

machine skills. All of this would be valuable to such an employer and would provide the competitive edge over someone who was less knowledgeable or experienced.

Career objectives

This is an optional component. Career goals should be included only if your career path has been thoroughly researched, and should not be overly optimistic. Of course the career objectives included should always be compatible with the position for which you are applying.

Education

The employer is mainly interested in your most recent education. There is no need to list schools, colleges or courses that were prerequisites for more recent study. If you are currently studying subjects that are relevant to the position, list them, even if you have not completed the course.

Work experience

Employers are interested in the duration of your employment and the duties performed in your previous roles. These should be explained in some detail. Contact names and numbers are needed to check your references.

Other interests

Interests that are relevant to employment should be listed, including team sports. Success in any endeavour will demonstrate that you are committed to achieving personal goals.

From the résumé presented in Fig. 26.4, you can see how the skills and knowledge acquired from completing the activities in this text can be used when applying for a job in tourism and hospitality. The knowledge and skills gained through any field of study can also be used in your résumé, course information documents being useful for this purpose. These show the topics you are learning about in the course and which skills will be developed by the time you have finished. This makes it easier for you to sell yourself to employers. There are a number of texts available on the subject of career planning in tourism and hospitality, including *Hospitality Careers* by the same author, which includes 84 questions you might be asked in an interview!

In general terms, there are some key things to check when preparing a résumé and the accompanying documentation:

- The information provided, including skills and knowledge, should be directly related to the position advertised.
- The résumé should be up to date, with the most recent education and work experience first.
- The résumé should be comprehensive but concise.
- Any information more than seven years old should be summarised briefly.
- Current study should be listed in detail.

- Duties and responsibilities for positions held should be provided in detail.
- Spelling and grammar should be checked carefully.
- The paper used should be top quality and printing should be strong and black (no second-rate copies).
- Attached documentation should be minimal and should appear in the order of the information in the résumé.

Research relevant industry information

At the start of this chapter it was suggested that a portfolio or file of press clippings would help you to monitor trends in the industry. In the same way, a collection of information about your local and surrounding areas, about events, attractions and the natural environment, can also be useful in developing your knowledge about the industry.

All of this information, if correctly categorised and easily accessible, forms the basis of the job interview and of the informational role of all tourism and hospitality professionals.

Activities

1 Develop a portfolio of current tourism and hospitality news by keeping press clippings. Label each one with the date and source. Categorise the clippings and provide a summary for each section.
2 Write a letter of application for the position below. Make sure that you sell your skills and knowledge and show why the job would suit you. Enclose your résumé and a maximum of three supporting documents.

INFORMATION CENTRE

Requires new trainee for a career in the hospitality industry.

Applicants should have the following essential attributes:
- ability to communicate clearly
- cross-cultural awareness
- ability to greet and thank customers in four languages
- team skills
- telephone skills
- extensive range of appropriate knowledge.

This is a full-time traineeship position for a high school graduate. Time will be allocated for completion of a related course through the local TAFE College. The successful applicant will be required to work on weekends.

All applications should be made to the Human Resources Manager
Private Bag 25 GPO
Brisbane 4000

3 Role play a telephone call to a busy Human Resources Director enquiring about career prospects in his organisation. Evaluate your telephone skills using the following guide—rate your skills 1 (poor) to 5 (excellent):

Speaking clearly

[ ]   [ ]   [ ]   [ ]   [ ]

Asking appropriate questions

[ ]   [ ]   [ ]   [ ]   [ ]

Speaking at an appropriate volume

[ ]   [ ]   [ ]   [ ]   [ ]

Using more formal language than usual

[ ]   [ ]   [ ]   [ ]   [ ]

Providing information in a structured way

[ ]   [ ]   [ ]   [ ]   [ ]

Listening attentively

[ ]   [ ]   [ ]   [ ]   [ ]

Recording information if necessary

[ ]   [ ]   [ ]   [ ]   [ ]

Showing enthusiasm through tone of voice

[ ]   [ ]   [ ]   [ ]   [ ]

Remembering and using the person's name

[ ]   [ ]   [ ]   [ ]   [ ]

Closing on a strong positive note

[ ]   [ ]   [ ]   [ ]   [ ]

CHAPTER TWENTY-SEVEN

Preparing for interviews

OBJECTIVES

The communication strategies described in this chapter build on the knowledge and skills developed in Parts 2 and 3. On completion of the chapter you will be able to:

- plan for a job interview
- prepare potential job interview questions and answers
- present appropriately for the interview
- participate in a job interview
- evaluate interview performance in relation to job requirements.

After I had been for a few interviews I discovered that each interviewer was different. Some made it really easy for you to sell yourself and others made it very difficult. As a result my performance in the interviews was up and down. I wanted to get to the stage where I could leave any interview feeling as though I had given it my best shot. The secret emerged when I studied Human Resources at college and discovered what good interviewing was about. With that in mind I was able to plan for interviews and prepare myself better. For example, the worst interviewer asks questions like 'Tell me about yourself' and 'What are your strengths and weaknesses?' A good interviewer asks questions like 'Can you tell me about a situation in which you had to provide information to a customer?' or 'Can you describe any problems you have solved in a work or team situation?' As a result, each time I prepare for an interview, I develop a list of skills and knowledge the interviewer might be looking for and then plan my answers. That way, even if they don't ask the right questions, I can try to find opportunities to talk about things that are relevant to the job. Interviews where you talk about things that are not relevant, like hobbies, are a waste of time.

HOSPITALITY TRAINEE

The above trainee has realised how important it is to prepare for an interview. The logical first step is to ascertain the minimum job requirements. These are generally available in the job description. Once they have been identified, it is possible to anticipate some of the interview questions.

The job description

A sample job description is given in Fig. 27.1. Although this information is unlikely to be available from the prospective place of employment, it can be found in numerous textbooks. Job descriptions are also available on disc in some libraries. A telephone call requesting information about the job can also help to develop some idea of the duties. Thus the starting point for preparing for an interview is the job description.

A job description lists the duties that are part of the job. Each item represents a specific task to be performed and starts with a verb. To this list you can add a number of duties which are assumed, such as answering telephone calls, providing information to customers, handling complaints, completing forms and paperwork, and so on.

From this stage of the investigation you can move on to the next, which is deciding on what skills and knowledge will be required for the job. In Human Resource Management this is called the person or job specification.

The person specification

The person specification describes the ideal person for the job. Thinking back to the job description, one of the duties mentioned was completing paperwork. The ideal person for this task would have legible handwriting and would be able to demonstrate attention to detail and accuracy during the selection process. Answering the telephone would require telephone techniques such as listening, questioning and using the customer's name. These skills would also need to be demonstrated in the selection process, in the interview in particular, for example by remembering the interviewer's name and using it. The ideal person for a job in tourism and hospitality would also need to be familiar with industry terminology.

The skills component for the position described in Fig. 27.1 would be most easily researched by observing someone in the role. The knowledge component could be researched by reading a textbook on the topic. Even for those who are skilled in a role, this research is often necessary to heighten awareness of unconscious skills and knowledge. The outcome of this research would look something like the person specification illustrated in Fig. 27.2.

Thus in planning for an interview, it is necessary to research the duties performed in the role (job description) and speculate on the skills/knowledge required for the role (person specification). This process is illustrated in Fig. 27.3.

This level of investigation would pay off in the interview—imagine the delight of the cafe owner if you were to mention that tea intake has declined by 22.5 per cent since 1992–93, while coffee consumption per capita has increased by 4.2 per cent (ABS, Cat No 4315.0). This would indicate an awareness of the importance of the cafe culture in Australia and would offer some interesting information to share with customers.

Analysis of the job in terms of the duties (job description) and ideal candidate (person specification) enables you to determine your suitability for the position and, most importantly, whether the position is compatible with your interests and career aspirations.

Job Description: Cafe Waiter.

Job Description

Title: Cafe Waiter/Espresso Expert

Duties
Take reservations
Greet and seat customers
Offer menus
Upsell food and drink items
Explain ingredients
Explain preparation methods
Operate espresso machine
Use standard recipes and procedures for:
    Espresso
    Cappuccino
    Caffe latte
    Macchiato
    Flat white
    Long black
    Short black
Demonstrate knowledge of coffee growing and
preparation of beans
Place food orders with the kitchen
Converse with customers
Seek feedback on customer satisfaction
Clear tables
Process payments

Person Specification: Cafe Waiter.

Person Specification

Cafe Waiter/Expresso Expert

Coffee-making skills
Setting up espresso machine for service
Operation of espresso machine for the range of
coffees advertised on the menu
Cleaning espresso machine
Basic machine maintenance
Storing coffee beans correctly

Communication skills
Effective verbal communication
Effective non-verbal communication
Listening
Questioning
Providing information as appropriate
Upselling
Seeking customer feedback
Problem-solving

Food and beverage skills
Taking reservations
Greeting and seating customers
Providing food and beverage service
Processing payment

Knowledge
History of coffee
The coffee plant
Roasting
Tasting and blending
Storage
Recipes and variations

Planning for the job interview, Stage 1.

Advertisement ➡ job description (duties) ➡ Person specification (skills/knowledge)

The questions

Having speculated on the contents of the job description and person specification for the role, the time has come to prepare some of the questions most likely to be asked in the interview. Even if the questions asked are not exactly as anticipated, there are likely to be opportunities to use the information you have prepared. Current trends in interviewing are based on the philosophy, 'In the past lies truth and honesty'. For this reason modern interviewers will probably not ask questions about what you would or should do. This is because we all know what we should do. If you asked a person what they should eat for lunch, they would say a salad sandwich. If you asked them what they had eaten for lunch, they would probably admit to hot chips or pizza! Many interviewers therefore ask for examples from your past so that they can predict how you will react in the future. Requests such as 'Give me an example of a situation in which a customer was unhappy with the service' and questions like 'Have you ever had to deal with equipment breakdowns during peak times—what happened?' illustrate the concept of predicting future behaviour from past behaviour.

In summary, the interviewer makes inferences based on your explanations. If you handled an equipment breakdown well, they would infer that you had good problem-solving skills. After all, you can't go into an interview and say 'I am good at solving problems' and then carry on listing all the things you are good at. The interviewer would prefer to reach this conclusion based on some evidence.

In preparing for the interview, you are therefore anticipating being asked for examples from your past which illustrate the skills required in the job. And even if the anticipated questions aren't asked, you can still use the information you have prepared to lead the interviewer to the correct conclusions! As illustrated in Fig. 27.4, you are providing examples from your past to allow the interviewer to make the right inferences.

As you can tell from the sample questions on page 319, planning for a job interview is essential if one hopes to perform well. Some of the outcomes in relation to communications skills listed at the start of each chapter may also be very useful in identifying the skills and knowledge required for professional performance in any customer relations role.

FIG. 27.4

Planning for the job interview, Stages I and II.

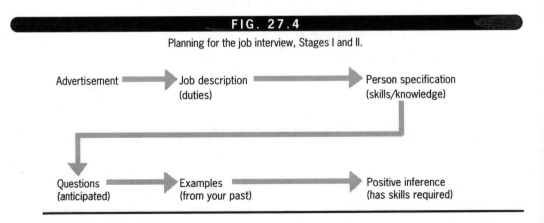

Examples of interview questions

How have you kept up to date with tourism and hospitality trends?

Can you give me a general idea of your knowledge of attractions, events and anything else a tourist might ask about?

How have your studies been relevant to work in this industry?

Can you tell me about any personal goals you have set for yourself and explain how you have achieved them?

Can you give me an example of a situation in which you have had to explain something to someone who spoke very little English?

How would you check that the person had understood you?

We work towards continuous improvement in customer service. Is there any way that you could assist in this?

Can you provide an example of a situation in which you have made a suggestion to improve the way things were done?

Can you describe a problem you have experienced in a team situation and explain your role in this?

Presentation for job interviews

Guidelines for preparation, presentation and participation in interviews have been provided by Australia Asia Pacific Hotels and are outlined in Fig. 27.5 on page 320. These give a very good indication of the professionalism that is expected in the job interview. As for presentation, applicants should attempt to dress in a way that is compatible with the requirements of the position, conservatively for some places, more informally for others.

Activities

1 Discuss the interview process with three people who have recently been involved (as an interviewer or applicant) in recruitment and selection. Find out the time span between the application, the response and the interview; the information (if any) provided before the interview; and the process and outcomes of the interview. Ask for tips and guidelines for successful interview performance and summarise them under the following headings:
   • Planning
   • Process
   • Communication.
2 Using the communication skills listed in the person specification for a cafe waiter in Fig. 27.2, develop a range of interview questions and prepare to answer them with specific examples from your own experience. The aim of this is to allow the interviewer to infer that you have the skills listed from the examples you provide.

FIG. 27.5

Interview techniques.

3 key steps to remember when attending an interview

PREPARATION, PRESENTATION, PARTICIPATION

PREPARATION

Find out information on the enterprise and the position you are applying for.

Clarify the time and place of the interview and any other requirements.

Allow yourself enough time to get to the interview. Applicants should arrive at least 15 minutes before the interview.

Make sure that you have immaculate personal presentation.

Remember to bring with you support documentation to back up your application.

PRESENTATION

Present a positive outlook through your body language and grooming standards.

Wear appropriate business clothing for the interview and remember courtesies.

Speak confidently.

Sell your strengths and abilities to the interviewer.

PARTICIPATION

Actively listen.

Respond informatively to questions and make your answers relevant to the position.

Don't be afraid to clarify questions if you don't understand.

Ask relevant questions of the interviewer regarding the position.

Thank the interviewer for their time to see you.

Reproduced with permission of ACADEMIE ACCOR.

3 Use the following check list to practise your interview performance with a partner. You can use the job description provided in Fig. 27.1 on page 317 or conduct your own research into a job that interests you. Rate your performance from 1 (poor) to 5 (excellent).

Job skills

[ ]   [ ]   [ ]   [ ]   [ ]

Verbal communication

[ ]   [ ]   [ ]   [ ]   [ ]

Non-verbal communication

[ ]   [ ]   [ ]   [ ]   [ ]

Customer awareness
[ ]   [ ]   [ ]   [ ]   [ ]
Industry knowledge
[ ]   [ ]   [ ]   [ ]   [ ]
Initiative
[ ]   [ ]   [ ]   [ ]   [ ]
Problem-solving skills
[ ]   [ ]   [ ]   [ ]   [ ]

Discussion questions

1 Do you agree with the philosophy of human behaviour that says that past behaviour can be used to predict future behaviour?

2 Is there any point in preparing responses to interview questions that you may never be asked? Explain your reasoning.

3 Do you think that different cultures have different coffee drinking habits? If so, how would you use this knowledge to further enhance your chances of obtaining the cafe waiter's job in Fig. 27.1?

4 A manager once said, 'The problem is that they dress fashionably and not appropriately for interviews'. What did she mean?

CHAPTER TWENTY-EIGHT

Planning your career

OBJECTIVES

This chapter links to Chapter 3, as research skills will be used to investigate work, career and training opportunities. On completion of this chapter you will be able to:

- identify a range of career paths in the industry
- identify a range of training opportunities for career development
- research job-related information
- interview a range of industry personnel to evaluate the positive and negative aspects of work in the industry
- develop a personal SWOT analysis (strengths, weaknesses, opportunities and threats).

was working as a banquet attendant at the Convention Centre while I was at college where I was doing a Hospitality Management diploma. I was worried at the time that I would not be able to use all the knowledge I was developing when everyone told me I would have to start at the bottom. However, soon after completing my course I was promoted to supervisor. A year later I applied for Assistant Food and Beverage Manager but was not successful until the following year. To cut a long story short, I became Food and Beverage Manager for one of the largest convention centres in Australia when I was twenty-six. And I can tell you that I use everything I have been taught—it is one of the most demanding jobs there is.

FOOD AND BEVERAGE MANAGER,
CONVENTION CENTRE

Food and Beverage Division provides an excellent career path for aspiring managers.

Worldwide growth in the services sector is very positive for anyone planning a career in the tourism and hospitality industry. In this chapter we will look at career opportunities in the industry and at new training arrangements under the national framework.

Employment trends

The identification of tourism-related jobs is extremely difficult. Some jobs, such as travel agents or tour guides, are clearly tourism related, but there are many others available in the following fields that are not so obvious:

- incentive travel planning
- meeting and convention planning
- corporate travel planning
- airline industry
- coach industry
- cruise industry
- car rental industry
- railways
- theme parks
- companies involved with natural attractions.

This list does not include many related fields such as the souvenir business and general retail, nor does it include entertainment. The tourism industry is thus hard to pin-point in terms of specific jobs since there are many services which are used by both local residents and tourists. Banking is a good example of a service provided to tourists as well as to residents and businesses.

The hospitality industry (which provides food, beverage and accommodation) is similar in that it caters to both tourists and local residents. The following list gives some idea of the scope of the hospitality industry:

- hotels
- motels
- guesthouses
- resorts
- clubs
- casinos
- pubs
- restaurants
- cafes and bistros
- fast food outlets
- convention centres
- entertainment centres
- catering operations.

The scope of employment in tourism and hospitality is thus extremely broad, but the common theme is customer service.

In 2000–2001 tourism directly employed 551,000 people in Australia, representing 6 per cent of total employment (ABS Cat No 5249.0), while Tourism Training Australia (2002) estimates that over 1.3 million people work in the combined fields of tourism and hospitality. The anticipated growth in both domestic and international tourism, as well as the trend towards eating outside the home, are further positive indicators for career planning in the tourism and hospitality industry.

Fig. 28.1 on page 324 provides an example of career progression in a particular establishment.

FIG. 28.1

Example of hospitality career progression.

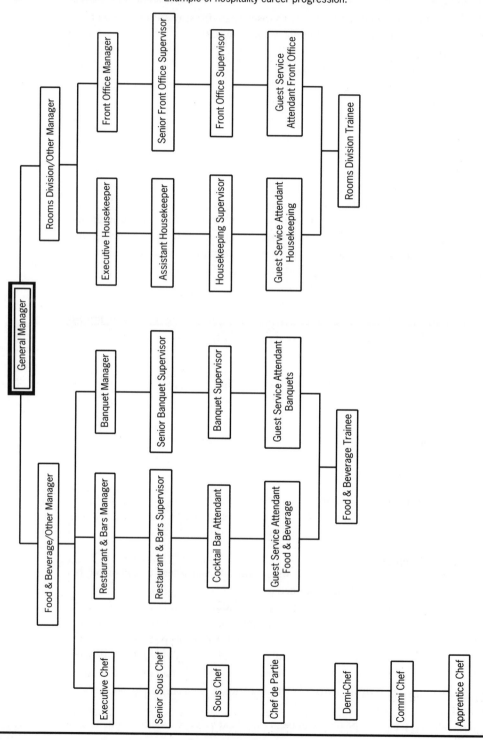

By permission of ACCOR Asia Pacific.

Training

The introduction of the new qualifications system has led to consistency in the award levels being offered by different institutions. This is illustrated in Fig. 28.2 on page 326. In tourism and hospitality, most training programs are based on competency standards developed by the industry (see Table 28.1), and courses are approved by industry bodies. The result of this has been portability of qualifications. Any approved training done in any state or territory is recognised Australia-wide. A list of approved courses is available from Tourism Training in your state or territory.

As each of the course components is based on competency standards agreed by industry, these units are also portable from one training institution to another. Many schools offer vocational courses that are competency based and recognised by other training institutions, thus earning credit towards a qualification.

It is also possible to combine on- and off-the-job training and assessment. This means that some parts of a course are conducted and assessed in the classroom while other skills are learned and assessed on the job. The tourism and hospitality industry is at the forefront of training reform, having undergone many changes in the past few years to achieve these goals.

TABLE 28.1

Brief description of the competencies applicable to each qualification in tourism and hospitality.

Certificate I represents a limited qualification, used in some industries as a baseline entry point. It often comprises generic industry competency requirements with a limited technical range, where work is routine and closely supervised.

Certificate II represents a base operational qualification that encompasses a range of functions/activities requiring fundamental operational knowledge and limited practical skills in a defined context.

Certificate III represents a qualification of the skilled operator, who applies a broad range of competencies within a more varied work context, possibly providing technical advice and support to a team and having team leader responsibilities.

Certificate IV represents a qualification that is based on more sophisticated technical applications, involving competencies requiring increased theoretical knowledge to be applied in a non-routine environment and may involve team leadership and management and increased responsibility for outcomes.

The Diploma represents a qualification that assumes a greater theoretical base and consists of specialised, technical or managerial competencies used to plan, carry out and evaluate work of self and/or team.

The Advanced Diploma represents a qualification involving technical, creative, conceptual or managerial applications built around competencies of either a broad or specialised base and related to a broader organisational focus.

Qualifications Framework, THHQ2 Hospitality Training Package ANTA.

FIG. 28.2
Hospitality qualifications framework.

Advanced Diploma of Hospitality Management

Diploma of Hospitality Management

Certificate IV in Hospitality
(Supervision)

Certificate IV in Hospitality
(Commercial Cookery)
(Catering Operations)
(Patisserie)
(Asian Cookery)

Certificate III in Hospitality
(Operations)

Certificate III in Hospitality
(Commercial Cookery)
(Catering Operations)
(Patisserie)
(Asian Cookery)

Certificate II in Hospitality
(Operations)

Certificate II in Hospitality
(Kitchen Operations)
(Asian Cookery)

Certificate I in Hospitality
(Operations)

Certificate I in Hospitality
(Kitchen Operations)

Personal SWOT analysis

A good strategy when planning a career is to conduct a SWOT analysis. SWOT stands for:

S trengths
W eaknesses
O pportunities
T hreats

An identification of your **strengths** will enable you to sell yourself in the employment market. You are likely to have made many positive assumptions about yourself and this is the time to take credit for them. Keep in mind that it is important to focus on attributes other than personality factors. After all, most candidates see themselves as having ideal personalities for the job! Judgements about personality are also hard to make. In general, identifying skills (including communication skills) and knowledge relevant to a particular job is likely to bring better results in a competitive environment.

Next you need to identify your **weaknesses** in terms of your employability in tourism and hospitality. This means identifying areas in which you still need training. The lack of a second language is an example of a weakness, but it is one that is not insurmountable, so it is the best type to admit to in an interview. As we have said regarding strengths, it is important to answer a question about weaknesses in terms of training needs rather than personality factors. Being specific about personal goals for obtaining relevant skills or knowledge can turn this rather negative question into an opportunity for you to sell yourself in terms of carefully planned training and career development.

You can identify **opportunities** by studying industry trends, looking for growth areas and identifying appropriate jobs in those growth areas. From these 'opportunities' you can select those that best suit your career needs.

Some of the areas in which growth has been predicted include:
- meetings, conventions and exhibitions
- restaurants
- hotels and motels
- caravan parks
- tourist attractions.

Finally, **threats** are stumbling blocks to the achievement of personal career goals. Working shift work is definitely a threat as it undoubtedly has an effect on family and social life. All jobs have some negative factors and it is essential to be realistic about them from the start. The third activity at the end of this chapter asks you to interview a number of industry staff to obtain their opinions about the downside of working in tourism and hospitality, which will be helpful in planning your career. Threats can be quite specific, such as the need to work unsociable hours, and also quite broad, such as an unexpected downturn in inbound international tourists following a marked change in the value of the dollar, which would ultimately reduce the number of jobs available.

Activities

1 Describe the impact that this book has had on planning your career in the hospitality industry?

2 Begin your own career planning by starting a portfolio of the following items:
- brochures of hospitality establishments
- information on tourist attractions
- local information
- hospitality news
- current affairs newspaper clippings
- personal documents.

3 Interview four people who work in the hospitality industry and discuss the positive and negative aspects of working in this field. At the same time, ask how they found their jobs and how they would recommend you go about it. A questionnaire designed for this purpose would be useful.

4 Conduct a personal SWOT analysis to identify your strengths and weaknesses, your training and career opportunities, and the threats that might face you in attempting to achieve your career goals.

5 Develop a career plan which links employment progression with training and educational achievements.

LINKS

TAFE NSW Workworlds—http://workworlds.ryde.tafensw.edu.au/

Tourism Training Australia—http://www.tourismtraining.com.au/

Sources of further information

Convention and visitors bureaus

Adelaide Convention and Tourism Authority—http://www.acta.com.au
Brisbane Marketing—http://www.brisbanetourism.com.au
Canberra Convention Bureau—http://www.canberraconvention.com.au/
Conventions New Zealand—
  http://www.conventionsnz.co.nz/conventions/index.asp
Melbourne Convention and Visitors Bureau—http://www.mcvb.net.au/
Northern Territory Convention Bureau—http://www.ntconventions.com.au
Perth Convention Bureau—http://www.pcb.com.au/
Sydney Conventions and Visitors Bureau—
  http://www.scvb.com.au/index_s.html
Tasmania Convention Bureau—http://www.comp2000.com.au/tcbwebsite.nsf

Government

ACT Government—http://www.act.gov.au/
Austrade—http://www.austrade.gov.au
Australian International Recruitment Service—http://www.detya.gov.au
Australian Local Government—http://www.algin.net.au
Northern Territory Government—http://www.nt.gov.au
NSW State Government—http://ww.nsw.gov.au
Queensland State Government—http://www.qld.gov.au
South Australian State Government—http://www.sa.gov.au
Tasmanian State Government—http://www.dpac.tas.gov.au
Victorian State Government—http://www.vic.gov.au
Western Australian State Government—http://www.wa.gov.au

Government tourism organisations

Australian Tourist Commission—http://www.atc.net.au
Canberra Tourism—http://www.canberratourism.com.au/welcome.html
Northern Territory Tourism Commission—http://www.nttc.com.au/
South Australian Tourism Commission—http://www.southaustralia.com/
Tourism NSW—http://www.tourism.nsw.gov.au/
Tourism New Zealand (market research)—http://www.tourisminfo.govt.nz/
Tourism New Zealand (travel)—http://www.purenz.com/indexnz.cfm

Tourism Queensland—http://www.queensland-holidays.com.au/pfm/index.htm
Tourism Tasmania—http://www.discovertasmania.com.au/
Tourism Victoria—http://www.tourismvictoria.com.au/
Western Australia Tourism Commission—http://www.westernaustralia.net/

Statistics and forecasts

Australian Bureau of Statistics—
    http://www.abs.gov.au/websitedbs/d3310114.nsf/Homepage
Bureau of Tourism Research—http://www.btr.gov.au/
Department of Industry, Tourism and Resources, Canberra—
    http://www.industry.gov.au/
World Tourism Organization—http://www.world-tourism.org/
World Travel and Tourism Council—http://www.wttc.org/

Tourism and hospitality associations and unions

Australian Council of Trade Unions—http://www.actu.asn.au
Australian Hotels Association—http://www.ahawa.asn.au
Liquor, Hospitality and Miscellaneous Workers Union—
    http://www.lhmu.org.au/
Restaurant and Catering Australia—http://www.restaurantcater.asn.au

Tourism training

NT Tourism Training Board—http://www.ntttb.org.au/
Tourism Training ACT & Region—Email: ttact@interact.net.au
Tourism Training Australia—http://www.tourismtraining.com.au/
Tourism Training NSW—http://www.ttnsw.com/
Tourism Training Queensland—http://www.ttq.org.au/
Tourism Training SA—http://www.ttsa.com.au/
Tourism Training Tasmania—Email: tourtraintas@bigpond.com.au
Tourism Training Victoria—http://www.ttvic.com.au/
WA Hospitality & Tourism Training Council—http://www.wahttc.com.au/

Bibliography

Australian National Training Authority. 'Training Package Resources for VET in Schools: Approaches to Assessment in Hospitality TH97'. Curriculum Corporation, Victoria, 1999.

Australian Hotels Association. *A History of the Australian Hotels Association, 1873–1988*. Australian Hotels Association, Sydney, 1988.

Axtell, Roger E. *Gestures: The DO's and TABOO's of Body Language Around the World*. John Wiley and Sons, New York, 1991.

Baker, S., Bradley, P. & Huyton, J. *Principles of Hotel Front Office Operations*. 2nd Aust. edn. Hospitality Press, Sydney, 1998.

Brown, G. & Hepner, K. *The Waiter's Handbook*. 2nd edn. Hospitality Press, Sydney, 2000.

Cassidy, N. Human Resource Practices in Hospitality—A Critical Review. Unpublished Masters paper. UNE, Armidale, 1997.

Chiplin, J. *Hospitality Core Units*. Hospitality Books, Sydney, 2001.

Collins, J. 'Migrant Hands in a Distant Land' in Whitlock, G. & Carter, D. *Images of Australia*. University of Queensland Press, St Lucia, 1992.

Commonwealth Department of Human Services and Health. *Dietary Guide for Australians*. AGPS, Canberra, 1994.

Commonwealth of Australia. *Development of Uniform Food Acts for Australia and New Zealand*. ANZFA, Canberra, 1999.

Commonwealth of Australia. *Food-borne Disease: Towards Reducing Food-borne Illness in Australia*. AusInfo, Canberra, 1997.

Cooper, Brian (ed.). *Early Australian Recipes*. Axiom, Sydney, 1996.

Cope, Bill & Kalantzis, Mary. *Productive Diversity*. Pluto Press, Sydney, 1997.

Deveau, L., Deveau, P., Portocarrero, N. & Escoffier, M. *Front Office Management and Operations*. Prentice Hall, New Jersey, 1996.

Drummond, K. *Nutrition for the Foodservice Professional*. Van Nostrand Reinhold, New York, 1994.

'Eating into Waste'. Tourism Training Australia, Sydney, 2001.

Engholm, Christopher. *When Business East Meets Business West*. John Wiley and Sons, New York, 1991.

Eunson, Baden. *Communicating with Customers*. John Wiley and Sons, Brisbane, 1995.

FitzGerald, H. *Cross-Cultural Communication for the Tourism & Hospitality Industry*. Hospitality Press, Sydney, 2002.

Gerkins, M. & Gerkins, R. *Food Law in Australia*. The Law Book Company, Sydney, 1985.

Hing, N., Breen, H. & Weeks, P. *Club Management in Australia—Administration, Operations & Gaming*. Hospitality Press, Sydney, 2002.

Hofstede, Geert. *Culture's Consequences: International Differences in Work Related Values*. Sage, Beverly Hills, 1980.

Hofstede, Geert. 'National Cultures in Four Dimensions' in *International Studies of Management and Organisation*, vol. 13, no. 1–2, 1983.

Howard, P. and Puckeridge, J. *The Professional Waiter*. 2nd edn. Hospitality Educational Services, Sydney, 1993.

Huyton, J. & Baker, S. *Case Studies in Rooms Operations and Management*. Hospitality Press, Sydney, 2001.

Industry Commission. *Tourism Accommodation and Training*. Report No. 50. AGPS, Melbourne, 1996.

Ive, J. *Food & Beverage—Achieving Excellence in Guest Service*. Hospitality Press, Sydney, 2000.

Kinton, R. & Ceserani, V. *Practical Cookery*. 7th edn. John Wiley and Sons, Brisbane, 1993.

Knowles, Tim, Diamantis, Dimitrios and El-Mourhabi, Joudallah Bey. *The Globalisation of Tourism and Hospitality: A Strategic Perspective*. Continuum, New York, 2001.

Kohr, R. *Accident Prevention for Hotels, Motels and Restaurants*. Van Nostrand Reinhold, New York, 1991.

McDowell, N. *An Introduction to the Hospitality Industry in Australia*, RMIT Publishing, Victoria, 1996.

Magris, M. & McCreery, C. *An Introduction to Food & Beverage Studies*, Hospitality Press, Sydney, 1995.

Mehrabian, A. *Silent Message*. Wadsworth, Los Angeles, 1971.

Merry, Greg. *Food Poisoning Prevention in Australia*. Macmillan Education Australia, Melbourne, 1989.

Mok, C., Armstrong, R. & Go, F. 'Taiwanese Travellers' Perception of Leisure Destination Attributes' in *Australian Journal of Hospitality Management*, vol. 2, Jan. 1995. Gatton College, Queensland.

Ninemeier, J. *Management of Food and Beverage Operations*. Educational Institute of the American Hotel and Motel Association, Michigan, 1990.

O'Shannessy, V. & Minett, D. *The Road to Hospitality*. Prentice Hall, Sydney, 1999.

O'Shannessy, V. & Minett, D. *The Road to Tourism*. Prentice Hall, Sydney, 1999.

Shaw, Julie. *Cultural Diversity at Work: Utilising a Unique Australian Resource*. Business and Professional Publishing, Sydney, 1995.

Smith, P. 'Migration, Ethnicity and Australian Aboriginality' in van Krieken, R., Smith, P., Davis, A. & Habibis, D. *Sociology: Themes and Perspectives*. Aust. edn. Longman, Melbourne, 1994.

Stewart, L. & Hunwick, H. *Nutrition in Foodservice*. Hospitality Press, Sydney, 1988.

Tourism Training Australia. Tourism and Hospitality Jobs to Rapidly Expand. http://www.tourismtraining.com.au/media_releases/release_03.html (3 July 2002).

Trickett, Jill. *Food Hygiene for Food Handlers*. The Macmillan Press, London, 1992.

Van Der Wagen, L. *Building Quality Service*. Butterworth-Heinemann, Sydney, 1994.

Van Der Wagen, L. *Hospitality Careers*. 3rd edn. Hospitality Press, Sydney, 1999.

'Vocational Education in Schools—Teaching Hospitality and Tourism'. Curriculum Corporation, Melbourne, 1995.

Walker, J. R. *Introduction to Hospitality*. Prentice Hall, New Jersey, 1996.

Glossary

abrasive a cleaning agent that has a rough texture for heavy-duty cleaning

accommodation sector the part of the tourism industry providing rooms, e.g. hotels, motels, bed and breakfast establishments, resorts

accommodation services provision of housekeeping and related services, e.g. laundry, babysitting

active listening taking positive steps, including paraphrasing, in order to better understand the speaker

add-ons extra products or services provided as part of the selling process

adjoining rooms adjacent rooms which do not connect through a private door within the rooms

à la carte style of menu offering choices for each course, with each item individually priced

anti-discrimination laws legislation to prevent discrimination on the basis of marital status, religion, cultural background, disability, age, etc.

attraction entertainment or natural geographical feature of interest to visitors

award rate/wage conditions of employment negotiated for an industry or profession, e.g. caterers

back of house departments of hotel or restaurant not seen by guests, usually referring to administration

banquets (department) department providing function rooms and catering, e.g. for meetings, weddings, seminars; also referred to as Functions Department

body language all elements of non-verbal expression involving the body, including posture and tone of voice

brand proprietary name of a product or service, e.g. restaurant or hotel chain such as Holiday Inn

buffet food set out for self-service, usually as an elaborate display

bumping sending a guest to another hotel when overbooked

carte de jour menu of the day; menu items available only on the day, often presented as 'Specials'

check-in arrival of guest and allocation of room, usually only after 2 p.m.; also known as registration

check-out departure of guest following payment, usually before 10 a.m.

colleagues people working on the team with you

commercial organisations that are operated 'for profit'

common law law evolved from court decisions and based on precedent

concierge person or department responsible for assisting with baggage, information and reservations with external agencies (theatres, tours, etc.)

confidentiality requirement not to divulge personal details, activities or room number of guests

confirmed booking hotel reservation confirmed verbally or in writing

conflict resolution solving incompatible views through negotiation and agreement

connecting rooms rooms that connect through a private door within the rooms

contamination food spoilt through mixing or blending with pollutants or growth of bacteria

contingency planning plans for dealing with things that go wrong, e.g. evacuation for fire practice

control systems systems for checking procedures, e.g. that guest accounts are accurate and up-to-date

cover a person served at a table, e.g. 25 covers (people) for lunch

cross-selling selling additional products and services, e.g. making meal bookings at the time of registration (compare up-selling)

cultural diversity variety of people of different cultural origins

culture way of life, including beliefs and activities of people from a particular region

customer expectations products and services anticipated by the guest

customer feedback information regarding level of satisfaction, obtained through formal or informal questioning

cut-off time time at which room is released for sale owing to non-arrival of guest

destination place a tourist plans to visit

detergent cleaning agent for removing dirt

disinfectant cleaning agent for destroying germs

diversity variety

domestic tourist person travelling in his/her own country

duty of care legal responsibility towards customers and staff, mainly for safety

emergency services fire brigade, ambulance, police and other services required in an emergency

empathising demonstrating comprehension (understanding) of another person's emotions

employer association group of employers (e.g. hotel operators) formed to achieve mutual goals (e.g. collective bargaining with unions regarding conditions of employment)

engineering department responsible for maintaining equipment such as air-conditioning

enterprise a business or organisation, large or small, e.g. hotel, coffee shop

enterprise agreement an agreement regarding terms and conditions of employment negotiated primarily between employers and employees in a single enterprise

enterprise policy statement of intent by a business, such as 'our policy is to provide training and career development for all employees'

environmental hygiene cleanliness of physical surroundings

equal employment opportunity (EEO) recruitment, training and promotion on merit; non-discrimination

ethics approach to issues, both legally and morally sound and well-regarded by society

etiquette standard polite forms of behaviour including verbal communication (e.g. greeting)

external customers customers originating from outside the enterprise or organisation, including guests, service providers and suppliers

food and beverage sector part of the tourism or hospitality industry providing food and beverage, including bars, restaurants, fast-food operations, caterers

food contamination food spoilt through mixing or blending with pollutants or bacteria

food poisoning physical illness resulting from poor food hygiene

food preparation all phases of preparing food including, for example, peeling and cooking

food spoilage food damaged physically or kept past its use-by date; food past peak quality

food storage process of ensuring that food is transported and kept in appropriate packaging, in appropriate store and at correct temperature

front office area in which hotel guests are greeted and allocated rooms on arrival and payment is processed on departure

front of house part of premises where guests are permitted, e.g. hotel lobby, reception, restaurant

function meeting, dinner, convention or similar occasion, usually with catering provided

functional area alternative name for a department, usually based on the function performed by the department, e.g. housekeeping

gaming forms of gambling activity; providing activities where winning is based on chance or luck, usually involving the placement of wagers or bets

grooming personal appearance, including care of hair and uniform

GST Goods and Services Tax; tax imposed on goods and services provided

guaranteed booking room guaranteed having received advance payment from customer; room guaranteed by credit-card payment even if guest fails to arrive

HACCP Hazard Analysis Critical Control Point; identification of points of measurement for hygiene purposes (e.g. temperature of food product on delivery)

hazard dangerous item or procedure

health and safety issues relating to prevention of illness or accidents to guests and/or staff

hospitality industry providing accommodation, food and beverage, and other related services such as entertainment

hotel provision of accommodation, usually rooms with en-suite bathrooms

hotel group/property management group organisation managing a hotel or motel; usually manages several such properties along the same guidelines with a single corporate management structure (usually leasing premises)

hotel owner owner of the hotel premises or building (the hotel owner might not be the property manager, just the lessee)

hygienic clean and free from germs

inbound tourist tourist arriving into the country

internal customers people who also work within the enterprise or organisation who require service/co-operation

international tourist tourist arriving from another country

itinerary list of dates and destinations; tourist's timetable

legislation laws passed by state, territory or federal governments

maintenance department responsible for repairs to hotel plant and equipment, furnishings, etc. (also known as engineering)

market segmentation process of grouping customers with similar characteristics

menu list of food and beverage items

motel accommodation provider, usually with rooms that have immediate access to parking

negotiation process of reaching agreement

night audit department or person responsible for checking and balancing hotel accounts during the night

non-commercial 'not for profit' organisation or enterprise, e.g. public hospital

non-verbal communication form of communication sending subliminal message, e.g. style or type of clothing, use of timing and decor; body language

occupancy number or percentage of rooms occupied

OHS occupational health and safety; health and safety precautions in the workplace; also legislation

outbound tourist tourist leaving the country

overbooking process of taking too many reservations, based on statistics of those who do not honour pre-booked tables or rooms

overstay a guest who stays beyond the date reserved

perishables items that quickly deteriorate or decay, e.g. fresh food products

personal hygiene cleanliness, body odour and personal presentation (nails, hair)

pest control prevention and eradication of vermin such as cockroaches and rats

point-of-sale terminal computer terminal used to process sales; provides customer receipts and management reports

policy statement of intent by a business, such as 'to undertake ongoing risk assessment and reduction strategies for improved occupational heath and safety'

posting adding expense items to a guest account

posture the way the body is held or used to communicate messages, preferably upright and attentive

problem-solving finding solutions to issues of concern to guests or other staff; a far better way of dealing with day-to-day issues than conflict management

procedures steps or processes to be followed such as setting up a bar for service or preparing a menu item to the required standard; also referred to as operational procedures

product combination of tangible and intangible elements that the customer pays for, e.g. food and restaurant ambience

promotion process of taking the marketing message to the customer

property hotel or motel, especially if part of a group or chain

protocol standard forms of polite behaviour (e.g. for answering the telephone)

quality assurance process of refining and improving products and services over time

quality control measurement of products and services to ensure adherence to standards

quality service meeting and exceeding customer expectations of service

registration process of checking in an arriving guest, confirming personal and payment details, and issuing room key or key card

regulations requirements of statutory bodies such as Office of Liquor and Gambling Commissioner (in South Australia) as an example

reservation booking a room in a hotel or restaurant in advance

resort accommodation provider, usually in association with a full range of sporting and/or other tourist activities

responsibilities obligations towards an employer, such as working safely

rights obligations of the employer towards employees, such as correct payment of wages

room nights number of nights stayed in a hotel

room rate amount charged for a room (often discounted in a competitive environment to less than full room rate)

safe handling technique process of handling heavy items to avoid injury

sanitation process of cleaning that removes and prevents bacterial development

sector distinct part of industry, e.g. transport sector, attractions sector

security department responsible for safety of guests, staff and physical assets

service ethic positive attitude towards achieving customer satisfaction

skipper a person who departs leaving an unpaid bill

standards levels to be attained, e.g. answering the telephone within three rings

support services services provided by other departments or enterprises, e.g. florist, doctor

table d'hôte fixed price menu with limited choices

tariff rate charged

teamwork group of employees working towards common goals

telecommunication equipment switchboard, pagers, alarms and other elements of communication

tourism people travelling to places outside their usual environment for purposes of leisure, business or other reasons (including visiting relatives)

union organisation formed to protect the interests of employees .

up-selling persuasive technique to encourage the customer to spend more (compare cross-selling)

vermin animals that cause contamination and damage, e.g. mice

waste disposal disposal of all waste including food scraps, bottles, paper, oil

waste management planned reduction of waste products; recycling or re-use of products to limit overall volume of waste material (reduce, re-use, recycle)

work ethic attitude towards work; working efficiently and effectively

Index